C of

C of E

The State It's In

MONICA FURLONG

First published in Great Britain in 2000

Second edition published in Great Britain in 2006

Society for Promoting Christian Knowledge
36 Causton Street
London SW1P 4ST

British Library Cataloguing-in-Publication Data
A catalogue record for this book is available from the British Library

ISBN-13: 978–0–281–05845–7
ISBN-10: 0–281–05845–8

1 3 5 7 9 10 8 6 4 2

Typeset by Graphicraft Ltd, Hong Kong
First printed and bound in Great Britain by Clays Ltd, St Ives plc
Reprinted and bound in Great Britain by Ashford Colour Press

To Nadir Dinshaw, a dear friend for more than thirty years, whose kindness to me has been beyond praise, and in memory of Joost de Blank, priest, bishop and archbishop (1908–1968) to whom I owe a debt of love and gratitude.

p83 education
p91 feminism

The door is sticking. Please push hard. The Church is open!

(*Notice on the church door of the parish church at Sidmouth, Devon*)

Our Church has a Purpose.
 To love God
 To serve our brothers and sisters
 To bring a message of God's love
      reconciliation
      peace
 to a world that desperately needs to hear it.

(*Handwritten notice on a church wall in Farningham, Kent, seen during the Kosovo crisis*)

Contents

Acknowledgments

I interviewed more than fifty people in the course of working on this book, bishops, including an archbishop, clergy, laity, and staff of Church House, and I mention them in the text when quoting them, except when I feel that what they have said might be damaging to them if they were identified. I was touched by their kindness, and willingness to talk to me, often in the middle of very busy lives, and touched and pleased too, that they trusted that I would not abuse their confidence. In particular I would like to mention His Grace the Archbishop of Canterbury, who was generous with his time. Even if those interviewed disagree with my conclusions I hope they will feel that I listened carefully to them, and wrote about them with fairness.

I could not have written the book at all without an intensive reading of writers who understood issues – historical, theological, ecclesial, financial and administrative – far better than I did (or do). Those whom I would particularly wish to thank, since I have learned from them shamelessly, are the historians Owen Chadwick, Eamon Duffy, David Edwards, Adrian Hastings, Diarmaid MacCulloch, and the late Brian Heeney (author of a very fine history of the women's movement in the Church of England between 1850 and 1930, who is rare among Anglican historians in finding women an interesting subject).

I was also helped very much by the writings of the sociologist Leslie Paul. His prognosis for the Church may not always have been right, but the combination of love, knowledge and objectivity with which he wrote, indicating the way a tormented history had shaped the Church of England, has helped, I believe, to develop critical and analytic writing about it. I have also valued the work of Robin Gill, and am much indebted to Terry Lovell's clear account of the Church Commissioners' debacle – *No. 1 Millbank: The Financial Downfall of the Church of England* – which can leave none of his readers any excuse for not understanding what went wrong and why.

I have had personal help from Frederick Shriver, a beloved American friend who is Professor Emeritus of General Theological Seminary, New York; also from other good friends, the Very Reverend Trevor Beeson, Canon Eric James, the Reverend Dr Judith Maltby, and the Reverend Dr Jane Shaw. Any errors or failures in this book are in no way due to them. My Vicar, Tony Rutherford, has been very supportive. Judith Longman of Hodder & Stoughton has been an inspiring and encouraging editor.

The first book I ever wrote was called *With Love to the Church* (1964), and it was a 'young woman's book', slightly wild in its criticisms it seems to me now, but nevertheless written with love as the title suggested. In the intervening thirty-five years, although I have had my ups and downs with the Church, the love has not abated. It has changed, however, as love does in long-haul relationships, and my changed views are what this book is about.

One of the people I interviewed in the course of preparing to write it was Sandy Millar, Vicar of Holy Trinity, Brompton, London, who courteously allowed me a generous amount of time. When the interview was finished, he said that he would like to pray with me, and he prayed 'O Lord, help Monica to write this book, and let her not go up too many blind alleys . . .' Blind alleys may be in the eye of the beholder, of course, but I have done my best to avoid them. I have no idea whether his prayer was granted.

Finally, I would like to apologise to other Christian churches in this country for referring to the Church of England as 'the Church' throughout this book. This is not because I believe it to be uniquely important, truer or more interesting than other Christian bodies in this country, but because I could not type out its full title every time I needed to refer to it – it was too laborious. Forgive me.

Monica Furlong
London, 1999

Foreword

Sometimes a vision can occur in the most unlikely place. I had one in Canterbury Cathedral at the enthronement of Rowan Williams as Archbishop. It brought together three themes that Monica Furlong identified in *C of E: The State It's In*, and which remain at the core of the Church's life today. Processing with the deans, four of us were directed to the north of the nave: it should have been to the south. We turned to go across, but found our way barred by a seemingly endless procession. It turned out to be three processions: the first was of members of the Archbishops' Council (I presumed all the clerical members were occupied elsewhere, for it looked as though it consisted of lay people); behind them came the diocesan bishops; and behind them came a long procession of well over 100 of those at whose desk the buck had never stopped – they were other bishops, suffragan and assistant. Here, visualised, were the issues which chiefly disturbed Monica: the Archbishops' Council, the appointment, place and support of diocesan bishops and the need for a stripped-down administration suitable to a more modest church. Today the issues are virtually the same.

The Archbishops' Council is the major structural development since Monica wrote *C of E*. Her interview with Michael Turnbull left her sceptical; she was right. The Church, instead of slimming down its systems, has in effect added another layer. Although this was denied from the first, the impact has made people more unsure where authority resides. The term 'Director', for example, is used of the senior officer of each department. But what and on whose authority does he or she direct? The organisation envisaged is roughly that the bishops as a body should have vision, which will be prioritised by the Council and translated into action. Somewhere along the line Synod has discussions. But the fudge between policy and execution, which is endemic in the Church, remains. In the face of, for example, a Director of Ministry being appointed by the Archbishops' Council without reference to the House of Bishops, we can see why the bishops feel impotent. For in an episcopal church, all ordained ministry derives from God through the bishop. What we have still not learned is the difference between an institution, which is an image in our minds of something in which we live or which we observe, and an organisation, which is the skeleton that enables it to do anything at all. The bishops are trapped between people who are 'professionally lay' and a host of others also called 'bishops', but they have no particular authority. One risk of this is that the bishops might desert the organisational heart of the Church and find their ministry far more in their diocese. The Church then withdraws from its still significant public role in society and becomes another denomination, of which we have quite enough already. Those who were sceptical about the Archbishops' Council seem to have been right. Given the fact that there is a central bureaucracy serving a scattered system (the dioceses and the bishops), it is inevitable that the civil servants will assume control, since there is no monitoring of their activities.

A new keynote word is 'leadership'. It is a model of ministry that is gaining ground. The argument runs that people respond to clear leadership and that the leadership skills of church leaders are insufficiently honed. At the end of George Carey's time as Archbishop of Canterbury, he received a sum of money, which has been used to found an Institute for Church Leadership. The aim of this is to clarify what leadership in the Church means and offer training. At present it is in the early stages, but it is noticeable that in his retirement, Michael Turnbull, former Bishop of Durham and chairman of the body which produced the idea of the Archbishops' Council, has been assigned a significant role. It remains to be seen what will come of this, but the mere fact of its existence indicates the direction in which some people see the Church developing. Leadership is important, but it is the way of discipleship that concerns the Church.

One differentiation that some seek to minimise is that between order and function. For example, from time to time the suffragans and other assistants join the diocesan bishops in conference. This is done on the grounds that a bishop is a bishop. At one point, Bishop Colin Buchanan sat as a member of the House of Bishops, although he was a parish priest. It is as if consecration confers a status. But the reality is that there is a difference of function, which is not smoothed over by a generic reference to bishops. A parish priest in the House of Bishops is anomalous.

The consequences of the ordination of women to the priesthood are becoming clear, and the issue continues to gather pace. As priests, many of them are effective in the parishes and a number are being preferred to cathedrals and archdeaconries. But the Act of Synod remains and is beginning to be used, as was anticipated by some, not to keep the unity of the Church but to encourage division. From the beginning, there seems to have been no real intention on the part of some to use this accommodation in order to facilitate transition. The so-called 'flying bishops' have been more pro-active than some expected, and it is clear that the debate on the ordination of women to the episcopate is likely to stir up emotions again. Yet now there looms Transferred Episcopal Authority, giving jurisdiction to a parallel episcopate. It is extraordinary in a Church that in its

Ordinal, rightly or wrongly, identifies three orders of ministry and seeks around them to build various unities, that the three orders should have been broken apart. It is also notable that current discussion of ministry and the mission of God says much about the order of deacon, its origins and its potential, possibly as a way of avoiding the issue of bishops.

A significant development has been the strength of the party groups that have emerged following the ordination of women to the priesthood: Forward in Faith represents a Catholic line opposed to their ordination; Affirming Catholicism represents Catholics who welcome this development; and on the evangelical wing, Reform has come into existence. The agenda of the latter group is larger than the single issue and attempts to claim the Church of England for its own. Money is a significant weapon and tool – a quota can always go unpaid or be diverted to some other purpose. They are like the Puritans, abandoning clerical dress and sitting lightly to the liturgy. Scarcely recognisable as part of the Church of England, the growth of their number among ordinands is ominous.

Ordination training, how it is to be provided and what it should consist of, remains a key issue. There seems to be quite a number of evangelical ordinands who have little understanding of orders and priesthood and see themselves as simply paid lay people and local leaders of a congregation. The Catholic ordinand is likely still to be caught up in the women's ordination issue, often seeking or being sought by a flying bishop. College versus course, integrated training in other institutions, local ordained ministry and NSM all remain prominent issues. Wherever the ordinand studies, however, he or she seems not to learn anything about the Church of England, its history and ethos, and is still embarrassingly ignorant of the history and development of his or her church. The average age of ordinands is rising and vocation seems blunted into a life-style choice.

An area to which Monica alluded in her chapter on the Church Commissioners, but which has come into greater prominence, is finance. After the notorious debacle of the Church Commissioners and their land purchases (which I now understand has been absorbed) as well as the cost of pensions, money has been a serious problem, affecting the church in all its parts. All the old problems re-emerge: quota (the 'family purse'), the money required by the diocese from the parishes and by the Central Board from the dioceses, building costs, housing. It is a remarkable testimony to the resilience of the Church that while there has been considerable anxiety and pain, clergy pensions, a massive charge, are covered. And although many a story implying the contrary could be told, the generality is that church people have somehow found the money. But it begins to look as though these costs might rise again and the future demand may be unsustainable. Nevertheless, the church has had to become more economically astute and there is always a danger of finance-driven policies.

Finance is also a major factor in the life of our cathedrals and greater churches. No dean (and incidentally all provosts have become deans) can be other than in some way a fund-raiser. Nevertheless, that demand has not distracted most cathedrals from their main task of worship and welcome to the visitor, as well as being the venue for significant local events. The Association of English Cathedrals (AEC), largely the conception of Hugh Dickinson (Dean of Salisbury) and me, began in a small way in order to generate a coherent view of the fabric of the cathedrals and to present a united front to English Heritage and any other government body. It was the first time in history that the cathedrals all acted as one – a major change in the life of the Church – and the AEC goes from strength to strength. Like all parts of the Church, these places have not been immune from reports and restructuring; but they have survived, and are probably better run than ever before. The days when a dean (as in the case of Armitage Robinson in 1902) could go back to the crown, ask for a more peaceful deanery than Westminster and be given Wells, have long gone.

What of the Church as it may become? There remain a large number of lively churches, with committed people and able clergy. We should not forget that the period under discussion is one in which there was similar turmoil in our political, educational and social institutions. A look at local age profiles can often explain the age spread of a congregation. For a while, it was believed that the odd grand gesture and bit of positive thinking would solve everything. It won't. The danger is, however, that the Church will be conceived increasingly in managerial terms drawn from another source such as industry or commerce. But a good organisational system is itself congruent with the ethos of the institution, and this is such an important point that it probably is the responsibility of the House of Bishops to point out when the church is particularly in danger.

'Fun' is an unusual word to use of life in the Church. Amid the sort of structural factors that I have discussed, fun seems a distant dream; we can become so deadly serious that we are, to others, dead. Yet whatever the central structures, bishops and councils, authority and power, the soul of the Church of England still resides in the parishes. Here the simplicity of faith is sought and lived. Strange things happen as people take part in the serious fun of worship: lives are transformed as men and women meet God, respond to his call and quietly serve their neighbour. It is indeed divine fun as they share with the angels in the laughter of the universe.

The Very Revd Dr Wesley Carr KCVO,
Former Dean of Westminster

Introduction

I have always enjoyed the way the abbreviation 'C of E' has been used in England. People going into hospital, obliged to declare for some sort of religion in case of collapse or sudden death, have notoriously used it as a hasty bit of descriptive shorthand, either to sum up their religious hopes and aspirations, or to avoid discussing the fact that religion did not figure much in their lives at all. The phrase appealed to me as a title because it sums up both the strength and weakness of the Church of England – its aspiration and willingness to include anyone who was prepared to be included, however nominally, but, by the same token, its shaky boundaries, its difficulty in requiring commitment from those who claimed to belong. 'What I like best about the Church of England' said an elderly friend of mine when I told her I was writing this book 'is that it leaves you alone.' I knew exactly what she meant, and realised that it was one of the things I liked about it too. But if it is to survive it may need to find new ways to breach some bastions of English diffidence and reserve.

I have added the subtitle *The State It's In* because I think it is the right time to look and speak honestly about the way it is responding to the huge changes in the world about it, and the resonances this sets up in its morale, discipline and structure. Within the year in which I am writing it has set in place structural changes said to be the most far-reaching since the Reformation.

It is not an easy time for the Church. Whatever the public assertions of the Church's Communications Department that all shall be well, and all manner of things shall be well any year now, the Church of England is between a rock and a hard place, and there are bitter pills to be swallowed. The most painful fact with which it has to deal (along with other churches) is the all-round drop in numbers: churchgoers, those on the electoral roles, numbers of baptisms, confirmations, church weddings – all have dropped steadily since the 1930s, with consequent loss both of morale and of income. Much

1

is made of the increase in the numbers of ordinands (those training for the priesthood), but this, the only good news on the table at the time of writing, seems an odd criterion of renewed life – many chiefs and few Indians will scarcely solve the problem.

The decline in membership is the more painful since it has continued inexorably in Britain during the Decade of Evangelism (1990–2000), a somewhat rash project, perhaps, at least so far as Britain was concerned (it is different in Africa). It is difficult not to see it as a sort of whistling in the dark that did not take proper account of the huge internal struggles of the Church in the 1980s and early 1990s, which it needed to resolve, however partially, before commending itself ostentatiously to others. Party struggles, struggles over authority and belief, rows about sexism and sexuality, though by no means new, did not present a serene and inviting picture, and the ordination of women, which commanded a lot of popular interest and respect in the population at large, caused so much uproar inside the Church that church leaders, at least, seemed unable to notice that outsiders liked the idea and actually admired the Church for doing it. The lowest point of all, the final shame, came when, in 1992, the story broke of a massive loss of money by the Church Commissioners as a result of unwise investment.

The obviousness of that failure produced action. Not only were the activities of the Commissioners investigated – by the House of Commons as well as by the Church itself – but a body was set up in 1993, the Turnbull Commission, which looked carefully at church finances, structure and organisation, and urged change. The Report it produced was debated in General Synod, and though its recommendations were not accepted in toto, it became the basis of a number of extensive changes. I discuss these at length in Part Two, though, within only a year or two of their being put into operation, it is too soon to decide conclusively whether they are simply cosmetic, or whether they have effectively addressed a new situation.

But despite a fluster of activity and the rather macho determination to 'take control', there are, on many levels, murmurings behind the scenes in the Church that we are simply moving the furniture around – rearranging the deckchairs on the *Titanic*, as they say. Like it or not, and how could anybody like it, the Church of England is undergoing a bewildering experience, that of 'coming down in the world', one which Britain herself has had to undergo since the Second World War. It threatens the sense of identity and self-esteem and is intermittently too painful to contemplate, yet a truthful self-awareness demands that it must be contemplated, and wisdom suggests that eventually it may actually be a relief, a laying down of a burden.

Like Britain, only later in the twentieth century and on into the twenty-first, the Church of England has to struggle with the unwelcome genie from the bottle of a different self-knowledge, the discovery that it may not be quite what, or who, it used to think it was.

Alongside this, what is having to be digested by a fairly conservative religious body is the extensive secularity of the society in which it now operates, and the new situation this creates. In the Britain of a generation or two ago there was a residue of Christian flavour – folk religion if you will – that seeped into many corners of life, from the lavish celebration of Christian festivals by the BBC to the fact that on Good Friday only the fishmonger and the baker were open (for those fasting on fish or breakfasting on hot cross buns), or that Whit Monday was one of the great public holidays of the year celebrated in the North by 'Whit Walks' and in other parts of the country by all kinds of ceremonies, some of them older than Christianity. As a child at a state school in the 1930s I was taught prayers and Bible stories, hymns and psalms – given, in fact, an extensive Christian education in what Churchill described as 'County Council religion'. Few, if any, modern children outside church schools are taught in this way (and in a multi-faith society it would no longer be politically correct), so that children who do not come from churchgoing homes – as I did not – now grow up largely ignorant of Christian ideas in a way unimaginable half a century ago. This is a lacuna with which the Church of England has never had to deal before in its long history. Love it or loathe it, most people until the last generation or so knew roughly what Christianity was about and what it stood for. The comments about religion by journalists in the press and on television, as they attempt to deal with religious information, suggest that even the basic Christian ideas are no longer understood by university-educated people, still less by others. Indeed even churchgoers can reveal an ignorance of the main elements of Christian belief. Some huge erosion of a central and common body of ideas and beliefs has taken place.

Other things have gone with it, not all of them to be regretted, for example a narrow morality which thought a married couple, however wretched their union, should stay together, which condemned children born out of wedlock (along with their mothers) to a painful stigma, and which refused to countenance the very existence of homosexual feeling. All these things forced people into pitiful acts of lying and concealment, and in the last case offered a thriving

3

industry of blackmail. The issue of secularisation, however, is not primarily a question of whether we are better or worse off, simply of the need to recognise that the change is enormous, something which all of us who lived through it know very well.

What was once respected and revered can quickly become the object of scorn and ridicule when the wind changes. The Church, which enjoyed huge influence in England for generations, is now quite often mocked in the press with a greater or lesser degree of spite. The mocking of authority – monarchy, the government, the Church – is a popular sport, part of the bread and circuses of a media-led world, and if the Church of England suffers more from it than, say, the Roman Catholic Church, it is because the wind has changed in that direction too – the cartoons of Victorian editions of *Punch* show how cruelly hilarious the middle classes found 'the Puseyites' and Roman Catholicism, along with Jews, and people who talked in Cockney accents, specially servants. The current fashion of mocking, now that, to a degree, it is the Church of England's turn, is often quite ignorant (as, of course, was the Victorian fashion), but it adds up to a sense that there is something faintly ludicrous about being a Christian, anyhow in the Church of England. The severity of the attacks on church leaders often seems wildly out of proportion to any offence, since the failings are minor – no flagrant examples of corruption, sexual perversity or grinding the faces of the poor. (There *are* clergy, of course, who have been convicted of sexually damaging acts, but except in the tabloids, who revel in this, these are not the targets.) The offence seems to be, as with unpopular children at school, that Christian leaders, like some royal figures, have been stereotyped as ridiculous, and then, in circular fashion, they are ridiculous because they are perceived to be so. In the case of both royalty and the Church it seems likely that some deeper disillusion is at work for which this unlucky few are being punished.

The other, and more attractive, face of this disillusion is the wistfulness with which many non-churchgoers approach the church – at baptisms, weddings, funerals – sometimes with memories of Sunday School or singing in the choir, sometimes with an obvious yearning for something the Church is thought to contain. 'I felt as if God was here' I read a few weeks ago in a visitors' book in an ancient church in a tiny Cornish parish. Cathedrals and old churches have never been so much visited, the hymn-singing programme *Songs of Praise* is a very popular television programme, and the BBC would omit the Christmas service of lessons and carols from King's College, Cambridge at its peril. There is a longing for some kind of spiritual expression, mixed with an ache for a more pious past, which so far does not translate, on the whole, into commitment to the Church, merely a regretful refusal.

There is, of course, quite a strong following that is deeply committed still to the Church – about a million probably – roughly the same number as those who follow football in Britain. Most of these committed Anglicans will go to church fairly regularly, receive Holy Communion with some regularity, celebrate Christmas, Easter, Pentecost (the old Whitsun) and other feasts, and usually engage in some kind of activity intended to help others. During the Kosovan crisis I noticed the following handwritten notice pasted up on a wall in the parish church in Farningham, Kent:

Our Church has a Purpose.
    To love God
    To serve our brothers and sisters
    To bring a message of God's love
                  reconciliation
                  peace
to a world that desperately needs to hear it.

This claim to love and service is no idle boast. Churches undertake an astonishing amount both of practical work and collecting of money to relieve suffering, the vast majority of this labour performed by volunteers. The parish church that I know best is actively concerned with homelessness, poverty, a children's hospice, the needs of the elderly and of mothers and children, the sick and the housebound and the needs of the developing world. It collects money or clothes, or Christmas toys for children who otherwise might not receive any, but it is ready for more practical effort too. It lays on a lunch for the elderly once a week, and a mothers and toddlers' group. It also watches out for the wellbeing of its frailer members – I can remember one occasion in which an elderly member who lived alone, and who had had a stroke, was found quickly because he was missed from church. I can think of other churches which offer enormous amounts of help to refugees (and in some cases have been prepared to hide refugees thought to be in danger if they returned home to their own countries, despite Home Office determination to get rid of them), and of others that operate credit unions in districts where loan sharks are particularly active. In one very poor parish described later in this book, the Vicar keeps a supply of tinned food always available for those who cannot quite afford to feed themselves if any unexpected expense overturns their frail economy before 'giro day'. All this represents a great deal of continuous hard work and some financial sacrifice. In a society taken up with 'market forces' and consumerism it suggests a very different emphasis – a desire to help others. Not only Christians do these things, of course, but church organisation makes it a great deal easier to do since it provides a structure and a building, and is simply taken for granted as part of the Christian way of life.

People do not join the Church primarily in order to help their neighbours, of course, though it arises very naturally within that context. As Farningham's mission statement makes clear, trying to serve one's neighbour is an offshoot of a larger purpose. The point of prayer, ritual, liturgy and reading the Bible, which all Christians do to a greater or lesser extent, is to open themselves to the perspective of a larger mystery – the mystery that is God. It is this mystery which summons people and which is the primary attraction even when people feel balked in understanding quite what it means. The bit that is easiest to understand is that the mystery requires some control of our rampant egotisms – others, after all, are children of God quite as much as we are – and the Gospels read in Church Sunday by Sunday drive this lesson home. The part that is harder to understand is that the relationship to the mystery is about transformation – of groups and of individuals; it is about the growth into wholeness and healing that is a possibility for us all, and it is this hope perhaps that leads people to regard the Church with a wistful 'if only'.

This is a difficult idea, and it is difficult to achieve. Most church-goers will have caught glimpses of it from time to time, in their community or their personal lives, and then have lost it again – a sense of unity with the world, of order and pattern and beauty, the same order that Chartres or Wells Cathedral or many a humble village church can seem to body forth.

Religion is difficult and dangerous stuff – the same hope of transformation, that can make it irresistible to those who have caught a glimpse of it, can turn it towards fanaticism or self-righteousness. It is too powerful a force to ignore, too capable of bringing energy where it is needed, yet its dangers need to be recognised.

It is on this deep foundation of energy and mystery that the Church of England, or any of the other churches, is going to have to build anew in order to survive. Skilful organisation, good works, a commitment to justice, are not going to do instead. If we look at the sections of the Church which are most successful in attracting energy and enthusiasm at present, we can see that the evangelical wing of the Church, particularly in its charismatic form, is far and away the most successful, attracting new congregations at several levels of society, and 'planting' new churches which quickly find large new congregations.

The response from other wings of the Church which are less successful is often a 'put down', a claim that what evangelicals 'peddle' is certainty, and in a frightening world where everything is changing fast, certainty is deeply attractive to people. I do not know whether this is fair, but I do think evangelical churches have put their finger on some key concerns – on the loneliness of the modern world, which makes the warm world of a friendly congregation a very attractive one, and on the need modern people have to receive instruction in the most basic of Christian ideas (through courses such as Alpha, for instance) before they are in a position to accept or refuse the Christian religion. Perhaps more important than either is the appeal to 'experience', a personal knowledge of God, the deep movement of the Spirit in a society where transcendence is suppressed and reason is king. And all that apart, charismatic churches in particular are often exciting to attend, with lively singing and preaching, and the possibility of witnessing healing or hearing someone 'speak with tongues'.

Not all of us would find evangelicalism the vehicle we would choose to carry forward the Christian enterprise – I would personally want to see the influence of Liberal tolerance and Catholic sacramentalism modifying and augmenting some of the Evangelical emphasis – but we would be foolish not to notice and prize the energy, love and vision that evangelicals are at present bringing to the Church of England. Despite their long history of devotion to the Church, at present they are the new kids on the block; they have a new style.

The days when the Church could be summed up quite easily in its three basic wings have gone (though maybe it was always much more complex and it is only with hindsight that it can be simplified). Other movements, even para-churches, have arisen, within, on the fringes, and outside the Church which, like all dissentient voices, say important things about what is getting left out of the frame. I am thinking of the 'post-evangelicals' and the Sea of Faith movement, as well as whole sections of churchgoing people – in particular women and gay people – who have simply moved on and out, driven by a sense of not being heard or wanted. It is curious, at a time when the lack of numbers worries church leaders so much, how little curiosity or dismay is ever expressed at an official level about this seepage, compared to the huge concern for, for instance, those (relatively few) clergy opposed to the ordination of women who leave or threaten to do so. It is difficult to avoid the conclusion that clergy matter more than lay people, or that those who ask the hardest questions are not really wanted. But, fortunately in my view, many women, and gay people too, refuse to vanish into the night, and stay within the Church asking the hard questions and expecting to be answered. Those who vote with their feet, as well as those who stay and argue, are perhaps the new heretics.

If history has taught us anything it is maybe that heretics, although not ultimately 'right' (none of us are that), were usually worth listening to, and the Church might have saved itself a lot of trouble if it had listened to them instead of crushing them. A list of heretics today might include Don Cupitt, a follower of a kind of *via negativa* who deserves more loving attention than has so far come his way. The scorn received by him, David Jenkins, and, in his day, by John Robinson, illustrates with painful clarity the kind of denial that is prized in the Church. Those who are really confident in their beliefs tend not to feel threatened by confrontation, and indeed, tend to play frequently with the essential doubts in their own minds. An ability to do this might be one definition of faith.

Gerald Arbuckle, a member of a Roman Catholic religious order, writing with feeling about the struggles in his own church, has coined the useful phrase 'loyal dissent'. Dissent, says Arbuckle, is vital for a living church since it 'proposes alternatives' and it is only by looking at alternatives that a body can evolve creatively.

> New ideas and ways of doing things may guarantee that life and vitality will continue. They are the seedlings out of which the future is born. However, seedlings are very fragile; they can be smothered long before they have had a chance to develop or become vigorous plants . . . Organisations, the Church included, are built to administer, maintain and protect from harm that which already exists; in contrast, creative or dissenting people are designed to give birth to that which has never been in existence before. Thus dissenters threaten the well-oiled structures . . . The alternatives they propose are seen as chaotic, something to be vigorously avoided by those taking comfort in the predictable and safe ways of tradition.[1]

No one can write about the Church of England without brooding upon Establishment. It is impossible to ignore the fact that the Church is well-connected, its top echelons mixing at the highest level of society – the monarchy and government – and having debating rights in the House of Lords. The privilege may be two-edged – what the Roman Catholic writer Adrian Hastings has called a *damnosa hereditas* – it has certainly meant in the past that the Church has been unable to order its own concerns without Parliamentary interference, even down to changing its Prayerbook. This is now greatly modified – a kind of 'creeping disestablishment', as some have called it, has set in; where the shoe pinches now is in a system where the prime minister chooses bishops (from a list provided for him by the Church). The Church has put up with this because it values its role at the centre of the British Establishment – it is flattering, of course, and it can be justified by passing the compliment on, as it were, to the Christian faith. Along with this, goes a conviction (galling to Free Church ministers and Roman Catholic priests) that Anglican churches are there for every person in the land, i.e., that everyone has the right to make use of their services. It is possible for the Church to get quite mystical about this – about the concept of everyone being part of it without any effort on their part – but it is difficult to see quite what it means in a society where the majority of people barely notice the Church. The discourtesy to other Christian churches as the Church of England congratulates itself on a 'special relationship' is, or should be, troubling. 'Establishment' itself, and not only as far as it concerns the Church, is, in any case, in for some serious scrutiny, and probably extensive change, and it is difficult to know where the Church will be at the end of all that – with luck, in a more realistic frame of mind about its place in the scheme of things.

I wrote this book out of a wish to make my own sense of the Church I belong to. I wanted to fill in some of the huge gaps I had about its history, and to have the excuse to talk to many different kinds of people about the Church as it is today. I think I expected some kind of consensus among those I talked to, but far from it – most people I talked to, whatever their particular area of knowledge, were themselves vigorously wondering and questioning, something I found unexpectedly heartening. I found myself looking at a Church in intelligent turmoil. Quite frequently, too, in the middle of the ebb and flow of argument, there were moments of clarity and simplicity when I felt deep admiration and love for the organisation itself, or for those who laboured on its behalf. I expected to find dead and empty churches, and although these certainly exist I was surprised again and again by the life and energy I found in parishes, as if a grass-roots revolution has begun as yet unrecognised by the press, or, more mysteriously, by statistics. There are some amazing pieces of work being done by churches up and down the country in holding together communities that have little else but shared desperation working for them. And for people in easier situations, many hopes, ambitions and ideals find a voice and a practical outworking in the

Church, which might otherwise remain dumb. If the Church did not exist, I thought more than once, it would have to be invented.

What interested me was to discover my own longing to see the Church lean, sober, effective, truthful. I was aware both of 'wary affection' (a phrase Diarmaid MacCulloch uses about the Church of England in his book *Thomas Cranmer*) and of frank exasperation, but then I have belonged to it for a long time, and perhaps wariness and exasperation properly belong to long-haul unions. To hang in and on when you know very well where the weaknesses and failures lie, is not the antithesis of love, but merely the realism of genuine relationship.

I also became aware of deep prejudices in myself, inculcated, of course, by my own particular brand of churchmanship, which, despite excellent qualities which I am prepared to defend, has its own blinkers. As I poked around in different corners of the Church it was immensely pleasurable to discover how much I could enjoy traditions different from my own – how moving and vital and interesting other kinds of liturgy were, and how nice people from other Anglican traditions (doubtless struggling with their own prejudices) were to me. It made me aware, believe it or not for the first time, how important it may be not simply to get to know our Roman Catholic, Methodist, United Reformed and Baptist fellow Christians, but also to forge much stronger links within the Church of England family. Some clergy, of course, already work at this, but the laity, I suspect, do so very little. The tendency is to find a church which suits our foibles and stay within it. We are going to need more generosity and imagination than that.

Even in my gloomier moments I had a persistent feeling that there was some secret, some magic, in the Church of England that I wanted to surprise – and I am glad to say that, here and there, I did surprise it, and I hope I have succeeded in describing it where I have found it.

The whole experience took me back to my own first inkling that the Church of England might be important to me, in a fairly low-key but moving experience that was all the stronger since I did not come of a churchgoing family. In my wartime early teens I spent a fine autumn Sunday walking in the Chilterns with some other girls of my own age. As it began to get dark we came down into Great Missenden in Buckinghamshire, and finding the tiny ancient parish church open, we went into it and found it decorated with sheaves of wheat, plaited loaves of bread, vegetables, fruit and all the trappings of harvest festival. We stayed on for evensong, and the simple ritual, the sense of history in the church, and of English history being present there, the beauty of the light surrounded by darkness, and the decorations, were a revelation to me and stayed in my mind as somehow the essence of what the Church of England was about.

Another vignette, by no means exclusively C of E in its nature, but perhaps evidence of the usefulness of church structure, in the sense of the church being there to be found, comes from many years later, in the 1970s. I was spending Christmas in a major Northern city with a clergyman friend of mine and his wife and family. The clergyman was preaching the sermon at a Christmas service in the cathedral early on Christmas morning, and we all went along. In the middle of the service the West door shot abruptly open and with maximum noise an eccentric figure stomped down the aisle – an elderly lady with her stockings wound about her legs and all her worldly possessions held in a variety of plastic bags. She muttered and interrupted at points in the service but no one took any notice – I guessed she was a regular visitor.

When the service was over and people were wishing one another a Merry Christmas before going home to their warm houses to eat large meals, my hostess went across and greeted the latecomer, and I heard her murmur to her in a voice only I could hear 'Would you like something to eat? Come down to the kitchen and I'll get you a bit of breakfast.' And as if it was the most natural thing in the world, without any of the patronising attitude the world associates with do-gooders, she made sure that one hungry and homeless person got fed. It did not solve the problems of the world, or of other hungry and homeless people, but it stuck in my mind, in its simplicity and unselfconsciousness, as an act of grace. It would have been a gesture difficult to offer if the church service, its congregation of worshippers, and a Christian habit of feeding those who need it, had not been there. Such gestures are widely practised in all the churches week after week with the minimum of publicity. I think it makes the world a better place.

The first recollection reveals the Church of England at its beautiful, mysterious and somehow profoundly English best, and the second, in my view, shows something true, some recognition of the human condition, some effort to resist our selfishness, that the Christian gospel, read week by week in the churches, insists that we need to make.

It is not all like that as we know, but the fact that it can be like that – a kind of statement of order, beauty, transcendence, tenderness, kindness, love – makes the Church precious and for me at least, makes it possible to forgive its failures of imagination. The Christian Church in history, and its English form in this country, has been a container for what in Europe, and its offshoots in other parts of the world, has been uniquely valuable. Law and medicine, science and art, poetry and philosophy, have been bred in this central nursery of suffering and joy. It has been our structure, our home, our mother tongue, our family, our meaning, our starting-off place, our identity. In Europe too, Christianity has been our starting point, and it feels to me foolish and psychologically dangerous to deny it, as it is psychologically dangerous to deny our own mother, family and home, whatever their incidental faults and failures. We cannot do this without denying important parts of ourselves. We need, as everybody does, a healing journey of return to our roots, before we can start the next phase of our journey.

It may, however, be time to take more risks with that identity, to relinquish antiquarian aspects of it that are no longer useful to us, to internalise it all in such a way that we overcome our fear of change and loss. We have also to find a way to open our arms to the many in our midst who hold different beliefs, or who feel different from us, and to admit and respect the doubts of those who hold no beliefs at all. We need, I suggest, a longer view, an attempt to look at the world, and the people within it, from outside, a perspective that religious people call God. As many have found over the centuries, living with one foot in mystery may make it possible to accommodate failure and disappointment and bereavement and hurt and fear in a way that nothing else can. It requires some attempt at selflessness and some attempt at forgiveness, that is to say to wish others well in their lives even when they have done us wrong.

I found that the final form of this book dictated itself. It came out a bit like Dickens's *Christmas Carol*, his study of three 'presences' who together bring about the repentance and joyful reform of Scrooge – the Ghost of Christmas Past, the Ghost of Christmas Present, and the Ghost of Christmas Yet to Come. The three major sections of the book are 'The Church as It Was', 'The Church as It Is', and 'The Church as It May Be'. I discovered that it was not possible to consider any one of these parts without becoming acutely aware of the others. I believe that the Church of England, though by no means as far gone on the route to destruction as Scrooge, here and there needs to see itself in the horrid example of Jacob Marley, as selfish, unloving, obsessive, and forging completely unnecessary chains for itself.

Part of the Christian mystery is an acknowledgment of what John Donne, an Anglican, says about our inescapable need for one another, and the underlying knowledge that all are linked, are part of 'the main'. This book is an exploration of that mystery in one small part, one province of the Christian whole, the Church of England.

Part One

The Church as It Was

Between 1530 and 1715 there was no single 'Reformation' but Christianity was reshaped, and reshaped again, and nothing was settled until the end of the period (only to be unsettled after it). Almost all of the English were then Christians, and some were Christians who lived and died with great courage in order to practise and defend their version of the faith, but if we are to be honest we must also say that their minds were clouded by hatreds. They were often brave under persecution but when they had the opportunity they, too, were intolerant: that, too, seemed to be their religious duty. And often they would think it their duty to use force. (David Edwards, *A Concise History of English Christianity*, p. 52)

The unending dialogue of Protestantism and Catholicism which forms Anglican identity . . . (Diarmaid MacCulloch, *Thomas Cranmer*, p. 629)

1

'An Old World of Devotion'

Soon after I became an Anglican, when I was in my early twenties, I was taken aback when a Ukrainian friend, a Roman Catholic, said contemptuously that the Church of England only came into existence because Henry VIII wanted to divorce Catherine of Aragon and marry Anne Boleyn. English history had not, of course, been taught this way in my English grammar school nor, I suspect in most other schools in Britain; it had had the slant evident in the historian A. G. Dickens and others, that the Catholic Church in England, at the time of Henry's secession, was seriously compromised by corruption, superstition, crude religious ideas and shameless money-grubbing, a point of view that fitted well into English anti-papal prejudices. Speaking at the Oxford Society for Historical Theology in 1996 about revisions of thought now being made by historians about the Reformation, and the ecumenical implications involved, the historian Judith Maltby discussed the way that 'interpretations', much more than actual events themselves, are what cause disputes in societies as much as in families. Using the family image to describe what happened in the Church of the sixteenth century, she says 'separation turned to divorce; there is certainly a history of domestic violence and abuse; plenty of estrangement and second marriages . . . in this divorce we see familiar patterns: from the demonizing of the other, the apportioning of blame, to pronouncements of "no fault divorce".'[1] It is a story of abuse across the Catholic/Protestant divide, a history from which we are still tentatively feeling our way towards healing, and a process in which any of us may be surprised at the depth of prejudices we uncover in ourselves.

The original remark by my Ukrainian friend, however, shook me and made me feel vulnerable. I loved my church and felt at home in it, and I shrank from exploring issues that might make it appear to be a sham. And how could it be a sham, I wondered, when I could see for myself that, as I put it, 'it worked'?

15

When I finally got round to examining the origins of the Church of England for myself it looked somewhat different. While it seemed useless to deny that Henry's personal crisis started the avalanche of the English Reformation, it was an avalanche that was ready to fall. But in abandoning Catherine and marrying Anne, together with creating the Act of Supremacy, Henry kicked the stone that set it in motion.

The Shock Waves of Reform
A religiously conservative man, Henry was, in a sense, a misfit in the huge struggle of the human spirit which the Reformation represented, a struggle which was intense in much of Europe, and which cost many lives. Events played dangerously into the King's character, and almost at once his 'natural cruelty and inherent assumption that clean breaks with the past could solve deep-rooted problems'[2] became evident.

The first movement towards reform came not from those who later became known as the 'Reformers', but from the wise and urbane Erasmus of Rotterdam (1467–1536) who wrote witty attacks on the Catholic Church, criticising its scholasticism, empty ritual and ecclesiastical abuses. Erasmus, the Christian humanist, advocated a 'simple biblical piety' instead of the existing complexities. He studied the Greek New Testament and produced a translation for the use of scholars that challenged some of the existing readings and interpretations of the text. This was part of the 'new learning' that took Europe by storm. Without intending to do more than change and improve the Catholic Church, Christian humanists like Erasmus, and his English friend John Colet, Dean of St Paul's, inadvertently paved the way for the wholesale actions of the Reformers who would bring about an irretrievable split. Luther, Calvin and others had an extremism beyond Erasmus's imagining.

The 'struggles over religion from the beginning of the 1520s up to the death of the Archbishop [Cranmer] in 1556, [revealed] an old world of devotion struggling . . . to maintain its identity against a new religious outlook which aimed to destroy it'.[3] Luther, Bucer, Zwingli, Calvin – the great names of the reforming movement on the Continent – sent shock waves through the whole of Europe as their actions and writings were widely reported; many interested in theology – like Thomas Cranmer and Thomas Cromwell – travelled to Germany or Switzerland and observed the religious phenomenon at first hand. In England the battle between the old way and the new swung this way and that under Tudor monarchs of different persuasions, until it achieved a kind of stability – the 'settlement' in the reign of Elizabeth.

The cataclysmic changes the Reformation brought about revealed how strong were the feelings, conscious and unconscious, of those who supported it and those who opposed it. With its sense of psychological upheaval one might perhaps liken it to an adolescence, a period in which new emotions, ideas and desires break through the unconsciousness of childhood bringing about an awkward, self-conscious and inevitable growth which is notoriously difficult to negotiate.

The Old Dispensation

In *The Stripping of the Altars* the historian Eamon Duffy has given a moving account of the kind of religious observance that preceded the Reformation – a description of Catholicism in medieval England in a number of small villages, as rediscovered by modern scholars. He describes a very unified world in which everything that mattered in people's lives found a place in the liturgy of the parish church. People lived, he suggests, in a world of symbols.

> Any study of late medieval religion must begin with the liturgy, for within that great seasonal cycle of fast and feast and festival, of ritual observance and symbolic gesture, lay Christians found the paradigms and the stories which shaped their perception of the world and their place in it. Within the liturgy birth, copulation, and death, journeying and homecoming, guilt and forgiveness, the blessing of homely things and the call to pass beyond them were all located, tested, and sanctioned. In the liturgy and in the sacramental celebrations which were its central moments, medieval people found the key to the meaning and purpose of their lives.[4]

The involvement of everyone, laity as well as clergy, in the annual cycle of festivals and fasts, was total.

Duffy goes on to describe a world now in many ways foreign to our own British culture, though it is possible to catch glimpses of it still in some Catholic countries on the Continent. Does Duffy over-emphasise the 'quaintness' of what he discovers of the history of rural churches? Would they necessarily have been typical of, for instance, religion in the cities? Is there a tendency anyway when considering the lost Catholicism of England to romanticise it in a way contemporaries might not have done?

Duffy describes how simple people used relics, or supposed relics, to help them with the most frightening aspects of their lives – sickness, childbirth, inclement weather whose effect on the harvest

17

might bring about starvation. A large number of relics consisted of 'girdles', many of them said to have belonged to saints or to the Virgin Mary, which women found comforting to wear in labour. There were images, particularly of the Virgin but also of saints, which were thought to be particularly effective if people prayed to them, pilgrimages which took years off a soul's presumptive years in purgatory, and miraculous phenomena which aroused deep interest. He speaks of practices and beliefs designed to ward off evil – it was thought, for example, that candles blessed in church at Candlemas might have efficacy in fending off the devil or might bring comfort if placed in the hands of a dying person.

Equally good at fending off evil were certain shrines noted for their healing properties, well worth taking long journeys in order to visit – Henry VIII in his devout youth walked to the shrine of Our Lady of Walsingham barefoot. Statues, 'images' as the Reformers contemptuously called them, were also thought to have special properties.

Duffy describes the round of feast days – Christmas, Easter, Pentecost, Candlemas, Trinity Sunday, Corpus Christi, All Saints, as well as the feasts for individual saints on which holidays would be taken, each preceded by its fast. Craftsmen or fishermen would celebrate the feast of their patron saint, churches and whole towns would make holiday on their patronal festival. Working people worked extremely hard on the land or at their crafts but their year was liberally sprinkled with holidays, at which licence and drunkenness were not unknown. There were other holidays in which pagan origins were thinly disguised, rituals at Easter using ancient fertility symbols such as eggs, balls and flowers, or the Plough festival when young men harnessed themselves to a plough and ploughed the ground up outside the home of a neighbour who would not give them money.

Rituals for the major Christian festivals often included intensely dramatic actions, as when, for example, during Holy Week, candles were snuffed out one by one to represent the gradual desertion of Jesus by his disciples. Palm Sunday included important processions, imitating Christ's original ride into Jerusalem, and on Holy Saturday a crucifix was placed in a sepulchre, often within the church itself, perhaps within a tomb prepared for a rich patron, only to be ritually removed on Easter Sunday. Duffy describes how a particular teaching method of the medieval period – that of encouraging worshippers to identify closely with Bible stories and to imagine themselves taking part in them – made a big impact on ordinary worshippers. Margery Kempe, a non-literate fourteenth-century woman, demonstrates this very well in her *Booke* in which she seems to believe herself actually living within the household of Mary and Joseph, helping to bath Jesus and wrap him in swaddling clothes. It was a method which moved over easily into telling ritual, which in turn, as Duffy describes, moved into acted drama. Candlemas, which in part celebrated the Purification of the Virgin Mary, in some places included actors dressed as Mary and Joseph carrying a doll which was placed on the altar. Guilds, with concerns for particular features of the Gospel or other Christian story, developed their processions and devotions into actual plays. In an era in which relatively few people could read, liturgy, ritual, processions and drama, along with the cycle of seasons and feast days, continuously taught the Christian story. Religious drama, a kind of extended ritual or story-telling, played its part in the creation of the English theatre.

Reading the Bible
The new Reformed tradition, or traditions, in contrast, would swerve away from elaborate ritual and dramatic presentation, with its colour, detail and symbolic appeal. The old tradition was one of priests translating or interpreting the Christian message, and passing it on to the people part-digested through the liturgy and other means. The Reformers set much store on the actual words of the Bible and of people being able to read and study them for themselves. By the Stuart period many farm labourers and working people had taught themselves to read principally so that they could read the new, Englished versions of the Bible. John Bunyan, in the mid-seventeenth century, shows the huge impact that its study had on a very intelligent, but basically uneducated mind. The Bible *was* his education, much as the classics were to become the education of innumerable Englishmen in the eighteenth and nineteenth century, and almost every sentence he writes shows evidence of its influence on his style, beliefs and outlook. Part of the effect of Reformed Christianity was to attract believers towards at least a semi-literacy. Perhaps inevitably that was a step away from the deep unconscious movements of drama and ritual with their own barely comprehensible magic, towards a more intellectual, and also a more democratic understanding of religion – understanding it was something within the believer's own compass and control. It presumed a less childlike, more adult, response to what was being taught.

The close devotion to the Bible also brought a critical eye to bear on many of the accepted beliefs and practices of the Christian religion which had accrued over the centuries, partly as a result of the assumption of pagan ideas but also because of popular interest

19

in miracles and magical ideas. This striking change of thought was true not only in England but in many other parts of Europe.

What Price Purgatory?
A particular target of the Reformers was the concept of purgatory – the place of correction and purification placed somewhere between hell and heaven, where it was assumed almost everyone would spend time after death. Even those who had confessed their sins, done penance for them and received absolution, were thought to have a residue of sinfulness for which a penalty had to be paid in a future state. As the Reformers pointed out, there was no mention of purgatory in the Bible, yet there was a huge ecclesiastical industry taken up, very profitably, with ways of promising worshippers release from purgatory. Indulgences, mortuary rites, masses said for the souls of the departed, pilgrimages to shrines, all revolved around this idea. These spiritual insurance policies naturally cost a lot of money.

It was generally recognised by even the most devout members of the old religion, by Thomas More for example, in his letters, that corruptions existed – in money-making in the sensitive area of people's love for their dead relatives or fear of the hereafter; in monasticism, in which monasteries, many of them extremely wealthy, allowed monks to live unedifying lives; in sexuality, in a system in which those who were supposedly celibate were often nothing of the kind. Erasmus in *In Praise of Folly* attacked some of the nonsensical theological questions beloved of scholastic theologians about whether God could have become incarnate in a cucumber, an ass, or a woman. In the female person of Folly, he depicted monks as

> so wicked that no virtuous man – like himself, for instance – could afford to consort with them . . . as illiterates, bound to the slavish devotion to nonsensical rules that produce a hypocritical display of piety without any substance of true godliness. They hear confession and babble the solemn secrets of the confessional to anyone who will listen. They are drunkards and womanizers, and they preach ridiculous sermons.[5]

No doubt he exaggerated for literary reasons (to the embarrassment of the careful More in whose house the book was written and to whom it was dedicated, thus linking his name to its statements irretrievably), but many contemporaries would presumably have agreed that the beauty and colour and imaginative power of the old form of religion was shot through with venality, greed and scandal; this helped to make change seem necessary and desirable.

The idea of change took people in different ways, and the arguments over it would cost many people their lives. Some, such as Thomas More himself, were adamant in their loyalty to the old ways, sure that the existing framework, held together by the authority of the Pope, was the only imaginable form of Christian truth. There was constancy, courage, integrity in their position, one famously dramatised in Robert Bolt's *A Man for All Seasons*, yet Richard Marius, More's biographer, calls him 'a disappointing hero'. He was a man deeply conflicted, ambitious, yet longing for the monastic life; witty, yet known for his wounding taunts and mockery which suggest hidden aggression; married, yet given to jeering unpleasantly at women. 'He felt a lifelong sensibility and repugnance to physical pain; yet he sent heretics to a flaming death with alacrity, and afterwards he mocked their torments . . . he refused to believe that even those heretics who died in witness to their hope could possibly be sincere.'[6] He was a repressive Lord Chancellor, refusing, for example, to permit any books in English published abroad to enter the country, and exercising a rigid censorship on books published in England. He was not willing to place Scripture in the hands of 'the common people'.

Others, such as Martin Luther, saw changes as necessarily radical. Nobody, at the beginning, not even Luther, thought in terms of a total break with the Church, or the setting up of a new Church, simply in terms of 'reforming' what was there. Luther had a fierce clarity about the need for reform.

Some, like Thomas Cranmer, for bad reasons and good, thought and worried and wriggled and argued and eased themselves into Reforming ideas until, almost to their own surprise perhaps, they found themselves a very long way indeed from the place where they had started. Eventually they could not find their way back even if they wanted to do so (and, at least when under pressure, Cranmer did sometimes wish he was back where he started). Thomas Cromwell, a devout man, who was a kind of secular equivalent of Cranmer, and certainly an equally important architect of the new English Church, lived with similar ambiguity – the painful price paid for surviving as a leader under a tyranny, though Cromwell did not last as long as Cranmer.

Cranmer – a Kind of Genius

Thomas Cranmer, one of the important ancestors of the Church of England, was a flawed genius – like Thomas More. Kindly, intelligent, scholarly, with an understanding (unusual in any generation) of the depth of Christian ideas, and how to express them in liturgy, he was wrenched from the quiet halls of Cambridge and thrust into the dangerous world of those who were close to the throne of Henry VIII and Edward VI. For twenty-five years or so he was like a man walking the edge of a precipice who watched many others – queens, statesmen, aristocrats, clergy, some of whom wielded great power and a number of whom he loved or cared for – crash to a horrible death in front of him. He nearly followed them in 1543 and was only saved by the King's own intervention – he was one of the very few whom the King liked and trusted – but he must have known that sooner or later he too might be doomed, and it showed extraordinary stability in him that he survived the inner terrors as well as the outer ones for so long. It lends a peculiar poignancy to one of the Prayer Book collects translated by him.

> O God, who knowest us to be set in the middle of so many and great dangers, that by reason of the frailty of our nature we cannot always stand upright: Grant to us such strength and protection, as may support us in all dangers, and carry us through all temptations: through Jesus Christ our Lord. Amen.

Cranmer was capable of 'frailty' – he would not have lasted, nor performed his task so well if he had not been – and it is difficult to admire him as he uses his excellent mind to wriggle the King out of his difficulty in his marriage to Catherine of Aragon and into the Act of Supremacy. Cranmer was certainly not a Daniel, not a religious hero in the usual sense – and yet in another way he was.

His devotion to King Henry is perhaps the most consistent emotion in his life – everything else is shaped around it – and yet within and alongside that central idea (and usually contrary to Henry's wishes) is his determination to lead England and the English Church into reformed ideas. He persisted in this often in the face of formidable difficulties. For Cranmer these ideas were not a static set of beliefs: he was engaged upon an inner process of argument and change from his early 'Catholic' phase right through to his death under Queen Mary, and he was open to different influences at different times. But within the rigid framework of Court, Church and State he worked persistently to bring about the kind of religion he had gradually come to believe in.

Like most of the other Reforming or Protestant enthusiasts (MacCulloch prefers the word 'evangelicals' for them on the grounds that the word 'Protestant' did not come into use until Mary's reign) Thomas Cranmer had begun life as a devout Catholic, shocked in the 1530s at an attack by Luther on the Pope. At the time Cranmer was a don at Cambridge, a fellow of Jesus College, bred largely in a scholastic tradition, a moderate man, gradually evolving, under Erasmus's influence, into a Catholic humanist. Cambridge was the breeding ground of evangelicals, many of whom in the 1520s met regularly in the White Horse Tavern, a pub so notorious for its Lutheran sympathies that it was nicknamed Little Germany. But there is no convincing evidence that Cranmer was a regular there, or, at this early stage of his career, that he had Reforming sympathies. For those interested in theology, however, the Continental debating issues were fascinating.

The changes in Cranmer's beliefs, his strengths and weaknesses, his pecular kind of genius with words and ideas, were to come into prominence in a particular context, the context of Henry's doubt and misery about his marriage to Catherine of Aragon.

The Royal Marriage
Catherine had been married to Henry's dead brother, Prince Arthur, the heir apparent to the throne of England, though whether the sick man had ever consummated the marriage was unknown. When Arthur died, it was decided with some haste by Henry VII that Prince Henry in his turn should marry Catherine in order to keep the Spanish alliance intact.

Henry married Catherine after he acceded to the throne in 1509, but it is known that he had already questioned the legality of such a marriage. Canon law, following Leviticus, forbade marriage to 'a deceased brother's wife', but a papal dispensation was issued to remove any impediment. Catherine's pitiful succession of miscarriages and stillbirths brought Henry to consider that maybe his marriage was under some kind of divine curse. The birth of Princess Mary in 1516 delayed any action – Henry hoped that Catherine might yet present him with a son – but as that hope faded his thoughts turned to annulment of his marriage. He charged Cardinal Wolsey with the task of persuading Rome to his point of view. From the first Rome seemed reluctant in the matter, presumably because they had earlier been persuaded to grant a dispensation for the marriage, and it made their authority look foolish. Also an annulment would not only cause great distress to Catherine, a devout Catholic, but would make her daughter Mary technically a bastard, and would doubtless anger the Spanish Emperor Charles V, the formidable Habsburg power in Europe.

In May 1529 there began a papal hearing of the King's case at Blackfriars with Cardinal Campeggio as the papal-representative extraordinary, and Cardinal Wolsey representing the King. By the end of July Campeggio adjourned the court until October, in circumstances which told Henry that his cause was lost and forced him to look for other solutions.

Cranmer in the Net

Cranmer was known to be in favour of the annulment from early on in the debate. Staying in the country to avoid an outbreak of plague in Cambridge, he met by chance with two distinguished clerics, Stephen Gardiner and Edward Foxe, both close to the King at the time, and they all fell into an animated discussion of the King's predicament. Cranmer advocated a canvassing of the opinion of European scholars as a way to soften the attitude in Rome, and so compellingly did he talk about the matter that his two companions mentioned his interest to Henry, who immediately invited him to London to talk about it.

It was, for Cranmer, to be the beginning of a great closeness to the King and his cause. (He had already worked for him on a minor diplomatic mission.) He now spent time in Rome trying to gather sympathy for Henry, followed by intervals working hard at home assembling arguments for an annulment, editing material which promoted the idea, and writing arguments of his own. A number of foreign observers remarked on Cranmer as an influence on the King. Others noted the clarity and precision of his thought.

It was during this period also that, both abroad and in England, Cranmer began to make the acquaintance of Reformers – Martin Bucer of Strassburg and Simon Grynaeus of Basel, a humanist and friend of Erasmus. Both of these men, a bit later in his life, would help form his thinking along Reformed lines, and therefore eventually shape the English Reformation along Bucerian rather than Lutheran lines, though in his early years of exploring reformist ideas Cranmer was more disposed to Lutheranism. Bucer, crucially, was a man who espoused 'the middle way'. Luther, as it happened, despised King Henry, and Henry had been alienated by his crass and offensive suggestion that Henry's way out of his problems was to commit bigamy, though in a sense Henry did so by marrying Anne secretly before his marriage to Catherine was annulled.

Cranmer for Archbishop

It was in 1532 that news came to Cranmer on the Continent that the King wanted him to succeed Archbishop Warham, who had just died, as Archbishop of Canterbury. It was an extraordinary thrust into the limelight for a man who only a year or two before had been a don barely known outside Cambridge circles. He, together with almost everyone else, was astonished at the idea of such promotion, and he tried to refuse. He was a man not really designed for power and intrigue but happiest working in his study; a man who could have no illusion of how complex and dangerous life could be around the King. Perhaps, on the other hand, the idea of power was also exciting, though in his later life Cranmer never seemed to be a keen power-broker.

From Henry's point of view Cranmer must have seemed a very suitable candidate. Intelligent, devout, weak in some ways or at least open to persuasion, poised between old and new ways of looking at religion, and therefore all the more persuadable, he had nevertheless sufficient scholarly and religious prestige to carry some conviction. He was also, as it happened, a friend of the Boleyn family, and Henry was later to tell Cranmer that it was Anne whom he had to thank for his appointment to Canterbury.

Cranmer the Married Man

But unknown to Henry, Cranmer brought a personal problem to the appointment. He had just got married – a step strictly forbidden to an ordained priest. It was not his first marriage. As a young don at Jesus he had married a woman called Joan, and although he was not ordained at the time he had been obliged to resign his Jesus fellowship, since only bachelors were permitted to be fellows. Joan had died in childbed relatively early in their marriage. That Cranmer should twice marry, in the first case at the cost of losing his fellowship (he was a poor man), and in the second at a time when the action carried incalculable risks, since Catholic priests were required to be celibate, suggests that he was a man with a very real need of marriage and that the need overcame his prudence.

It happened while he was on the Continent in 1532. He used this journey to learn more of the Continental Reformers, in particular at Lutheran Nuremberg. He struck up a friendship with the Lutheran Osiander, and very shortly afterwards married a young relative of his, Margarete. MacCulloch attributes this uncharacteristic impulsiveness to the infectious mood of Nuremberg. But Cranmer had not only acquired a hostage to fortune by getting married, he had in a sense already declared himself as a would-be Reformer by dismissing the strict requirement of his orders to remain celibate. It was as if, on some level, he knew the way he was going to go. And yet he was still thought of as a theologically conservative man – his attraction to the thinking of his new-found Continental friends had not begun to reveal itself very much and he still appeared like a regular Catholic with the sole reservation of his support for the King's annulment.

25

Cranmer tried refusing the new appointment without success. However, he delayed his return to England for as long as he decently could.

Cranmer at Lambeth

Cranmer finally returned home in the winter of 1532–3 to an England in a state of political and theological upheaval. Anne Boleyn was pregnant, and it was vital that Henry's annulment with Catherine should go through before the child was born, so as to make it legitimate. The same committee that struggled with this problem and on which Cranmer sat, was also struggling with the intermittent influence of evangelicalism. The most prominent evangelical was Hugh Latimer, whose sermons were in danger of rousing his listeners, by harsh criticisms of the religious status quo, to no one knew quite what acts of folly. Some bishops banned him from their dioceses. Latimer was one of the two whose name would eventually be linked with that of Cranmer in death, along with Ridley – they became the three most famous Protestant martyrs.

Cranmer had a political problem about becoming Archbishop, to which he and Henry between them found a devious and not really honest answer. No previous Archbishop of Canterbury had taken office without papal authority in the form of bulls. Since Henry was in the process of flouting papal authority, how could that same authority be used to grant him, Cranmer, office? And without authority how could he be Archbishop? Henry had thought of this, knowing it to be a delicate point with Cranmer, and to get his own way he used the fact that the Pope, and the papal nuncio in England, were desperate to avert a final break between England and Rome, and he thought correctly that this might make them biddable. Henry applied for bulls to make it possible to make Cranmer Archbishop, agreeing to finance the huge cost of this out of his own pocket.

In April 1532 Cranmer was made Archbishop at a ceremony in the Palace of Westminster in which he swore first an oath of loyalty to the papacy, followed incredibly by 'a solemn protestation' declaring that his oath would not override the law of God and his loyalty to the King, or act to the hindrance of 'reformation of the Christian religion, the government of the English Church, or the prerogative of the Crown or the well-being of the same Commonwealth'; and he swore 'to prosecute and reform matters wheresoever they seem to me to be for the reform of the English Church'. It was an example of eating one's cake and having it, what MacCulloch calls a 'morally dubious manoeuvre'. Cranmer was then vested with a *pallium* (the woollen robe that proclaimed archiepiscopal status) specially sent from Rome for his consecration. 'In a procedure which can reflect no credit on him at all,' MacCulloch goes on, 'Cranmer had formally benefited from papal bulls while equally formally rejecting their authority.'[7]

2

Anglicana Ecclesia

Meanwhile Henry had secretly married Anne Boleyn. The realisation that the child she was carrying would not be legitimate without marriage forced Henry's hand. He set about the process of making himself head of the Church in England in place of the Pope. Of course there was opposition, which Henry crushed. Using the statute known as *Praemunire* he fined the Convocations of Canterbury and York for accepting Wolsey's authority as papal legate (what MacCulloch calls 'one of Henry's little tricks'), and forbade appeals to Rome except with his consent. This was later enforced unconditionally in the Restraint of Appeals Act of 1533, which also served to prevent Catherine appealing to Rome. Cardinal Wolsey, who had failed to get permission for the King's annulment, was, inevitably, destroyed. In a highly significant action in 1532 known as 'the submission of clergy', usually regarded as the true beginning of the Reformation in England, Henry had forced the clergy to meet, and to do so only under licence from him, and to secure his assent to any new canons they sought to promulgate. All this abrogation of the authority of Rome, and any independence of the Church as an independent legal entity in England, was sealed in the Act of Supremacy of 1534, which named Henry and his successors as 'the only supreme head in earth of the Church of England, called Anglicana Ecclesia'. Although not a Reformer at heart at all, but driven by desires partly personal and partly national, Henry had inadvertently brought about the beginnings of a Reformed church in England. The Pope's unsurprising response to this was a Bill of Excommunication.

The Convocation of Canterbury was required formally to end papal authority in England, voting that 'the Bishop of Rome has no greater jurisdiction given him by God in holy scripture in this realm of England than has any other foreign bishop'. In the lower house thirty-two voted for the motion, one was uncertain and four brave men voted against. Of the senior clergy eleven bishops including Cranmer signed and ninety-one others – abbots, archdeacons, etc. – some of whom signed on the spot and others who signed later.[1]

Now the machinery of an independent church began to be set up. Cranmer consecrated bishops by royal authority alone, without the papal bulls which would once have been necessary. Chancellor Thomas More resigned and with John Fisher, Bishop of Rochester, refused to sign the Act of Succession which denied both the Pope and the existence of the King's first marriage. Consequently both were sent to the Tower. Three years later, in 1535, they were executed for refusing to sign the oath which required them to accept Anne Boleyn as a legitimate wife of Henry, and her offspring as heirs to the throne.

There were other denials of the new status quo. When Cranmer attempted a visitation of the province of Canterbury in his role as Metropolitan, a number of bishops refused to recognise his authority, most notably the Bishop of London, John Stokesley, at St Paul's Cathedral, who pointed out that Cranmer was still describing himself as 'Legate of the Apostolic See'. Other bishops protested also, and the ill-conceived visitation gradually petered out. The most potent, and moving, of any protest was the Pilgrimage of Grace, that series of risings in the North, of great, if fatal, courage, which emerged from deeply held beliefs, but also from, as we should say now, 'secular' causes, economic and regional concerns. The pilgrims held Cranmer and Cromwell responsible for the damage done to the Church, and sang ribald songs about them. For a while the Pilgrimage seemed to threaten the whole precarious structure built up since the break with Rome, but in the end it failed completely, only indicating to others that resistance was useless. The Crown always had the advantage in putting down local rebellions. Not only could it raise troops, but the ethos of society was against rebellion – the fear of disorder was profound, and revolt against authority was thought to be sinful.

The 'High Vicar over Spirituality'
Thomas Cromwell, the vicegerent, was the other key player with Cranmer on the church stage. In 1536 he was 'high vicar over spirituality under the King', a grandiose title difficult to translate into modern terms – perhaps to be described as the senior administrative officer dealing with religion, a political figure, as opposed to the more ecclesial role of the Archbishop. The structure of a church and state without the authority of the Pope, a bewildering concept at first to almost everyone involved, was gradually falling into place. Archbishop and Vicegerent, Cranmer and Cromwell,

under the King now represented church authority in different guises, religious and political. From 1535, when appointed the King's vicegerent, meaning that he exercised all Henry VIII's authority over the Church, Cromwell actually ranked above Cranmer as the wielder of Henry's authority. Cranmer and Cromwell got on well, despite some land deals that Cromwell did at Cranmer's expense, and perhaps both recognised that they needed the other – Cranmer was deeply religious, Cromwell a shrewd politician but also a profoundly pious man who read the New Testament in Greek. Both had Reforming tendencies.

The period after the annulment of the marriage to Catherine, the 'reign' of Anne Boleyn, was one in which evangelicalism in England began to burgeon and grow. Anne herself had many links with evangelicals, particularly in France, and the twin influences of Cromwell and Cranmer itself encouraged change. Hugh Latimer, who not long since had been *persona non grata* in a number of dioceses, actually preached to Convocation, attacking the doctrine of purgatory, shrines and devotion to images. He also suggested the use of English at weddings and baptisms.

Ten Articles
During this period Convocation issued the 'Ten Articles'. They were a result of intense argument between conservatives and evangelicals, argument so fierce that Cromwell and Henry avoided such confrontations in future. Partly as a result of horse-trading in trying to agree on a common statement, the finished document typically annoyed everybody and pleased nobody. Influenced in part by Continental statements of belief, and in particular the Augsburg Confession of 1530, the Articles had a strongly Lutheran flavour. They admitted only three sacraments, baptism, eucharist and penance; they advocated justification by grace alone, and there was disparaging discussion of images, saints, ceremonies and the doctrine of purgatory. There was an attempt to encourage people to read the (Coverdale) Bible.

Anne had given birth to Elizabeth, the future Elizabeth I, another blow to Henry in his ambition to have a son. Anne was perhaps too intelligent to please Henry, too little the submissive wife for the marriage to succeed, and she held religious theories that did not appeal to her husband, but she might have survived if she had borne him the longed-for son. On the day that Catherine of Aragon died, when it might have seemed that the couple could feel a more auspicious time was beginning, Anne miscarried her second child, an event which played into Henry's superstition. It was only a short step from there to unsubstantiated accusations of unfaithfulness. Cranmer, who was close to Anne, heard her confession in the Tower on the night before she was beheaded.

At first sight Anne's fall from grace and execution felt like a severe blow to the evangelical cause. 'Anne's conservative enemies had originally intended to rehabilitate Princess Mary, use for their own ends the pliancy of Jane Seymour, and thereby establish their own ascendancy' writes MacCulloch. 'Instead they found themselves in political oblivion' with 'Cromwell in a still stronger position at Court'.[2]

Bucer of Strassburg was trying to link together countries with evangelical ideas, and to repair dissensions between Luther and others. He was very flattering to Cranmer and other English theologians. Bucer himself was essentially a moderate, a proposer of a reformism that modified the past, and respected it, but also respected the authority of secular rulers and the social stability they could provide. Through Cranmer he undoubtedly helped to form the Church of England in this image.

Destruction of the Monasteries

In the 1530s, perhaps driven by not much more than greed, Henry set in train the destruction of monastic life in England with Thomas Cromwell as his tool. The monks were accused of 'manifest sin, vicious, carnal and abominable living'. It was the excuse for the expropriation of all that they owned, to the benefit of Henry's exchequer. 'In the course of three years', wrote J. R. H. Moorman,

> was expunged from the face of England one of the greatest and most ancient of her institutions. It was monks who had evangelized England, whether from Rome or from Iona. It was monks who had kept scholarship alive in the Dark Ages, who had established the earliest schools, who had provided hospitality for the traveller and the pilgrim, who had fed the poor and nursed the sick. Now by the rapacity of a King and the subservience of Parliament the whole thing was brought to an end, the monastic buildings sunk into decay and ruin, a useful quarry for farmers who wanted good stone to build their barns and fences.[3]

Whatever the glories of monasticism in the past, and they had been considerable, the evidence seems to suggest that the monasteries were in a parlous state by Henry's reign, and Moorman is somewhat overstating the situation. Yet given Henry's devout character in youth, and his considerable learning, it seems appalling that he could so coldbloodedly set about destroying monasticism in England. He was not interested in reforming the monasteries, merely in plundering them. Though not himself involved in the destruction of the monasteries, one wonders what Cranmer, a scholar, made of it.

The 'Englished' Bible

William Tyndale was the first translator of the Bible into English, completing only the New Testament at first, and parts of the Old Testament later. Miles Coverdale used Tyndale nearly verbatim, adding the missing parts of the Old Testament, and published the first complete English Bible in Zurich in 1531, an edition published in England in 1536. In 1537 John Rogers published an English Bible, often known as 'Matthew's Bible' which was printed in Antwerp, overseen by an English printer, Richard Grafton. It was plainly derivative from Coverdale's Bible. MacCulloch suggests that Grafton had been corresponding with both Thomas Cromwell and Cranmer, and Cranmer was probably unaware when he took the Bible to Cromwell how much he already knew about it. Cromwell gained Henry VIII's permission to sell both 'Matthew's Bible' and Coverdale's Zurich Bible.

Meanwhile an official Bible was in preparation, translated by Coverdale. The 'Great Bible' or 'Cranmer's Bible' as it was known, was issued in April 1539, and it was ordered to be set up in every church so that people could read it for themselves, or be read to. The evangelical wish that the Bible should be available widely in the vernacular was on the way to becoming a reality. In the same year Jane Seymour gave birth to Prince Edward, Edward VI to be, and died shortly afterwards.

In 1538 Thomas Cromwell started a campaign of iconoclasm – of statues, roods and sacred objects. One or two people who opposed the regime were burned as an example – in one case alongside a wooden 'image' from Wales. Alongside this sort of assault on folk and religious tradition was the fact that so many of the old feast days were now banned – people had many fewer holidays and naturally felt resentful of this.

At an official level church life was incredibly busy – endless committees, discussions, correspondence emanating from Lambeth Palace. Cranmer, and a number of his bishops, were ceaselessly drafting and redrafting documents defining their theology. Cranmer, who had been a Catholic humanist, and then had Lutheran and Bucerian enthusiasms which had both marked him, now, according to Diarmaid MacCulloch, was exploring predestinarian ideas, as shown by his comments in the margins of his books. Salvation was a major theme in his thinking.

King Henry, though he used people to read books for him and comment upon them, was a critical and energetic reader of theology himself. One historian says of him that he suffered as a thinker from a 'combination of a relatively able but distinctly second-rate mind and a prominent inferiority complex'.[4] (His father had much preferred his older brother.) His limitations became particularly evident in 1538 when, provoked by the enquiries of the German princes about why England still insisted on clerical celibacy, the withholding of the chalice from the laity, and masses for the dead, Henry moved into belligerent theological mood. A year later, probably conniving with the 'conservatives', Katharine Howard's uncle Norfolk, Bishop Gardiner and others, he issued the Six Articles, 'the bloody whip with six strings' as the evangelicals called it, which effectively slammed the door on the evangelical doctrinal ferment for the rest of his reign. Cut off from Rome he might be, but otherwise his ideas were very little changed. He reiterated his belief in transubstantiation ('after the consecration there remaineth no substance of bread and wine, nor any other substance, but the substance of Christ, God and man'), communion in one kind only, celibacy of clergy, the observance of vows of chastity made by laity, private masses, and auricular confession.

For the evangelicals, and for Cranmer in particular, 1539 and 1540 were to be hard years. The downfall and execution in 1540 of his colleague Cromwell propelled Cranmer himself further into the forefront of things. Part of the reason for Cromwell's lightning descent had been his pushing the suit of Anne of Cleves as a wife for the King. Henry found her repulsive and he and his Archbishop were once again faced with the humiliating process of annulment, though by this time the process ran on oiled wheels. Persecution against evangelicals followed the Six Articles, and two bishops, one of them Latimer, resigned. But Henry was oddly even-handed in dealing out misery, and was not fond of arch-conservatives, who were a threat to his supremacy. MacCulloch speaks of his 'murderous lunges against representatives of either religious wing'.[5]

The Authority of the Prince

An interesting development in 1540 was the arguments Cranmer was putting forward about authority, about where power lay in the Christian Church. He had no belief in Apostolic Succession, and he saw the creation of bishops in the early centuries of the Church as a device of structure and authority forced upon them because there was no Christian monarch – a curiously 'own goal' sort of argument, we may think, since the creation of a Pope might have seemed as good a way as any of supplying an overarching power. The idea of the 'godly prince' was not a new one – King Alfred had believed that the role of the king was to be Christ's deputy on earth. Cranmer built upon this ancient idea of princes and governors as the ultimate authority; it was but an extension of it to suggest that they had the right to create their own bishops and priests. Henry was unlikely to quarrel with this theory of royal supremacy in the Christian world, though many would later wonder about it. Although the debate about authority was to surface repeatedly in the Church of England up to the present day, the Erastian undertone was never completely to disappear. The power of 'the Prince' was a curiously strong and persistent one in England, and is not entirely dead yet, however much its form has changed.

Cranmer the Liturgist
The year 1544 saw the first officially authorised service in the vernacular, the litany. Put together by Cranmer from a number of sources, it was to be sung to a simple plainsong setting; Cranmer favoured simple musical settings in which the congregation could join. Though the litany is not much used nowadays, it can still be found in almost identical form to that of 1544 in the Book of Common Prayer. But here, for the first time in a liturgical setting, was the superb language of Cranmer, which was to be one of the chief glories of the Church he helped to create. Odd phrases from this comprehensive prayer which touches upon so many aspects of life, public and private, as well as later phrases from Cranmer's prayers, have a way of lingering on in the secular consciousness up to the present day – 'have mercy upon us miserable sinners', 'we beseech thee to hear us, good Lord', ' women labouring of child', 'we have left undone those things we ought to have done, and we have done those things we ought not to have done', 'erred and strayed from thy ways like lost sheep', 'not worthy to gather up the crumbs under thy table', and so on.

The end of Henry's reign was marked with persecution of evangelicals, his conservative subjects furiously building up evidence against them, mainly in connection with doctrine about the eucharist. Writing of the English Reformation as a whole David Edwards, discussing the repeated shaping and reshaping of the Church which went on in this intense period, makes the haunting point of how many

> lived and died with great courage in order to practise and defend
> their version of the faith, but if we are to be honest we must also

say that their minds were clouded by hatreds. They were often brave under persecution but when they had their opportunity they, too, were intolerant: that, too, seemed to be their religious duty. And often they would think it their duty to use force.[6]

It is not easy for the modern mind to make sense of the passion of religious intolerance and persecution, yet we ourselves might summon a somewhat similar passion over, for example, the irruption of Fascist ideas into our own democracy – the anger aroused by the violence of a Fascist bomber in Brixton and Soho in 1999 being a case in point.

Leslie Paul, commenting on the gradual coming into being of the Church of England over four reigns, those of Henry himself, Edward VI, Mary and Elizabeth I, says that for Henry (unlike the others), the Church was still 'in all essentials the Catholic Church he had worshipped in as a boy... with one important difference, the severing of allegiance to Rome'.[7] In other words the change was, for him, political rather than doctrinal or liturgical. He still believed in almost everything that the Reformers were to question. Yet Geoffrey Elton notes that by the spring of 1543 the King's companions at court were of 'the more reformist wing'.[8] In the same year there appeared a revised formulary of the Christian religion, *A Necessary Doctrine and Erudition for any Christian Man* (i.e. it was meant for laypeople, not just clerics), which was popularly known as *The King's Book*. Henry, having had continuing debates with his theologians since a similar book known as *The Bishops' Book* in 1537, had contributed extensively to its composition.

On his deathbed Henry sent for Cranmer – it was a fitting end to their long association. Towards the end of his life Henry observed with distaste the way that religious argument was spreading like wildfire amongst his subjects: 'That most precious jewel the Word of God is disputed, rhymed, sung and jangled in every Ale-house and tavern.'[9]

3

The Evangelical Hour

Having alienated all the Catholic countries in Europe, and removed the stability lent by the support of Rome, when he died in 1547 Henry left his son Edward, a ten-year-old minor, the inheritance of a country seething with debate. But for the evangelicals it was like coming out into the sunlight. In the last year of Henry's reign, when he was too feeble to hold the religious balance, many of them had suffered torture and imprisonment. Cranmer, undoubtedly in the conservative sights, was vulnerable, since, following the lead of the Six Articles, they were using the 'real presence' as a sign of appropriate orthodoxy, and Cranmer probably by this time could not have said that he believed in it. Yet in the last years of his life Henry seemed to turn more kindly towards evangelicals, and as he died it was Cranmer he chose as his companion and priest. Very soon after Henry's death, in the new evangelical climate that was almost palpable, Cranmer at last publicly acknowledged his wife. By now he had three children by her.

King Josiah
Edward Seymour, Duke of Somerset, the uncle of the new young King, was appointed as Protector, and under him the country was to be run by a Regency Council until the boy came of age. The young King had been educated by evangelical divines and was precociously inclined to such ideas. Somerset, and some others who now rose to prominence, noted that in moving the country in this direction there might be financial gains for themselves. Many did, in fact, gain substantially in properties and wealth. In the struggle for profit, Cranmer himself made, and seemed content to make, modest gains. He crowned Edward, his godson, King in 1547, and preached a sermon in which he likened his new majesty to the biblical king Josiah who had been a remover of images. Later that year he published a book of homilies which spelled out what were now his

key ideas: that salvation came through faith, not works (the classic example of this was the thief on the cross) – a subject on which he and Henry had strongly disagreed – although this did not at all in itself imply the forsaking of the need for goodness. This was the main thrust of the book, and it was contemptuous of some favourites of Catholic piety, such as rosaries, 'feigned' relics, purgatory, indulgences, prolonged fasting, and of excessive use of bells, candles and festivals. The book was in fact polemical, and thus exaggerated. As a teaching tool, it was to be imitated and plundered by less expert preachers.

Teams of 'visitors' were sent out by the administration through England, partly to preach, partly to find out what was going on. Their labours were driven by Injunctions which took up ideas already current in Henry's reign, but more strongly emphasised and including newer and harsher prohibitions. All recitations of the rosary were now condemned, as were all images (some had been defended in the past as 'the books of unlearned men'), and all candles were forbidden except two on the altar. The appalling Injunction 28 ordered the removal of relics, images, pictures and paintings and the destruction of images not only on the walls of churches but in windows.[1] Even the niches which had held images were to be blocked up and churches were to be whitewashed. Parishioners were required to destroy images in their own houses. Processions were forbidden and only one bell allowed to be rung in church, just before the sermon. The visitation itself 'was thorough, in many places aggressive, and it was consistently used to push through a radical reading of the Injunctions. Everywhere they went the commissioners enforced the destruction of images, the extinguishing of lights, the abolition of . . . ceremonies.'[2] Such aggressive acts of destruction suggest that the iconoclasts were destroying something childlike in their own faith. But the wanton destruction of so many beautiful objects and loved practices seems to indicate a fear and dislike of beauty itself, as well as of sensuality and the deep wells touched upon by ritual. It was a war against feeling, or at least against feeling not filtered or expressed through the medium of words. Fortunately the destruction was not quite so total as it appeared. Leslie Paul describes how parish churches were to become quite adept at hiding or burying treasures and statues, evidence for which was that they reappeared briefly in Queen Mary's reign, only to disappear again after that.

Those who had ordered the massacre of images themselves became frightened at what they had started and tried to halt the wholesale destruction. But the momentum had become unstoppable. 'The work went on, statues and niches were pulled down, windows painted over

37

or broken, walls whitewashed and covered with texts against idolatry.'[3] Two conservative bishops, Bonner of London, and Gardiner of Winchester, who protested about the image-smashing and much else, found themselves in prison, Gardiner until the end of Edward's reign. Meanwhile, Parliament had experienced the novelty of a mass in the vernacular.

'The Bread and Wine do not Change in their Nature . . .'
The diffidence that Cranmer had necessarily shown while Henry was still alive in exploring ideas close to the heartland of Catholic belief was dissolving somewhat in the new evangelical climate. MacCulloch believes that under Henry his ideas of the eucharist were already changing, but secretly. Now he was ready to look openly at the whole issue. He began by consulting Bucer.

> We acknowledge that the bread and wine do not change in their nature, but that they become signs . . . by which signs [Christ] indeed with his own benefits and gifts may be offered to everyone . . . We do not consider that Christ descends from heaven, nor that he is joined with the symbols, nor that he is included in them . . . [Christ] is Lord, and he remains in the heavens until he will show himself openly to all as judge'.[4]

The faithful worshipper is drawn up into Christ in the eucharist, Christ is not drawn down to him.

Cranmer's First Prayer Book
Cranmer had been working on a form of eucharist which was to find its way into the first of his prayer books, that of 1549. Considerably influenced by the Sarum Canon of the Mass, it was a sort of halfway house towards the new form of liturgy Cranmer hoped to see. It brought problems from both wings of theological thought, from the evangelicals because it was still too 'romish', and from the conservatives because it departed too far from the mass. It was in English. The people took communion 'in both kinds'. This service was referred to as 'The supper of the Lord and the holy communion, commonly called the mass'.

Some of the most remarkable prayers in the book are the Collects, translations for the most part from ancient sources – three bishops of Rome including Gregory the Great in the late sixth century – thus linking the English Church very firmly with its forebears. Cranmer translated these brief prayers for particular seasons of the Church's year with a marvellous economy and often unforgettable language, as in the following to be used in one of the Sundays after Trinity.

> Grant, we beseech thee, merciful Lord, to thy faithful people pardon and peace; that they may be cleansed from all their sins, and serve thee with a quiet mind; through Jesus Christ our Lord. Amen.

Or the beautiful Collect for Purity that opened every communion service.

> Almighty God, unto whom all hearts are open, all desires known, and from whom no secrets are hid: Cleanse the thoughts of our hearts by the inspiration of thy Holy Spirit, that we may perfectly love thee, and worthily magnify thy holy Name; through Christ our Lord. Amen.

Or the Collect for Good Friday:

> Almighty God, we beseech thee graciously to behold this thy family, for which our Lord Jesus Christ was contented to be betrayed, and given up into the hands of wicked men, and to suffer death upon the cross, who now liveth and reigneth with thee and the Holy Ghost, ever one God, world without end. Amen.

Parliament approved the new prayer book in 1548 and it began to be used across the country in the following year. It was a collection of acts of worship, of course, but it was also, inevitably in its context, a tool of theological instruction which, in the circumstances, was highly political.

That apart, it was the first vernacular expression, apart from much shorter prayers such as the litany of 1544, of Cranmer's literary and liturgical genius. Cranmer acted as editor, but key parts of it were his work. 'There is little doubt' says MacCulloch,

> that we owe him the present form of the sequence of eighty-four seasonal collects and a dozen or so further examples embedded elsewhere in the 1549 services: no doubt either that these jewelled miniatures are one of the chief glories of the Anglican liturgical tradition, a particularly distinguished development of the genre of brief prayer which is peculiar to the Western Church.[5]

They are original, in the peculiar sense that Cranmer used a wide range of sources from his reading and scholarship and turned them into the language of prayer. A handful of them he is thought to have written himself.

A new marriage service was a feature of the book, in which, for the first time, marriage was stated to be 'for the mutual society, help and comfort, that the one ought to have of the other', an emphasis on enjoyment in marriage that was entirely new, and perhaps owes something to the life Cranmer had lived with Margaret Cranmer.

Cranmer would continue to work on this first model, partly in the light of criticism, from Martin Bucer among others, and continuing liturgical argument. It revealed, as others have noted, a deep understanding of the purpose of worship, of the direction of the congregation's hearts and minds towards the mystery of God.

Judith Maltby describes the Prayer Book as 'more than a text; it provided a framework of words and actions to address a wide range of human needs and was intended to involve the participants fully. To appreciate this is analogous to the transformation of understanding that can take place between reading a play and watching a particular production.'[6] Though, of course, worshippers, as she goes on to say, are participators as well as actors. Later in the century those who despised the Prayer Book would compare it scornfully to a tennis match (they were speaking specifically of the antiphonal saying of Psalms), a backhanded compliment, since it recognised the dialogic nature of the new Anglican liturgy and what an innovation this was.

> The medieval mass involved a set of parallel liturgical activities, with the clergy involved in one set of devotions and the laity in another: the great moment of union of priest and people coming at the elevation of the consecrated host. Cranmer and others promoted a different understanding of corporate prayer. It was to be 'common', not only in the sense of a uniform rite for the nation, but also in the sense that the priest and people attended to the same aspects of the liturgy together. Hence the repeated emphasis not only on the vernacular but on clerical audibility, as the opening rubrics for Morning Prayer direct that: 'the minister shall read with a loud voice.'[7]

The congregation learned the virtue of active participation.

Protest

The new Prayer Book produced religious protest almost at once, particularly in the West Country but also in other parts of the country. The protesters wanted the old Catholic Church and its practices to continue. Eamon Duffy describes a 'bloody Sunday' at Clyst St Mary near Exeter in which many local protesters were killed and the village was burned down. Later in the same year the Government was to set up a sort of amnesty in which people might hand over missals, books of various kinds, primers and other material which belonged to the old dispensation. Local officials – mayors, bailiffs, constables and churchwardens – were held responsible for this event as also for the removal of any still existing 'images', with severe penalties if they were found to be negligent in their duty. It was a holocaust of the old religion and of all that had been precious to it, violent in its emotion, and sometimes in actual shedding of blood – a hateful pogrom driven by fear, suspicion and, above all, a self-righteous zeal. Yet there must have been a resentment of that old religion to fuel so much anger. There was also, it must be said, a huge greed at large, with valuable church plate, vestments and other precious objects gradually getting swept into the coffers of the Crown under pretext of religious principles. Historians differ about how much the Protector himself was driven by evangelical piety and how much by self-interest – the temptations created by the pickings of the Protestant ascendancy were considerable.

The furore of the late 1540s brought down Somerset and for a while the Catholic party hoped that their fortunes might improve, for example by making Princess Mary the Regent for the young prince. Somerset, driven by what Geoffrey Elton calls 'convention, self-interest and irresolution', was ruined by a coup led by Northumberland, himself probably committed for mercenary reasons to Reform yet playing along with the 'Catholic party' when this seemed to work diplomatically. Yet by 1550 the evangelical status quo which had seemed distinctly shaky was established again. Nicholas Ridley, a safe evangelical, had replaced Bonner, the rebellious Bishop of London. Latin service books were widely burned on government orders.

Cranmer's Prayer Book of 1552 represented a giant stride forward into evangelicalism from the book he had edited three years previously. Duffy notes how the new book banished the baptismal prayer that drove the unclean spirit out of the child about to be baptised, 'along with all anointings, in baptism, the visitation of the sick, and ordination'. In the service of confirmation it 'omitted the ceremonial signing of those confirmed with the sign of the cross on their foreheads',[8] though it retained it, with an important variation of its place in the service, in baptism. Provision for music had been neglectfully, or intentionally, overlooked, and indeed the music choirs and clergy had been accustomed to sing was now mostly politically incorrect or rather, against the law, since the new Prayer Book was the only worship book allowed. At communion, unsurprisingly, there were a number of significant changes. The prayer of invocation, in which the priest called upon God to bless and sanctify the bread and wine, disappeared, together with two signs of the cross made over the elements as an act of blessing. There was a shift from the old idea that the priest could celebrate all by himself to the different emphasis that there must be a 'good noumbre to communicate with the Priest'. The priest was to wear a simple surplice, not a cope nor any other vestment. The celebration was to happen not at an altar but at a table in the body of the church with the priest standing on the north side. Ordinary bread, not a wafer, was to be used, and bread left over was casually disposed of, removing the idea that the bread had actually been consecrated. There would no longer be a reserved sacrament, which meant that it could not be conveyed through the streets to the sick. The priest would celebrate afresh in the house of the sick, though this had the drawback that the emphasis on numbers meant that a sick or dying person might not be able to receive communion at all. Plague was the only exception to this rule, since neighbours were not likely to partake in such a communion service. Duffy emphasises that one of the most striking changes of thought occurred in the attitude to the dead. 'Funerals in late medieval England . . . were intensely concerned with the notion of community, a community in which living and dead were not separated, in which the bonds of affection, duty, and blood continued to bind . . . The dead, whose names were recited week by week in the bede-roll at the parish Mass, remained part of the communities they had once lived in.'[9] The beautiful objects they had left behind for use in worship kept their names and memories alive. Now these ideas changed.

The evangelicals were uncomfortable with any suggestion that the prayers of the living 'might effect any change in the state of the dead' and while the first Prayer Book allowed for prayer for them, the second ruled this out. 'In the world of the 1552 book the dead were no longer with us'[10] is how Duffy puts it. He makes the interesting point that from 1552, the corpse is spoken about but is not addressed directly as was hitherto the case: 'I commend thy soule to God . . .' etc.

The Presence of the Dead

MacCulloch takes up the fundamental issue of the difference between old church and new church in attitudes to the dead, and finds the nub of the matter in the eucharist, whose meaning has now shifted, he suggests, for both Catholic and Protestant alike.

For modern Western Christians it is primarily the service of the living, when those who love the Lord gather to give thanks, to make offering and to celebrate with him. For the late medieval Church, the mass had become as much something for the dead as for the living; it had broken down the barrier between life and death in a very particular, concrete sense. Behind the crowds of the faithful in a medieval parish church . . . jostled invisible crowds, the crowds of the dead. And they crowded in because the Church maintained a model of the afterlife in which the mass could speed the souls of the faithful departed through purgatory. A gigantic consumer demand of the dead fuelled the services of the Church.

It was to change this that the reformers struggled. Insisting that the just shall live by faith alone, they believed that the medieval Church, with the papacy as its evil genius, had played a gigantic confidence trick on the living by claiming to aid the dead in this way. They sought to banish the dead, and to banish the theology which had summoned them into the circle of the living faithful gathered round the Lord's table.[11]

The Reformers, however, wished to replace the commerce of masses and indulgences on behalf of the dead with the concept of 'free' grace offered to dead and living alike.

For Duffy the difference between the two Prayer Books is a decisive one, providing 'a telling index of the distance which the reform had travelled in just three years from the thought world of medieval Catholicism, and therefore from the instincts of the vast majority of people'.[12]

MacCulloch says that churchgoers felt uneasy with the new requirement to receive communion weekly, and started staying away, or sending a servant to be the liturgical representative of their household. Churchwardens, too, were thought to be unhappy at the expense of providing so much bread and wine on a regular basis.

The Pattern is Set
This brought about what was to be of great significance for Anglican worship, a new importance for mattins and evensong, liturgies taking features from the old monastic offices, and designed for the daily use of clergy or for particularly zealous parishioners. What began to be established was 'a morning marathon of prayer, scripture reading and praise, consisting of mattins, litany and ante-communion, preferably as the matrix for a sermon to proclaim the message of scripture anew week by week'.[13] The parish priest was told to say the office of mattins publicly in church and 'from this hint in the Prayer book preface sprang a characteristic pattern of Sunday worship in

the Church of England, morning and evening prayer; this dominated the mainstream devotional life of the Church for four centuries between the accession of two Queen Elizabeths, before the modern emphasis on restoring the central place of the eucharist changed the shape of worship once more.'[14] Many older readers will remember the reciting of mattins and evensong with great pleasure, as I do myself, and can often be heard to say that they miss them.

What was the response of the population at large to the considerable change in their experience of churchgoing? Of course, the loss of feasts, holidays, well-loved ceremonies and rituals, beautiful objects with rich local associations must have been deeply upsetting – one has only to think how much fuss it causes to change almost anything in the furnishings and habits of a modern parish church, to guess what mayhem, what desperate committee meetings, what lobbying behind the scenes, what talking behind people's backs, must have attended the wholesale and chaotic changes of Edward's reign. And it would be a mistake to underestimate the effect of force majeure in silencing protest, in an era of drastic punishment, and no doubt many did keep quiet from a need to keep their jobs, and protect their families and their homes.

But in fact it would be possible to argue that in the sixteenth and seventeenth centuries, when religious ideas were powerfully held and debated throughout society, that people were more, rather than less, capable of protest than our contemporaries.

Which suggests that the evangelical reforms were not simply imposed on the religious culture against the will of nearly everyone, but did, in fact, touch a nerve or feel like an outward expression of ideas already familiar and attractive to large numbers of people. And of course, the wave of reforming enthusiasm from the Continent in its several different forms helped people to feel that this was the way things were going. There seems no doubt that many intelligent and learned people, like Cranmer himself, really did feel a need to question and re-examine their faith, and to make changes in the light of their questioning.

Judith Maltby has written about the response of those who 'conformed', and used the Prayer Book as it was designed to be used, 'whose conformity grew beyond mere obedience to the prince (though we must never lost sight of the *religious* significance of obedience) into an attachment, perhaps even love, for the Church of England'.[15] They did not believe that the Prayer Book was the word of God, but rather that 'when they worshipped according to the lawful liturgy, they were worshipping God'.[16] Such people used the Prayer Book and, in many cases, even owned a copy of it, although it was costly in terms of most people's incomes. She contrasts this with those who did not accept it, the 'spiritually disgruntled' who have tended to interest historians more.

Interesting evidence about the way the laity accepted the Prayer Book comes from a number of complaints parishes made about their clergy in the years following its publication when they felt that their vicar was not doing it justice. For example, at Flixton in Suffolk, parishioners brought their Prayer Books to church with them in order to try to shame their Vicar into conforming. Eventually he was deprived of his living for not doing so. Later there would be a crop of such complaints at the grass roots with vicars (from various motives and theological points of view) trying to show their contempt for the form they were obliged to use by coming late, coming early (so that parishioners arriving on time missed most of the service), refusing to conduct funerals properly, and other such devices. An indignant laity was simply wanting to get on with its prayers in the decent style laid down.[17] It would later be used secretly by Protestants under Queen Mary and again during the era of Cromwell. Roughly 290 editions of the Prayer Book were produced between 1549 and 1642, and something like half a million Prayer Books are thought to have been in circulation before the Civil War in the mid-seventeenth century.[18]

A Coming of Age?

The old practices, however beautiful or charming, did inculcate a passive attitude in worshippers, along with the parental corollary that the priest knew best. Many must have privately thought their local relics of dubious authenticity, or have resented the fat profits made out of indulgences, even while they felt nostalgia for the old rituals of Christmas, Candlemas, Easter and Corpus Christi which they had loved as children. In what was a sort of 'coming of age' of religion (to borrow anachronistically from Bonhoeffer) it seemed natural to begin to ask what *really* happened in the mass or communion service. Few people, of course, had the knowledge and intelligence of men like Cranmer and Bucer, but in the way ideas 'trickle down' from intellectuals and people in the forefront of ideas, first to the middle class, and then to less educated people, it seems likely that ferment, doubts, questions, worked their way through sixteenth-century England. Outside the Church, too, the stew of ideas beginning to brew among the radicals would ferment into the next century.

It was not the unpopularity of evangelical reform that stopped it in its tracks but the failing health of King Edward, whose physical

45

frailty had yielded to tuberculosis. When it became obvious, to the fifteen-year-old King as well as his doctors and courtiers, that death was imminent, he made a will that the succession should pass to his evangelical cousin Lady Jane Grey. This was in contradiction of his father's wish that the succession after Edward should pass to Princess Mary. Unwillingly Cranmer agreed to sign this document, in spite of the fact that by facilitating Henry's annulment he had declared Mary a bastard. In the frenzied days that followed Edward's death, first Jane was proclaimed Queen, only for there to be such a revolt through most of the country that Mary, who had gone into hiding, was quickly named as Queen in her place.

4

The Fall of Cranmer – Queen Mary

From that moment Cranmer knew that he was a lost man. He remained free for a month or two before being summoned to the Star Chamber and taken from there to the Tower on a charge of treason. He would be executed, however, for heresy. His possessions were disposed of, including his magnificent library.

Queen Mary moved tentatively for a little, allowing a funeral for her brother, according to the new Cranmerian rite, with Cranmer himself officiating, though she had a requiem sung for him in the Tower. Many influential people quickly turned their coats and proclaimed Catholic allegiance, while the evangelical leaders waited in dread for the blows to fall. They were picked off one by one, Cranmer, Ridley and Latimer being in the Tower together. A little later on they actually shared a prison apartment, there reading the Bible together and discussing the nature of the eucharistic presence. Outside in the world Cranmer's old enemies openly crowed over him. Within a month the mass in Latin was back.

There was, of course, no question of any compromise between the two forms of religion. For the first time the word 'Protestant' began to be used in contradistinction to 'Catholic', as the polarisation became ever more marked. Events were set in train to realign England with Rome, so that the Queen could make Cardinal Pole Archbishop in Cranmer's place. Parish churches restored altars – there were fierce disputes in some places between those who wanted to keep the tables introduced by Cranmer and those who wanted their altars back – along with whatever survived of the pre-Edwardian 'images'. Those who had acquired 'church goods' for their own profit were discovered, some of them giving back such possessions freely, others having to be pursued and forced to return them. Articles necessary for the re-Romanisation of the churches were also loaned by individuals and between churches. Some two thousand parish clergy were dismissed for having got married.

At the same time Bibles were impounded. Writing of this last move Duffy suggests, perhaps unintentionally, why ultimately England would move away from Catholicism in the form in which Mary and her predecessors had known it. It was not the Bible, as such, that traditional Catholicism disapproved of, he says.

> [Pole] abhorred religious argument and the spirit of self-sufficiency which he believed indiscriminate Bible-reading by lay people was likely to encourage. Better for the people to absorb the faith through the liturgy, to find in attentive and receptive participation in the ceremonies and sacraments of the Church the grace and instruction on which to found the Christian life. This was the true Catholic way, the spirit of the *parvuli*, the 'little ones' of Christ, for whom penitence, not knowledge, was the true and only way to salvation.[1]

Yet it seemed as if the main thrust of the Reformation, in all its forms, was a sense of the *parvuli* striving to become adult, not without the usual difficulties of maturation, but unstoppably and inevitably. But Duffy also puts his finger on the weakness of the evangelical reform. 'Behind the repudiation of ceremonial by the reformers lay a radically different conceptual world, a world in which text was everything, sign nothing.'[2] Celebrating and valuing what it had found at the Reformation, it would take centuries for the Church of England to acknowledge and try to recover what it had lost – the world of signs. In its place text ('the word') became in its own way a different sort of worshipped image, one which sometimes excluded feeling and the deep movements of the unconscious mind which ritual had faithfully fed. It is not, of course, that poetry or powerful preaching cannot express feeling, but that part of our human consciousness is pre-literate, both historically and in our personal childhood experience, and the whole of our experience cannot necessarily be captured in words. It may be important to lay wordless experiences alongside the wordy ones, as in music, colour, form, movement and smell.

Meanwhile the Marian church took up the idea of the use of English. Congregations were to be instructed in the Lord's Prayer, the Hail Mary, the Creed and the Ten Commandments in their own tongue. This idea did not derive from the Reformers, though they had used it to effect. The idea of instructing the faithful in the basic texts of the faith had been around since at least the fourth Lateran Council of 1215. As in Cranmer's time, there was a book of homilies for use by preachers, and naturally they tackled the themes the whole huge dispute had been about – salvation, authority, the papacy, the presence of Christ in the sacrament. One or two of the homilies

48

on less controversial subjects 'were slightly revised versions of the homilies . . . from Cranmer's book'.[3] There were also echoes in the writing in some places of Cranmer's immaculate prose, as if it had engraved itself indelibly on the minds of the writers.

Cranmer Heretic and Hero

Cranmer himself spent two years in prison in varying degrees of discomfort and hardship. Worse than any physical distress was his endless preoccupation with trying to save himself by argument which became a form of mental torture. His mind was clear, some of his arguments excellent, and the political expertise he had learned in his years as Archbishop stood him in as good a stead as anything could. In the main he was to conduct himself with great courage, though the dreadful predicament in which he found himself, and the pressures to which he was subjected, often in isolation, caused him to waver at times between a guilty sense that maybe after all his opponents were right, and he had betrayed Catholic truth, and then a comforting certainty that, after all, he had deeply believed in reform and continued so to believe in it. The trouble was that the latter led ineluctably to his death, and the idea was unbearable to him.

When Latimer and Ridley were burned at the stake, Cranmer was forced to watch the horror from a gatehouse in the town walls of Oxford, undoubtedly in an attempt to frighten him out of his defiance. Fascinated, the crowds watched him as well as the two being executed. He was deeply distressed by what he saw, in particular the long-drawn-out agony of Ridley, whose brother-in-law, in attempting to hasten the death by piling on more fuel, inadvertently prolonged it by using green wood. A contemporary commentator observed that 'Cranmer was very publicly traumatized by the awful sight, tearing off his cap, falling to his knees and desperately bewailing what was happening'.[4] It was the final fixing of the date of his death by burning, MacCulloch suggests, which led Cranmer to a humiliating recantation in which he declared that he had been wrong to deny transubstantiation and to defy the Pope. It is worth remembering in this context that both Joan of Arc and Savanarola each recanted several times – loneliness and intolerable pressure caused even the strongest to break.

In early stages of his imprisonment Cranmer had been subjected to what would be thought of now as brain-washing. On top of his isolation and fear he suffered a great deal of harrying and questioning. When this seemed to result in a degree of penitence his persecutors thought they had got him where they wanted him and he was subjected to a humiliating 'trial' conducted in Christ Church

Cathedral in February 1556. 'To begin with, the prisoner was placed dramatically high up in the Cathedral rood-loft itself, as if in a show case, while John Harpsfield preached on his crimes.'[5] This did not have the expected result. Cranmer turned to the rood beside him, and said that he acknowledged it as his sole judge. He complained of being given no chance to defend himself at Rome, and shouted that he appealed to the next General Council. He was dressed at first in his archiepiscopal robes only to have them stripped off him as a form of humiliation, but he remained impenitent, interrupting comments made by others, calling on people present as witnesses, and questioning the right of the papal delegates to exercise authority as they were trying to do. Following interminable interrogations and wrangles with Catholic dignitaries, Cranmer appeared to weaken at the last and to say that he had been wrong all along in espousing a reformed Catholicism.

Cranmer as Martyr

In order to parade his change of heart Cranmer was given what, in our day, would be called a 'show trial' at the University Church in Oxford. He was led there through the March rain with psalms being chanted antiphonally. From a special stand in a church packed with dignitaries he was treated to a sermon by a Dr Cole which explained, among other things, the dubious rightness of why a sinner who had repented as Cranmer had done should still suffer burning for heresy. Cranmer then took up his agreed text, a mixture of prayers and sermon which covered a good deal of ground. He began by saying that he would treat of 'the great thing, which so much troubleth my conscience' and then went on to other matters, including a recital of the creed. What the authorities were waiting for was to hear him denounce his 'untrue books and writings, contrary to the truth of God's word', and to hear him speak of his recovered belief in transubstantiation. Instead Cranmer denounced his own recantation, and all the papers he had signed to prove it. He then, amid increasing hubbub, said that the Pope was Christ's enemy, and that he did not believe in transubstantiation, just as he had written in the past. He was dragged off the stand and hustled out through the streets of Oxford to his death at the stake, in the place where the Martyrs' Memorial now stands. Famously he held his right hand to the fire, claiming that this was the hand that had betrayed him. He died with the words of the first martyr, Stephen, on his lips: 'Lord Jesus, receive my spirit.'

Diarmaid MacCulloch writes of 'the huge repercussion of the rainy Saturday on which Cranmer died' and of the moving statement which had preceded his death. 'It spread through the centuries like ripples from a stone thrown into a pool, from immediate unfinished business through to the creation of religious and cultural identities for England and for the English-speaking world . . . The Catholic Church's publicity coup lay in ruins.'[6]

The immediate response to the debacle at Oxford was that the government published Cranmer's recantations, and the text of the sermon he was supposed to have delivered on the day of his execution. In vain. In no time at all the true story of what happened was known throughout the country. Later the story of Cranmer's life and death would be graphically told by the Protestant martyrologist John Foxe. Some three hundred others who could not accede to Catholicism also died at the stake – four other bishops, twenty-one clergymen, eight gentlemen, eighty-four tradesmen, one hundred husbandmen, servants and labourers, along with fifty-five women and four children. In addition to this holocaust, many were fined or imprisoned, and goods were confiscated. This rigour did incalculable harm to the way in which Roman Catholicism was henceforth to be viewed in England. 'The stench of faggots was stronger than the smell of incense. Roman Catholicism killed its own cause by the savagery to which it had recourse. After Mary, it was not to be freed from hostility and impediments until the nineteenth century.'[7]

5

The Elizabethan Settlement – the Golden Mediocrity

When Queen Mary died and Queen Elizabeth ascended the throne of England in 1558 she had the unenviable task of governing a bitterly divided country, not a simple polarisation of Catholic and Protestant, but of many smaller groups of dissidents, whose numbers on the Protestant side, fomented by similar movements on the Continent, had been building up ever since Henry's reign – different forms of Puritanism, each with its distinctive set of convictions. So far as religion was concerned she was wary – in her situation a sensible form of shrewdness – and reluctant to move very fast in any direction at all. Religious debate was bound to create storms, and storms were dangerous for the stability of the country. At first there were defiant sayings of mass, and processions through the streets.

Elizabeth set about establishing a new status quo quite quickly. An Act of Supremacy once again severed the link with Rome (in 1559) and a new Prayer Book was authorised – one which was very similar to Cranmer's book of 1552, but more conservative in its understanding of the eucharist. This may have been a sop to the traditionally inclined, but also perhaps reflected a traditional streak in the Queen. She liked her religion middle of the road, preferring an altar with cross and candlesticks to a table. She had a sophisticated taste in choral music and employed Catholic composers and musicians to supply it.

Parishioners were obliged to attend the new/old liturgy on pain of being fined if they did not, and having all their possessions confiscated if they continued the offence. Clergy were allowed to wear a cope to celebrate holy communion. Some feasts were restored. But in other respects things were what they had been in Edward's reign – no images were allowed, or processions, and any pursuit of the cult of the dead was forbidden. There was, however, a softening of iconoclastic practices, and genuflections at the name of Jesus were now permitted. Elizabeth set aside the work Cranmer had done on changing canon law – to open that can of worms offered too much scope for theological and political quarrels, no doubt. Like her father before her she believed that the Church of England was part of the mainstream of Christendom and not a radical break from it, and like her father too, she saw the need for independence from Rome. Elizabeth chose not to be 'head' of the Church, like her father and brother, but 'supreme governor'.

> The queen's highness is the only supreme governor of this realm, and of all other her highness's dominions and countries, as well in all spiritual or ecclesiastical things or causes, as temporal, and that no foreign prince, person, prelate, state or potentate, has, or ought to have, any jurisdiction, power, superiority, pre-eminence, or authority ecclesiastical or spiritual within this realm.[1]

David Edwards describes how it was at this point that 'a tension between Catholic and Protestant became built into the English Church'[2] – MacCulloch alternatively describes this as 'the unending dialogue of Protestantism and Catholicism which forms Anglican identity'. Priests trained abroad who returned to England or people harbouring priests in their homes were liable to the death penalty. The fear was not so much of Catholics, as of political disloyalty or treason. But the flame of Catholic devotion remained strong, and remained an important current of English life, an underground stream, until it began to appear above ground in the nineteenth and twentieth centuries. The force of Puritanism, now increasingly evident in English life, was also biding its time to complete, as the Puritans saw it, the reform already begun.

Yet, partly because of the influence of the Bible, and partly because of a sense of things gradually settling down (though there would be many upheavals to come), the new Protestant way of religion began to achieve what church people nowadays call 'reception'. 'New pieties were forming' says Eamon Duffy 'and something of the old sense of the sacred was transferring itself from the sacramentals to the scriptures.'[3] At any rate, by the 1570s there is a perceptible sense of a changing of the guard, even in many traditional parishes. Duffy uses the example of Morebath, a parish which had done its best to resist the changes, and the way in which its records of expenditure and acquisitions 'record the passing of a world'.

> Slowly the Elizabethan order had been accepted. Chalice gave way to communion cup, altar to table, and the vestments, hoarded so long against the day of restoration, were eventually unstitched and resewn to adorn the table of the supper. And as these external changes had been accepted, so attitudes had shifted. By 1573 the old priest, who had urged his flock on to set silver shoes on St Sidwell and lights before the Jesus altar, had come to see in the gift to his church of a handsome communion book and psalter for the new service a cause for prayerful rejoicing. In a thousand parishes in the 1570s and 1580s the same victory of a reformed over traditional religion was silently and imperceptibly enacted.[4]

Owen Chadwick describes the breach with Rome as appearing to the Reformers like 'the cutting out of a moth-eaten patch of the cloth and the renewal or cleansing of the remainder'. It was the beginning of a huge English hostility to the tradition they had excised. '[They] saw in the Pope of Rome the Scarlet Woman, or the Beast, Antichrist sitting upon the throne destined for another.'[5]

It must have seemed a notable victory to the Protestants. Public religion had re-formed itself around monarch, Scripture, the Prayer Book and holy communion, instead of around the papacy, ritual, the mass, and a particular understanding of the dead. 'The new generation of the 1590s and 1600s had known no other Church, and had come to love the rhythms of the Anglican liturgical year, and the cadences of Cranmer's liturgy.'[6]

Undoubtedly the Prayer Book became of huge significance to the Church of England, and those of us – a dwindling band – whose introduction to Christian liturgy it was, know something of its power and beauty. Yet some of the sense of 'traditional religion' went underground in Elizabethan England, to be carried by the folk memory like a stream, and to resurface four centuries later. Most people did not have the courage, the certainty or the obstinacy of the Catholic recusants – they went with the new status quo and came to enjoy it and discover that it had its own spiritual qualities. But it neglected some things important to the human psyche, as traditional religion had itself neglected other things.

There were other reasons for the success of Protestantism. It was as if the individual worshipper was reaching for a new independence from the power of the priest, the terrors of purgatory, and the influence of 'the dead'. This independence, and the growth in humanism, appeared to express or at least parallel a rising confidence in nationhood, which found expression both in exploration of the world, and in a great flowering of poetry and drama. Perhaps the years of bitter religious conflict encouraged a turning away to learned and aesthetic pursuits, many of them far removed from an obsessive interest in religion. When Matthew Parker, Elizabeth's first Archbishop of Canterbury, talked of the young English church as 'a golden mediocrity', which was to say a golden mean or *via media,* he caught something essential about people's attraction to it, or perhaps a quality that was growing in the English character. Religious extremists caused enormous havoc in the sixteenth and seventeenth century, and possibly for this reason a dislike of extremism began to mark the Church of England. There have been many extremists since, of course, and they have had their hour and have sometimes given precious insights to the Church which have become incorporated into its ideas and practices, yet there seems to be a need for the pendulum to swing back in its own good time to the golden mediocrity.

There seems to have been a final willingness to accept a church not too aggressively Protestant, and not entirely devoid of its Catholic virtues. The new independent and quasi-secular thought liked the idea of a national church, that is to say one that had mastery in its own house and was not under the authority of the Pope.

> There was a genuine swing away from a priest-ridden hocus-pocus religion, exploiting the poor and ignorant, and obscuring, even dishonouring its biblical origins and a longing for a faith which was above board and gentlemanly and kept in its place ... in a Christian community not yet split into a multitude of sects but all contained within the one *Ecclesia Anglicana* Elizabeth's problem was to find a settlement so satisfactory to all factions that it would drive none into rebellion or recusancy.[7]

It was to be episcopal rather than presbyterian in form.

Scripture, Tradition and Reason

The theologian Richard Hooker, second only perhaps to Cranmer as a founding father of the Church of England, came to prominence in Elizabeth's reign. 'Hooker formulated what was to become the classic Anglican reliance on Scripture, on "Tradition" meaning the whole inspired experience of the Church of Christ, and on Reason as the God-given glory of humanity.'[8] In his writings he said that 'the laws made by the monarch with the consent of Parliament were in effect the laws of God for the people of England'. As Tudor subjects knew very well, this might just be exchanging one tyranny for another, though it was, in a sense, an advantage that the tyrant was closer to home. It would be a couple of centuries before England learned to remove the possibility of tyranny, at least in the old form. The sense of a national church with the monarch as 'supreme governor' both appealed to England's instinct for independence, and also helped to nourish the idea.

The True Church

Hooker and the bishops of his circle believed that the Church of England was more truly Catholic than the Roman Church, having scraped away the barnacles of superfluous doctrines and dubious practices and returned to Scripture and the purity of the early Church. It was a bigger and more generous way of understanding what they were about than that of the earlier Reformers, a religion of intelligence, graciousness and generosity which allowed a certain flexibility. What might be seen as the more settled 'Anglican' view, which was similar to that of the Lutheran and Erasmian view, was that rites and ceremonies (water in baptism, the use of the surplice, bowing at the name of Jesus) are permissible if not expressly against Scripture. Hooker and his bishops

> presented the Church of England as the best of all churches, claiming an apostolic descent and an uninterrupted history from the Celtic Church which gave it a greater authority than the schismatic Protestant churches, and a superiority over Rome in that it had sloughed off the corruptions of the usurped authority of the bishops of Rome. The Church of England had an authority as ancient and as apostolic as Rome's, and a practice more true to the injunctions of Christ.[9]

This confident view was threatened by Puritanism, a Calvinist form of religion, which emphasized that more was needed than the simple practice of churchgoing and prayers. What the Puritans, like the present day evangelicals, preached was 'conversion' – an 'experience' of God that indicated one was 'chosen', or 'saved'.

The Thirty-Nine Articles

The Thirty-Nine Articles, meant as a kind of definition of what the Church of England stood for, were put together in 1571, and never again revised despite attempts to do so, for example in 1922. A revision of the Forty-Two Articles written by Cranmer, they have the profoundly Protestant emphasis one might expect – the reliance upon Scripture, justification by faith, not good works, the authority of 'the Prince', the rejection of purgatory, the use of the vernacular, the administering of communion 'in both kinds', the idea of Christ's death as a 'satisfaction', that is to say a propitiation for all the sin of the world, and the denial of 'transubstantiation'. Many of these things would still be acceptable to many Anglican church-goers, though there might be reservations about 'Princes', about how Scripture was to be interpreted, and about the doctrine of 'satisfaction', not necessarily all by the same people. And no doubt some Anglo-Catholics believe in purgatory. The Articles from which most of the Church of England has silently departed long ago, though some extreme Protestants create difficulties by incon-veniently remembering them, are Article XVII which, in the late Cranmerian style, embraces predestination, and Article XXV which recognises only two sacraments, baptism and holy communion, leaving out confirmation, penance, ordination, marriage and extreme unction.

The King James's Bible

Despite the Calvinistic note in the Articles, Elizabeth did not have Calvinist sympathies, though she knew that many of her subjects did. Her instinct for moderation and that of her successor, James I, were themselves facts which helped to shape the Church of England. James insisted on bishops, and the obedience owed to them by clergy and laity, and appointed a Calvinist archbishop. He set a group of scholars to work on revising the existing forms of the English Bible, leaning heavily upon Tyndale's translation, and the 'Authorised Version', worked upon in Westminster Abbey's Jerusalem Chamber, was published in 1611, a book of extraordinary influence, on religion itself, obviously, but also on the whole formation and use of the English language. It took only two years and nine months to complete.

As significant as anything else in the whole story of the English Reformation is the way that more and more people were learning to read. It was particularly effective to appeal to the authority of the Scriptures when they were no longer transmitted at second-hand.

> The man who could sit by his own fire and con his Bible, or bring his family together and read it to them at prayers, or study it with his friends, was not only going to be affected by it at the deepest spiritual level, but was made in a measure independent of Church and priest and critically armed against both.[10]

The oral tradition had been largely superseded.

Great religious poetry was beginning to emerge from *ecclesia anglicana* – that of John Donne, George Herbert and Henry Vaughan. Donne, Dean of St Paul's, had the appeal of the reformed rake; as a young man he wrote erotic poetry, as a middle-aged cleric he wrote wonderful sermons. Herbert was the gentleman and courtier who turned away from the world of power and glamour to the pious life of a country priest. Rather like the 'poor parson' in Chaucer's Prologue, Herbert, at Bemerton, became a model of the good clergyman, constant in prayer, dutiful in his public speaking and prayers, kind to the poor. Vaughan was the visionary and mystic.

The Middle Way

At the beginning of the Stuart period there were three main religious groups – the traditional Catholic group, depleted by suffering, persecution and the general drift towards what might, though so far it was not, called 'Anglicanism', the Puritans, in various forms, who wanted to change the Church much more extensively, many of whom abhorred bishops, and a middle group who did not wish the extremism and fanaticism of either of the others.

> No one at the beginning of the Stuart era, or when the struggle between king and parliament, bishop and puritan, was at its height could have imagined that it would be this third party, the middle of the road group, which would emerge victorious by the end of the century, retaining the monarchy, a catholic but reformed Church on the one side but on the other a supreme parliament and a modest degree of religious toleration. It would have seemed the least, the most absurd possibility.[11]

Much bloody water was to pass under the bridge before that happened, however. Under James and Charles I bishops again became powerful. Archbishop William Laud dismayed Calvinists by adopting what David Edwards calls the 'more optimistic' approach to salvation, the idea that more, rather than fewer, might hope to be saved – not a popular idea with Puritans. The Arminians also looked more kindly on the 'old religion', which meant in practice that Laud allowed 'altars' to be used again in a sense, that is to say 'tables', not stone altars, could be placed at the east end of the churches and railed in. Churches were permitted to be more beautiful and services more aesthetic. Strict Sunday observance was also softened.

Arminian ideas and the anger they produced among the Puritans helped precipitate the Civil War and Charles was executed. It was a shocking end to the idea that monarchs ruled by divine right, a powerful blow at a church which depended upon a monarch as 'supreme governor'.

The Puritan Chance

It was the great chance of the Puritans to complete, as they saw it, the work of religious reform, and, on the way to doing that, to extirpate all prelates and ecclesiastical offices. The Book of Common Prayer was banned, and thousands of clergy were dismissed from parishes and from the universities. The Cromwellian era unleashed yet another phase of violent philistinism on the churches; once again there was smashing, desecrating and defacing. One instance of this is the beautiful Blythburgh church in Suffolk where horses were stabled in the church – a deliberate fouling of a sacred place – and soldiers took potshots at the beautiful carved angels in the roof. Another is the systematic destruction of the Lady Chapel in Ely Cathedral. Acting, singing, dancing, the celebration of Christmas and other festivals, were all forbidden.

The great hope of the Presbyterians to achieve a 'Settlement' was foiled, partly by Cromwell's gift for playing one party off against another, partly because he feared that the 'freedom of conscience' he believed in would be denied by such a Settlement.

'Ordinary people', craftsmen, farm labourers, Congregationalists, Quakers, Independents like the very 'unordinary' tinker John Bunyan, were not only reading the Bible for themselves by now but had a very powerful sense of themselves as 'chosen by the Spirit', which gave them an extraordinary new mood of confidence.

The Puritan Collapse – the Legitimate King Recalled

Yet in the middle of the seventeenth century hope, energy, purpose, certainty, failed the Puritan cause, an unexpected collapse, which made way for the Restoration of the monarchy. The Parliament summoned after Cromwell's death came to feel 'that there was no alternative open to those who wanted stability: the legitimate king must be recalled and with him the establishment of the Church of England must be restored'.[12] It was a choice for the less extreme, one which one might feel was typical of the English character, or alternatively that the English character, and the taste for *via media*, was itself shaped by a series of such decisions.

1662

After the dramas and reverses and the very real suffering of the Civil War and its aftermath, life slowly settled back into something like normality. The Church of England, less Calvinist than it had been, moved centre stage. The Act of Uniformity of 1662, together with the revised Prayer Book, which was essentially the old Prayer Book of 1549, with additions by Bishop Cosin and others, enforced Anglican worship upon everyone. David Edwards paints a picture of the post-Restoration parish which

> now depended more on the 'squire' than on the 'parson' . . . The priest was often poorly paid, either because he had been appointed in one of the many parishes which were too small or because he was a 'curate' paid by a rector who, being a graduate with a family, might think himself entitled to receive the income of more than one parish and to live where a decent house was available.[13]

Most of the people in the parish accepted the Church of England – as they had to, for baptism was the only way of registering a birth, a wedding in church was the only way of making a marriage legal, and there was no alternative to being buried in the churchyard. But not all attended the Sunday services, and in most parishes only about a tenth communicated at the celebrations of holy communion, usually four a year. The Church of England was a success in political terms, but a qualified one in religious terms. The law was harsh on dissenters, who were forbidden to meet in their own homes or to preach. Bunyan was one of those put in prison for continuing to preach, and he spent twelve years there altogether. Under the Five Mile Act of 1665 dispossessed Puritan incumbents were forbidden to go within five miles of their former livings. The Roman party suffered equally, the Test Act of 1673 forcing all prominent men to swear against transubstantiation. James II's Declaration of Indulgence in 1687 giving Romans and Nonconformists the right to worship in their own way brought about his downfall, and he fled to Europe. The invitation by Parliament to William and Mary to take the throne of England in 1688 led to a revolt by a large group of bishops, clergy and lay people. Nine bishops and four hundred clergy refused to take the Oath of Allegiance to the new monarchs on the grounds that by doing so they would break their earlier oaths to James and to his successors. The Non-jurors, as they were called, suffered severely for their refusal, being sent to the Tower and deprived of their office in the case of bishops, and losing their livings in the case of clergy. The integrity of their position still casts a glow of heroism over their action, though it achieved no result, and it is difficult not to feel with hindsight that William and Mary were a much better bet as monarchs than James II.

6

A Different Debate

Some of the energy was going out of the religious debate that had raged for two hundred years – it was like a great fire gradually dying down. The squabbles had more the character of grievances than issues of life and death or heresy. In Purcell's short opera *King Arthur*, full of fairies and rural idyll, there is a sudden outburst of rage against the Church in a comic harvest drinking song from a bunch of farmers. Drinking, as they say, 'till they cannot stand, All for the glory of old England', they go on to complain of tithing.

One in ten. One in ten. Why should a blockhead have one in ten?

They also protest against the boredom of church services and sermons and the laxity of the clergy.

Why sit and hark to a drunken sot,
While pie and pudden are burnt to pot?

One can almost smell the burning Sunday dinners. Hogarth satirised the Church as mercilessly as many other aspects of eighteenth-century life – there are pictures of sleeping congregations which bear out the whinge of Purcell's farm labourers. Nevertheless there is abundant evidence that eighteenth-century clergy were respected figures in their communities. Sermons, in fact, were extremely popular, and sold well in printed form.

The eighteenth century has often been presented as a 'tunnel period' in the history of the Church, a time when its particular genius was eclipsed, and it was somnolent and careless. Recent studies suggest something different and make it seem very possible that this negative view of it stemmed partially from the need of ideologues – the Evangelical and Oxford Movements – to see themselves in a flattering light. What appears striking now is that parish life in the period was still at the heart of rural and urban communities in a way we can only just imagine, with the pulpit a place where important shared ideals were articulated. Parishioners had a deep attachment to their church. Very possibly the Church reached the all-time zenith of popular allegiance in England and Wales in the first half of the eighteenth century.

'The social and economic life of the early eighteenth century was relatively small-scale. Most people lived in villages and small towns . . . In relatively small-scale societies people knew one another, or at least knew about one another. There was potential for a much greater sense of social solidarity and cohesion . . .'[1] The parish church was the nucleus of that cohesion.

The peculiar intimacy of the society came not from the fact that nobody ever went away – it was not uncommon for one or more members of a provincial family to live or work in London, and travel was quite common – as that 'most people worked in the context of a household or family, their own or someone else's'.[2] Some historians say that the early years of the eighteenth century were the last remnant of 'the old world', a close society where Christian beliefs and imperatives existed by 'universally held opinion'.[3] More recent research suggests that, despite the influence of sceptic philosophers among intellectuals, a commonalty of Christian opinion held its own for most of the century.

'The parish church provided a focus for neighbourhood life and pride . . . welfare and religion were allied forces, and the secular wealth and spiritual energy of the period were directed towards charity and church building.'[4] Those who enjoyed wealth felt it was mandatory justice to provide for poorer people. They were not alone. 'The vision of a Christian community tied together by gratitude and acts of kindness, by brotherly (and sisterly) feelings in Christ's name, continued to occupy an important place in social thought.'[5] The church was the place of local government. The 'vestry' set rates for the property owners of the parish which were used to care for the poor, to tend to the highways and secure law and order, and they also appointed church wardens (some of whom were women) to oversee the church building itself, and to look to the conduct of the clergy and the spiritual welfare of the parishioners.

Parish churches were important expressions of communal pride, and much money was spent on beautifying them. People often learned first of national and local events through announcements at services, and sermons might provide political as well as spiritual commentary. Material facts underlined the centrality of the church. It was usually the biggest building for miles around, and as such an appropriate meeting place. It was also the storage place for the community's possessions, provided and maintained by the vestry – the fire engine and fire buckets, and the standard weights and measures. Going to church was an important part of social life, and not to attend was to cut oneself off from what was going on around one. This seems to have applied to the labouring classes as well as the better off. One curate describes his congregation as made up of 'farmers, labourers, mechanics and fishermen', all of whom attended church regularly. Citizenship and Christianity were coterminous in a way that is surely gone for ever, though the Church of England has a sort of folk memory of this period, and still appears to hanker for it.

Communion was often celebrated monthly, with very large numbers at Easter. Depending somewhat on what sort of work people did, many people attended church daily. Even Dissenters attended parish churches from time to time (and Anglicans sometimes attended Dissenting meeting-houses). There was more movement between the two groups than has been popularly supposed, and, by this stage of English history, a more relaxed relationship between them.

A series of social changes slowly accumulating during the eighteenth century, however, were to affect the Church profoundly. A gradual moving apart of social groups, including the clergy, who were becoming more affluent and acquiring more status, began to break up the unity of the earlier society, and segregation of housing for different groups was literally moving them apart. The expansion of towns, migration with consequent disruption of the family, new and more commercial patterns of work in workshops rather than in the home, all helped to break down the old communal values, together with the morality that went with them. 'These factors were probably quite as important in diminishing the role of the Church in the lives of English people as the attacks on the Church of England's political power, and the slow growth of Enlightenment ideas in England.'[6]

The Enlightenment spoke in many voices. One of them was satire, the satire of Voltaire, Gibbon and Swift. In his 'Voyage to the Houyhnhnms' (the last part of *Gulliver's Travels*), Jonathan Swift reviews English religious history.

> Differences of opinion hath cost many millions of lives; for instance, whether flesh be bread, or bread be flesh; whether the juice of a certain berry be blood or wine; whether it be better to kiss a post, or throw it into the fire; what is the best colour for a coat, whether black, white, red or grey; and whether it should be

long or short, narrow or wide, dirty or clean; and with many more. Neither are any wars so furious and bloody, or of so long continuance, as those occasioned by difference in opinion, especially if it be in things indifferent.[7]

Put like that, the religious disputes over transubstantiation, visual images, Puritanism and the Prayer Book, all look foolish exposed to the cold light of reason and Swift's clever tongue, though the things that seemed to Swift indifferent were projections of very deep disagreements, some of them, perhaps, arising from profound differences of religious temperament.

Perhaps the most influential philosopher of the Enlightenment was John Locke. He was born in 1632, but his book *Two Treatises on Civil Government* published in 1690 was profoundly influential in the eighteenth century, and disturbed the assumptions of a Church-focused society as surely as economic and industrial change. Arguing against the biblical arguments of Robert Filmer who saw government as a monarchic organisation with a paternal role, one to which all were required to submit themselves, Locke saw 'man' as a free sovereign being, gifted with reason in order to understand and arrange his life for his own good, surrendering his freedom to 'society' only in return for various kinds of shared protection – of property, rights and person. 'Society' is not a mystical body in Locke's view, but a convenience rationally consented to. Similarly the individual, according to the *Essay Concerning Human Understanding*, is not an immortal soul, trailing clouds of glory, but, famously, a *tabula rasa*, with everything to learn from his or her senses.

One might argue that England had been moving against a monarchical philosophy from the day in the previous century when it had struck against 'divine right' – monarchical and paternal government – by beheading King Charles. Locke was not, or did not see himself as being, anti-Christian. He thought, as perhaps many Christians think today, that the essence of Christianity was belief in Jesus as the Messiah sent by the Creator. He saw believers as giving themselves up to him, to be his subjects, and to obey the moral laws which he taught.

From the seventeenth century onwards there was much discussion of Deist philosophy, a system of 'natural religion' which, to begin with, included a diverse group of people who believed slightly different things, but which eventually crystallised into a body of belief which granted God the primal act of creation, and little else in terms of further intervention in the world. Deism was a great talking-point, but never as popular as a belief in England as on the Continent.

In the mid-eighteenth century scepticism reached its apogee in the work of the Scottish philosopher David Hume, who thought that there was no such thing as real knowledge – the best we could hope for was an appearance of probability. Belief in the existence of God and of the physical world could not be proved by reason. Reason itself 'is nothing but a species of sensation'. He denied any underlying purpose or unity in the world. 'Objects have no discoverable connexion together; nor is it from any other principle but custom operating upon the imagination, that we can draw any inference from the appearance of one to the existence of another.'[8]

While these new ideas were being put forward, many intelligent people stuck with their beliefs. Dr Johnson's Toryish Anglicanism has something very appealing about it, as he gives all his loose change to beggars, cares for a blind old woman, Mrs Williams, in his own home with great devotion, or rails at the cruel way England was treating the Irish Catholics. There is a simplicity in his love for his Church and its disciplines, and a patient application to the idea of loving his neighbour that is very moving. Some would say that this sort of 'practical Christianity' was entirely typical of the period.

The clergyman James Woodforde (1740–1803), a Norfolk rector, wrote a famous diary[9] in which he recorded the domestic pleasures and pains and bits of gossip of parish life – the planting of his vegetables in his garden, and the making of beer, the shooting of a sick dog as an act of mercy, dealing with the problem of a parishioner who had got a girl pregnant and then did not wish to marry her, enjoying merry rounds of whist with local friends as well as evenings of charades, suffering over a brief infatuation with a woman who hurt his feelings badly, keeping his record of who attends his church, and his equally meticulous record of what he ate. It is this latter predilection of his for the pleasures of the table – the last entry in his diary, as death comes to claim him, is 'For dinner today, roast beef!' – that makes him slightly despised by those who like clergy to be spiritual and austere. As a great admirer of Woodforde's, I only wish more parish priests were like him. He was a modest man, meticulous in his work, moderately happy in an everyday sort of way, loving life. He was kind to his servants and relatives, endlessly thoughtful for the poor of his parish, inviting them to a good meal at Christmas and making sure they had enough to eat at other times. He refused to join in a petition to give a local highwayman an extra cruel whipping on the way to his execution, and he visited the man in prison and gave him sixpence to ensure he had a few last comforts. Woodforde was a man incapable of extremes. Perhaps there is something more earthy, more run-of-the-mill, and therefore more durable, about such priests than about the extremists of one kind or another. I think of them as a sort of backbone of the Church of England.

Woodforde lived in a world still recognisable in Jane Austen's *Sense and Sensibility*, published only a few years after his death, in which domestic and local life was woven with the life of the Church, and in which even major events did not seem to intrude very much on the pleasant lives of the gentry or the much harder lives of the rural poor. The clergy, of course, like Jane Austen's Edward Ferrers, were gentry themselves, and there were vestiges of this tendency up until the 1960s. Different from Woodforde (though not very much) were the high churchmen of the eighteenth century, the ancestors of the Oxford Movement, though little loved or admired by them. (As originally used, from about 1688, the word 'high' meant 'strict' or 'stiff' and described a person meticulous in following the rules of the Church, and a staunch defender of the Establishment.[10]) John Keble referred contemptuously to their 'two bottle orthodoxy', presumably with reference to their drinking habits as well as their supposed half-hearted quality. Modern historians do not tend to see eighteenth-century high churchmen like this, but suggest that, since they tended to antagonise Roman Catholics on the one hand, and Dissenters on the other, because of their impartial suspicion of both, they made considerable enemies in a way that influenced their later reputation.[11]

Tories almost to a man, and lovers of the quiet life, the high churchmen distanced themselves from excesses of all kinds, but particularly those of the sixteenth century. They would be described with some justice by their nineteenth-century successors as 'theologically ambiguous, Erastian, "high and dry" '. They were said to be worldly, and in matters of ritual and spirituality cold and and dull.[12] They were, however, devoted to the Book of Common Prayer, regarded the Church of England as a branch of the Church universal, clung closely to the creeds and believed in canonical obedience in a way the Oxford Movement certainly did not emulate. They followed carefully the Church's rubrics about how to conduct matters in church. 'Careful adherence to the rubricks was seen . . . as the most distinctive characteristic of high churchmen . . . The readiness to subordinate private preferences to the greater needs of unity constituted one of the greatest differences between the eighteenth century high churchmen and their nineteenth century successors.'[13]

Shading off from the higher churchmen were the 'latitudinarians' (a term first applied in the seventeenth century). Influenced by the ideas of Locke, with his emphasis on reason, they were uninterested in some of the old dogmatisms. High churchmen, by contrast, followed in the steps of Laud, believing in an apostolic order and a static deposit of doctrine, and evangelicals harked back to the Reformers and Calvinistically inclined bishops of the early seventeenth century.

For the first time in England it was possible, if not quite fashionable, at least among intellectuals, not to believe in God. The belief in reason, Hume excepted, led to a confident belief in progress – the idea that by casting away the superstition and intolerance of the past it would be possible for humanity to improve itself and bring about happier societies.

There were new philosophical and scientific preoccupations around in Enlightenment England, new secular interests, a new pleasure in enjoying oneself. Intellectually, and also humanly speaking, there were striking gains. The total preoccupation with what people believed, and the sense that this was all that mattered about them, and that it might consign them to heaven or hell after death, retreated somewhat. There was the beginning of an understanding that everyone could not be pressed into the same mould, and with that a developed sense of the value, and usefulness, of tolerance. Along with this went ideas about human rights and freedom, and the beginnings of the concept of the emancipation of women. The arts, music, literature, the theatre, flourished. The eighteenth century was a great century for talk, and the coffeehouses flourished as places of social gathering. Well-to-do people in great houses occupied themselves with scientific research, as well as social and aesthetic pleasures. Their interest in botany and agricultural method helped to precipitate change, as they came to understood new methods of growing crops and breeding animals. None of this could have taken place in the largely feudal society, with its peasants and its strip farming, which had been typical of England since the Middle Ages. So 'enclosure' – the appropriation of common land – came about, which brought about an agricultural revolution with new and improved crops and healthier breeds of cattle.

By the end of the eighteenth century belief in 'reason' or even in 'reasonableness' took a tremendous tumble with the hideous spectacle of the French Revolution, which began by deposing a king and a political system which certainly ground the faces of the poor, but ended in a blood bath in which no one felt safe. The fear that that produced had repercussions in England, when any attempt to protest about poverty and injustice by the underclass was seen as the first step on a slippery slope, and was harshly put down.

A landless Proletariat

Changes in agricultural methods, together with 'enclosure', created an indigent peasant class, a whole generation suddenly unemployed, what Marx was to call 'a landless proletariat'. The combination of new invention and a large group of impoverished peasants helped bring about the Industrial Revolution, which herded the lower classes into the factory towns of the North. To start with they were much better off in terms both of health and prosperity, a fact evident in the doubling of the population over seventy years around 1850. Later, living conditions became worse; children in particular were severely exploited, and most workers were grossly overworked by greedy employers.

Gin and Sin

'Was the Church aware of this vast social and economic trans-formation?' Leslie Paul asks.

> On the whole it would seem not, at least until well into the nineteenth century. There was, of course, a piecemeal awareness. Many priests must have know of, and connived in, the sale of poor law children to the new factories. Many were magistrates, all were members of the parish vestry, the organ of local government. The clergy could hardly ignore the invasion of their parishes by factories and industrial housing . . . They were torn between pride in local progress and the wealth it would bring, alarm lest the invasion of the poor in search of work meant a higher poor law rate and a genuine but unworthy fear of the already alienated masses . . . The poor in the towns were being brutalized by their living conditions, particularly the overcrowding in disease-ridden houses . . . which they took to gin and sin to escape – abandoning the Church . . . The Church of England has never overcome this social heritage from the nineteenth century, this identification with masters and landed gentry *against* the poor. I would say that this, more than anything, was the great watershed in the history of the Church: a great class, both patronized and despised, then decided that 'the Church is not for us'.[14]

Yet against this view of the Church of England as indifferent to the suffering of the labouring poor is strong evidence of innumerable small 'societies' of religious people, who met regularly within parish churches to pray and read the Bible together, and who also worked to help the poor in various ways – in education, charity schools and religious education, in the form of arranging for young people to be 'catechised' and receive religious books, collecting money to relieve suffering, suppressing 'houses of ill fame', etc. This work, like much individual charity, did relieve poverty and its effects, but it has an atmosphere of 'improvement' about it – improving both of those who belonged to the religious societies and the poor themselves – which has a feeling of *de haut en bas* about it, and is a long way from perceiving and striving to correct the social wrongs that brutalised the poor. The societies may have been motivated partly by fear of Dissenters – the Act of Toleration of 1689 which removed the old sanctions against Dissenters made many devout Anglicans fearful.

The reports which eventually drew attention to the appalling lives of the industrial workers came not from the churches but from government sources.

In this seedbed the Evangelical Movement and Methodism were both to grow; both placed less emphasis on 'communality' than parish church religion had done, and more on individual piety and discipline. The individual's relationship to God, rather than the relationship of the community with God, became paramount.

The Method

It has often been suggested that revolution was avoided in England by the power of the Wesleyan revival. John Wesley, the son of an Anglican clergyman in Lincolnshire, and an Anglican clergyman himself, began his spiritual life very much under the influence of the heroism of the Non-jurors. As a young man he lived a life of prayer and fasting, regular offices and a daily eucharist – a set of disciplines and beliefs very like those that were the Tractarian starting point. (The Methodist Gordon Wakefield says of John Wesley and John Henry Newman that they were 'by any standards the two outstanding English Christians since the Reformation – and the Church of England could contain neither of them'.[15]) Wesley first had a conversion experience as a young don at Oxford, and then some years later, after considerable inner distress (like Newman he had neurotic tendencies, evidenced not least by his habit of working himself continually to collapse), he underwent a second conversion, strongly influenced by Lutheran ideas, which prepared the way for his distinctive life's work. From the age of thirty-five he devoted himself to a lifetime of journeys as exhausting as those of St Paul, covering, it has been estimated, about a quarter of a million miles in his travels about Britain on horseback and preaching some 40,000 sermons. He spoke to the poor, to miners and factory workers, to gin-drinkers and slum-dwellers, and his powers as an orator were so extraordinary that, particularly in the early years, his listeners fell into ecstatic trances.

Individuals changed colour, cried out, fell insensible, were overwhelmed with simultaneous conviction of guilt and salvation,
roared out their hallelujahs and their hymns in the certainty of the
presence of the Lord. Britain had never witnessed before such a
wave of religious fervour as brought together twenty thousand
poor to listen together in one place to one Church of England
priest.[16]

As time went on Wesley, whose gifts of organisation were as
remarkable as his gifts as a preacher, developed his 'method' of
organising worship and teaching people about Christianity. It
depended very largely on lay leadership and on meeting in people's
own homes – what was known as 'the class system' – and it
developed an important tradition of lay preaching. In 1850, apart
from its full-time ministers, it had '20,000 local preachers, over
50,000 class leaders, together with trustees, stewards, prayer leaders
and Sunday School teachers'.[17] The aristocracy and the non-
labouring poor were little influenced by Methodism, but in the
middle class and the working class it established itself firmly.
Harrison describes farm labourers feeling at home in the Methodist
setting 'in the way they seldom did in the parish church with its
liturgy, ritual and sermon by a middle-class parson'.[18] Dignity,
knowledge, an exercise of responsibility came, via Methodism, to a
group of people who had been excluded from such opportunities.
Like the religion of the Independents of the previous century it
invited poor people, as Bunyan had been, not simply to be preached
to, but to preach, to comprehend and to convey religious truths
themselves. It was a 'layman's religion'. What Wesley taught, he
said was 'plain truth for plain people', a truth of assurance that, by
way of the cross, salvation was for everyone, everyone was 'justified'.
    Methodism thus had an Arminian tinge to it, and a warmth that
swept through the working classes of Britain with extraordinary
power. 'My heart it doth dance at the sound of his name', as a
Wesleyan hymn had it.
    It also had repercussions that went beyond religion. 'It is not an
accident that almost every self-educated working man in early and
mid-Victorian England who came to write his memoirs, paid tribute
to the beneficial influence of Methodism in his youth.'[19] What they
describe, together with some later accounts, is 'a pattern of Methodist
domestic piety, help in a local Sunday school, conversion, membership of a Methodist class, preaching and then (usually) a progression
beyond the original Methodism to some new intellectual position.
Methodism for them was almost a natural stage in their educational

and moral development.'[20] In addition to this it offered a model for Chartist and radical organisations (both of which adopted something like the 'class' system), and it trained its followers in public speaking. Methodist ideas became adopted into plans for social and political reform.

Wesley's other great Methodist contemporary and fellow-preacher, George Whitefield, had his own chapel in London, enjoyed extraordinary esteem in America, and was supported by the patronage of the Countess of Huntingdon, who set up her own religious institution – the Countess of Huntingdon's Connexion – after Whitefield's death. A very gifted speaker, as capable as Wesley of attracting huge working-class audiences, Whitefield's beliefs had a stronger Calvinist note, with a belief that only some could be saved and that these were a predestined elite. Closely allied at first, the two men drifted apart in their beliefs, and the formal break between them came in 1741. There were to be a number of other Methodist secessions with consequent fragmentation over the next century.

But the achievement was immense. 'The Church of England', says Leslie Paul, 'did not know what to do with the religious revival that John Wesley handed to it on a plate.'[21] Regretfully Wesley began himself to ordain ministers to carry on his work after his death. A great opportunity to contain the vitality and working-class appeal of Wesleyism was lost.

Parallel to the working-class appeal of Methodism, was the growing working-class Roman Catholic community as more and more Catholics crossed the Irish Sea in search of work. 'Instead of a church composed of a few ancient families, mostly in the North, the Roman communion became a body catering to the needs of predominantly working class congregations of Irish origin.'[22] As a result of this rapid increase in numbers the Roman hierarchy was reintroduced into Britain in 1850, amid huge misgivings in the Church of England.

It might have been thought that Wesley and the evangelicals within the Church of England would make common cause, but it did not work out like that. The evangelicals had a strongly Calvinist streak that was different from Wesley's more optimistic view of salvation, but it was similar in important respects, in particular the classlessness that came naturally to it. There was no sense of 'status' in their beliefs, as in the hierarchical distinctions of the historic church – or rather, the status came from something quite different, the sense of 'election'. Chosen by God, convinced of salvation, the believers felt inferior to no one. Democracy had its cradle in the confidence of 'assurance', as the Labour Party, it has often been suggested, was born in the nursery of Methodism.

The Evangelical Movement

Evangelicalism did not only cross classes – it also crossed denominations. Anglican evangelicals were closer to Calvinists and biblical fundamentalists of other denominations (with whom they founded the Evangelical Alliance in 1846, which continues to this day) than they were to the Tractarians and high churchmen in general. This did not mean that they were not loyal to the Church of England. Within it they maintained a powerful low church conscience. They were the backbone of the temperance movement, the driving force in Wilberforce's campaign against slavery, and the inspiration of Lord Shaftesbury's admirable and successful fight on behalf of child chimney-sweeps, and against the inhumanity of working conditions in factories and mines. Shaftesbury, as a schoolboy at Harrow, was so shocked when by chance he saw the drunken indifference of a pauper's funeral as it passed in the street, that he devoted his life to relieving the suffering of the poor.

Evangelicals believed in a strict private morality (in contrast to the bawdiness and heavy drinking of Georgian England).

> Sexual frankness went underground ... The ideal of the nineteenth century was the modest, puritan professional gentleman with a house and garden in the suburbs, and the high esteem of his chapel or church ... it was called *respectablility* which did not in its heyday carry a derisory ring but meant precisely 'worthy of respect'. It gave birth to the solemn English Sunday ...[23]

By the end of the nineteenth century this attitude had produced a Civil Service known for its lack of corruption and a police force widely admired for its ability to keep order without brutality. Protestant evangelicalism seemed to have seeped into most areas of English life.

Early in the nineteenth century, partly as a response to the Hogarthian corruption of politics and private morals, England had began to put its house in order, transforming its political system with the Reform Act of 1832, the Act forced through by the Whigs which decisively destroyed the rotten fabric of Parliamentary representation. The bishops, strongly identified with a very reactionary Tory party, were mostly against it, as indeed were many parochial clergy. In 1828 the Anglican clergy had tended to be against the Roman Catholic Emancipation Act which allowed Roman Catholics and Jews to participate fully in education and public life for the first time. The natural supporters of the Whigs were the Dissenters, and the Church of England had never been more unpopular. Bishops and Archbishops were mobbed in the streets, and the Bishop of Bristol had his house burned down. Dr Arnold, the influential Headmaster of Rugby, famously wrote in 1832: 'The Church, as it now stands, no human power can save.'[24]

7

'The Stammering Lips of Ambiguous Formularies'

Just as Dr Arnold predicted the imminent collapse of the Church of England (in the year of the Reform Bill), a new force was stirring in Anglican religion which was to have considerable consequences. In July 1833, John Keble, a Fellow of Oriel College, preached a sermon before the judges at the Assize at Oxford, in St Mary's, the University Church. The sermon had the title 'National Apostasy' – like so many movements in religion it began from the always dubious premise that everything was worse than it used to be – and, although untypical of much that the Oxford Movement would come to stand for, it was a ringing call for change. Everything was not worse than it used to be, of course – in fact, Britain was in the middle of a number of very important reforms, though it was partly these reforms that worried Keble and others, and breathed drama into his words.

His sermon was, in part, a protest against a bill to reduce the number of Irish bishoprics by half, mainly to save money. Since the Irish Church was established at the time, the bill felt like the first shot fired, on the part of the Government, in a war against Establishment in general. Thus the first sighting of the Oxford Movement is the improbable one of its defending the Tory Party, as well as church and state.

The deeper preoccupation was with Erastianism, the ascendancy of state over church. It was this which Keble was primarily preaching against, possibly inspired by the example of the Non-jurors, the last Anglicans to protest effectively against state interference in church matters, but seeing things differently from the high churchmen of the previous century.

Then too, Keble and his fellows were offended by the particular brand of liberalism that had emerged from the Enlightenment in general and the French Revolution in particular, the sense of an inevitable progress in human affairs which would emerge from education and rational thinking of all kinds, and to which religion was simply an outmoded form of superstition, to be treated with scorn. The members of the Movement felt profoundly threatened by 'the tendencies of modern thought to destroy the basis of revealed religion, and ultimately of all that can be called religion at all.'[1] 'Reason' did not appeal to them.

At this stage in its life the Movement was anti-Roman, confident in the rightness of the Church of England, 'against Popery and Dissent', as they put it. Oddly, they believed, with many others, that the Catholic Emancipation Act would drive people into the arms of Rome – a singular lack of trust in people's commitment to the Church of England. But clearly they were sensitive, as their descendants in the Anglo-Catholic wing have been ever since, to the suggestion that the Church of England was 'a mere Parliamentarian Church'. Far from believing this, they thought, as some sections of the Church of England had believed all along, that, on the contrary, they were a part of the 'Holy Catholic Church'.

Truth on Horseback
What emerges as one studies the beginnings of the Oxford Movement is the immense seriousness of their commitment to the rather ambitious project of changing the way in which the Church of England saw itself. Its members were scholarly, all university men, mainly from Oxford, and they defended their ideas with sermons and writing, most famously in their series of *Tracts for the Times* – by different hands, of course, and an odd mishmash of different kinds of writing. Either the Church was part of the historical and traditional Church, despite its history of reform, or it was nothing. Reaching back into the medieval past, but beyond that to the traditions of the primitive Church, the Movement's members embraced the writing of the Fathers, the habit of frequent communion, the practice of fasting, and the observation of saints' days. John Keble, John Henry Newman, Edward Bouverie Pusey (the highly respectable Professor and Canon of Christ Church), Hurrell Froude, were the men whose vision and enthusiasm fired these ideas into a fairly supine church. The intensity of the Movement – they seemed incapable of doing or saying anything that was not intense – derived from the Romantic Movement and its dramatising of everything that it touched, from love to landscape, from nature to religion. Two leading lights, Isaac Williams and John Keble, were practising poets, and a strong vein of poetry

ran through the whole Movement. As time went on a striking feature of the sermons and writings of the leaders was their sense of their own spiritual authority.

The *Tracts* of the Oxford Movement began to appear in 1833, little four-page booklets to start with, published at one penny; members of the Movement rode around the country on horseback delivering their messages to vicarages and bishops' palaces alike. It is difficult for a twentieth-century person, deluged daily with paper through the letterbox, to imagine a less interesting or appealing form of mission, but the *Tracts* caused instant furore wherever they were seen, and in that sense were about as effective as advertising can possibly be. The Movement's hagiographer, S. L. Ollard, says that 'the *Tracts* rang out like pistol shots', a curiously aggressive image, but then Tractarian theology did have a very combative air about it.

Newman's Revolution

By 1835 the Movement was widely known, helped along by the highly gifted preaching of Keble, Newman and Pusey. To begin with, the vigour appealed to people, particularly the young. Before the more contemptuous term 'Puseyites' took over, the movement was colloquially known as 'Newmania' – a description of Newman's extraordinary influence at Oxford.

> The undergraduates paid him the compliment of crowding his sermons, of imitating his gliding gait, of holding their heads on one side and pausing long between sentences, of reading in hurried impersonal monotony, of kneeling down with a bump as he knelt, of arguing endlessly over his teaching. In later years nostalgic disciples remembered how every subject of discussion seemed to come round to Newman's doctrine, and how you could not talk of novels or philosophy, poetry or painting, Walter Scott or Jane Austen, Gothic architecture or German literature, without finding yourself in an argument about Newman.[2]

In 1839 it was said that two-thirds of the serious undergraduates at Oxford were followers of Newman. 'Young men will not become disciples unless they sense something revolutionary. Newman, high Tory defender of the established church, had a streak of revolution.'[3] The revolution was the 'appeal to the ancient fathers of undivided Christendom'.

But slowly things began to change. After the early death of Hurrell Froude from tuberculosis, when his admirer Newman rashly published some outspoken autobiographical writings of his, it became clear that the Movement was contemptuous of the Reformation and the legacy it had left. 'The Reformation was a limb badly set,' Froude had written. 'It must be broken again to be righted.'[4] The Movement were the new Reformers preparing to perform the vital surgery.

The attraction to traditional Christianity led Newman to establish a quasi-monasticism at Littlemore, near Oxford, in 1840. It was not a monastic foundation, he insisted – he assured the Bishop of Oxford that he was not trying to revive the monastic orders – but a group of young men who lived at Littlemore with him, said the monastic offices, observed Lent austerely, and used hairshirts and scourges – practices with an oddly gothic feel in the Church of England. Before the end of the nineteenth century, the Anglo-Catholic movement would set up Anglican religious orders for both men and women.

At a time when Roman Catholicism was still very unpopular in England this sense that the Tractarians spat on the reform that helped create the Church of England could not make for warm feeling. It felt un-English. Convinced Protestants, and particularly the Evangelical wing of the Church, began to take alarm.

To complicate things further, some of the newer and younger members of the Movement had a genuine enthusiasm for the Roman Catholic Church which the founders had not had. (Newman was, of course, later to change his mind, but at the beginning he was still shaped very much by his evangelical background.) At Oxford in particular the senior academic world began to sneer comprehensively at the Movement.

Tract 90

By 1841 Newman, a neurasthenic who seemed always to be inwardly suffering, was struggling with doubts about whether the Church of England was truly Catholic. In that year he published 'Tract 90', *Remarks on certain passages in the Thirty Nine Articles,* that thorn in the flesh of the Church of England, which most sensible people preferred not to debate. For some time, mostly withdrawn from life at Oriel and living mostly at Littlemore, Newman had been trying to prove to his own satisfaction that the English Church held the Catholic faith.

Tract 90 was the outcome of his deliberations. It used a phrase that was difficult to forget, just because it did put its finger on the hesitancy and awkwardness which the Church of England inherited from its ambivalent past – 'the stammering lips of ambiguous formularies'. Newman withdrew this from the second edition of the Tract because it caused such offence.

When the Tract was published Oxford was plunged into controversy, with many of the colleges fiercely condemning the Tract. This was followed by a series of attacks from bishops. Already showing many signs of depressive tendencies, Newman slunk miserably away to Littlemore, describing himself as a 'wounded brute'. There was no doubt, however, that within the terms of theological debate he did suffer a sort of persecution. In 1843 he ceased to preach. Meanwhile Pusey had been accused to the Oxford Vice-Chancellor of preaching heresy and suspended from preaching for two years.

The younger members of the Oxford Movement adopted a very different approach to Roman Catholicism from the original Tractarians. W. G. Ward, Fellow and Tutor of Balliol, published in 1844 a book *The Ideal of a Christian Church* which was not only highly critical of 'the English church' but suggested that only the Roman Catholic Church fulfilled the conditions of what a church ought to be. Ward was not proposing to go across to Rome like Newman, but rather to stay where he was while holding and teaching all Roman doctrine, a reforming from within, as he would have seen it. Again there was uproar. At Convocation in 1845 the principal officials of the University, together with politicians, peers and others, heard Ward defend his book. Convocation condemned it by 777 votes to 386.

In a move reminiscent of earlier theological cruelties, though not physically violent, Ward was deprived of his degrees as Bachelor and Master of Arts. There was a proposal to tar Newman with the same brush by condemning Tract 90, which was forestalled by a sympathetic Proctor. But Newman now resigned his Fellowship at Oriel. Five days later he asked for 'admission into the One Fold of Christ'.

Going to Rome

Newman's movement to Rome was a cause célèbre within and without the Church, and aroused a storm of which Gladstone observed that it 'left wrecks on every shore', and Disraeli that it was a blow under which the English Church continued to reel. Some four hundred and fifty clergy followed Newman on his journey; others felt unable to do so, but felt weakened and bereft by his departure. The remaining leaders and followers of 'the Revival', as they called it, were stricken. 'We sat glumly at our breakfasts every morning,' wrote Dean Church, 'and then someone came in with news of something disagreeable, someone gone, someone sure to go . . . we who stayed were voted impostors.'[5] Over the next ten years or so a number of clergy, including Manning (later Cardinal), and a number of lay people

79

continued to 'go over' to Rome. Between 1833 and 1933 they would number about a thousand.

The Seeds of Revivalism

The work of revival that the initiators of the Oxford Movement had begun had already seeded itself effectively in the English Church, however, and up and down the country clergy began to recover a lost sense of ritual. 'The Reformation pushed the focus of worship from altar towards pulpit,' says Owen Chadwick.[6] The Revivalists took it back to the altar, an altar on which until recently had stood only a fair linen cloth, possibly a couple of candles not often lit, and possibly, though not certainly, a cross. In the 1850s came the introduction of chancel screens, sanctuary rails, lighted candles and the beginning of the use of vestments. Such ideas did not originate with the Oxford Movement, but were part of a much wider movement. 'Cambridge, as the original centre of that group of church-restorers and decorators and designers known as the Cambridge Camden Society, was till 1845 more important than Oxford in the matter' (of elaborate church furnishings).[7] At the beginning, around 1837 or 1838, the Oxford Revivalists were still experimenting with 'little signs', like 'the wearing of a scarf embroidered at the ends with crosses'.[8]

There was considerable resistance to the Revivalists from the Evangelical Alliance, and a later body, the Church Association, and there was also popular prejudice against them, with bands of roughs and hooligans invading choral services to interrupt them and cause fear and chaos. Longstanding English fears of popery were fanned by, amongst others, the Prime Minister, Lord John Russell. Queen Victoria was known to deplore the influence of the Tractarians, and tried to prevent them being given senior appointments in the Church.

Meanwhile the mob had fun. 'Between June 1859 and May 1860', except for a period when the Bishop closed the church,

> Sunday afternoons at St George's in the East (in London's East End) were the zoo and horror and coconut-shy of London. The best days witnessed pew doors banging or feet scraping or hissing or coughing or syncopated responses. The worst days witnessed gleeful rows of boys shooting with peas from the gallery, fireworks, flaming speeches during service, bleating as of goats, spitting on choirboys, a pair of hounds howling gin-silly round the nave, cushions hurled at the altar, orange-peel and butter, kicking or hustling of clergy . . . pew number 16 was used a privy.[9]

The clergy – Bryan King, Charles Lowder and Alexander

Mackonochie – were physically attacked. This horror went on Sunday by Sunday for more than a year, despite police intervention, and eventually the Rector was induced to leave and did not return. But the controversy had hardened the resolve of the Ritualists. 'The riots ensured that in the long run, unless Parliament devised some form of high commission to maintain discipline, chasubles and incense and roods and tabernacles would be established more widely in the Church of England.'[10]

Cartoons in *Punch* reveal the merciless ridicule this invited. There were legal threats too. There were prosecutions in ecclesiastical courts on grounds of 'teaching doctrine contrary to the English church', with the danger of a clergyman losing job and home if found guilty. The main bone of contention was the teaching of the doctrine of 'the Real Presence', the doctrine that the body and blood of Christ were actually present in the eucharist, as opposed to being there figuratively or symbolically. The hearing of confessions too, and the granting of absolution, though not difficult to justify from the Book of Common Prayer, also aroused great resistance because of the 'Romish' flavour of the practice. Mackonochie, who had moved on to St Alban's Holborn from St George's in the East, was prosecuted for using the 'mixed chalice' (the Roman practice of mixing a little water with the wine in the chalice at the 'preparation of the elements'), and also for using altar lights, kneeling during the Prayer of Consecration, elevating the chalice and paten, and censing (using incense over) persons and things. He might equally have been arraigned for using 'the eastward position' or wearing eucharistic vestments, both common Revivalist practices.

The years of the 1870s, when Tait was Archbishop, proved to be particularly painful for the Movement, with an Act of Parliament restricting what might be performed in church, and strong opposition from the Archbishop himself. Members continued to secede to Rome, but Pusey remained faithful to the English Church and managed to preserve some hope for those who stood alongside him. Dr Liddon, in the second wave of the Movement, unforgettably, if uncharitably, remarked, 'We shall live to see the drowned Egyptians on the shore even yet.'[11] I wonder which Egyptians he had in mind? Lord John Russell and Queen Victoria, the Archbishop, those who had gone over to Rome, or the parts of the Church of England which had not taken up the Movement's ideas?

What saved the Movement and caused its teaching to have a permanent influence on the Church of England which survives into the present, even among churches who have little idea of where some of their ideas and practices come from, was not the doctrinal bickering or even the courage which Ollard inflates to high heroism, but the simple devotion of many priests up and down the country.

Charles Marriott in Oxford, for example, showed himself fearless in the face of cholera and smallpox epidemics, as he went around ministering to the sick. Edward King, an undergraduate at Oriel during the days of high drama, became an inspiring teacher of ordinands, and a much loved Bishop of Lincoln. St Saviour's, Leeds, a new church which was the personal gift of Dr Pusey, became the first attempt to reach working men in industrial towns. Walter Kerr Hamilton was the first follower of the Movement to become a diocesan bishop. At Salisbury he imbued his diocese with 'sound Catholic teaching' which included 'the Real Presence', the eucharistic sacrifice and absolution. In slum parishes, tough city parishes, industrial wastelands, the Ritualists worked, and showed concern for the poverty of their parishioners which they did their best to alleviate. Quite often, it seemed, these men came from 'good families', but they chose to use their background, education, influence and social confidence to minister to others less privileged. Not surprisingly, they became legends of which it is still possible to hear old people speak, and their funerals through the crowded streets of their parishes were an extraordinary sight, with the entire local population turning out to line the route. One such priest was Arthur Henry Stanton, who served for fifty years at St Albans, Holborn. Robert William Radclyffe Dolling equally gave his life to work in the slums of Portsmouth. The mission of the Movement, says the sociologist W. S. F. Pickering, was not the catholicising of the Church but of reaching the masses who had nothing to do with any church at all. 'Their aim was not so much to turn Evangelicals and ordinary Church of England people into Anglo-Catholics but to convert to Christianity people who had little idea what it was all about.'[12] The slums, where the Established Church had failed, were a particular concern, also the overseas mission. 'In many respects Anglo-catholicism seemed to work better in Africa or Korea than in English villages.'[13]

The legacy of priests like the slum priests, whose parishes illustrated the kind of vivid Christianity in which they believed, was that a number of churches up and down the country became inextricably associated with what became known as Anglo-Catholicism and continued the tradition they had established. All Saints, Margaret Street, in London's West End, St Albans, Holborn, All Saints, Clifton, a number of churches in Brighton, and many more, continued their witness.

To read the hagiographist Ollard on the Tractarians might make you think that the only Christian energy and goodness around at the time of Keble's Assize Sermon in 1833 was the little band of Oxford academics who, perhaps carrying some of the passion of the Romantic Movement into the field of religion, set the Church of England by the ears. But of course this was by no means the case.

If Anglo-Catholicism stressed the 'symbolism' of religion, the finding of appropriate settings, gestures, clothes, rituals in which to carry out the holiest rites of the Christian religion, the evangelical influence worked at a more public level of trying to bring truth, honesty, fairness and compassion into elections, government, the Civil Service, and the lives of the poor.

Education ◀—
The evangelicals were also active in education. In, for example, Sheffield, in 1840, almost all education was provided by the churches. Nearly thirteen thousand children were in Christian Sunday Schools and another six thousand in Christian day schools. As a result of all this activity few children missed education altogether. The Sheffield evangelicals were also active in promoting libraries, working men's clubs, savings banks, medical care and literary and philosophical concerns, as well as being active leaders in many secular concerns. Their underlying temperament was puritan, suspicious of art, colour, sensuality and eroticism, but their sense of duty and the need for hard work was powerful and helped bring about important changes. As the nineteenth century wore on their identity was strengthened by their disapproval of the 'Ritualists' with their supposedly dangerous leaning to Rome.

Reading Victorian religious history now is to be impressed by the energy and innovation it revealed, but also by the intensity of its rows and religious struggles which are hard to reconstruct in more modern terms. It is a little like reading Hardy novels in which so much of people's misery seems somewhat gratuitous and often avoidable. We may wonder a little how much they needed the drama, a bit like the drama of the Victorian woman on her couch with a headache.

Longer than Six Days
Nearly all Victorian clergy, of whatever persuasion, believed in the inerrancy of the Bible, and were in that sense, fundamentalist. It was this which lent extraordinary power to the debate on evolution, most churchmen believing, with Disraeli, that they were asked to choose between the apes and the angels, 'And I', said Disraeli, 'am on the

side of the angels.' Evolution was deeply shocking to Christians in the first place because it suggested that the Bible was quite simply wrong about the beginning the world. 'Geology disproved Genesis,' as Owen Chadwick succinctly puts it. The composer Vaughan Williams, a relative of Darwin, at the age of six became aware of the public debate and asked his mother what it all meant. 'The Bible says that the world was made in six days,' she told him, 'but your great-uncle Charles thinks it took a little longer.'

Since the eighteenth century at least there had been a growing interest in science among educated people and now, it felt, at least to some of them, they had to make a cruel choice between science and the Bible. To knock away one of the props of faith like that seemed to undermine all else that the Bible said. Though, as Chadwick makes clear, many distinguished scientists went on more or less happily with their Christian beliefs.

The second problem about evolutionary theory, rather like the Christian problem about Galileo, was that it made human beings feel so much less important. Galileo's insistence on the Copernican view of the solar system – that the earth moved round the sun – or the suggestion that humanity was merely at the top of the animal chain, was a blow to human identity and to cherished ideas about being specially chosen by God. And evolutionary discussion opened the way to another appalling vista. How could a God of love design so hideous a universe in which everything preyed on its neighbour and only the strongest could survive? 'The very plants are at war', as T. H. Huxley said.

The battle between Bishop Wilberforce and T. H. Huxley in 1860 was widely misreported many years later by Huxley in a way that made Wilberforce look a fool. Christians are rarely at their best, in any case, when on the defensive, but there *were* intelligent Christians (some of them scientists) who could think beyond the immediate situation, who could speak in terms of the slow revelation of the Spirit, who could contemplate biblical errancy without having their faith overthrown, or who could welcome the new learning. But Convocation solemnly condemned *The Origin of Species* in 1864, eleven thousand clergy and one hundred and thirty-seven thousand laity having signed a petition against it. There was an unsuccessful attempt to arraign it for heresy in the Privy Council.

Yet, with a capacity for adaptation which indicates either the slipperiness of the Christian mind, or some deep truth which is still found to reside within Christian belief even when what once seemed essential props have been knocked away, this profound change of thought happened. 'Western Christianity . . . accepted that man is part of nature and has emerged within the evolution of the forms of life on this earth; and it accepted that the books of the Bible were written by a variety of human beings in a variety of circumstances . . .'[14]

8

New Definitions and Structures

In 1851 a census of churchgoing was taken for the first time,[1] and it was shown that, on Sunday, March 30 of that year, seven million people attended public worship of some kind out of a population of eighteen million. (It must be said that the methodology of this census has come under criticism in recent years.) Allowing for those who could not attend church – young children, elderly people, invalids and those who would have attended but were prevented because of being in service or other necessary work – the census estimated that those who attended represented about 60 per cent of would-be worshippers.

> Attendance in rural areas and small towns was noticeably higher than in towns of more than 10,000 people. Most of the absentees lived in the large towns of the industrial area. As between different denominations, the Church of England was shown to be strongest in the villages and country towns, the Nonconformists in certain of the recently expanded towns of the 'chief manufacturing districts'.[2]

Impressive as the figures may seem by modern standards, contemporaries were troubled that 'religion did not have a firm hold on a large part of the population', though it would have had a much lesser one if it were not for the labours of Wesley and his followers. It was noted that it was the working-class population who tended to stay away. 'In cities and large towns', wrote Horace Mann, the author of the report that accompanied the census, 'it is observable how absolutely insignificant a portion of the congregation is composed of artisans.'[3] He commented that although most of them had attended schools and Sunday Schools which commended religious observance to them, by the time they became adults they were no more drawn to churches than were 'the people of a heathen country'. Certainly, as he observes, they felt the Church of England at least to be a middle-class preserve, and the Anglican clergy were perceived, with justice, to be Tory in their sympathies. There was anger at the width of the social and economic divides; a vicar might be paid, in some cases, as much as £1,000 a year, and a handloom weaver would possibly get twelve shillings a week. Payment of clergy was extremely uneven, however. There were curates whose annual stipend amounted to £81.

The simplistic class divisions of the census have been criticised since Mann's time. There were, for instance, rich Nonconformist manufacturers, who because of their religious allegiance were regarded as working class. It was also noticed at the time, as it had been by Wesley, that personal religious commitment often made families more economically viable, what we should call 'upwardly mobile' in terms of class.

By the late Victorian era, music-halls, sports, clubs and newspapers were thought to wean working people away from the churches. There were doubtless other reasons – pew rents, class resentments, and the difficulty of following the services, in the case of the Church of England. Surprisingly little seems to be said by historians about the physical exhaustion of the labouring classes and the effect this might have had upon how they wished to spend Sunday. An interminable working week might have made a day in bed, or a walk in the country with the family, a more attractive proposition than a religious service and sermon that may have been barely understood.

Yet recent research suggests that it is all more complicated than has often been suggested, that it is very possible, for instance, that working people got missed from the census figures by, for example, attending weekday religious meetings or religious groupings unknown to the researchers. Certain religious ceremonies – baptisms, funerals, the churching of women, harvest festival and probably others, were always popular among working people. Churchgoing in general had reached the lowest point to date in about 1880, together with a marked decline in candidates for ordination in the Church of England. (Britain had more clerics of various kinds, however, in the 1880s, than any country in Europe except Spain and Italy.) 'To informed foreign visitors it appeared that the ordinary people of Britain were among the most Christianized in Europe.'[4] Ironically, the 'middle-class' nature of Victorian churchgoing, that historians have commented on unfavourably, seemed to Continental observers an advantage – the fact that religion 'flourished among the educated and "progressive" classes rather than the poor and ignorant classes was a sign of life and strength'.[5]

The Edwardian period was far from being the slide into

secularisation it has sometimes been portrayed. 'In the late 1900s . . . the Anglican Church was attracting a higher proportion of the population as Easter communicants than at any time in the previous century.'[6] By 1910 the combined membership of the established churches of England and Scotland and the Protestant Nonconformist denominations was 3 per cent higher than it had been in 1860.[7] Roman Catholic and Jewish communities also increased rapidly at this period, not entirely because of immigration.

Attendance at Sunday Schools nearly trebled between the 1860s and 1906. Membership of the innumerable organisations of the period – Band of Hope, Girls' Friendly Societies, Men's Societies, etc. – ran into millions. 'The British people constituted a rather *more* religious society in the Edwardian period than they had done half a century before.'[8]

Perhaps the Edwardian success was built on the formidable Victorian energies that had tried to bridge social gaps in the last seventy years or so of the nineteenth century. New parishes were created in industrial areas, churches were built or repaired. There was a growing sense that the middle classes, clerical and lay, had a duty to ease the lot of the labouring population. 'Clothing clubs, soup kitchens, parochial schools were alike products of this relationship.'[9] From about the middle 1830s 'the slum parson' began to emerge, working alongside Chartists and radicals at social reform. Richard Oastler campaigned against the brutality of child labour in the Yorkshire mills, and fought against the New Poor Law. Walter Farquhar Hook, the evangelical Vicar of Leeds from 1837 to 1859, campaigned for shorter working hours, public parks and general education, and was loved for his labours, despite living in the heart of the Dissenting West Riding. Hook was a 'Tory-radical'.

The Christian Socialist Movement of the 1840s and 1850s had a different emphasis, seeking not so much political change as a lifting of the working man through education to a new sense of his own ability and worth. It organised Working Men's Associations for self-help, self-governing workshops, provident associations, and a Working Men's College with F. D. Maurice (sacked from King's College, London for alleged heresy) as its principal. Many brilliant teachers – Ruskin and Rossetti among them – taught there. In itself a failure, the Christian Socialist Movement identified the Church of England with the poor, and sowed seeds which bore fruit in various ways – in the Oxford Movement with *its* concern for the slum poor, and in the Co-operative Movement.

Like F. D. Maurice, its founder, Stewart Headlam, held that 'all men were brothers', and set up the influential Guild of St Matthew, at St Matthew's, Bethnal Green, to which many clergy belonged, which encouraged viewing social programmes in the light of the gospel and the sacraments – Headlam's beliefs were dubbed 'sacramental socialism'. 'Priesthood binds me to radicalism,' he was famous for saying. 'In his mind there were no dazzling constructions of intellectual penetration, but a perception of the fearful effects on human lives of the appalling conditions in which the masses of working people were obliged to live. His influence continued after his death "setting social priorities" in the English Christianity of the first decades of the twentieth century.'[10] It is still quite easy to find clergy who, whether they know it or not, and most of them do, are still living out Headlam's 'sacramental socialism'.

In 1888 the American Episcopal Church had urged the codifying in simple terms of the beliefs of the churches who derived from Anglicanism. The result was the drawing up of the 'Lambeth Quadrilateral'. This was itself the outcome of the first ever Lambeth Conference in the previous year. It saw the four essentials of all Anglican churches as the Old and New Testaments, the Nicene Creed, the sacraments of baptism and eucharist, and the historic episcopacy. This was, and had to be, a kind of lowest common denominator.

It managed to find its way round the Thirty-Nine Articles, with their almost infinite capacity to promote controversy, embalming as they did so many painful memories and disagreements; for the Church of England they were, and perhaps still are, a theological Drumcree. Yet the existence of the Lambeth Conference, with the wider concerns that it forced upon the Church, was the beginning of a new consciousness, an attempt to understand life outside Britain in a way which was not entirely driven by imperial considerations.

Becoming Democratic – the Representative Church Council
Among the many significant events for the Church of England of the nineteenth century was a democratisation of the church – a belief that power must be shared among Church people, or at any rate church men, outside hierarchical or governmental structures. Of course lay men at the top level of society had played a huge role in the nineteenth century in determining the course of the Church, particularly in Parliament. Shaftesbury, Gladstone, Arthur Balfour, the Cecil family and others had been as influential as any bishop. But by the end of the century there was a growing sense that power needed to be more widely shared, as also that the Church was getting restive at being almost totally dependent for change on a Parliament that was too busy, too indifferent, or not necessarily well enough

informed, to give the necessary attention to its business.

In 1899 Arthur Balfour declared in Parliament his desire to see 'greater spiritual autonomy' given to the Church of England, and this was the beginning of the huge change that would lead to synodical government and a degree of freedom to order its affairs in the next century, though a bill discussed by Parliament in 1900, to set up an authoritative church legislature with lay representation, failed miserably. Change was in the air, however, and two years later Archbishop Randall Davidson, the two Convocations, and the associated new Houses of Laymen, met to create a representative legislative body. It had no statutory power and could pass no laws for the Church, but it was a movement towards the sort of power the Church quite properly wished to appropriate to itself.

From the 1860s lay people had met regularly in annual Church Congresses – meetings with no powers, which nevertheless discussed issues of general interest to church people, and which anyone might attend. Women might contribute to discussion, though only through male proxies, an example of the peculiar terror in the Church of England of letting women speak in public. Brian Heeney describes how revolutionary history was made in this respect in 1885, when 'Miss Agnes Weston read her own paper, a practice which was customary from then on'.[11]

Voluntary Parish Councils

The abolition of compulsory church rates in 1868, and the establishment of secular parish councils later in the century, stripped the vestries of political and civil power. This paved the way for something new – voluntary parish councils to look after local church matters, to be composed of lay people (with clerical participation), perhaps by way of a reflection of the Victorian love of committees. 'As interest in these gained momentum in the 1890s they became an important means by which laymen were included in Church affairs at the parochial level. Beginning at Ely in 1866, diocesan conferences extended this form of lay participation; by the early 1880s nearly all dioceses held such conferences regularly.'[12] In the beginning, Heeney suggests, this invitation to lay men was not so much about democratisation as a way to beat off calls for disestablishment or defend against the success of dissent, but it quickly took off, as lay people grasped the power that was offered to them.

Parochial Church Councils

In the 1890s the voluntary parish councils changed their form to what we know as the parochial church council today, with members holding their position by election. In 1897 the Canterbury Convocation had stipulated that the councils would consist of 'elected councillors by male communicants of the Church of England of full age'. This exclusion of women even as electors had caused some debate among the bishops. Since there were already a number of women churchwardens, as there had been for over a century, and since churchwardens were to be ex officio members of the councils, the decision to exclude women as councillors or voters did not make sense.

The Rise of Feminism

Their exclusion provoked what Heeney calls 'the first clear expression of Church feminism'.[13] One thousand one hundred churchwomen signed a petition of objection to the ban of women candidates for election in February 1898, but subsequent discussion, though it revealed some warm supporters of women among the male clergy, also showed chilling levels of prejudice. Archdeacon Lightfoot feared that 'the most truly feminine women' would not be the ones to apply, and that, once the door was open, 'there was no limit to the number of places on the council that women might occupy'.[14] They would be useless in local public affairs. Archdeacon Sandford opined that women were not made by God to engage in public discussion, as the Bible made clear. There was 'a real danger lest the distinction between sex and sex should be forgotten'[15] – witness the growing agitation at the time for women's suffrage and other women's causes. The mild comments of Dean Gregory of St Paul's that women often knew most and worked hardest on practical matters in the parish, that they were often 'the most devotional persons of the parish', and that they would not be required to make public speeches in order to be elected, cut no ice. It would be another sixteen years before women were admitted to parochial church councils. In that sixteen years, so strong was the sense of injustice that church feminism was forced into being.

It was further strengthened early in the twentieth century by the fact that women were not permitted to vote for representatives to Davidson's Representative Church Council, the modest precursor of Church Assembly and the later General Synod.

Clergy prejudices against women affected women's life in society as well as within the Church. In the same period as the parish council debates, Bishop Christopher Wordsworth (he whose daughter

Elizabeth was to become the first Principal of Lady Margaret Hall, Oxford) reminded women that they could never be independent beings since they were *exousia* (that is, taken out of another being, Adam) and not *ousia*, an independent being. '[Woman's] true strength is in loyal submission, her true power is in love and dutiful obedience.'[16] John William Burgon, the Bishop of Chichester, meanwhile, deplored the setting up of a new college for women at Oxford in 1897, worried, as well he might be, that education might make women less amenable. 'Woman is intended to be man's "helpmeet" – Man's helper . . . not a rival self; for as the Spirit pointed out some 4,000 years later [i.e. after Adam and Eve] man was not created for the woman, *but the woman for the man* and from this very consideration the Spirit deduces woman's inferiority.'[17] Burgon thought that 'being an influence' was woman's true role, a consolatory sop, presumably, for not having any real power. Others were subtler. Charles Gore thought that woman's place involved 'a subordination which . . . involved no inferiority whatever in nature or essence, but only difference of function'.[18]

However, there was much that was beginning to undermine these patronising diktats about women. There was the slow fuse lit in the Enlightenment (though not by the Church) that saw women as equal if different. There was the growth in effective education for girls. North London Collegiate School, Cheltenham Ladies' College, Somerville College and Lady Margaret Hall at Oxford, Girton at Cambridge, all of them founded in the nineteenth century, between them offered superb secondary and tertiary education for girls and women. Another factor that helped change opinion was the incredible feats performed by women in the foreign missions, and equally valiant feats at home, where a great deal of the Church's work was done for it unpaid by women parishioners in slums and Sunday Schools and as 'district visitors'. Emily Wilding Davison mentions that, in 1917, of eighty-five thousand district visitors (people who dealt at first-hand with various sorts of 'rescue' work), seventy-five thousand were women. Church statistics of 1883 show that of the 113,412 Sunday School teachers then employed, 100,000 were women.[19] This huge army of voluntary church workers, in part a witness to the fact that many middle- and upper-class women had more time on their hands than ever before, was to keep marching well into the twentieth century. In a period when drunkenness caused great suffering within the family, many women worked together in temperance organisations. Other women's enterprises were the Girls' Friendly Society (founded in 1874 by Mrs Townsend) whose original function was to offer society and help to girls working or studying away from home, and a whole spate of other girls' clubs attached to the Church. Anglicans were also very much involved in the setting up of the YWCA. The Mothers' Union, with its emphasis, naturally, on mothering and on the concerns of the family, was founded in 1887 by Mrs Sumner and gradually took in a wide range of further concerns beyond the primary one of Christian faith. The Church Army (founded in 1883) as an Anglican imitation of the Salvation Army, soon developed work for women, but without equality of gender. Women might not become Captains in the Army and did not preach, although they took meetings. The horror of women speaking in public, though ostensibly deriving from St Paul's strictures in the Epistle to the Corinthians, seemed to spring from deep irrational fears. Women were not permitted to read the lessons, even in country churches where no suitable man could be found to do so. The National Mission of Repentance and Hope, instigated by the Archbishops in 1916 to bring a little religious comfort in a dark time, initially involved women speaking as 'witnesses' in church, but this caused so much trouble (including Anglo-Catholic claims that this was a 'plot' to get women into the priesthood) that Bishop Winnington-Ingram retracted his original permission. Women might only speak to 'other women and children'.

Just how costly it was for women to try to change this state of affairs is shown by Sheila Fletcher's moving little picture of Maude Royden reading the lesson for the first time at St Botolph's, Bishopsgate, the church of which her friend Hudson Shaw was Rector. She was a confident woman from a well-to-do family, educated at Oxford, with a brilliant reputation and a great deal of experience as a public speaker, and yet she read 'with trembling lips'. 'She feared there would be some interruption or protest.'[20]

There was more cause for trembling when Shaw asked Maude Royden to deliver the Three Hours Service on Good Friday at St Botolph's. Hearing of this revolutionary event in advance, Bishop Winnington-Ingram forbade her to speak in the church. Shaw therefore closed the church for the day and held the service in the parish room, a service so hugely popular, largely as a result of the publicity caused by the furore, that there was no room for anyone to kneel down, and many listened through the windows.

The official Church, as so often, had completely misread the signs of the times; the spirit of the age was on women's side. On the other hand, many Christians, both women and men, played an important role in the women's suffrage movement. The League for Women's Suffrage was founded in 1910 and in the few years that remained before the First World War many women demonstrated that they were profoundly unhappy with the status quo, and were ready to suffer to change it. Wartime work took many women out of the home, in some cases into jobs of considerable responsibility, and by the time the First World War was over there had been a perceptible change in public attitudes to female emancipation. The suffragists were pushing at an open door, though it took another ten years for their longings to take full effect.

Although repressive and prejudiced about women, the churches were, in many other aspects of their life at this time, forward looking and adventurous. The extraordinary energy, success and vitality of all the mainstream churches at the beginning of the twentieth century cannot be denied, although many historians see this period as the beginning of the time when the churches would start to fail as a dominant social force, would become 'recessive', to quote the Marxist historian Hobsbawm. Historians do, of course, look through the spectacles of hindsight, and through the particular prejudices of the late twentieth century, yet it is a useful and possibly fruitful exercise to consider that changing social structure and the churches' own awkwardness in adapting to it had already set the churches' feet on a road that would make them increasingly marginal. 'Buoyant church membership, booming social and evangelizing activity, aggressive political mobilization',[21] were the success story of the Edwardian churches as they set out to open themselves to 'the material, institutional and organizational world' and yet deep fault lines may have already been invisibly present. Stick a hair over the crack at this point, as one does in a house to discover the rate of subsidence, and twenty, thirty and fifty years later the extent of the damage will have become plain. Indeed many intelligent churchpeople from the Victorian and Edwardian periods onwards had already anticipated the difficulties to come, feeling in their own persons the tensions between 'spiritual and material pressures, between tradition and modernity, between belief in "individualism" and acknowledgment of the mass reality of social class'.[22] Democracy, general education, 'the era of the common man', materialism, consumerism, the destruction of small communities, the human devastation of two huge world wars, the growing power of science, the atom bomb, the motor car, the aeroplane, tourism, mass media, were gradually to dissolve the strong foundations of Edwardian religion.

9

The Twentieth Century

The growing confidence of women as they asked more and more questions about their role was only one of a number of threats of the modern era that put the Church on the defensive, and in fact was regarded as one of the minor problems since there seemed little doubt at first of the ease with which women could be kept in their place. Sigmund Freud, beginning to be published and read from early in the twentieth century, proposed a very different view of humanity from that current among contemporary Christians of almost any shade of belief, and he appeared to do so with the authority of science. In particular his view of the baby and child as a sexual being – 'polymorphously perverse' as he put it – shook the Victorian view of the child as an innocent (though St Augustine took a view not unlike Freud's), or a *tabula rasa* upon which parents, teachers and clergy might print their own moral views. He also shook Christian confidence in free will, depicting all human beings as somewhat, and in some cases, entirely, controlled by complexes, unconscious impulses, and the dark amoral influence of the Id. He set up a new form of confession (was it seen in this way by Christians at the time? I am not sure) in which patients spent hours talking to the doctor, alienist, analyst or therapist about themselves. It tended to worry the Christians, then and later, that Freud believed it was the role of the doctor to be unjudgmental, no matter what was confided to him. Freud, who was in any case suspect to Christians of the period as a Jew, though not a believing one, was to go on to define religion as a form of wish-fulfilment.

Carl Gustav Jung, who had grown up as the son of a Protestant pastor in Switzerland, became first a disciple and then a rival of Freud. He was particularly interested in the power of the unconscious – the part of the mind of which we are unaware except through dreams, art and aspects of our own behaviour. He thought that all of us were connected by means of 'the Collective Unconscious' (this

95

idea occurred to him when he noticed how all cultures repeatedly made use of the same symbols in their art and religion), and that within the Collective Unconscious resided 'the archetypes', symbols of tremendous power, which might work through humanity for creative or destructive purposes. Part of the point of 'therapy' was to recognise which archetypes influenced the patient, so that some control over their power could be achieved. One of the symbols Jung cited was that of Jesus – 'the archetype of the Self' – that is to say the symbol which helped us as individuals or as groups to become what is in us to become. As an old man in a television interview in the late 1950s Jung was asked whether he believed in God. 'I don't believe, I know,' he replied, and this statement seemed to lead to a kind of adoption of Jung by many Christians who managed to convince themselves that he was 'on their side'. Conveniently they lost sight of the Jung who described modern religion as a kind of puppet which had no intrinsic life of its own, and could only be activated by energetic manipulation.

Karl Marx, leading his poverty-stricken life in London and working on *Das Kapital* at the British Museum, was to be another threat to Christian complacency. Proposing revolution, to be followed by a totally new social organisation in which the 'alienation' of the masses would be overcome, he became the father of a vast political movement which now is seen to have fatal flaws. So far, at least, it has only been associated with tyrannies and dictatorships and wooden social systems in which motives of love and caring seemed to disappear into terror or indifference. In the early decades of the twentieth century many Christians, as well as other thinking people like George Bernard Shaw and Beatrice Webb, felt the attraction of the out-workings of Marx's ideas, and were supportive of the great Russian experiment, but already by the late 1930s writers like George Orwell had written clearly about the inhumanity, brutality, mindlessness and dishonesty of Stalin's state.

Imperial England

Edwardian England was prosperous, at a certain level of society, conscious of the glory and burden of Empire, and, according to recent historical studies, more religious than the Victorian era that preceded it, at least in terms of the numbers who attended places of worship. Rudyard Kipling is perhaps its most revealing writer, catching in poems and stories the extraordinary confidence of the era, and its upper class educated in public schools, with its own (in some ways admirable) mores, rigidly divided by education, custom and speech from the classes below it. Ironically it mirrored the Indian caste system of which Kipling wrote. The lowest caste of Edwardian England toiled as servants for long hours in the basements of large houses, or as 'hands' in factories. Galsworthy too, particularly in *The Forsyte Saga*, captures the Edwardian world with its heartless and hypocritical morality, its certainty that Irene should stay wretchedly with Soames, yet its blind eye turned to married men who 'had a little piece on the side'. Galsworthy understood very well the obsession with money, the snobbish divisions between inherited money and 'trade' (the Forsytes, for all their money, were trade), as well as racial and religious prejudice. Religion, never badmouthed by Kipling or Galsworthy, seemed at least partly a device for maintaining the status quo, and keeping the lower classes in order. However intelligent or gifted members of the lower classes might happen to be, it was extraordinarily difficult for them to secure jobs worthy of their abilities because they were handicapped by a meagre education that ended at thirteen or earlier.

The First World War
The First World War dealt a shattering blow to the confident Britain of Edwardian England, one from which it never quite recovered. It shook up the class system, as young officers fresh from public schools fought alongside privates from working-class backgrounds. Both sides learned much more about each other.

Religion was caught up in the euphoria of the beginning of the war. Adrian Hastings describes Arthur Winnington-Ingram, the Bishop of London, 'drumming the nation into the army', a patriotic gesture for which many a wife and mother must have lived to curse him. 'What is the Church to do?' he asked in a religious newspaper. 'I answer, Mobilise the Nation for a Holy War.' He was later, in a sermon, to make a demand 'to kill the good as well as the bad, to kill the young men as well as the old'.[1] Clergy played a disturbing role in the early stages of the war in encouraging working-class men to enlist.

Many clergy enlisted as chaplains, and some performed admirably the role demanded of them, writing endless letters on behalf of the troops, taking services, administering communion, providing cigarettes, sitting with the wounded and dying. Others were incompetent, cowardly, or bellicose. There were men like the Reverend G. A. Studdert Kennedy ('Woodbine Willie') whose loving exemplary Christian presence made him a legend among the men. The awareness of a great gulf both in terms of class and of religion had, however, begun to appear. 'What war chaplaining did do', Adrian Hastings remarks, 'was to convince the more clear-minded of padres just how non-religious England was. The war did not create irreligion so much as reveal it.'[2]

The damage to religious faith came not only from the failures of its representatives, but from the utter horror and disillusion of the war itself, from the millions of young men from Britain, the Empire, France and Germany who were killed by being shot, bayoneted, blown up, buried alive, crushed beneath tanks or drowned in mud, not to mention the thousands who returned home with terrible wounds to bodies and minds. How could people reconcile a God of love with such evil, so much suffering, such hopelessness?

> There was no genuine religious revival during the war nor after the war nor was there a pastoral or theological revival – though these things were sought for and even claimed to be coming, at the time. The war unleashed bewilderment and hate, and the churches had done very little to help with either . . . What the war did was to shatter [the] social and political role [of the churches]: to unveil the truth to high and low alike of ecclesiastical near-irrelevance. When it was over the churches had simply to start again, from a weaker position and with next to no new resources or inspiration.[3]

Yet inadequate as religion seemed to meet the extent of the tragedy, the vastness of the disillusion that had succeeded the golden Edwardian age, churches did carry much of the burden of remembering the sorrow and horror of what had happened, and all churches of the period have some memorial of the massacre of the First World War. The grave of the Unknown Warrior in Westminster Abbey provided a focus at which to reflect on the unimaginable horror of trench warfare.

The war was followed by further tragedy, of men returning from the suffering of the trenches to find that there was no work for them.

An Attempt at Democratisation – Church Assembly

Among many other changes which seemed overdue by the end of the war was an increased liberty for the Church of England to make its own decisions. The Life and Liberty Movement had promoted the idea that the collecting of opinion at the grass roots and the debating of it at the national level would reinvigorate the Church. The Enabling Act of 1919 allowed for the setting up of Church Assembly, a forum foreshadowed by the Representative Council but with some legislative power, and largely masterminded by the Cecil family, which accounted for its Tory stamp. For the first time the Church was permitted to 'promote Measures' – that is to make proposals to Parliament for legal changes which it wished to bring about. This important, if limited, decision-making was, at least theoretically, to be shared among all sections of the Church. According to Leslie Paul the war had jolted people out of a long complacency into a readiness to take on board new ideas. 'There was a great longing to have the workers and the lower middle class represented [on Church Assembly], to have a national forum from which to address the people, and to bring to an end what many saw as an upper class monopoly of the leadership of the Church.'[4] Unfortunately, it could not work in those terms. Three weeks a year of full-time service confined membership almost entirely to the rich, the retired, and wives whose husbands supported them.

The Failed Prayer Book
Church Assembly's well meaning idealism came a cropper rather quickly when its horse fell at the first fence. In 1927 and again in 1928, Parliament rejected the new Prayer Book, a modification and updating of the 1662 Book of Common Prayer. The new book would be widely used, in practice, of course, in many churches up until the Alternative Service Book arrived in 1980. To defeat the attempt to introduce it in 1928, Anglo-Catholics and Evangelicals combined (not for the last time) to whip up fear and resentment of the idea in Parliament. They did not share common principles, of course. According to Leslie Paul, the Anglo-Catholics joined the unholy alliance because they feared they might be prevented from saying the Latin mass in their churches and the Evangelicals because they feared the mass! This defeat was a serious rebuff to the Church's new-found autonomy. A minority, again not for the last time, had got together 'to defeat the will of the Church's own supreme chamber and were prepared to see it crushed rather than submit to the legitimate decision of a majority'.[5]

Commission on Doctrine
In 1922 a Commission on Doctrine was set up, with the unenviable task of trying to reconcile the Church's endemic tendency to polarise between 'Catholics' and 'Protestants'. W. R. Matthews described the reasons for it in his book *Memories and Meanings*.

It is clear that one of the dominant purposes of the Archbishop in setting up the Commission was a practical one. The conflicting currents in the Church of England had become violent. The extremes on either side aimed at purging their opposites from the

Church and both agreed that the majority who were attached to the middle way and hoped that they were both Catholic and Reformed were feeble compromisers. The expressed aim of the Commission was to formulate the limits within which disagreements were tolerable.[6]

After four hundred years the old wounds within the Church of England remained unhealed. The profound English attraction to the middle way was, and continues, in the Church of England, to be attacked in an almost cyclical way by those who crave a more dramatic, more extrovert expression of faith. Yet the middle way enforces an extraordinary stability, even inertia, as it did in the case of the Commission, which did not get round to reporting its findings till 1938, the year of Munich, when everyone had other things to worry about. The Commission's conclusions were anodyne, not daring to tackle the thorniest subject of all, the Thirty-Nine Articles. Of the Articles' statement of humanity's total depravity, Leslie Paul says drily, 'The Commission repudiated total depravity.'[7] It did however, accept a human bias towards evil, and one did not have to look very far in the 1930s to see appalling evidence of it. But of course the attempt by people of widely dissimilar views on a Commission to agree tends to lead to a nullity of thought and a feebleness of language and the findings of this Commission were no exception.

Anglo-Catholicism
Pickering, speaking at the Keble Conference of 1983 which celebrated one hundred and fifty years of the Oxford Movement, examined the longer-term fortunes of Anglo-Catholicism. He noted the huge success it enjoyed in its heyday between the two World Wars. 'As a result of the terrible First World War, Anglo-Catholics found themselves free from the legal harassment and social ostracism of earlier decades and achieved a respected and legitimate place within the national Church of which they were members.'[8] In the 1920s and 1930s there were powerful leaders, and vast congresses were held in places like the Albert Hall. As many as seventy thousand attended the congress in 1933 – the centenary of Keble's Assize sermon and the start of the Movement – and forty-five thousand attended a mass at Wembley Stadium. It was the hour of triumph, with the Archbishop of Canterbury preaching on the Oxford Movement in a service broadcast by the BBC.

Pickering contrasts this former glory with the later relative collapse of Anglo-Catholic fervour – six or seven hundred people attended the 150th anniversary in 1983. Searching for equivalent power in contemporary Anglo-Catholicism, Pickering can only point to the forestalling tactics of clergy over Methodist unity. Writing at a later date he could have added tactics to forestall women's ordination.

Pickering does not think the decline of Anglo-Catholic influence can be ascribed purely to the secularism which has hit other parts of the Church of England, as well as other Christian churches. This, he says, is merely a description, not an explanation, of what has occurred. He points out that even when the Anglo-Catholic movement was riding high, there were those in their own ranks who were uneasy about its future. Too much concentration on liturgical and ecclesiological matters at the expense of matters of belief was one criticism. Alec Vidler, an influential theologian in the 1960s and 1970s, once an Anglo-Catholic, complained that theological stance was narrow and backward-looking, unable to meet the scientific and secular challenges of the twentieth century.

Pickering suggests that part of the difficulty is that although many liked the idea of developing a Catholic ethos within the Church of England, the actual doctrines and practices seemed bizarre in the English context. Such people did not want to cross the divide between Anglo-Catholicism and Roman Catholicism, and were troubled by the excessive devotions to the Virgin Mary at the major congresses of the 1920s and 1930s, and the sending of a telegram to the Pope, addressing him as 'Holy Father'. It took them farther than they wanted to go.

Pickering also suggests that there is a residual, and possibly ineradicable, reluctance in England about the word 'Catholic'. Even when its meaning is explained, it is difficult to separate it from its Roman origins. English history, together with a church whose sense of itself as 'Protestant' had been strong and as 'Catholic', dormant for nearly four hundred years, made it at best a difficult and implausible transition. The resumption of the idea of being 'Catholic' resulted in followers going in several different directions – trying to restore what they believed were the practices of the 'primitive Church', copying medieval practices, along with architecture and other medieval conceits, and imitating what the Roman Catholics were doing. This last practice suffered a *bouleversement* at the Second Vatican Council.

> They were suddenly thrust into the embarassing position of having to argue, in line with Vatican II, against old practices which they had so slavishly sacralised. If, on the other hand, they rejected the changes demanded by Vatican II and continued in the Counter-

101

Reformation ethos, they would in their own eyes alienate themselves from contemporary Roman Catholicism and would be charged with even greater sectarianism by being in the Lefebvre wing of Anglo-Catholicism. They would thus become a sect within a sect and supporters of a dying form of catholicism.[9]

Pickering wrote this in in 1983 – Vatican II itself has taken some hard knocks under the current Pope.

Pickering goes on to discuss whether Anglo-Catholicism is, in fact, a sect 'keen to create lines of demarcation between themselves and others, to speak of "we" and "they" even with reference to those within the Anglican Church'. Anglo-Catholicism, he points out, has its own private language, with special titles – 'father' – and other in-phrases not used elsewhere in the Church – 'celebrating mass' etc. It is a subculture which may be seen, by those both within and without, as 'foreign to the general culture which the Church of England has nurtured and in which it is set'.[10]

This is not necessarily to condemn it – the Church of England itself, because of the relatively few people that attend it, has sect-like qualities. But there is, as Pickering points out, something ambiguous in adopting 'a sect-like position in the name of catholicism'. All of this is given an odd sort of poignancy by the fact that the Roman Catholic Church is alive and tolerably well on the very doorstep of Anglo-Catholicism, rarely criticised by its admirer even when criticism seems called for. Pickering concludes: 'Can a Church with approximately four hundred years of history in which protestantism has played such a prominent, decisive, but not exclusive part – can a Church which is a veritable melange ever be catholicised in a genuine or widely accepted sense?'[11]

Whatever the eventual outcome, it must be said that the Tractarians, Puseyites, Oxford Movement, Revivalists, Ritualists and Anglo-Catholics as they were eventually called, took the rather staid and grey English Church of the 1830s, and over a period of seventy years took it and coloured it quite differently. Their beliefs were embodied in architecture by a genius of Gothic, Augustus Welby Pugin (1812–52) and others.

Perhaps the greatest achievement of the Oxford Movement was to put the Church of England in a much bigger context, 'set its feet in a large room', as it says in the Psalms. 'By their insistent affirmation of the oneness and catholicity of their Church, while remaining out of communion with Constantinople and Rome, the Tractarians put a great question mark against the finality of the separations both of the eleventh and the sixteenth centuries', wrote A.M. Allchin.[12] It was a position which led inevitably, and happily, to ecumenism, an ecumenism to which the Second Vatican Council would give a welcome fillip.

The Student Christian Movement

In the early years of the century there was a real vigour of ideas to be found in the Student Christian Movement. Founded in the 1890s, called then the Inter-University Christian Union, it had a strongly evangelical flavour to start with, and was concerned with encouraging the young to go overseas as missionaries. Its oft-repeated (and incredible) aim was 'the evangelisation of the world in this generation'. It had the great merit, as Adrian Hastings points out, of bringing together Anglicans and Freechurchmen in a common Christian enterprise, which gradually grew away from the missionary emphasis to one of a growing social conscience, and awareness of the acute poverty and need nearer home. As time went on more and more Anglo-Catholics were attracted into the Movement, and the different sacramental emphasis this produced in turn repelled the conservative evangelical section of the SCM. So CICCU – the Cambridge Inter-Collegiate Christian Union – came into being, having disaffiliated from the SCM in 1910. Subsequent attempts at reconciliation between the two groups proved fruitless. The SCM did not consider that the atoning blood of Jesus Christ was the central point of their message. CICCU did, and regarded SCM as apostatisers.

SCM gave a platform, however, for many of the most influential Christians of the late Edwardian and the Georgian period – William Temple, J. H. Oldham and William Paton among others. Until well after the Second World War the SCM maintained an intellectual and spiritual vigour that inspired the young.

Evangelicalism in the Wilderness

Conservative evangelicalism, on the other hand, was in for a long period in the desert. There was a growing mood in the country to improve social conditions for the poorest members of society (a mood which was to find its vehicle in the Labour Government of 1945), and consequently a gospel which concentrated on conversion rather than on social issues was unlikely to appeal. There was a lack of intellectualism, a fear and suspicion of ideas, which many Evangelicals themselves have since noted and deplored. Both CICCU and other Christian Unions faltered, and Evangelicalism was further depleted by the secession, temporary in some cases, of some of its members to the Oxford Group, the moralist organisation set up by Frank Buchman during the 1920s.

Writing of a slightly later period, Oliver Barclay, a committed member of the IVF, describes with moving honesty how, feeling marginalised by others, Evangelicals became defensively unwilling to change. They tended to be legalistic about drink, tobacco, the cinema and theatre, make-up and dancing in a way incomprehensible to others who thought these things harmless. 'No responsible evangelical would be seen going into a pub.'[13] For years my own parents repeated the story, with some indignation, of how Evangelical relatives, invited for Christmas lunch, reproved them for drinking wine, something which, at that period, they did once a year! It did not commend the beliefs which brought about the ungracious rebuke.

Barclay points out how these ideas isolated Evangelicals from much social and cultural life, and often caused the livelier spirits to leave and adopt a more human form of religion. The life of the intellect was also treated with great suspicion.

> There was generally among Conservative Evangelicals something of an intellectual inferiority complex and a negative attitude to contemporary 'high' culture. This helped to produce an anti-intellectualism that was fed by seeing some promising people turned away from the old paths by wider interests. The older leaders often advised people (including myself) not to read theology because it never seemed to do anyone any good unless they positively needed it for the ministry. When, as a first year science student, I mentioned my interest in current poetry (T. S. Eliot and W. H. Auden) I was told that it would be best not to broadcast it or I would be thought to be 'unsound'.[14]

Barclay goes on to make the very good point that this philistine attitude was close to that of the vast majority of working people in the pre-Second World War era, most of whom had a very modest education. Many children of his background, however, were lost to the cause as soon as they went to university, or developed broader intellectual interests.

George Bell and William Temple
The eyes of Anglicans at this time were not on the Evangelicals, however, but on men like Bell of Chichester and Temple of York and later of Canterbury. Bell, in the pre-war period and during the war, had emerged as a just man, a prophetic influence, seeing the approaching holocaust at a time when others preferred to bury their heads, and holding out a hand of love to Jews in desperate peril in Europe. Temple, with his huge intellectual gifts, his background in the Life and Liberty Movement, his experience as Bishop of

Manchester and Archbishop of York, and his ability to reach out across class and comprehend the sufferings of the poor, seemed the very model of a Christian leader when he went to Canterbury in 1942. He had famously been described by Churchill as 'the only sixpenny article in a penny bazaar'. In the year he became Archbishop he published a best-selling religious book *Christianity and Social Order*, a book which, if it did not influence the country's swing to Labour in 1945, at least anticipated the mood which brought the Welfare State into being. Adrian Hastings writes of him as 'a modern man' (as well as a modernist in religion), comparing him to the 'Victorians' – Lang, Winnington-Ingram, Headlam and Henson – who had preceded him.

> He was modern intellectually, but still more socially, in his personal behaviour, able to participate with sympathy, with a sense of real identification and confidence, in the new world of the Labour Party, the BBC, the cinema, the League of Nations. Nothing is more important to remember about him than that he was president of the Workers' Educational Association before ever he was ordained. There was a quite extraordinary wholeness about Temple, a profoundly serious concern for all things and everyone: the interpretation of the gospel, the immediate needs of the common man, the reunion of Christendom, philosophy, the educational system, the Church's pastoral care.[15]

He had friends in high intellectual circles, in Britain and abroad, who gave him a perspective that stretched beyond Britain and immediate church concerns. He 'provided leadership as no one else in the Christian Church of the twentieth century has quite managed to do'. He 'never lost for long the confidence of left or right'. Two years after going to Canterbury, this huge genial and lovable figure died in office, to be succeeded, apparently at Churchill's whim, not by George Bell, the obvious choice, but Geoffrey Fisher.

Geoffrey Fisher

Fisher, a famous flogging headmaster of Repton (Archbishop Ramsey, his one-time pupil, could not bear to have Fisher's portrait around when he went to live at Lambeth, according to Robert Runcie), proceeded to run the Church rather like a public school, with huge amounts of hard work, attention to detail, and a willingness to chastise where he thought it was deserved. As a young journalist writing for the *Spectator* in 1960 and uttering some, possibly foolish, remark about the Church of England (unfortunately I no longer remember what it was), I received three pages of single-spaced typescript setting me right, an extraordinary use of a busy arch-bishop's time. The Archbishop's schoolmasterly habit of correction reached into many insignificant corners of the Church of which he was Primate.

10

Postwar Christianity

Archbishop Fisher's great labour was to reform canon law, a task, we may think now, a bit like distraction therapy, forgetting how much more positive the future of the Church still seemed at the time. The Church felt less like the *Titanic* than it was to feel a decade or so later; the experience was more like being at sea with a captain entirely lacking in nerves, less worried about storms, rocks and whirlpools than spit and polish. However, he did sort out and equalise clergy stipends, a very real achievement. Alongside the Labour landslide of 1945, however, was a stirring of excitement and vigour in the churches. Both of these things were to do with the postwar mood of hope. There was certainly a fear of 'atheistic' Communism, against which Christianity was seen as the only hope. I remember a curate in my local church solemnly warning us in a sermon in 1949 that within twenty years we might find ourselves as Christian martyrs in the fight against Communism. Equally solemnly we all digested this; at twenty, I found it a rather exciting and romantic thought. There was also, I think, a genuine desire to find a deeper faith, stimulated, in some cases, by people's wartime experiences. My own suburban church, St John's, Greenhill, in Harrow – a large building – had a huge congregation for mattins and evensong and was packed to the doors at Midnight Communion at Christmas. There was no weekday congregation to speak of, though as time went on, and the Vicar, rather 'Broad Church' at first, became noticeably more 'Catholic' in his time among us, there was encouragement to attend communion on saints' days. There were regular parish meetings to discuss church matters which were very well attended, and there was the clutch of successful church-dependent organisations common at the period – the Mothers' Union, the Young Wives, Scouts and Guides, a Youth Fellowship and a dramatic society. There was also a network which involved calling on and, to some extent, keeping in touch with, every household in the parish.

The late 1940s and early 1950s were a period of austerity, in some ways worse than the austerity of the war itself. There was little money to spend, and little to spend it on. Europe was still largely in chaos. There was, however, a powerful sense of hope: the war was over and it was going to be possible to shape a different sort of society. Already it was clear that it would be much less class-bound than Edwardian and pre-war Georgian society.

County Council Religion
The 1944 Education Act, known as 'the Butler Act', enjoined a weekly religious assembly (it was assumed it would be Christian in nature) on Britain's state schools. Many schools went far beyond this. My own County Council grammar school had a daily religious service, known as 'Prayers', which always included a hymn, a Bible reading and prayers. Every girl, unless prevented by other religious affiliation (which meant, in those days, Catholics and Jews), was also expected to pass the School Certificate Examination in 'Scripture', which involved knowing one of the Gospels really well. The morality to which our teachers appealed when we misbehaved, was of a kindly, but somewhat sheltered kind – I remember their sense of outrage when, in some impromptu end of term play, some pupils acted as if they were drunk! What shocked our teachers was that anyone might consider drunkenness funny – which the audience patently did. There was also a general sexual naïveté unimaginable today. Until I was thirteen and 'did' human reproduction in 'Science', I was not quite certain how babies were conceived and born, and nor, I believe, were most of my contemporaries. My best friend and I gleaned information from all possible sources and passed it on to each other. Most of our teachers were unmarried, and most them almost certainly celibate. The teacher who taught us about human reproduction was, I think I am right in saying, the only married member of staff at the time.

Too much questioning of Christian ideas was not encouraged. Once, when I asked in a 'Scripture' lesson how one could be sure that God existed, the teacher, who happened to be the headmistress, replied crushingly, 'We haven't got time to keep going back to first principles, Monica.' Yet at the time I had begun to be deeply doubtful about God's existence, and badly wanted a helpful answer, or at least an admission that one might have doubts. Despairing of a Christianity that seemed mixed up with obeying school rules and general propriety, I started reading haphazardly in an attempt to answer my own questions. I started with C. S. Lewis, whose clear expositions of Christian ideas, although I find them too simplistic nowadays, at least helped me to grasp what basic Christian theology was all about. I tried Dorothy L. Sayers, whose theological work felt too rhetorical, and also too obscurely angry, to help much, though I loved *The Man Born to be King*. I liked the feel of William Temple's *Readings in St John's Gospel* and *Christianity and Social Order*. Finally, and most important for me at the time, the novels of Charles Williams and his 'history of the Holy Spirit', *The Descent of the Dove*, caught something of the passion I was seeking in religion. There was, it seems to me now, an arrogance about all of these writers, except Temple – most of them seem extraordinarily defensive and rather bad-tempered. (The correspondence between Dorothy Sayers and the unfortunate BBC staff over *The Man Born to be King*, to be found in recent biographies of her, captures the bossy mood exactly. It is difficult to pin down quite why they felt that way, but Sayers at least seems unpleasantly certain of her intellectual and educational superiority to most of the people she was writing for, as well as producers at the BBC who were trying to work with her.) All the same, I am grateful to Sayers, Williams, Lewis, etc. At least they made Christianity interesting and intellectually exciting.

When I did eventually decide, in 1950, that I was a Christian – something I had been uncertain of for several years – my Vicar, Joost de Blank, who was not arrogant at all, started me reading the French worker-priests whose writing had a very different feel from the writing of the Oxford alumni. Thomas Merton's *Elected Silence* both fascinated and frightened me. Did loving God entail living one's life as Merton had chosen to do in considerable austerity and deprived of speech? A year or two later I was enthralled by the writing of T. S. Eliot, and particularly *The Cocktail Party* with its theme of a modern crucifixion. It played to full houses on the London stage.

The *Church Times*

Another instance of arrogance was evident in the *Church Times* of the period, which used to make me blink at its extraordinary rudeness about Roman Catholics, and indeed about anyone who did not quite see the world as they did. This was, I think, the intellectual Christian ethos of the period. In around 1951 I applied for a job as a reporter on the paper. I was interviewed by the Editor, Rosamund Essex, a stout middle-aged lady dressed in a sort of gym tunic, with a very jolly manner, who asked me the difference between a cope and a chasuble. I did not get the job.

The Coronation

The crowning of a young Queen in 1953 seemed to usher in a new phase of English history. The coronation itself, in Westminster Abbey, with its solemn anointing as a spiritual sign, and its bestowing of the tokens of rule – the orb and sceptre – on the Queen, was a mixture of religion and state ceremony. It was profoundly moving and beautifully staged and performed and people bought and rented television sets or watched with neighbours to share the experience. As so often with the Church of England, the difficult questions were not asked. Was the new Queen's job in fact a religious one at all or was it largely a presidential one? Did these particular ceremonies imply not only that she had spiritual status, but that she might even have 'divine right', an idea that had apparently been jettisoned several centuries previously? Was Britain still so Christian a country that state and church had a symbiotic role which made such ceremonies appropriate? The issues were blurred, perhaps because no one was quite sure of any of the answers, and all were caught up in the huge drama of the Coronation itself. Only out and out anti-royalists, of which there were few, seemed prepared to demur. I think it would be true to say, however, that, as so often with major Anglican ceremony, most people felt the occasion 'worked'.

Morals

Britain's conservatism over morals was still a striking feature, or would have been if we had not taken it entirely for granted. Going to be fitted for a contraceptive device at a National Health Service clinic in 1953 I was asked by the doctor whether I was married, or about to be so. If the answer had been no, I do not think she would have been prepared to help. A year or two before that, I remember going to sing carols with a church group at a 'mother and baby home' run, I think, by the Church of England. There were perhaps half a dozen very pregnant young women there, all of whom, so I was told, had been unable to remain in their parents' homes either because they had been turned out, or because the families could not face 'the disgrace'. The mothers kept the babies for six weeks and then gave them up for adoption, and I remember a curate who was pastorally responsible for the mothers in the home telling me what a cruel business he thought it, since the young women had grown fond of their babies by then, and it was agony to surrender them. The moral pressure of a society which forbade children (and sex) out of wedlock forced this appalling choice. Yet birth control, as I discovered, was only available to those who were married or about to be so. This was a society prepared to go to extreme lengths to discourage sex outside marriage. (The Anglican Communion had approved the use of 'artificial means' of birth control, for married couples of course, at the Lambeth Conference of 1930.) My parish church embarked on a campaign to oppose the sale of condoms in slot machines which appeared on the streets in about 1952. I remember timidly asking whether it might not be better for such a sale to take place than for a woman to have an unwanted baby. The Vicar did not see it that way – he believed that the machines encouraged sex outside marriage.

In 1954 the nation had a mini-crisis over the fact that Princess Margaret was in love with, and wished to marry Group Captain Peter Townsend, the 'innocent party' in a divorce case, as people said then. The pressures were such that she was obliged to separate from him. In a statement announcing this, she said that she acted as she did because she was 'mindful of the Church's teaching'. Nowadays it would be difficult to imagine the same situation arising with a member of the royal family who was not even likely to ascend the throne.

Homosexuality

If sex outside marriage, or to divorced people, was frowned upon, homosexuality was an entirely taboo topic, rarely mentioned even between close friends, still less between relatives. In the changing climate of the 1960s, I remember a priest I had known since the late 1940s telling me how much this forced concealment had cost him, a man in his early forties at the time: 'I remember the endless jokes in the parish about my getting married. I longed to be able to talk frankly about myself – I felt a sham – but I dared not do so. One night, at a dinner party at Xs, I drank a glass too much, and realised that I had said something that gave the game away. Nobody said anything, but I worried about it for months. I became a compulsive workaholic – it was my escape, except that I was also beginning to drink too much.'

At an earlier stage of his life, wishing to be completely honest, he had tried to tell his (devout) parents about his sexuality, and had written them a letter explaining his feelings. Neither of them ever referred to the matter. Their willed blindness would have been echoed by the congregation at his church if he had attempted to 'come clean' with them. They would have been amazed (whether shocked or not) that a man whom they loved and admired so much, and who was a devoted priest, could possibly have been homosexual (the word 'gay' had not yet come into common use). In 1967 the Homosexual Law Reform Act was passed, not without resistance from the churches. By declaring that sex that took place in private

111

between 'consenting adults' was outside the remit of the law, the Act stopped the practice of homosexual men being sent to prison, simply for having sexual intercourse, and to a large extent, the widespread use of blackmail against those known to be homosexual (by photographing them in compromising situations in clubs, for example). It did not remove the possibility of the police acting as agents provocateurs and trying to incriminate men in public lavatories. The fact that homosexuality was such a closely guarded secret, however, meant that the Church was happy to recruit and employ men who were homosexual, knowing and not-knowing, rather like my friend's parents. This was the Church's gain, since many fine priests then, as now, happened to be homosexual.

The Nuclear Issue
There were two great 'causes' among Christians and others in the 1950s. One, the most gut-wrenching of all, was about the use of nuclear weapons. Ever since the dropping of the two atom bombs on Hiroshima and Nagasaki in 1945, some awareness of the terrible potential of nuclear weapons to wipe out life on earth had got through to everyone. Subsequent research, some of it a study of the long-term effects on the surviving Japanese victims, some as a result of further testing on Christmas Island and at Woomera, in Australia, made it clear that the danger, and horror, was greater even than we had guessed. Nuclear explosions not only caused unspeakable injuries to any human being or animal suffering the attack but poisoned the environment irretrievably for miles around, a catastrophe later linked to cancers and troubling changes in climate and ecology. CND – the Campaign for Nuclear Disarmament – found many supporters from all walks of life who marched and demonstrated, many of them Christians, like Canon John Collins, Diana Collins and Michael Scott. They joined with others, like Bertrand Russell, in what Adrian Hastings calls 'a rather amateur alliance of Christian and humanist radicals'.[1] In the late 1950s and early 1960s 'the Aldermaston March was the focal point of all political and intellectual dissent'.[2] It was frequently argued, with how much truth it is difficult to say, that disaffectedness, disrespect for authority and various kinds of dissipation among the young came from 'the Bomb', since they felt that their lives were going to be short. It was only much later, perhaps in the early 1980s, and particularly, of course, after the end of the Cold War, that the sense of the imminent horror of nuclear attack began to diminish, and it seemed possible, by a kind of reverse ethic, that it might have helped reduce the possibilities of international war.

Immigration

From the mid 1950s a striking change occurred in British society. Two hundred and sixty thousand Caribbean immigrants entered the country between 1955 and 1962, many of them to take up jobs on the railways, in hospitals and factories that native Britons were unwilling to undertake. The virtually all-white society of pre-war Britain became multi-racial quite quickly, and eventually multi-faith, as the Caribbeans were followed by immigrants from other countries, a number of them Muslim, Sikh or Hindu. Racism, which previously had been largely concentrated on Jews, now had a wider target. Later, in the 1960s, Enoch Powell made public references to 'piccaninnies', and prophesied 'rivers of blood' if Britain did not immediately send all immigrants home.

In the late 1940s and early 1950s the worsening situation in South Africa was also becoming evident in Britain. Christians read Alan Paton's *Cry, the Beloved Country*, and learned, in particular from the Mirfield Fathers who had worked and taught in South Africa, of the gross cruelties and injustices imposed by apartheid and a brutal police force. Again Canon Collins and Diana Collins were active in establishing the Defence and Aid Fund, designed to help the oppressed in legal and other ways. Another important Anglican organisation was Christian Action, which published and campaigned tirelessly for 'causes'.

Ecumenism

The ecumenical movement was still in its infancy. The sense of division between the Church of England and the Roman Catholic Church seemed huge and unbridgeable. I remember a solemn discussion between myself and a woman friend in the mid-1950s about whether it would be wrong of her (from a Catholic point of view) to attend my daughter's baptism. She did so, amid jokes to the effect that we would not tell the Pope.

The uncrossable divide between Roman Catholics and Anglicans would change, however, with the election of Cardinal Roncalli in 1958. As Pope John XXIII he met with Archbishop Fisher in Rome in 1960, a meeting hedged about, on the Archbishop's side, with 'Protestant' suspicion and fear. Significantly, no photographs exist of the famous meeting. Yet it went extraordinarily well, largely because of Pope John's famous warmth. Adrian Hastings goes so far as to say that it was 'a turning of the tide'[3] in the long and painful history between the Church of England and the Roman Catholic Church. Even the crusty Fisher recognised that some fundamental change had occurred, almost in spite of himself, and that relations between

113

the two churches could never again be as they had been. Pope John went on to call for *aggiornamento* – a bringing up to date of the Catholic Church – and this was to be achieved, or at any rate started by a Vatican Council, only the second to be so called. This would include an innovation, a Secretariat of Unity, which would look towards Christian unity, a coming together of the Catholic Church and the 'separated brethren'. The Council opened in 1962. Anglicans and others from other major Christian traditions were permitted as observers. 'Whatever the future had in store' (for the Catholic Church and the Church of England) 'it must be something very different from the mutual disregard which, at both official and local levels had hitherto characterized that relationship.'[4] There would be all sorts of setbacks, of course, as the Curia later took back some of the power they lost when Pope John took charge, and some of his successors were of a different mind from him, but certain kinds of rapprochement can never be entirely forgotten. Too much hope is aroused for the old prejudices and pretences ever quite to convince again.

South Bank Religion
'You know that quote about "bliss was it in that dawn to be alive"?' said Canon Eric James.[5]

When I arrived in London from Cambridge in 1959, with Mervyn Stockwood as Bishop of Southwark, and John Robinson as suffragan, to be Vicar of St George's, Camberwell, we were extremely hopeful about starting a reform movement – everything seemed bright with hope. Though we were surrounded by some terrible social problems. I remember asking myself 'What is the first problem I have to deal with here?' And the answer was 'Housing'. There was a backlog of people waiting to be married as a result of the interregnum, and not one of the couples had a place to go to. I set up a group of people I knew from Cambridge – students I had known up there who had come to work in London – as a housing group, to work on the problems of solving the shortage. What went on liturgically at St George's when I got there was amazingly old-fashioned. I remember the churching of women service – marvellous women kneeling there while I spoke the most awful stuff – 'All men are liars' came into it somewhere, I remember – Psalm 116. And the baptism service was pretty archaic too. So we changed those things. There was a little group that met with John Robinson on Wednesdays to work at liturgical reform. There was a strong sense of being in a new time. The Southwark Ordination Course started then too – a real innovation.

114

John was the theological brain behind that. Mervyn called the Course 'an ordination course for people in night school'. He wanted me to run it, and I had to tell him that with a parish of 10,000 I couldn't do it.

The thinking was that there were lots of people who had vocations for ordination that had never been looked at because they had to pursue secular jobs. But that was only half of it. The more important idea was that the theology of the priesthood should be thought out from a secular base, with people who knew the working world. I was on the Council of the Course and it was very exciting. Naïvely exciting. John tended to think that because there had been a return to religion in Cambridge a similar thing might well happen in South London. I always felt that John's Cambridge background was a disadvantage in that sort of way. You needed to see the South London world almost against the background of Dickens. I had worked as a boy on a riverside wharf on the Thames and knew that none of the people I worked with there even thought of going to church. But John was very quick to grasp what was going on – he picked up the urban problem of the Church immediately. Woolwich was the right place for him.

There were some very bright people around – Nick Stacey at St Mary's, Woolwich, and Ernie Southcott had come from being Provost of Sheffield to be Provost of Southwark. He was very useful, though he and Mervyn did not get on. As well as liturgical experiment there was new theological thinking. Douglas Rhymes wrote a book on ethics, *The New Morality*. John was very interested in ethics, he lectured on it at Liverpool and there was a lot about it in *Honest to God,* but people were so knocked over by his idea that 'their image of God must go' that they didn't notice, though it was as important as the narrowly theological ideas. John also aroused a lot of interest by appearing in defence of publishing *Lady Chatterley*, of course.

The Southwark reforms opened into a larger world and turned into more organisational reforms. Nick Stacey organised the Keble Conference in 1960 with people like Tim Beaumont, Peter Whiteley and, of course, John Robinson. The Conference was interested in institutional reform. For example, there was pressure for a Synod instead of Church Assembly, and a better deployment of the clergy which pushed on to the Paul Report.

I was released from Southwark in 1964 to go and stump the country to head up the Parish and People Movement – the English equivalent of the Liturgical Movement in France. This was on the assumption that there was a reform movement in the Church of England waiting to happen. After I had been doing it for about a year and a half, I realised that there was no reform movement. Eric Abbott, who was Dean of Westminster, called a meeting of bishops in the Jerusalem Chamber during Convocation, and I remember saying to them, 'Well, it may just be me, but I don't think there is a real movement.' What I kept coming across was clergy who hated John Robinson. It seemed to me that they felt he had breached the sacred/secular divide, had tried to join together work and what went on at the far end of the church, and that was unforgivable.

Eucharist Replaces Mattins

The Parish and People Movement had a large impact. In 1950 my own church, St John's, Greenhill, made a move – like many other churches around the same period – away from mattins and evensong as the central Sunday liturgy of the church to a mid-morning eucharist. Previously holy communion had only been available at 8 a.m. ('the early service') or, once a month or so, after mattins on a Sunday. Now it was the central act of worship. At the same time the presiding priest ceased to celebrate with his back to us, and stood behind the altar facing the congregation. For a while a table was placed at the top of the nave – the 'nave altar' of the Elizabethan period, from which ordinary bread rather than wafers was dispensed – but later St John's returned, as did others, to distributing communion from the 'high altar', though with the priest facing the congregation. The congregation, with rare exceptions, were enthusiastic, feeling that a rather dry liturgical experience had come alive for them. It was interesting how, with very little opposition, this radical change in Anglican practice (which, of course, owed much to Anglo-Catholic witness) happened so quickly and easily. Since it required no legal sanction it came about without the usual arguments. There were those opposed to the move, A. M. Ramsey among them, rather surprisingly. Ramsey was concerned about the negligence of unprepared communions – what he called 'tripping to the altar'. There was very little general opposition, however. The idea took off quickly in many churches.

The Sixties

The 1960s seemed to herald tremendous change. Perhaps it was partly that the exhaustion and trauma of war had moved into the past and there were new perspectives and new arguments. There was new music too – the music of the Beatles and other pop musicians. People had become more aware that they were living in a huge technological revolution. Television, labour-saving devices, automation in working environments, and, just over the horizon, the cyber revolution, produced public discussion about what we should all do with the huge amount of leisure which would be available to us when most of the work was done by machines. (It is one of the cruel tricks of life that precisely the opposite result has occurred.)

The Church had a new Archbishop, A. M. (Michael) Ramsey, previously Bishop of Durham and Archbishop of York, a writer and scholar and an Anglo-Catholic. He was eccentric in appearance, large and, at first glance, formidable, with beetling eyebrows, unnerving silences and no small talk. Without precisely having a speech impediment, he had a strange, and much imitated, repetitive style of talk, punctuated with curious brooding noises. (He once opened the conversation with the young woman seated next to him at a formal dinner by saying – after a series of humming noises, small grunts and attempts at speech – 'Tell me, Miss X, do you prefer the *Iliad* to the *Odyssey*, or the *Odyssey* to the *Iliad*?') He had a smile of astonishing sweetness, a way of giving whoever he was talking to his undivided attention, however many other people were milling about, and an underlying warmth that was irresistible. He might easily have been a figure of public mockery, yet, a bit like Dr Johnson, his spiritual stature somehow forbade that, his intelligence and integrity enforcing an overwhelming sense of respect from almost everyone. No one could have shown less inclination to cut a public figure, less interest in 'image'. At a lunch for the press in the late 1960s he was asked by one journalist whether he thought the Church of England would survive into the next century.

'Well, you know, that is not certain, not certain, not certain, at all. Not certain. It might easily, easily, it might easily, quite easily, just fall away after twenty years or so. Just fall away.' His audience listened in stunned silence. Here was the Archbishop of a major church, a primary figure in state and society, straightforwardly admitting (not without a certain cheerfulness) that the body that he led was not merely vulnerable but possibly terminally unwell. Nobody knew what to make of it and, almost incredibly, none of them reported it – it was as if they had decided not to hear. Or perhaps they recognised the kind of integrity that could not tell a lie, at least about something so important, and felt an instinct to protect it. It is, God knows, a rare enough commodity in public figures.

In the late 1950s a young Anglican ginger group had set up a magazine called *Prism* which was both committed to, and critical about, the Church. Adopted financially by the Reverend Timothy Beaumont, this moved on to become *New Christian,* a lively radical magazine edited by Trevor Beeson. It was a period in which there was much to discuss, theologically and morally.

One of the discussion points of the 1960s was the 'death of God' movement, an odd misnomer since its proponents were not saying that God had once been alive but was now dead, but rather that God was a dead issue for modern people. 'Demythologising' became a popular word. Christianity, it was felt, had existed in a fog of stories through which it was difficult to discern essential facts. The stories needed to be thrown overboard, leaving us with something harder, more rational, more modern.

In 1962 a group of Cambridge theologians published *Soundings*.[6] It touched both on old themes that needed looking at anew, such as comparative religion, and new themes that had not yet been taken fully into Christian consciousness – the impact of psychoanalytical ideas (Harry Williams), among others. Ironically, the editors of this book felt that John Robinson was too conservative to be invited to contribute.

Honest to God

In 1963 John Robinson's *Honest to God* was published,[7] and rapidly became a bestseller. The huge publicity for the book came about partly by the fury and venom of his opponents – the *Church Times* letters' column was filled up for weeks by their screams of disapproval and betrayal – partly by the fact that the writer was a bishop, and many who had given up the churches felt suddenly that this authority figure understood their difficulties. Robinson attacked childish ideas of God, in particular as an old man with a beard 'up above the bright blue sky', and suggested that belief had become more difficult because would-be believers were stuck with images of God that misled them. Borrowing from the German theologian Paul Tillich he suggested what he believed to be a more fruitful way of thinking about God, as 'the ground of our being', what we experience in our hearts and in the most profound moments of our lives.

Drugs and Hippies

Other spiritual ideas, not specifically Christian, surfaced during the 1960s and 1970s. There was, among the young in Britain and America, growing up in a period of considerable middle-class prosperity, an interest in poverty, in the idea of a life without 'things'. As the 1960s moved into the 1970s, opposition to the Vietnam war among the American young spearheaded a general revolt against the idea of going to war. ('All we are saying, is give peace a chance', as the Beatles sang.) The enormously popular musical *Hair* took up the theme both of Vietnam, and of a general freedom from the old repressive taboos which were believed to have made the older generation so unhappy. The Beatles also helped encourage the movement towards meditation; for a while they employed an Indian teacher as their guru. The Christian churches were not seen as relevant to this spiritual revolution, but as too sexually repressive, too bound up with authority and Establishment, yet *Godspell* and *Jesus Christ Superstar* were enormously successful on the London stage. The quarrel of the young was not with Jesus, but with the churches, it seemed.

There was a great longing for 'spiritual experience' among the young and this was sought in drug-taking. Where they were not nightmarish, the experiences often were profoundly spiritual. A member of The Who pop group, describing a God experience he had had, with or without the help of 'substances', was asked what was needed for such an experience, and he replied, memorably, 'desperation', something a good many more orthodox believers – Paul, Augustine, Francis of Assisi, Ignatius Loyola, Teresa of Avila, John Bunyan – had also found.

Desperate or not, many Harvard students of the 1970s phoned home to say that (under drugs) they had seen the beatific vision, not, it seemed to their parents, the reason for which they had sent them to Harvard at considerable expernse. Experimenting with the drug LSD, people reported moments of religious ecstasy, and also of hellish terror. At this period (not perhaps later when 'altered states' were a fashion), drug experimentation seemed to be a longing for a unified vision of the world, *ek-stasis* – the ability to stand outside the humdrum world and see it differently – a function that religion had always existed to perform, by a great variety of methods. Now it was being taken out of the hands of the churches.

One of the grandfathers of this change was Aldous Huxley. Another might have been William James, the turn-of-the-century psychologist whose *Varieties of Religious Experience*[8] not only made a fascinating religious distinction between those he described as the 'once-born' and the 'twice-born' – believers who believed because they had grown up with a set of beliefs, and those who had some sort of 'God-experience' which confirmed the beliefs – but also gave superb descriptions of mystical experience, some induced chemically, by 'laughing gas', for instance, and some by other methods: prayer, religious practices, or 'desperation'. In 1953 Aldous Huxley, not a religious man, agreed to take part in some research conducted by a university department, which involved swallowing 'four tenths of a gram of mescalin dissolved in half a glass of water'.[9] Within an hour, Huxley, a man who claimed to have a poor visual imagination, found himself focused in total concentration on three flowers, an iris, a rose and a carnation, on the table. 'I was not looking now at an

119

unusual flower arrangement. I was seeing what Adam had seen on the morning of his creation – the miracle, moment by moment, of naked existence.'[10] This, Huxley went on to say, seemed to him to be what Meister Eckhart had mean by 'Istigkeit' ('Isness'), or what Plato had meant by 'Being'.

In the period after Huxley wrote of his vision, and later on in the 1960s when more and more people began to experiment with LSD, the possibility of its dangers as a street drug, of its being slipped into someone's drink 'as a joke', or in reducing some people to break-down, schizophrenic experiences or 'flashbacks', was not at first apparent. What religious people objected to was that people who had put no work into 'being spiritual' seemed to be enjoying similar experiences to the saints. Huxley's answer to this was that human beings are chemical creatures. Fasting, sleeplessness, pain, lack of external stimulation (as in a bare, possibly dark cell), or, in somewhat different circumstances, dancing and singing, could all bring about chemical changes in the brain which produced hallucination or vision. The psychiatrist R. D. Laing, asked what was the difference between a saint's vision, an LSD experience and a schizophrenic episode, said 'A holy person will have a holy experience, a sick person will have a sick experience.'[11]

The 'flower children', meditating, theoretically living in poverty (but often, at least in part, off their conventional parents), taking drugs which they hoped would open them up to God, tried to shift power away from capitalism, power politics, greed. Protest at universities about injustices within and without the campus, and, in some parts of Europe, as in France, political demonstrations by students on the streets, attacked the domination by the middle-aged and elderly. Sexual experimentation became commonplace, aided by more effective contraception than had been available in the past. The churches' protests about the loss of a 'high ideal' of sexual intercourse, that is to say, refraining from sex until marriage, and remaining faithful to one partner, fell on deaf ears. Divorce became easier.

Another aspect of the sexuality of the 1960s and 1970s was feminism. Betty Friedan's famous book, *The Feminine Mystique*,[12] described one woman's dissatisfaction with her lot in a way that caught the mood of postwar women. Encouraged to give up their wartime jobs so that the men could have them, to go back to the home, to be traditionally feminine, and to have large families, many women found themselves miserable in a life virtually confined to housework and the company of tiny children. Education had led them to expect work that used their particular gifts, and their biology seemed to deny them this, allowing nothing more individual than child-bearing and rearing. There must be more to being an adult woman than being a wife and a mother. Germaine Greer's *The Female Eunuch*[13] looked at the political, economic and sexual situation of women and found it wanting.

These two set off a revolution, with many other women suddenly refusing to fit the conventional and stereotypical mould of daughter, wife, mother or employee. Women campaigned for equal pay for equal work and the end of other forms of discrimination, which culminated in legislation in the Sex Discrimination Act of 1975, an Act from which the Church of England, not at all to its credit, and apparently blind to the implications of what it does, has shown itself determined to claim exemption.

The Ordination of Women
Partly because of the feminist movement – there would not have been the will and the courage otherwise – but in another sense separate from it since there were many reasons involved which had little to do with feminism, women throughout the Anglican Church and in England itself in the 1970s were coming forward and saying that they wanted to be priests. This idea had been firmly on the Church of England's back burner for many years. For most of its history women were not permitted to speak in church in any public capacity (this was true up to the 1950s).

The Reverend Florence Lee Tim-Oi, who had been ordained priest in the Hong Kong diocese in 1944 mainly because of a shortage of priests in the exigencies of war, was forbidden after the war to practise as a priest until 1974, when Hong Kong, following a statement by the Anglican Consultative Council, officially accepted women priests. In the Episcopal Church of the USA, eleven women got themselves ordained priest 'irregularly' in 1974 with the help of sympathetic bishops. Two years later the American Church agreed officially to ordain women. In the 1960s the demand in Britain for women to 'have their vocations tested' started to grow, slowly at first. Male clergy who were in favour of this, and women who wanted to be priests, gradually began to speak out.

In 1975, interestingly the year of the Sex Discrimination Act, after much work behind the scenes, General Synod voted that 'there was no fundamental objection' to women being ordained. Perhaps this was meant as a sop, a delaying tactic (in the years that followed there seemed little official desire to implement the realisation), but the fact that it had happened was inevitably read quite differently by the supporters of women's ordination. The vote encouraged the reasonable assumption that the ordination of women was approaching. Some women began training on, for example, the new Southwark Ordination Course (a part-time course for people working at other jobs). In 1978, however, Synod voted 'not to move forward', an action which produced tremendous disappointment.

'We asked you for bread and you gave us a stone,' Dr Una Kroll memorably shouted from the gallery when the result was announced, a mild intervention that was received at Church House with as much panic as if the barricades were going up in Great Smith Street. Perhaps in a sense they were.

The End of Barchester

Derek Pattinson became Assistant Secretary-General of the Church of England in 1970, the year that General Synod was up and running. He was a civil servant who had worked in the Administrative Civil Service in Revenue and the Treasury, and at the age of forty took on the task of following two long-serving church officials, Sir John Guillum Scott and his father.

He became Secretary-General in 1972, but regarded 1970, with the coming of the General Synod, as the key date in a huge transformation in the Church – 'Barchester came to an end', as he put it.

> It has to be said that Synodical government was oversold . . . it wasn't quite what many of those who joined thought it was going to be, but nevertheless between 1970 and the early 1980s, I would say the Church of England was transformed. There was the new system of government, and the fact that though the Fenton Morley Commission which followed the Paul Report had done its work in the 1960s, all that had now to be translated into action. The Synod getting control of worship and doctrine, stipend reform, reform of appointments, the Church getting a say on the appointments of bishops – all this just came in a great rush. We ran into a lot of difficulties over worship and doctrine. I used to say 'Parliamentary powers to the Church to delegate by Measure were given to the Church in 1919 by the Parliament of a busy Empire; by the 1970s we did not have a busy Empire, and Parliamentarians were looking for things to do.' Parliamentarians became very aggressive about worship and doctrine, particularly Conservatives.
>
> The atmosphere on the Ecclesiastical Committee became increasingly difficult and one felt the hostility. However, we got it through. The changes were cumulative – reform of money matters, stipends, changes in the freehold – it was a total operation. All these things hung together to change the Church. It left the

diocesan bishop with more, not less, power, particularly since bishops have come to take the lead in appointments, even where they are not the patrons.[14]

Pattinson was to serve under three archbishops. His undoubted favourite was Michael Ramsey, with Runcie a close second.

Ramsey presented the Worship and Doctrine Measure to the House of Lords in November 1973 – his last day as archbishop. It was striking how he dominated the House of Bishops. He was someone around whom other dogs really did not bark very much. There were a lot of good bishops who were very much in awe of him. Towards the end of Ramsey's time he became a bit contemptuous of the vapourings of some of the bishops of his own age group, whom he described as so many old sheep, but he was interested in the ideas of the new wave who were coming along – Robert Runcie, Kenneth Woollcombe and Patrick Rodger. He would draw them out in discussion because he wanted to know what these younger ones were thinking.

When Coggan came in it was just for five years. He was an old man in a hurry – he came too late. He had a need to do everything himself – he couldn't delegate. Of the three I served under he was the one I was least happy with. I would be explaining something to him, and he'd look at me with those cold blue eyes of his and say 'Ye-ss, Ye-ss. I see what you mean.' And I knew that he didn't see at all, and I might as well have saved my breath.

He went to Canada, to a theological college job before the war, and he was out of England during the war, and came back to be principal of a theological college after the war, and I've always felt that he missed out on that experience that we all had. In contrast I always felt how helpful it was that Robert Runcie had had the kind of war he had. What Coggan didn't understand at all was what had happened to the evangelical movement in which he'd been brought up – he didn't understand all the new exuberance. His was the world of sung mattins and very formal pre-war evangelicalism.

He got on to the idea of the Call to the Nation mission. He planned that totally outside the structures of the Church of England and the other churches, although he was wanting to draw in the other churches. A select group was invited to Lambeth to discuss the mission – Christian Howard and I were invited to the first meeting, but not to any subsequent meetings. The mission was planned on the back stairs at Lambeth. Then, of course, when it burst out on the world, the Church of England was vexed, but the other churches were scandalised. The British Council of Churches was up in arms. Christian and I reckoned that it would take five years to rebuild the confidence. In the next twelve months he had to move on fast – he was first unwell and then was out of England quite a lot – and the whole impetus dissipated because it had all revolved around him and a few henchmen, so The Call was soon forgotten about.

He was a good preacher, a deeply honest man, and he carried off public occasions well. He was often a force for good, but he was not a good team man. If he was rattled he kicked into touch, which took the form of setting up another committee, even if there was a committee already doing the work. He almost lost control of the Lambeth Conference of 1978, they were so obstreperous and bolshie.

The Myth of God Incarnate

In 1977 a group of theologians from the 'liberal' wing of the Church of England published a collection of essays *The Myth of God Incarnate*.[15] Its editor, John Hick, expressed the belief in the preface that many would find the book 'disquietingly negative and destructive', and he was right. He suggested that, far from being a fixed and final religion, Christianity 'was from the first very diverse, and has never ceased developing in its diversity'. Absorbing changes in religious thought in the past had usually been traumatic, as, for instance, in the recognition in the nineteenth century that the world had not been made in six days, yet the vast majority of Christians had adjusted to the transition. The transition the book was asking Christians to make was to accept that, Jesus was not, in fact, the Son of God, the Second Person of the Trinity, though nevertheless a person of huge importance. Adrian Hastings compares this Anglican theology, with its slightly smug academic enjoyment in knowing better than most ordinary Christians, and its lack of any kind of social commitment, with the costly and experimental 'liberation theology' being hammered out in Latin America and other parts of the world (mostly, though not exclusively, in a Roman Catholic context) at the same time. It felt 'privileged', the musing of well-fed dons, in contrast to the costly struggles of the oppressed. On the other hand, it may be there are important questions one only gets to ask on a full stomach.

Ecumenism

Another failed attempt at inclusiveness that had preceded the women's ordination disappointment was that of Anglican/Methodist unity – both debacles masterminded, I heard a leading Methodist recently observe bitterly, by the same man, Bishop Graham Leonard, now a Roman Catholic. Both Anglicans and Methodists prepared slowly and carefully for a day of historic reunion, with the prospect of healing the 200-year-old schism. 'The final scheme for a two stage reunification preceded by a Service of Reconciliation appeared in 1968. It included what could be taken as a conditional reordination of the Methodist clergy . . . Almost all the real and painful concessions had come from its side.'[16] When the vote was taken in July 1969 it obtained the necessary majority in the case of the Methodists, but failed in the Church of England because of the combination of Anglo-Catholics, some Evangelicals and diehards (the same combination that did its best to scuttle the Synod motion for women's ordination). Adrian Hastings says that if it had gone through it would have stood out as 'the principal ecclesiastical achievement of the sixties, and it would have constituted "radical change" '. The failure of this loving and careful scheme did Methodism in Britain great harm. Marking time as a church while they waited for the expected change to come, hurt and humiliated by the rejection, they suffered a damaging reverse. The Church of England seemed indifferent to the false expectations it had aroused and the pain that it had brought about by not fulfilling them.

Relations with the Roman Catholic Church seemed promising. The Second Vatican Council of the 1960s, which had bravely taken the lid off internal dissent, stimulated interest in theological ideas in a way that excited other churches, not least as the Council itself revealed a new attitude of friendliness towards 'the separated brethren'. Representatives from other churches were invited as 'observers'. Pope John Paul II visited Britain in 1982, the first Pope ever to do so.

In the previous year ARCIC (the Anglican-Roman Catholic International Commission) had reported after eleven years of debate on all the sensitive areas of disagreement: eucharist, ministry and authority. On both sides very distinguished theologians and senior churchmen took part. The Report noted the growing closeness and charity between the two churches and for a while it looked as if a path had been laid theologically that might lead to intercommunion. But despite the warmth of the new Archbishop, Robert Runcie, and his visit to Rome in the mid-1980s, nothing except the intangibles changed. Maybe it was, as Runcie and others suggested, because of the growing movement in the Church of England towards ordaining women. It would be impossible to deny the problems this would entail for Rome, yet it seems unlikely that even deeper fears and doubts were not at work, which expressed themselves in a refusal to accept Anglican orders. Yet the Cold War between the two churches was clearly over – the Berlin Wall between them had come down. Sooner or later a closer rapprochement would take place.

Increasingly, almost in spite of the leaders and theologians, Christians were coming together at the grass roots to make a Christian contribution in their neighbourhood. The liveliness of Christians working together in many districts has been extraordinary, with Christians, using bigger resources than those available to a single parish, setting up counselling centres, coffee shops, bookshops, credit unions, days of prayer together and much else.

11

The End of the Century

The 1980s began promisingly for the Church with the consecration of Robert Runcie as the 102nd Archbishop in 1980. A liberal Catholic, trained at Westcott House, Cambridge, who had been Principal of Cuddesdon and Bishop of St Albans, he was known particularly for his ecumenical interests, and more particularly for his links with the Orthodox Churches. He was a graceful incumbent, intelligent, witty, humanly attractive and socially adroit. Derek Pattinson describes him as 'a joy to work with' and said that it was like working for a very competent minister of the Crown.

> The only time he would be cross with you would be if you hadn't given him a good brief. I gave him briefs for General Synod, for Standing Committee, for the bishops and so on. He made wonderful use of any brief I gave him. Sometimes if the bishops or others had known that it was me speaking they would have reacted in a hostile way, but the way he hummed and hahed and spouted it, it was his own![1]

Up till Runcie's time Lambeth had a very small staff – he expanded it considerably. In this, as in other ways, he created a new style of being archbishop, seeing his staff as a kind of 'family' chosen to help him with his difficult job, adding new technological gadgets to make the operation of Lambeth more efficient, responding effectively to press and public relations demands, while being a man who took his own spirituality seriously. Famously, he asked others to contribute ideas for his speeches and sermons, which he then made his own, both by changing the text and by the way he spoke it. Pattinson felt that he valued the stimulus of others' ideas. He found him particularly impressive in Synod. 'Time and again he would get up – he usually spoke about sixth – and make a speech and then you knew which way Synod would go.'[2]

An exception to this was one of the early debates in the 1980s on women's ordination, when Runcie spoke against the issue and said he would not vote for it, and Habgood spoke in favour and said he would vote for it. Pattinson felt that, if anything, this indicated the closeness of the trust between the two archbishops. The Canterbury/York partnership is not an easy one. Fisher and Ramsey, Ramsey and Coggan, Coggan and Blanch, had all been, to various degrees, incompatible, but the working relations between Runcie and Habgood were excellent. Neither would take the other by surprise. 'Runcie would say at Synod, "Oh John, you take the chair this afternoon." Neither Coggan nor Ramsey would have surrendered the chair like that.'

The Archbishop was also very good at the Lambeth Conference. 'You never knew what would happen next!'

Runcie was shrewd about people.

Michael Ramsey knew the clergy of the Church of England remarkably. Donald Coggan knew a few of the evangelicals, but he didn't even know the up-and-coming ones. Robert Runcie knew all the clergy of the Church of England, of whatever party, who had any pretension to brains, so he knew exactly where to go when he needed someone.

He could be very affirming of work done by the Church House Boards or by anybody else which he thought was on the right lines. Coggan, on the other hand, was not supportive in that way. When a Board produced a Report, like the Board of Social Responsibility did on dying, for example, Coggan was capable of making a speech with a completely different thrust from what they had said. I think he saw the offerings of Church House Boards or others, as attempts to quench the Spirit.

One of the most important things Runcie seemed to me to bring to his archbishopric was his idea of 'critical solidarity' – a sense of supporting the Government while being critical of it, something the other churches joined in with.[3]

It was Runcie's misfortune, however, to preside in one of the more difficult decades, one in which the Church introduced a new Prayer Book, and dealt with a number of extremely thorny issues while simultaneously becoming more conscious of declining numbers – between 1960 and 1985 it lost more than a third of its active membership. This was all hard enough, but Runcie was the first, probably, of a number of archbishops to become something of a target for the press in a way that had not quite happened before, at least not in the twentieth century. It was part of a trend in which other leading figures in the country, particularly the royal family, suffered endless speculation and prurient curiosity about their private lives, and maybe it was a sort of backhanded compliment that the leader of the Church of England was thought interesting enough to pursue. Runcie lent fuel to the fires of intrusion by commissioning a biography towards the end of his term of office from Humphrey Carpenter, the son of an old friend of his, who wrote an immensely entertaining book about the Archbishop in which he published a number of conversational indiscretions made by Runcie and others which seriously undervalued the hard work and abilities of his subject.[4] It was a puzzle that the Archbishop, with all his shrewdness, connived at a book about himself which didn't do him justice, when there was no shortage of other writers who might have done a better job. It was as if he had commissioned a formal portrait of himself from the cartoonist Giles.

Another misfortune, from Runcie's point of view, was that although the pressure to ordain women had been slowly building up for years, it was in the 1980s that it reached its peak, with consequent panic among some Anglo-Catholics and Evangelicals who were strongly opposed. Himself a man who liked women and got on well with them, Runcie was sufficiently traditional not to be enthusiastic about ordaining them (as his predecessor Donald Coggan had been), and his foot-dragging, designed to preserve the Church, perhaps endangered it more by giving time for a powerful backlash to build up.

Finally, Runcie was obliged to work alongside a Prime Minister, Mrs Thatcher, who was thought not to like or approve of him very much. The low point between them came when, at a service at St Paul's in 1982, marking the end of the Falklands War, his sermon made a point of remembering the relatives of the 'young Argentinian soldiers' killed in battle, as well as British soldiers, of course. He suggested that the bereaved of both sides needed the prayers of the congregation. Runcie was no pacifist – he had fought as a tank commander in the Second World War – and perhaps therefore knew more at first hand of the cost of war than some of those who criticised him. It did not seem particularly surprising that an archbishop should make it obvious that that he believed in love and forgiveness. Denis Thatcher famously remarked after the service that 'the boss was spitting blood', and other Tories spoke furiously of 'wet', 'cringing' clergy and their 'divisive liberalism',[5] suggesting that the sermon was an insult to the British dead. Runcie's words were, of course, the opposite of 'cringing', which was what so annoyed a party riding high on its power.

Faith in the City

Another church initiative ill received by the Conservative Government was the report *Faith in the City*,[6] regarded by Adrian Hastings in his biography[7] as possibly the chief glory of the Archbishop's time in office. In 1981 there was rioting in Brixton, which drew public attention to the conflict and distress of the inner cities. This provoked a letter from Canon Eric James, who had been Canon Missioner at St Albans when Runcie was bishop, and who had worked closely with him there, urging an Archbishops' Commission on the inner cities. The Archbishop, under advice from his urban bishops, particularly David Sheppard, went ahead with the idea, and by 1983 the Commission was up and running under the chairmanship of Sir Richard O'Brien, the former Chairman of the Manpower Services Commission, its brief to 'examine the strengths, insights, problems and needs of the church's life and mission in Urban Priority Areas' and to make appropriate recommendations. Its members included academics, theologians, social workers, a headmaster, a Trade Union Assistant General Secretary, clergy, laity and a significant black presence. In no way could it be said to have been assembled with political bias – it was remarkable for its balance. The Report commented on 'a grave and fundamental injustice in the Urban Priority Areas . . . the sense of alienation' (of those who lived in them, particularly the young), and of the devastating impact of 'unemployment, decayed housing, sub-standard educational and medical provision and social disintegration'.[8] Those who collected evidence for the Report and assessed it, many of them from very different backgrounds from Brixton or Tottenham or Toxteth, claimed that their own lives and attitudes were profoundly changed by the conditions they found. Derek Pattinson suggests how important it was that the Archbishop headed up the idea and stuck to it.

The Commission recommended, among thirty-eight other suggestions, that the Church of England should set up a Church Urban Fund to finance appropriate projects in the inner cities, and it made twenty-three recommendations to the Government, on themes like job creation, increased child benefit, positive measures against racial discrimination in employment and housing, the raising of the rate support grant, and an inquiry into mortgage tax relief which worked solely to the advantage of the better off.

Immediately, on its appearance in 1985, the Report was condemned by Conservative MPs, including a Cabinet Minister, as 'a Marxist document', and violently attacked by the Tory press in whom it evoked an intense paranoia, as if the Church had been guilty of a left-wing conspiracy against it. The immediate result was best-selling sales of the Report, warm support from a number of distinguished and knowledgeable people, and a very fair assessment of it by, among others, the *Financial Times*, which pointed out that one of the major insights of the Report was how ill-equipped a prevailingly middle-class clergy were to deal with the miseries of the inner city. The Church had not spared itself in the Report, and there were more recommendations for its own members than for the Government. It was as if the Government chose to regard the Church as conveniently impotent and could not forgive it for its virility in its strong recommendations of a way forward.

The expertise evident in the Report was to have far-reaching results, not only stimulating some government action, but including the raising of £18 million from charitable trusts, business, and by churchgoers themselves, to create the Church Urban Fund which would enable inner city projects over twenty years.

The whole enterprise, together with *Faith in the Countryside*, which followed it in 1990, showed the Church of England in an attractive light (except to those affronted by the suggestion that something was very wrong in the inner cities) putting considerable expertise into examining a serious social problem, prepared to admit to its own failures, ready to raise money to take the action it thought necessary. It was a triumph for the Archbishop, and might be seen, in its thoroughness, intelligence, openness and practical suggestions, as a model for the Church in the future.

The Kidnapping of Terry Waite

In January 1987 the Archbishop's envoy Terry Waite was kidnapped in Beirut. Originally employed by Robert Runcie as Assistant for Anglican Communion Affairs, Waite had already embarked on missions outside that job, playing a significant part in obtaining the release of several hostages, four missionaries in Iran in 1981, four captive Britons in Libya in 1984, and two men in Beirut.

Waite was working to free the remaining hostages in Beirut – British, Irish and American – and although aware of the growing dangers of the situation, he returned there in the hope of resuming negotiations, which turned out to be one act of daring too many. The Archbishop had for a while been increasingly uneasy about Waite's activities, feeling that he was getting taken over by the heroic aspects of his role, and his need to be 'centre stage', and that he was not, in any case, employed by him primarily as a negotiator. Against the Archbishop's advice Waite returned to Beirut, and almost immediately was kidnapped, partly because of a link with American intelligence, which did not emerge until much later. He was to spend four miserable years in the hands of Muslim extremists. He left a young family at home.

The *Crockford's* Preface

A painful episode in 1986 concerned, ludicrously to begin with, the Preface to *Crockford's*, the directory of Church of England clergy. By established custom this annual volume always had a preface written by an anonymous author, which was sometimes more critical of the Church than might have been the case if the author was named. The publication of *Crockford's* was awaited with mild interest by the press, who hoped for, and sometimes found, an element of scandal in the introduction. In 1986 the preface was sharply critical of the Archbishop as a man who lacked principle, taking 'the line of least resistance on each issue', vulnerable to pressure groups. His worst fault, however, the article claimed, was that he did not appoint men of different churchmanship from his own to senior appointments, but chose moderate Catholics like himself, who were 'good with the media'. The article had all the marks of being what it actually was, the work of an ambitious, but disappointed man, who had realised that he had been passed over for promotion and felt animus towards Robert Runcie for not helping him to a bishopric or a deanery.

The author was Gareth Bennett, a clergyman and don at New College, Oxford, a man active on the Standing Committee of General Synod. He knew Robert Runcie well, both as a friend and as an occasional helper, in framing speeches, papers and sermons. Perhaps he hoped that this closeness would lead him to the senior appointment that he coveted. There was much evidence in what he wrote to identify him, for those who understood how the Church worked and who knew his opinions. The press seemed baffled by the tone of the Preface, in particular at the extraordinary fact of the Church attacking itself in this way in a publication produced by itself – 'shooting itself in the foot' as people say. It whetted the appetite of journalists to find the author.

The press got wind of the fact that those in the know believed that the author was Gareth Bennett, but when they asked him if this was the case, he denied it. It was a lie that would have fatal consequences for him, because the hunt for the author continued. Bennett apparently panicked, unable to take the heat of intensive press interest, and committed suicide. It was an incident of considerable pathos – a man 'willing to wound and yet afraid to strike', who secretly vented his rage, lied about what he had done, and then had not the inner stability to ride out the storm.

He was an odd choice of a hero, but was immediately taken up as one by a disgruntled Anglo-Catholic group, and William Oddie wrote an intemperate book about the incident,[9] which not only described the incident in detail but went on from it to extrapolate extraordinary and grandiose significances, including 'the death of the Anglican mind'. The sadness of the human tragedy apart, it was a storm in a teacup, but one which indicated the level of paranoia in a small group of clergy increasingly worried, by the mid-1980s, that women were likely to be ordained, and feeling themselves more and more as a 'remnant'.

Derek Pattinson, who had invited Bennett to write the Preface, noted that it picked up what had been the gossip of Church House for the previous three years.

> When it arrived I thought to myself, 'It is strong stuff. It'll sell', and I was delighted with it. I didn't begin to anticipate the catastrophe that would follow. The mood, however, changed between Bennett writing it and its publication; there was the first major challenge from the evangelicals – Higton and so on – and the mood in the Church was an unhappy sort of mood. In that climate there was no chance of the Preface being taken 'light-heartedly', as it were. Of course, Robert knew all the time who had written it. He had just had a sabbatical term in Oxford in which he had dined with Bennett every week, and had bounced his ideas off so that he knew what he thought. He knew Gary's disgruntlement about lack of preferment and so on.
>
> When the guns began to fire I was at the point when I was going to say to Gary next time we spoke that I thought we should face the music together, and after the first furore the whole thing would all blow over in a couple of months. On the Saturday on which he died early in the morning I heard a snippet of an interview with him on the radio in which he, Gary, was criticising the author of the Preface!
>
> I went out on that Saturday to a Quiet Day, and I came home to a message from him on the answerphone. I rang back, and got no reply, and of course, he was dead by then. It was a desperate tragedy. Later when I talked to Robert I said to him that I thought Gary had been fearful that he had destroyed his friendship with him. Robert said 'Of course, he hadn't done that. He misunderstood.' Later I got a letter from Robert, dated Christmas Day, setting out his thoughts on it all in a way which made it possible for our working relationship, his and mine, to continue.[10]

The Women

Church and Archbishop were faced with a 'gentle revolt' from a large constituency of women, and a smaller but influential constituency of men, who had formed the Movement for the Ordination of Women in 1979 under the Secretaryship of Mrs Margaret Webster. Since there had been no effective action to take forward the Synod resolution of 1975 that 'there was no fundamental objection to the ordination of women' and since another resolution designed to advance the matter was rejected in 1978, something more dynamic seemed called for.

The Movement had an impressive mix of 'the great and the good' – members of the House of Lords, a judge or two, a handful of sympathetic bishops and theologians. Equally important, it quickly acquired impressive support at the grass roots, among ordinary churchgoers and parish clergy. Unusually for a contemporary church movement its numbers increased rapidly to around five thousand. Its members demonstrated (silently) for the first time at an ordination in St Paul's Cathedral at Petertide 1980, and suddenly they found themselves in the news.

Some of the bishops were outraged by this event. Archbishop Runcie, newly consecrated, was not, and courteously invited a group of the demonstrators to Lambeth to talk the matter over with him. He told them that while he sympathised with their point of view, if they persisted in pushing for the ordination of women it would split the Church and *of course* they would not wish that. Kindly and intelligent as he was, he seemed unaware of the implications of what he said – that even if God was calling women to be priests, and some of those present felt themselves to be called, this was of lesser importance than upsetting the Church of England. To the women it seemed yet another request that they should 'be silent in the churches' and simply accommodate themselves to men, regardless of their own needs and longings. It was too late in history for such a plea, however. Women knew their own ability too well, and could no longer stifle it.

The Debates about Women

As a result the 1980s were punctuated with a series of debates in General Synod as women, and those who championed them, tried to press the issue of ordaining them. At every debate women were always told by one or more speakers that there were far more important and pressing issues than ordaining them, with the implication that they were wasting everybody's time. More bizarre things than that were said – charges that they wanted to 'mutilate' the Church, that women priests (those already ordained in other countries) were 'a virus in the bloodstream of the universal Church'. To hear some of the fathers of the Church in full spate was like listening to a textbook of psychological pathology. To women who had been faithful churchgoers, and who thought that women had good things to offer the Church as priests, it came as a shock to find themselves spoken of with such loathing and contempt. It was a revelation about the male-centred culture of the Church that was hard to assimilate, not least because relatively few men seemed to grasp how shocking it was.

In 1986 the Movement received a setback when Synod refused to allow women lawfully ordained abroad to celebrate communion in this country, a courtesy usually extended to priests ordained elsewhere. In 1987, despairing of progress, a group called the St Hilda Community, meeting at St Benet's, the ecumenical chapel of Queen Mary College in East London, decided to invite women priests from abroad to visit them openly, and to defy Synod by holding communion services at which the women celebrated and which they advertised in the church press. (This was in distinction from the many privately and secretly celebrated communions already held in people's houses when women priests from abroad were visiting the country.) As a result of the *Sunday Times* drawing attention to this, the Bishop of London, Graham Leonard, threatened legal proceedings (for trespass) against the Community if they continued to meet in the chapel. The London diocese happened to own the ground on which it stood, and the women were, in fact, forced out, with maximum and useful publicity, to be received warmly by an Anglican/Methodist church down the road.

Another furore, in 1989, was when the Movement itself held a communion service at its Annual General Meeting at Church House. It was celebrated by Joyce Bennett, a priest working in England who had been ordained in Hong Kong. Part of the fuss was because a bishop, Peter Selby, a loyal member of the Movement, was present. There was also an attempt to whip up horror about the event on the grounds (erroneous) that the part of Church House in which the service was held belonged to the Queen. The Home Secretary, egregiously, apologised to the Queen. Her Majesty's feelings about a woman celebrating communion were not known.

It must have been obvious to those in authority that the issue was 'hotting up'. The Lambeth Conference in 1988 had been the setting for vigorous demonstration and no meeting of General Synod was complete without a line of women and men standing outside holding up placards spelling out WAITING. Voting on the issue in the dioceses showed that thirty-eight out of forty-four dioceses were in favour.

In 1987 General Synod voted that women might become deacons, and the almost immediate presence of women as clergy helped make their later acceptance as priests seem natural and appropriate.

In November 1992 General Synod voted, with an unprecedented two-thirds majority, for the Ordination of Women Measure.

This event was received with huge applause and interest in the national press ('Vicars in Knickers' was the headline in the *Sun*), and among many of the laity. By all accounts it was less than enthusiastically received by bishops and many clergy, who kept warning the women against 'triumphalism' (but after more than sixty years of campaigning a little excitement seemed natural enough), and prophesying gloom and doom for the Church. The success of the vote was followed by vigorous campaigning from those opposed to women's ordination, who threatened that 'up to 3,000' might leave. (This turned out to be excessive – fewer than four hundred clergy have done so at the time of writing, fewer than followed Newman in 1845, and a number of those who left are retired. Some forty have since returned to the Church of England.) Distressed by the atmosphere of conflict, the bishops in unseemly haste put together a new legal package, the Act of Synod. In defiance of common sense or logic, it tried to encompass 'two integrities', to say in effect that the Church gave equal standing both to those who did and those who did not approve of women priests. This seemed rather to miss the point of the Measure for ordaining women as priests, so painstakingly worked out over a long period (unlike the Act). The Measure which made it possible for women to be ordained had made generous provision – Resolutions A and B – for parishes which did not wish to have women as priests, to refuse to have them. The Act of Synod (1993) went far beyond this, effectively setting up a church within a church by appointing provincial episcopal visitors (PEVs) popularly known as 'flying bishops', who were to officiate in parishes who did not want women, and, more significantly, ordain those who must not be touched by bishops who had laid hands on women. Although bishops and opponents denied that they were working from any premise of a 'doctrine of taint', the taint idea continued to haunt all further dealings with those opposed to women priests.

The Act was hailed by its enthusiasts as a great victory for the Church of England's inclusiveness, without the slightest apology or even recognition in official speeches that it was, in effect, a kick in the teeth for women priests that would make their future standing precarious and their work harder – it makes it immeasurably harder for them to become bishops, to give one example. An alternative to the triumphalist view is that the Act was a shameful retreat from what had been carefully decided, an inability to stand up manfully (sic) to those who opposed women's ordination. It was a victory for the 'old-boy network' – when the chips were down it came more naturally to the bishops to empathise with the feelings of men who might leave than with women who might stay and serve the Church. Morally pusillanimous, they chose nature before principle.

A new Prayer Book

In 1980, without any of the political drama of the 1920s, a new prayer book, the Alternative Service Book (usually known as the ASB) was introduced, one which, for most members of the Church of England, created the first radical break with the Book of Common Prayer they had known. The 1928 book, though widely used, was extraordinarily similar to its great progenitor of 1662. The change was startling and was driven by two considerations: one, the considerable changes in the use of language since the Book of Common Prayer had come into existence, and two, the need to move ecumenically closer. At a time when the Church longed to find new adherents it was felt that seventeenth-century language did not help, and in any case the Church of England was, traditionally, a 'vernacular' church. At the same time, scholarship suggested that it would be possible to move further towards what was believed to be the practice of the early Church (moving back behind all the Catholic/Protestant quarrels of the sixteenth and seventeenth centuries), and certainly one of the encouraging things that came out of the change was that Anglican and Catholic practices in celebrating holy communion or the mass became remarkably similar. The wholesale way in which the new prayer book was received – 'sweeping the board' as Derek Pattinson puts it – suggests that there was a long-standing desire for something of the kind well before it actually arrived.

What was less encouraging was that the Church of England had exchanged the glorious language of Cranmer for a deadness and dullness which suggested that the compilers – the Liturgical Commission – had cloth ears. I still remember the brutal shock of attending a wedding just after the ASB had come into existence. One gets used to the deadness and dullness, of course, and many churchgoers appear to have little awareness of the problem, yet for some of us the sense of loss has never gone away, even though we cannot imagine going back to the status quo ante. The Prayer Book Society, who fought a rearguard action against the new forms, seem so far to have had the last laugh. (A new prayer book – *Common Worship* – has begun to be introduced while I have been writing this book, though so far I have only been present at its baptism form of service, about which I shall say more in Chapter 22.)

The Decade of Evangelism

Part of the consequences of decline in the number of churchgoers in Britain and the anxiety it precipitated, was the Decade of Evangelism, a decision for a sustained campaign in the Anglican Communion made by the bishops of the Lambeth Conference of 1988, with the intention, as they thought of it, of shifting the emphasis of the Anglican Church as a whole from 'maintenance to evangelism'. There seemed to be little or no discussion of this potentially far-reaching initiative at the grass roots, or awareness that for church leaders to utter the wish for evangelism might be a long way from galvanising ordinary Christians to action. It could more effectively have been preceded by widespread discussion about what evangelism consisted of in the 1990s, and how those 'on the ground' felt like setting about it. It was given strong support by the leadership of the Church.

Tactlessly, the prospective Decade largely coincided in time with another Decade which had begun two years earlier – the Ecumenical Decade of Solidarity with Women, and a telling cartoon as the second Decade started showed Big Brother Evangelism trampling on Little Sister Solidarity. When Jean Mayland, an influential Synod member, urged support for the Solidarity Decade in Synod, Derek Pattinson, the then General Secretary, set up a small group to help the process along. With the bizarre contrariness so often evident in the Church where women are concerned, however, the late Margaret Hewitt was appointed as chairperson, a woman known for her lack of sympathy with feminism and her opposition to the ordination of women. Little happened. With the help of Mary Tanner, then Secretary of the Council for Christian Unity, but a supporter of women's issues in the Church, Jean tried to get the Archbishops to agree on a prayer that might be used for the initiative. The first one written was so woolly that it was unusable. A second, better, version was completed, but this disappeared into the bureaucracy of Lambeth and was never seen again. So ended the Archbishops' participation. This was in sharp distinction to the leadership of the Methodist, Baptist and Roman Catholic Churches, who all made a point of welcoming the idea warmly. In the Decade itself the initiative continued to be very poorly supported by the Church of England, again unlike at least some of the other churches. It was made clear that it was seen to be simply irrelevant, something that was frequently said in debate about the women's ordination issue itself. Jean Mayland remembers how the Wakefield Diocese, keen at the time to be seen as a 'missionary' diocese, refused even to replace the contact for the Decade of Solidarity when the existing one had to give up. It was amazing, she comments, how they could not see that supporting women had any role to play in missionary endeavours. They were not alone in this in the Church. At the very least such attitudes gave women who understood the underlying issues a sour attitude to the Decade of Evangelism – another lost opportunity.

At the mid-point of the Decade of Evangelism, in 1985, a pan-Anglican conference was held at Kanuga in Carolina, USA, to review the results so far, and these were published the following year in a book called *The Cutting Edge of Mission*.[11] As one might expect, experiences differed widely in different parts of the world. In some countries – many parts of Africa, Latin America and parts of the Far East – Christianity is on a roll with booming numbers that Western countries can only look at with wonder and envy, and their evangelism seemed as natural as breathing. 'The "typical" communicant Anglican is African, female, and does not speak English as a first language.'[12]

Janice Price of the Board of Mission of the Church of England, on the other hand, wrote that Britain was 'in the midst of massive cultural changes . . . we are having to look at culturally relevant new ways of being a church in our context'.[13] The most hopeful thing she could manage to say was that 'there are encouraging signs here and there'. Some of them were reported in *The Cutting Edge*: Lady Brentford's work with Christian groups within Parliament, Alpha courses and evangelical expansion, but the example given of improvement in a routine church situation seemed pitiful – for example, a 1 per cent increase in churchgoing in a year reported by Nigel McCulloch, the Bishop of Wakefield in his diocese. 'God is doing great things even in the Church of England.'[14] Over the period of the Decade the Church of England continued to lose members, and it seems impossible not to conclude either that its nature was ill conceived, at least for Britain, perhaps employing an outdated understanding of evangelism, or that it came at a time when the mood was entirely wrong. Whistling in the dark had become an art form.

Needless to say, nothing negative got said at Kanuga, or at least nothing negative made it to the final report. It was 'a week of unusual blessings', 'a time of deep spiritual enrichment', 'a remarkable harmony and mutual concern', 'a unique experience in the life of the Anglican Communion'.[15] The language followed a Christian custom of talking in ideals. No one, it seemed, dared to whisper that the Emperor might be naked, that in the West, at least, one could make out a good case that the Church is dying, that, so far as the Church of England was concerned, the Decade of Evangelism was, by and large, a flop.

The Shrinking Clergy

The turn of the century has seen a decline in the numbers of clergy, though there has been a recent small upturn. By the year 2000 the Church will have around a thousand less clergy than it had in 1980 – around ten thousand. The organisation of parishes has also changed considerably with fewer and fewer clergy having the 'parson's freehold', and around 50 per cent of clergy stipends being provided by parishes. Both of these changes represent a shift of power away from the clergy themselves, some of it towards the bishop and some of it towards the laity.

Human Sexuality

In 1988 Lambeth Conference called on bishops of the Anglican Communion to undertake in the next decade a 'deep and dispassionate study of the question of homosexuality'. Partly in response to this, but more in response to growing confrontations in the Church at home, the House of Bishops produced a statement in 1991, *Issues in Human Sexuality*.[16] In the late 1970s a working party on homosexuality met under the then Bishop of Gloucester, which published a Report in 1979, *Homosexual Relationships*, which provoked, as *Issues* remarks, more controversy than reasoned debate, in particular the controversy of the Higton debate of 1987, in which Reform[17] mounted its guns against homosexuals. The *Church Times* in 1990 noted that this had been

> a useful reminder that numbers of churchpeople simply disapprove of it (homosexuality). But enough fresh testimony has come to hand since then to show that this is no longer an adequate response. Homosexuals themselves are too numerous, and known to be. There are probably at least a million of them in the United Kingdom. The Church of England has homosexuals among its priests, among its ordinands, among its worshippers. These are people who have the same need of sexual expression in its many forms, for companionship, for acceptance, as heterosexuals. It becomes increasingly difficult to deny them those things and argue the denial is merciful or truthful or practical... The scriptural prohibitions were drawn up for an era when it was believed that homosexuality could be avoided by taking thought. Many other

140

scriptural prohibitions have been reinterpreted: truth to the best
lights available may require that this one should be too ... The
Church of England cannot long defer the time when it will have to
consider withdrawing the disapproval of homosexuals. That would
mean, most notably, that homosexuality ceased to be an obstacle
to ordination.[18]

When a second working party reported in 1989 (*The Osborne Report*)
the House of Bishops rather unwisely refused to publish it, though it
did, inevitably, get leaked to the press. In both Reports homosexuals
had considerable opportunity to make their views known, but *Issues*
gloomily reported that no progress seemed to have been made: 'of
any substantial agreement there seems as yet little sign'. On the one
hand there were those who felt sure, using biblical texts, that those
who expressed physical feeling for people of their own sex were
sinful. On the other there were those to whom it seemed evident
that homosexuals did not appear to have 'chosen' their sexual
orientation more than the colour of their hair, and that it was not for
others to demand their celibacy. In between were many, as in society
itself, who found the idea of homosexuality distasteful and worrying,
and did not want to have to think about it.

Issues was not unsympathetic; it moved a few inches, but predictably came down more or less in a conventional position. Lay people
must do as they thought best about their sexuality (a tacit admission
that they would do this anyhow?), but clergy

cannot claim the liberty to enter into sexually active homophile
relationships. Because of the distinctive nature of their calling,
status and consecration, to allow such a claim on their part would
be seen as placing that way of life in all respects on a par with
heterosexual marriage as a reflection of God's purposes in
creation. The Church cannot accept such a parity ...[19]

This painfully arrived at conclusion upset almost everyone. Those
who wanted a straightforward statement about the wickedness or
even disgustingness of homosexuality did not get it. Laity discovered
that there was a 'double standard' for them, which did not necessarily
accord with their view of the priesthood or the Christian life. Many
clergy were already living with partners, particularly in certain
dioceses, in some cases with the full knowledge of their parishioners.
This new diktat placed them in an impossible position (not unlike
the position of married clergy in the eleventh century when Pope
Gregory VII suddenly laid down celibacy as the rule for all clergy).
Some resigned, others carried on feeling very vulnerable. Some

committed suicide. Bishops who knew very well that they had ordained homosexuals in the past, and that many had made a fine contribution to the Church, including some at the highest levels, suddenly became cautious. In the years since, however, a number of clergy, including Archbishop Runcie, have admitted to knowingly ordaining homosexuals, and feeling that they were right to do so.

The Church had got by for years by turning a blind eye to the issue, but hardening attitudes in the Church to homosexuality were indicated in 1988 when the Archdeacon of London, acting on the Bishop's instructions, turned the Lesbian and Gay Christian Movement out of its offices at St Botolph's, Aldgate. The Rector of St Botolph's, Malcolm Johnson, refused to evict them, and the London Diocese, in a litigious mood, as it had been in the case of the St Hilda Community, took them to court. They won the case, and St Botolph's was required to pay. Many loyal friends of LGCM subscribed to pay the fine. That this organisation had done a great deal of good was hardly to be questioned.

As the 1990s wore on Peter Tatchell's *OutRage* hit on the desperate device of 'outing' senior clergy, bishops in particular, whom they had reason to believe were homosexual. This was a huge affront to episcopal dignity, and offended many people's sense of fair play, but, as the Lesbian and Gay Christian Movement (which had never gone in for outing people) was later to point out, it pushed things along quite a bit from the bland and complacent statements mentioning 'compassion' which had been so irritating in the past. It made it impossible to continue to shuffle the issue from working party to working party, and from statement to statement.

The Coming of AIDS

Rumours of AIDS began to reach Britain from America slowly in the early 1980s and then to make a devastating impact as 'people we know' began to fall sick and die of it, often at shocking speed. Clergy, supposedly celibate members of religious communities, well-known Christians, became victims of this appalling illness just as others did. This 'blew the cover' of the hypocritical way the Church had dealt with homosexuality for decades, if not centuries, apparently not minding too much what people got up to in their private lives so long as it did not frighten the horses. Now the horses were well and truly frightened. It was tempting for evangelicals in particular, always particularly hard on homosexuality, to imply that AIDS was a sign that God was angry. Lesbians could not resist pointing out that at least he did not appear to be angry with them. The gay community itself organised its considerable resources to take care of AIDS victims – as in institutions like London Lighthouse. Many Christian organisations also showed loving care, for example, the Mildmay Hospital in East London. Sympathy for AIDS grew as more was understood about the way it was transmitted: the unforgettable image of Princess Diana embracing an AIDS patient helped to change public prejudice. In a number of parishes up and down the country there was the problem of what to do when it became apparent that the vicar had AIDS. In the earliest cases vicars tended to resign or disappear. Later some decided to share it with their parishioners and invite their help. Simon Bailey, a Yorkshire vicar, a desperately sick man by the time the programme was made, appeared on a television programme with his parishioners discussing the issue of AIDS.

Lambeth Against
Although the important issue of Third World Debt was ostensibly the centrepiece of the 1998 Lambeth Conference, it was upstaged by the major battle which took place on homosexuality, and in fact this is the issue for which this Conference will be remembered. For some of the participants other issues were inextricably involved with the central issue: political, fundamentalist and Muslim attitudes in countries some of the bishops came from. Bishop Jack Spong complained of the African bishops who were quite certain that homosexuals must be sinful that 'they've yet to face the intellectual revolution of Copernicus and Einstein . . . that is just not on their radar screen', and was forced to make a muted apology. Others worried about the conservative way Scripture was being interpreted. The gap between Europe and America and 'the South' as it came to called, which largely meant Africa, seemed unbridgeable: two groups with no language in common, but both suspicious of the other. Homosexuality was seen by the South as a perversion peculiar to developed countries, one which the southern bishops seemed to imagine was unknown in Africa or Asia. The Conference ended with a resolution that pleased nobody – the old saluting base of assuring homosexuals that though they are loved by God, they, and their sexuality, are not quite up to the mark. There was the usual cry that homosexuals must observe chastity, a word which got changed in debate to 'abstinence', 'for fear the understanding of chastity could shift'. Abstinence, we were assured by a married bishop, was a glorious and splendid state.

What reached and shocked a British audience that extended far beyond churchgoers, was an African bishop, Emmanuel Chukwana, Bishop of Enugu in Nigeria, encountering the Lesbian and Gay

Christian Movement outside the sports hall of the University of Kent and shouting at them the text from Leviticus about stoning homosexuals to death. He followed this by laying his hands on the head of the Reverend Richard Kirker and attempting to exorcise his gayness out of him. 'Father, I pray that you deliver him from homosexuality in the name of Jesus', etc. As far as I know, the exorcism did not work.

The statement issued about homosexuality by the Conference, which had troubled many of the bishops, although endorsed by the Archbishop of Canterbury, together with the revelatory and hate-filled scene of exorcism shown on television, aroused such deep feelings both inside and outside the homosexual community that the matter could not simply rest there. Shortly after the conference a group of bishops published a letter to Lesbian and Gay Anglicans, apologising for the fact that their point of view had not been heard 'and we apologize for any sense of rejection that has occurred because of this reality. This letter is a sign of our commitment to listen to you and reflect with you theologically and spiritually on your lives and ministries. It is our deep concern that you do not feel abandoned by your Church and that you know of our continued respect and support.'[20] It pledged that they would continue 'to reflect, pray and work for your full inclusion in the life of the Church', and called for more conversations throughout the Communion. In England it was signed by forty-two bishops, including suffragans, many of whom had, of course, already signed the original hard-line Lambeth report approved by the Conference.

The Death of a Princess
An incident which provoked much debate in and out of the Church was the death of Princess Diana and the public response that it evoked. The Princess, a much loved and very popular figure in the country, died tragically in August 1997. A huge grieving process began immediately with thousands of people lining up for hours to sign a memorial book for her, or laying flowers outside Kensington Palace and Buckingham Palace. The funeral service, conducted in Westminster Abbey, was watched, either along the route or on television, by a vast audience, and as the cortège left the Abbey and drove slowly through north London on its way to Althorp, the road was lined for miles with flowers, and the driver had to stop at intervals to remove the flowers piling up against the windscreen. In a society often said to be fragmented, there was the astonishing experience of a collective mourning process for a woman seen to be good and loving, though not morally perfect in a way that would

have once seemed to be de rigueur. In a country where around 1 per cent are churchgoers, the church service, though inevitably criticised by some, was felt by many to express the public mood in a way that nothing else could have done. It is not really possible to draw conclusions from this episode, only to derive questions from it.

Part Two

The Church as It Is

Every part of the life of the Church, the totality of the system of communication by which it promotes its own coherence and effectiveness, ought to stand for a facet of the Gospel. There should not be a sharp division between what a Church teaches and how it manages its institutional arrangements... (Stephen Sykes, *Unashamed Anglicanism* (DLT, 1995), p. xi)

Management. The new science. We all make obeisance to it. In the old days we got on with the job, jollied staff along if they needed it, kicked the sluggards in the backside, encouraged the unconfident... It seemed to work all right. The service didn't collapse. Have you ever considered what exactly is the difference between administration and management? (P. D. James, *Death of an Expert Witness* (1977))

The early Christian communities saw themselves as a special and distinct form of corporate existence. They spoke of themselves as a people or nation, but one without any racial or social qualifications. They were ridiculed as a 'third race', neither Greek nor barbarian. Much of their distinctiveness consisted in the quality of their personal relationships, and their at least partial re-ordering of systems of status and rank, based on conversion to Christ and baptism. The letters of the New Testament were written to, and reflect the struggles of, the new communities to realise this vision in a complex and hostile environment. (*Working as One Body*, The Turnbull Report (Church House Publishing, 1995))

12

The Lambeth Walk

The Church of England has just undergone considerable structural change as a result of the recommendations of the Turnbull Report, *Working as One Body* (1995). There is now a central executive council, the Archbishops' Council, which is at the heart of a web of organisational change. This has far-reaching effects on the Church Commissioners, General Synod and the staff of Church House. Of the three courts which run the Church of England, Lambeth is the least affected. The following three chapters describe the power structure of the Church as it was and as it is now, and the way the changes are seen, both by those who designed them and those who now work within them.

Court No. 1 – Lambeth Palace, London SE1
The Church of England is run by three courts: the court of the Archbishop of Canterbury at Lambeth Palace, often called 'Lambeth' for short, the court of the Church Commissioners at No. 1 Millbank, Westminster, often just called 'Millbank', and the court of General Synod, underpinned by the staff of Church House. Here, divided a little awkwardly between prelate, clergy and lay people, lies the power of the Church of England. Synod is, of course, the late arrival, only coming into existence in its present form in 1968 after a long struggle (more than seventy years) to democratise the Church and give lay people a say in its decisions, and free it, at least partially, from the whims of Parliament. The Church is modern in patches. Sometimes you can still catch a glimpse of England's unreconstructed feudal past.

For example, Lambeth. Of the three courts of the Church of England, Lambeth is the only one that looks the part. It is a huge building, partly medieval, approached by gatehouse and courtyard and a formidable flight of steps. Placed a little way up river from the Houses of Parliament, it occupies a geographical location which for centuries has proclaimed the closeness of the Church to the monarchy and to Parliament. Thomas à Becket was the first Archbishop to live at Lambeth. Thomas Cranmer, the father of the Church of England, also lived there – oh, the constant crossings by ferry to the Palace of Whitehall to talk to King Henry and his successor, before the final trip to the Tower en route for the terrible months of humiliation and bullying under Queen Mary and the dreadful death at Oxford.

This haunted residence has continued to be the home of subsequent archbishops. The Archbishop of Canterbury ranks first in the nation after the royal family, and takes precedence over every other subject of the Crown. Next comes the Lord Chancellor, and, after him, the Archbishop of York.

The Archbishop has the ringing title of Primate of All England and Metropolitan, and signs himself 'Cantuar'. (A Primate is the chief bishop of a country, a Metropolitan is one who oversees a 'province'. Ecclesiastical England is divided into two provinces, Canterbury and York.) Cantuar has a number of important functions. He is Archbishop of the Church and Bishop of his own see of Canterbury. He crowns the monarch, is the state's leading representative, has a seat, along with twenty-five other bishops, in the House of Lords, and speaks there on issues where his opinion seems relevant. He ordains bishops within his own province, is responsible for a variety of appointments, licences, faculties and dispensations which may or may not be important. (I remember a notary, whom I needed to consult in order to have a signature formally witnessed, showing me a certificate from Lambeth Palace which validated his professional status – an absurd vestige of medieval England that might have been removed long ago without anyone being a whit the worse.) When not signing certificates for notaries, the archbishop, as the Turnbull Report, *Working as One Body*, puts it, with a touch of grandeur, 'is regarded as "vicar to the nation", articulating spiritual and moral guidance to the nation as a whole'.[1]

He also holds a position of seniority among the bishops of the worldwide Anglican Communion, but it is a position of respect rather than hierarchy in this case: he is *primus inter pares* as the phrase has it, the first among equals. His role there is an essentially unifying one.

Centred at Lambeth, like a queen bee maintained by a busy hive of workers, the archbishop does church business, entertains, holds interviews and meetings, issues statements to the press, prays (there is a fine chapel, recently restored during Archbishop Runcie's tenure) and, together with his staff, prepares his tours, speeches, sermons and ideas on policy. It is also his home – he and his family have an upstairs flat – though he has another home, or rather palace, in Canterbury, the place where he officiates as a bishop in his own diocese in addition to his archiepiscopal work.

The sheer size and seedy splendour of Lambeth Palace apart, the whole arrangement is reminiscent of the working arrangements of the prime minister, with 10 Downing Street as combined home and office, Chequers as a working home and country retreat, and a constituency to be run as well as the country. The administrative expenses of Lambeth Palace are considerable – in 1994 they amounted to £732,000.

It is not a cosy residence. For example, there is a Guards' Room, where archbishops used to keep a private army, and vast corridors, rooms and stairs designed to be the appurtenances of a quasi-prince, a role now *démodé*. As if to disclaim so much splendour within a Christian context, for a good many years those who administered Lambeth cultivated an aristocratic shabbiness. Humphrey Carpenter's life of Robert Runcie described the appalling decorative state of the palace at the time Runcie took over as Archbishop in 1980. 'Blackout curtains on the windows, cork tiles on the floor of that great drawing room, and so on.'[2] These were the words of Lord Laing, a millionaire friend of Runcie sufficiently concerned about his welfare to set up a fund – the Lambeth Fund – to help him and subsequent archbishops with their impossible legacy. Laing did not only help to arrange finance for refurbishment but also for properly equipping the offices. 'Lambeth was terribly primitive in terms of telephones and intercoms. There were oldfashioned typewriters, no wordprocessors.'[3] Laing also helped to fund an increase in staff, including financing a secretary for the archbishop (a bill which, incredibly, the Church Commissioners refused to pick up), and Lambeth's own press officer.

Each incoming archbishop appoints his own personal staff. In Ramsey's day this was not much more than a chaplain and a secretary. Nowadays, it is around twelve people, not counting domestic staff. Since Runcie's day this has continued to include a press officer (now known as Secretary for Broadcasting, Press and Communications) as well as a 'Bishop at Lambeth', a kind of glorified chaplain and head of staff, who can lift some of the more routine tasks off the archbishop. There is also the more usual kind of chaplain who is also the Diocesan Missioner. There is a Public Affairs Officer, a Secretary for Public Affairs (both), a Secretary for Ecumenical Affairs, a Secretary for Anglican Communion Affairs, an Assistant Secretary for Ecumenism and Anglican Communion Affairs, an Archbishop's

Officer for Mission and Evangelism, and others employed as chaplains, secretaries, steward and bursar. The Archbishop of York, the other Primate, in contrast, appears only to employ a Chaplain and a Private Secretary, which seems modest. However, looking at the Archbishop's of Canterbury's quadruple workload, as head of the Church of England, Bishop of the Canterbury Diocese, *primus inter pares* of the Anglican Communion, and member of the House of Lords, the number of helpers does not seem vast, though some of them might seem to overlap with the staff of Church House.

Carpenter asked Runcie whether when he was Archbishop he had felt a need for a *familia* – an old expression, used for the household of a bishop in the Middle Ages – a group of staff around him that were 'on his side' in the way that a kindly family might be.

'I tried to do that more than I achieved it,' Runcie replied. 'I wanted to have a sort of penumbra of people who came in from positions in the outside world, with whom we would enjoy easy relations, and they in turn would bring in others.'[4] For Runcie this was not just a question of 'support', though in twentieth-century Britain any archbishop might be forgiven for feeling that he needed it, but of employing fully informed advisers who could talk to him about important issues – nuclear power was one instance he gave – so that any utterance he made on the subject was made from knowledge.

A modern archbishop is expected to produce soundbites on a whole range of subjects, as well as all his other duties. Instant opinions are required of him on some of the most sensitive issues of the day. Runcie dealt with some of these in sermons, famously inviting well-informed friends and others to draft material for him. Perhaps because of unrecognised assumptions of a feudal past, Archbishops of Canterbury have tended to operate at times somewhat independently of the Church of England, making statements off their own bat, sometimes brave and insightful, occasionally of an appalling crassness, usually just rather banal and predictable. Hence the whiskery joke which goes: 'The archbishop has just preached a sermon about adultery.' 'Oh? What did he say?' 'He was against it.'

An obituary of Cardinal Hume said 'he was never anxious to rush into print, and his silences were frequently as eloquent as his public statements',[5] a restraint not often shown in the Church of England. Not every archbishop has a natural skill for the soundbite (and it would be a pity for him (or her – though there is little sign of a her in the offing) to be appointed for such a reason), and not every archbishop is prepared to take advice from his staff.

Whatever the personal skill of an archbishop, however, he is liable to suffer from the tendency of our time for the media, and indeed all the chattering classes, to be critical, sometimes harshly so, of people in authority, and to forget, or ignore the fact, that inside every leader or eminent figure there is a human being who, at least to start with, feels scorn, ridicule and unkindness as much as any of the rest of us. (High office and power may eventually inure people to that sort of pain, however.) Archbishop Ramsey was perhaps the first to feel the sting of this sort of attack. Archbishop Runcie had to put up with more of it, with comments on the success or otherwise of his marriage, the rehearsing of bitter details of the Gareth Bennett affair, and public speculation about how he and Mrs Thatcher got along together. Perhaps archbishops nowadays need thick skins more than any other quality – a sensitive person could be destroyed.

Essex Man Comes to Lambeth

At first things augured rather well in this respect for George Carey, the 103rd Archbishop who was consecrated and enthroned in 1991 at the age of fifty-six. There was genuine interest and approval that he was not in the public school and Oxbridge mould, that he had grown up on a Dagenham housing estate, the son of a Ford worker, had left his secondary modern school at fifteen, and worked as an office boy for the London Electricity Board. He went on from this humble start to complete a more distinguished academic education than many of his predecessors, culminating in a PhD from London University, an achievement which argues unusual guts, self-confidence and courage.

He served a curacy at St Mary's, Islington, a well-known nursery for unusually gifted evangelicals, lectured in a number of evangelical colleges, took time out from academia, and accepted a drop in salary to be vicar of a rundown parish in Durham, and went on to become Principal of Trinity College, Bristol, a theological college.

Carey has been a staunch supporter of women's ordination, and been a good example in this to others in the evangelical wing of the Church who were, back in the 1980s, much less certain of the idea than he was. Canon June Osborne remarked to me that he is the first archbishop we have had who actually knows how to 'treat women as peers. George is perfectly comfortable about simply *attending* to women.' She meant this in contrast to either behaving flatteringly or seductively with them, or treating them as potentially risky and alarming – widespread clerical attitudes which many women will recognise with a grimace. To Carey women were simply, and refreshingly, fellow human beings. She went on to say that 'you can actually imagine him knowing what it's like to go round Tesco's, can't you? Whereas you feel that some of the leadership of the Church have not got any roughage in their lives at all, and people recognise that and feel uneasy with it.'

Carey moved on from Trinity College not, as is usual with new bishops, to be a suffragan bishop, but to a senior diocesan post, that of Bishop of Bath and Wells, a rather grand posting which included one of the poshest of episcopal houses, the one where the swans come swimming up the river and ring the bell when they want to be fed.

After only four years there, he became Archbishop of Canterbury, an amazingly swift rise to the top job. To be of working-class background, in a time where humble beginnings and meritocratic achievement are admired, and to be an evangelical at a time in the Church's life when the evangelicals are riding significantly high, is to be, at least in theory, the archbishop of the moment, and Carey has clearly felt himself to be matched to the hour, and has thanked God for it.

Carey was, and is, a man to whom his Christian conversion was overwhelmingly important for both religious and social reasons. As Madeleine Bunting noted in an article in the *Guardian*,[6] Carey discovered himself as a seventeen-year-old when he became a believer in an evangelical church, and it was a movement of the spirit that swept him out of his modest background and on into a larger landscape. As much as any collier or factory-worker converted by Wesley in the eighteenth century, everything suddenly seemed to be possible for him. 'My conversion opened a wider world. If I was thirsty for knowledge as a child, Christianity was like a drug. It made me aware of the power of language, and it gave me a focus for my education.'[7]

Others who grew up in the 1930s and 1940s in humble backgrounds will recognise the dogged faith in learning – the feeling, much rarer nowadays at least in that particular form, that learning was the way to a richer life for many who had not been generously endowed with opportunity to start with. Others again will recognise the special role that the churches played at the time in helping and encouraging effort and confidence in those without many other social advantages. But the sheer wonder of the conversion experience was perhaps rarer in the immediate postwar world (though it was to return with Billy Graham within a few years). For Carey it was the most important happening of his late adolescent years, and continues to be the key to much that he says and does.

This seminal experience, together with intelligence and a huge capacity for work and enthusiasm, Carey brought to his rundown parish, St Nicholas in Durham, perhaps the most significant experience in his ministry in forming him. He made key friends there who are still among his strongest supporters. He moved on to his increasingly prestigious jobs in the Church. A faithful pastor, a good teacher, a kindly and able bishop, Carey had a lot going for him when he was appointed to Canterbury.

Carey's Drum

The jury is still out on whether he has 'made it' in this now almost impossible job. Evangelicals say that he has, or that, rather, in twenty years he will be recognised as a great reforming Archbishop. Many others, in and out of the Church, find the earnestness, the 'black and white' quality of his thinking, an almost insurmountable hindrance to acceptance. It is not simply that he lacks the adaptability and diplomatic finesse of his predecessor – the great Michael Ramsey did not have those qualities either. It is more that he is formidably earnest in his conviction that it is his job to convert the nation to Christianity, and he shows little awareness of the complexity and even ambiguity of such an ambition at the turn of the twentieth century.

Yet there are always many voices, especially among politicians, loudly wondering why 'the Church' does not give the country a lead, and no one could accuse Carey of not doing his best to do that. So why is he not the answer to their dreams? I guess what might have made him more acceptable or his early passage as Archbishop easier, is diffidence – modesty, genuine or fake, being a quality prized in Britain as almost nowhere else, with Tim Henman representing a sort of *beau ideal*. It seems to act as a necessary social oil, smoothing away the rough edges of envy or spite. But Carey was not diffident and is incapable of faking. At last he had got his chance to do what his evangelical predecessor Donald Coggan had tried and failed miserably to do in his 'Call to the Nation' of 1975. The evangelicals had got a second chance and Carey meant to make the most of it. For a year or two he seemed to have something public to say about everything.

Archbishops, like schoolteachers, often get judged, fairly or otherwise, in a crucial early period from which there is then no going back, or only a partial one. It might be said that in the first year or two Carey missed his mark. Bunting describes how when Carey was a young man doing his National Service he knelt to say his prayers every night in the barracks under the eyes of his mocking fellows. It was brave, as Carey's performance as Archbishop is brave, but one might ask 'Did it work?' or might it have been more effective

155

to live out his Christian convictions unobtrusively and say his prayers quietly in bed? Did the gesture produce much more than embarrassment in the barracks, a hardening against whatever it was that the young Carey was seen to stand (or kneel) for? In a nation where people do not like a naked parade of religious feeling, does 'going on about it' alienate more than attract? May it even be experienced as a kind of emotional intrusion or assault upon others? In this area of life courage and suffering, like patriotism, are not enough, or even perhaps the point.

Bunting quotes 'senior cabinet ministers' saying that 'George is helluva nice guy out of his depth' and senior clerics saying 'He's off the plot . . . he lacks the width and breadth of Anglican ecclesiology.' 'There's a lack of subtlety in Carey's mind . . . things are driven through passionately, crudely . . .' Even more damningly, she quotes: 'He is an unmitigated disaster . . . the wrong man in the wrong job.'[8] Old Durham friends – Ruth Etchells, Pete Broadbent, Christina Baxter, Pete Ward – proclaim their faith in him, a faith that they believe, in time, others may come to share. Journalists, on the other hand, have found the Archbishop an irresistible victim. 'He is like one of those people you see waiting with cardboard placards at airports,' one of them wrote. 'His placard has "Archbishop" printed on it.'

If the implication of this is that Carey is uncertain of who he is, I think that is quite wrong. He knows exactly who he is and what he is trying to do – to convert Britain – and he is full of loving thoughts towards those he wants to convert. The trouble is that it makes people cross and uneasy, and they blame him for this – they would rather have a suave, debonair archbishop like Runcie who would not dream of behaving in such an ungentlemanly way. But Carey is not a gentleman and, to do him credit, is not in the least interested in trying to be one. He is still the Ford worker's son, and a convinced evangelical, and he knows, because he has experienced it, what a certain kind of religious experience can do for a person. And he longs to to share this particular vision.

He goes on banging the same drum – the drum of bringing Jesus Christ to the nation. It could, I suppose, be a bit like Drake's drum, sounding its note of alarm when the nation is in danger, but it is not a drum that the nation as a whole so far seems to want to march to; in fact it may have the effect of turning people off any kind of Christian expression. In spite of the promising conversions in evangelical churches, which lend credence to his hopes, it feels improbable that there will be wholesale conversions, or that all sections of the Church would feel able to put that kind of emphasis before all else. They would feel, perhaps, that such events are not simply a matter of willpower, hard work, enthusiasm and prayer alone. There are deep and partly mysterious psychological springs which bring about huge movements within a population, such as Wesley's extraordinary effect on the working classes of the late eighteenth century. In any case, twentieth-century people are nervous, with reason, of huge popular movements, knowing how quickly important controls can be lost in the turmoil.

In its resolute idealism, the idea of wholesale conversion is reminiscent of the naïve and fruitless fantasy of the Student Christian Federation in the 1890s, who spurred one another on to heroic missionary endeavours with the cry of 'the evangelisation of the world in this generation'. Carey, despite living in the era of what the business guru Charles Handy has called 'post-heroic leadership', is still cast in the heroic mould, but is a hero what is needed?

Begging so many questions of what Christianisation, in all its many different manifestations, might actually mean beyond getting people into churches, it fills many within and without the churches with dread, irritation, rage, cynicism or laughter according to their temperament and point of view. And this is something I do not believe George Carey will ever understand.

It has implications within the Church, of course, as well as in Christian relations to non-Christians. The message is of a rather worrying closing of ranks. In Madeleine Bunting's words, '[The archbishop] firmly believes everyone has to sing from the same song sheet for the Church to communicate a clear message, and conveys this to bishops and clergy.'[9] She likens this insistence on 'coherence' and 'staying on message' to Blair's Labour Party. It is a new, and worrying departure for those who had seen the Church's strength as 'always having been its diverse, unwieldy, almost anarchic' self.[10]

'If we are leaders together,' she quotes the Archbishop's own words, 'we must stand together, we must not be irresponsible by questioning the faith of the Church.' The Archbishop is addressing the bishops here, offering a word to the wise about the kind of bishop – we know the sort he means – who dares to put into words the very real doubts about the Christian faith which are in ordinary people's minds. Yet the bishops who have done this – Robinson, Jenkins – have found a fascinated and grateful following among many who stood outside or on the fringes of the Church, and have provoked useful theological debate. Is a rigid conformity likely to work better, with all lips buttoned and uncertainties ignored? I very much doubt it, and if it happens, and there are worrying signs that bishops are less bolshie than they used to be, then the Church we have known and loved may have gone for ever.

Clearly there is an issue about power here. Madeleine Bunting quotes Carey complaining, when he first arrived at Lambeth, 'I have less power than I did as a curate'; and she goes on to say that the office of archbishop, as Carey inherited it, was not primarily one of power but of influence, informal influence, something which a man like Temple or Runcie knew how to manoeuvre. A man of a hundred and one bright ideas (as one of his staff informed me) Carey was not content with this back-stairs method of operating, and it may be that, using the Church Commissioners' failure as a lever, all the very extensive changes which the Church is now undergoing spring from the simple fact that the Church has acquired a 'hands-on' Archbishop who is determined to steer the ship himself. This may be an exaggeration, but there is a sense in which one feels he wants to run the Church of England as if it was St Nicholas, Durham.

In His Own Words – an Interview with His Grace the Archbishop of Canterbury

I asked for, and was granted, an interview with the Archbishop,[11] and we met in his study at Lambeth Palace, where we sat in armchairs and drank coffee. Carey is a courteous, pleasant man, without bombast or condescension, and he answered questions acutely and straightforwardly, apologising as he did so for suffering from both jet lag and a cold. I was specially curious both about how he melded his strong evangelical convictions with a Church where very different kinds of convictions were held equally strongly, and also about how he saw the new Archbishops' Council, which had started early in 1999. I shall go into the subject of the Council at greater length in the General Synod section, but it is necessary to know that it is one of the reforms started as a result of the work of the Turnbull Commission, and it is an attempt to make the Church more 'coherent' and 'transparent' by gathering up some key decisions into the hands of the two archbishops and a committee of nineteen whose major task will be to decide on priorities.

I began by speaking of the Archbishop's own religious background and his longing to see Britain evangelised. I wondered if he was hoping for a takeover of the Church by the evangelicals? Not at all.

> I appreciate all that my Evangelical background has given me, but I regard it as simply one valuable and important tradition within the Church. We need the Catholic tradition and also the Liberal and Charismatic. I believe that the Church is big enough to hold all these disparate traditions together. I have grown myself in my

understanding of the Church and of theology through coming to understand the breadth of it all. Not only is Cranmer important, as one of the first reformed evangelicals, but people like Jeremy Taylor, F. D. Maurice, and a number of my predecessors from different backgrounds – William Temple, Donald Coggan, Robert Runcie.

Was this simply what an archbishop *would* say? I asked him. It was, was it not, his job to hold the Church together? Would he have felt so inclusive twenty years ago?

Carey laughed and hesitated for a moment, and said that ever since he wrote his PhD thesis in the 1960s he had been appreciative of the Catholic tradition, and it was impossible to study theology in any depth without seeing the richness of Liberal thinking. 'I don't like labels, though I am happy to be described as an Evangelical if people understand how that shaped and formed me.'

Was he thinking of a journey that every Christian ought to be making when he spoke of the way different traditions formed people? I asked.

Exactly. But I'd like to say a bit more about the Evangelicals. Their real growth in this century has happened since the 1950s. There used to be very few Evangelical bishops, very few Evangelical scholars, and that has changed a lot in the last few decades. There has been the influence of Tyndale House in Cambridge which encouraged advanced Evangelical scholarship – John Stott played a remarkable role in that, as did Michael Green. Julian Charley, who served on ARCIC as an Evangelical, affirmed the great value of Catholic spirituality and life and so on. Evangelicals have played a key role on General Synod.

One of the most important watersheds in Evangelical life was the Keele Conference of 1967. It was an affirmation of social theology, with Evangelicals saying 'people like Wilberforce in the last century made a contribution to social life, and Evangelicals since then have been too separatist, too focused on the spiritual. It is time we developed our social theology.' That movement has been very important.

The Evangelical wing is a sign of hope for the Church of England at present – it is the tradition that is growing fastest. I think that is because its theology is 'mission-orientated', and the Church of England is now, of course, in a missionary situation. I want the Church to grow, and I welcome Evangelical growth, but I don't want it to be at the expense of the other traditions. I wish more people in the other traditions were focused on the idea of sharing the faith with others. I am afraid that if they don't change in this direction, developing their own traditions appropriately, there could be further decline in those traditions. Evangelicals feel a vocation to share their faith. If there is a danger in their methods it is that they are sometimes too simplistic.

The Archbishop remembered at this point that I had once written a book called *Christian Uncertainties*, a book about subjects on which Christians disagreed, and I took his next remark as a metaphorical wagging of a finger.

Liberals, on the other hand, can bring too many uncertainties into the matter of faith, where Evangelicals will say 'Here is a clear way forward.' The message is more black and white, and therefore is attractive in a world where there are so many uncertainties, and people are looking for sound foundations. But the Evangelicals must also develop an understanding of complexity, and I do believe that they have changed a good deal in this respect, that they are less simplistic than they were in my teenage years, for instance. My great dream for the Church of England is that every church in this land, whatever their theological tradition or colour, will be aware that we are in a missionary situation, that we have got to build bridges into the wider community, and each tradition has a role to play.

I want the whole Church to work closely together. I'd like to see it becoming a bit more Catholic, a bit more Evangelical, more Liberal, more Charismatic. All these things – but the Church of England more authentically, genuinely itself, genuinely themselves. And all of us learning together.

The Catholic tradition, for instance, has enormous reserves to draw on and I think its emphasis on the sacramental quality of life, the emphasis on mystery and colour and beauty is tremendously attractive. The numinous has an important place in the spiritual life. Icons, candles, silence, etc., can contribute greatly to the quality of worship. You don't have to go back to the Latin, but calm, silence, candles, light, a change of mood . . .

I remembered that it was said that when Carey was Principal of Trinity College, Bristol, he encouraged ordinands to have a close knowledge of Catholic spirituality and its rich contribution to life and spiritual formation.

Prompted by me, Carey also talked about the Liberal tradition with its willingness to raise questions, of being unafraid of where they might lead. 'If Jesus Christ is the way, the truth and the life, no Christian should ever avoid questions, since he leads us into more truth.' The Archbishop spoke about Springboard, the organisation he started in 1991 specifically to 'encourage, renew and mobilise the church for evangelism'. The aim was to bring together those with a belief in evangelism from the three major traditions of the Church, and although he found representatives of the Catholic and Evangelical traditions ready to join, he couldn't locate a Liberal would-be evangelist. He had wanted someone with a flavour of David Jenkins about him – 'someone who can speak with enthusiasm about a living faith in God, from a liberal tradition'. He pointed to John Saxbee, the Bishop of Ludlow, as a contemporary who shared the Springboard vision, and was now on the Springboard executive.

I wondered what the Archbishop thought about the Charismatic movement.

> In the 1970s and 1980s what it did to the evangelical wing was to make the sacramental more significant in evangelicalism. It also challenged what some evangelicals had taught about attitudes to the Creation as it brought colour and awareness of the sacramentality of life into worship. It helped to remove some of the old materialism and divisiveness. If God is the author of life, life is to be enjoyed, theatre is to be enjoyed, beauty is to be enjoyed. That means that beauty comes into the churches. It made the Evangelical churches focus more on the sacramental, and as a result they could look more affirmingly at Catholic tradition. So I think that helped enormously. And still does.

Carey thought that there was still too great a tendency for the Church to be an inward-looking, though pastoral, body with 'people expected to come to our churches because they want to come to our churches ... In a very competitive world where leisure dominates, we've got to go out and get people. We cannot expect them to come to us automatically now.'

I mentioned the much greater mobility of modern people, as well as the many activities open to people on Sundays.

'Yes, before the 1950s and 1960s you had a more or less stationary population. My parents, for example, never owned a car at all.'

Carey went on to recall a time that both of us remembered when the Church was much more at the centre of its community.

> I became Vicar of St Nicholas, Durham in 1975. Looking back through its records I saw that in the 1920s and 30s that church used to take whole train-loads of Sunday School kids to the seaside in the summer. Used to hire special trains to take them. I had a pretty active church there in the 1970s, but the Sunday School was down from hundreds of children to forty or fifty. That reflects a

161

change in society itself, and is not something simply to do with the Church.

I asked whether he thought that in the days when going to church was the conventional thing to do, at least for middle-class people, or when it provided a major source of recreation for those who may not have had much other opportunity for enjoyment, as when it took train loads of children to the seaside, its membership might have been somewhat compromised. Something that *everyone* does is not really about commitment, but about habit and fashion and enjoying the advantages of belonging.

The Archbishop seemed to warm to this idea.

I think the Church of England is more authentically itself today, and more itself, than perhaps it was a hundred years ago. Then, if you were English, you were Church of England. Now people make a choice about that. Nowadays, over the past ten or fifteen years, you hear people say 'I am a Christian.' If you had said that thirty to forty years ago, people would have blinked at you 'Well, of course, you're a Christian. Why do you have to say that?'

I suggested that the different groups in the Church did not get on all that well together, or rather that, so far as they can, they ignore one another. The Archbishop, while admitting that in his situation he tends to be removed from parish life, said that his impression was that they were all getting along much better together.

I'd like to argue, you know, that the broad church that we are now is probably a foretaste of what is to come. If we want to think about the coming great Church, then it is going to be one in which we have to accept huge differences within the family, and we are not going to have final answers this side of eternity. Living with differences I think is actually the genius of Anglicanism.

We moved the conversation from this high level to the present organisation of the Church of England, in particular the structural changes which had resulted in the Archbishops' Council, the new central body which will initiate action. I expressed my concern that power was being taken from General Synod.

Well, I hope not. I have been criticised for being a bureaucrat, a manager, for simply moving the furniture around, and putting in another layer of bureaucracy. I resist that. Let me put in a bit of background. Over the past fifteen or twenty years it seems to me that the Church has been seeking for a greater coherence. When I became a member of General Synod in 1985 I felt quite perplexed by all the disparate parts of the Church of England. You know, the Church Commissioners, which seemed to be an independent body, the Central Board of Finance, General Synod itself and two Archbishops. It seemed to be a very odd way of running something. And then when I became Archbishop in charge of the Standing Committee, I used to find that there was so much rivalry between the constituencies. So antagonism gets built into the thing, and the parties go to battle, which was the tendency of the old Synod, in my view. And then the Policy Committee often acted like the Budget Committee, and the Budget Committee operated like the Policy Committee. When the Church Commissioners lost money, the occasion provided a catalyst for us to look at the structure of the Church of England. I believe that the *Working as One Body* Report gave us a theological rationale of a coherent, transparent Church which is accountable to the people of God. And I do not believe for one moment that the Archbishops' Council is taking power away from any other body. General Synod will remain the major legislative body of the Church of England and the Archbishops' Council must report to that General Synod and be accountable to it.

We are also accountable to the House of Bishops, which must remain the major theological and leadership body. The Archbishops' Council feels that its job is to focus on priorities. We will be able to say, for example, 'We have got to focus on vocation.' That will mean that we might have to say to another body 'Sorry, you can't have your money because it is going to go elsewhere', something we have not been able to do up till now. We are there to focus priorities, we have got to determine where our limited financial resources should go, and we should try to express what we want the local church to do.

I am all for empowering the local, diminishing the central, and I am pretty sure that that is where we are going to see a lot of changes in the days ahead.

We are good as a Church at changing our minds, but I don't think we are going to change our minds about the Archbishops' Council. I hope that it will lead the Church, but it cannot do that alone. We look to Synod to do the job it is best at – debating issues. It is not a good body for deciding priorities. We can't expect 580 people to do that. Whereas I think you *can* expect nineteen people working closely together to focus on how we can serve the Church better. On the Archbishops' Council we have all the traditions represented, and have already reached a remarkable unity.

Members of the Church House staff had expressed uncertainty to me about how successfully in the future they would be able to initiate debate on topics that they were concerned about. This was because the various departments, under the new organisation, no longer each have representation at the highest level, and this may mean that they are represented by someone who does not thoroughly understand the work of a particular department or may not even be particularly sympathetic to it. This might mean that a matter of concern never got as far as the Archbishops' Council. It also struck me as possible that however 'open' both Archbishops might be at the present time, the Council might create difficulties if some future Archbishop was determined to do things his way. I asked the Archbishop whether he thought there was any danger of these developments, with the consequent loss of democratic expression.

No, I don't think there is a danger, because anything that comes up in the usual way through General Synod, Diocesan Synod, or Private Members' motions has to be discussed, and it would be the Synod Business Committee which will insist that a subject has to be debated. As the Presidents of Synod we can't stop it, and the Archbishops' Council cannot stop it. I don't think, actually, the Council has any power to stop any kind of democratic process, because, as I have said, we are transparent . . . Synod has its own mechanism for full debates and that is unchanged. The House of Bishops will have its own mechanism, also unchanged.

The Archbishops' Council has very limited business, actually. We must decide options of where the budget is spent on priorities. For example, we will decide over the next five years whether education will be a priority, or whatever. The Archbishop of York and I would want to lead initiatives on missionary development, evangelism and other areas. In addition to those things, we have had a huge amount of business handed on to us. Liturgy, for example. We have got to complete all that.

Let me just add to that. Let us just suppose that a very sensitive matter came up, say an ecumenical matter or something to do with the ordination of women as bishops, for example. I am just thinking out loud here. We would have no role in opposing anything, but what we could do is to exercise leadership and say, now our sensitivity regarding this might be so-and-so. We might well help the Archbishops' Council decide its strategy on a given thing, but we couldn't dominate it. We are in the early days, of course. Who knows? But I do not have any really major worries regarding this, though I know that some people do.

I said to the Archbishop that I felt some concern at the huge variety of liturgy now being used in the Church of England. Whereas, at one time, the Book of Common Prayer had meant that every church except a few very high Anglo-Catholic ones were using a similar liturgy Sunday by Sunday, now there seemed to be increasing 'pick and mix', particularly at both ends of the spectrum – the Anglo-Catholic churches at one end of the scale and Evangelical churches at the other, who felt free to add or cut or drastically change the nature of the service. Did he feel anxious that some essential unity had been lost, or, equally worrying, that some extraordinary things were being done and said in churches that theologically and aesthetically did little credit to the Church of England?

I want to preface my comment by saying that, even in the old days before 1960 when most of us used the Book of Common Prayer, the way different churches used it was vastly different. Evangelicals often truncated it. I remember my old Vicar – I never heard him say the Prayer Book Communion service in its entirety. He would add it to Morning Prayer, starting with 'Ye that do truly and earnestly repent you of your sins'.

The Catholics, of course, would often add bits on to the Prayer Book because they felt it was deficient in terms of the mass. So I just want to qualify my answer by saying I don't think it ever was the case that the Church of England was truly, down to the last man and woman, all saying the same thing. I think there was an enormous *richness*, richness rather than diversity, in the way we used the Prayer Book.

Having said that, it is undeniably the case that when the 1980 Alternative Service Book presented us with four different eucharist prayers, and the Book of Common Prayer and the 1928 Prayer Book are still potentially in use, that diversity and variety are being encouraged. And the new Prayer Book – *Common Worship* – will encourage it still further.

So what holds us together? Well, it is still 'common prayer'. We are still a liturgical, credal church, so the central component is very important.

I get very cross with two groups in the Church. I get cross with the Catholic wing who use the Roman Catholic mass when they know they shouldn't be doing so. It is theologically and ecclesiologically bizarre and they don't get any marks from the Roman Catholic Church for doing so. And on the other hand I get cross with the Evangelicals who will use alternative forms of liturgy which are not official and do not have canonical permission, since they swear to the bishop at their institutions that they will use the rites of the Church and no other. I hope the new services are going to give the Church one or two forms of family worship that people can use, which will be good forms in themselves, because I think the family service is very much a growth area. Part of the success of the Evangelical churches is due to the fact they have a very simple liturgy that people can understand. Coming from a working-class background I know that if you try to impose on people 'this is the way you should pray' it doesn't necessarily work. What I think we should look for is establishing a central core of legal services there to be used, wearing similar things (though chasubles will vary, dress will vary), and it should be possible to say 'This is an Anglican way of doing things.' Freedom within a framework is what I would look for.

To go back to the Evangelicals. I think the Evangelical church is an easy church for newcomers to find their way into, because it is so relaxed. Maybe its failure is that it cannot always hold people within the family of Evangelicalism, because people move on. They may move into a Liberal churchmanship. For example, David Jenkins and John Habgood both came to faith through the Evangelical movement, I think in both cases through CICCU (the Cambridge Evangelical student body). The fact that people move on does not bother me. It may be the role of Evangelicals simply to bring them in to the Christian family. But it might be that Evangelicals may have to look to themselves and to say what is lacking in our tradition that we do not seem to have the breadth of mystery to carry on the whole thing? That is something we may look at in the future.

Finally, I asked the Archbishop about the difficulties of actually doing his job.

An Archbishop at the beginning of the century – I think it was Davidson – said that the job was impossible for one man to do but only one man could do it. Being Bishop of the Canterbury diocese, for instance, is a job in itself. I have to delegate there, and I do so willingly, but I go there regularly. This coming weekend I'll be in the parish of Blean the entire weekend leading a teaching mission – something I do three or four times a year.

The job of being Archbishop has, of course, continued to grow since Davidson's day, with travelling, international problems and the responsibility of the Anglican Communion.

I said that the Archbishop often had a bad Press.

It happened in Ramsey's time, it happened in Robert's time, it happens in my time, and I think you have just got to expect it – it is par for the course. And, of course, political figures also get hammered. It can be very disagreeable, but that is part of it.

I asked if it caused him personal pain.

> I found it difficult to begin with because I could not understand what was happening. I think one gains in knowledge in how to deal with it as time goes on, and I pay attention to the people I respect, my friends and so on. Some people out there just hate the Church and hate the Church of England in particular, and do not want Christianity to be a formidable force in our land. They obviously want to ridicule it, and try to diminish it by writing it out of the picture . . . but these days I regard them as more pinpricks than anything else. You have to get on, you can't brood, there is too much to do.

Did the Archbishop see the Church being disestablished in the foreseeable future?

> Establishment is an evolving thing. If you look back a hundred and twenty years to Archbishop Tait's time it is clear that it was very different then. You know, I have now worked with two Governments – Conservative and Labour – and neither of them expressed any desire to change the existing church–state relationship. In fact, they seemed to value it. You might have thought that the present Government would say 'We really want to become modern and break away. Why are we holding on to this curious anachronism?' But they welcome us in Parliament, and are delighted when bishops speak out in the House of Lords. I think the reason is that they think we are doing a good job. On our side, I feel that Establishment is not a matter of privilege but of responsible service. Should the country say, one day, 'We don't want an established church,' well, we will still carry on doing our work much as we have done in the past. But I do not see any sign of that happening.

I said that I felt some concern about the other Christian churches in this country and what the Establishment status of one church said about them and to them.

> We have what we have inherited and we have to make appropriate changes to bring others in, in a uniform way. We will have to wait and see, but certainly there is no opposition to that sort of change from me or from the Church of England. In fact we wish to co-operate and help in any way we can. What often happens at present is that when bishops speak in the House of Lords, they often speak for other religious groups too, at their request. Of course, we are happy to do that, but if there is a possibility of working with them in the days to come it will make sense to change things.

Ruritania Revisited

Court No. 2 – The Church Commissioners, 1, Millbank, London SW1

The second influential court of the Church of England is the Church Commissioners, responsible for a payroll of nearly 18,000 serving clergy and pensioners, as well as other important areas of finance. In 1997, for instance, the latest year listed, they disposed of income from their assets of £143.7 million. £19.5 million went to pay stipends of parochial clergy, £82.1 for clergy and widows' pensions, £10.6 for episcopal administration, and much smaller sums to bishops' housing, bishops' and cathedral clergy stipends, financial provision for resigning clergy (£2.4 million), church buildings and administration. Income exceeded expenditure by £3.8 million, a satisfactory and financially virtuous end to the year.

The Commissioners' well-known headquarters – No. 1 Millbank – is a notable Grade II listed Edwardian building with the Commissioners' name beautifully engraved in stone over the door. Being on the north side of the Thames it is physically more accessible than Lambeth to Parliament, just down the street, and this feels symbolically all too right – the moneybags of the Church perhaps speaking louder in the 'real world' than the spiritual murmurings from Lambeth. While the Church Commissioners' office has the dignity of most of the buildings along London's Embankment, it is not by any stretch of imagination a palace, being rather more in the style of a small Whitehall department. It has operated with a fairly modest staff considering the size and complexity of its work – around three hundred people. However, as a result of the recent shifts and deliberations in the Church, and perhaps a dim sense that since it has blotted its copybook it needs to be punished, a slimmed-down model will be moving eventually to Westminster to share Church House, for long its sparring partner. 'We despise the Church Commissioners for thinking of nothing but money,' a member of the staff of Church House told me, 'and they despise us as a bunch of wholly impractical ideologues.'

The Church Commissioners, though they have the feel of an ancient institution, were only created in 1948, out of two older bodies, the Ecclesiastical Commissioners, founded in 1836, and Queen Anne's Bounty, offered and accepted in 1794. The Church of England, although an established church, receives little money from the state, except in the very limited form whereby those directly employed by the state, as prison or hospital chaplains or chaplains to the Forces, are paid a salary. However, a million or so pounds is paid by Government into the Redundant Churches Fund annually and a further four million or so to the repair of historic churches still in use.

Otherwise, to take care of a huge number of buildings and paid workers the Church depends upon investment income or upon voluntary giving. A useful form of income, used exclusively to pay clergy stipends, was Queen Anne's Bounty mentioned above. Before the sixteenth-century breach with Rome clergy paid taxes to the Pope, which were known as 'first fruits', the year's profit on their benefice or living, as well as a tithe. Henry VIII transferred these payments into his own coffers, and the devout Queen Anne, in recognition that they rightly belonged to the Church, restored them, with the request that they should be used for 'the maintenance of poor clergy'.

The nineteenth-century rearrangement of wealth and property in the Church and the reapportioning of incomes was placed in the hands of the Ecclesiastical Commissioners. When they were dissolved in 1948 the responsibility of administering the Church's money and property, together with administering Queen Anne's Bounty, was placed in the hands of the Church Commissioners, who continued to invest it in whatever seemed appropriate. The Church Commissioners quickly became an extraordinarily prestigious body of ninety-five members. These included both archbishops, forty-one diocesan bishops, the three Church Estates Commissioners, five deans or provosts, ten clergy, ten laymen appointed by Synod and four by the Queen, four people nominated by the Archbishop of Canterbury, and representatives of London, York, Oxford and Cambridge. There were fifteen officers of state including the Prime Minister, the Home Secretary, the Chancellor of the Exchequer, the Lord President of the Privy Council, the Speaker of the House of Commons, the Lord Chief Justice, the Master of the Rolls, the Attorney-General, the Solicitor-General and the Lord Mayors of London and York. There is something distinctly comic about this list, whose members seem to qualify for Ruritania or a Gilbert and Sullivan opera, complete with colourful braided uniforms, and songs crammed with sly digs, rather than for the management of a modern institution and its assets. Not surprisingly the vast array of officials were ill-qualified to offer advice and tended to rubber-stamp decisions previously made – this latter activity would make a particularly effective ensemble scene.

One of them, Viscountess Brentford, is a much respected chartered accountant who became a Church Commissioner in 1991. At the time of writing she has just been appointed the Third Estates Commissioner. She had earlier revealed just how impossible being a conscientious Church Commissioner was in the early 1990s. She was 'horrified by the level of borrowings and the size of the property portfolio' when she read the Commissioners' annual report and accounts for 1991. She began asking questions in Millbank about risk evaluation procedure and the Asset Committee's long-term plans,

> but I was shunted to one side as if the questions had never been asked. You had to be enormously self-confident to get past an extremely patronizing attitude . . . you were left wondering what was going on. To find things out, you would either have to be very aggressive or have powerful friends, and at that time I didn't know anybody.
>
> I think it was one of the problems all the Commissioners faced. You were treated like . . . a minor irritant.[1]

Unable to obtain the information she required, she found herself helpless to take her doubts and criticisms further.

The real power in the 1980s and early 1990s belonged to the First Church Estates Commissioner, Sir Douglas Lovelock, who had been formally recommended by the Prime Minister and appointed by the Crown, and to a lesser extent to the Second Church Estates Commissioner, Michael Allison, appointed by the archbishop. Sir Douglas was effectively the company chairman in a corporate structure, and was, by all accounts, a supremely self-confident and rather overbearing man. Michael Allison, an MP, had the task of answering questions on behalf of the Commissioners in Parliament. There was also a Third Estates Commissioner, Mrs Margaret Laird, who had responsibility for rectories, vicarages and bishops' houses. Sir Douglas was paid a salary of £62,000 a year, and his principal concern was the Assets Committee, a body over which he had been granted almost total control with the idea, originally, of generating efficiency. 'The First Church Estates Commissioner was established as a person of almost supreme authority whom few within the Church of England, including the Archbishop of Canterbury, could openly challenge without creating a constitutional crisis.'[2] In the 1980s the three Church Estates Commissioners had virtually exclusive power over assets valued at the time at nearly £303 million.

Under the authority of the three Estates Commissioners the staff at No. 1 Millbank busied themselves with managing historic assets, providing money for clergy stipends and pensions and administration and, after 1983, pastoral reorganisation, making churches redundant, and buying and selling clergy houses and church land.

Even a cursory look at the Commissioners' history makes disturbing reading, and it is evidence of a huge conflict within the Church itself between those who think that the Church should be a model of financial rectitude, using its investment to promote a good society, or a fairer world, and those who simply feel that the Commissioners must play the financial game much as it is played in the City, in order to keep the Church solvent and pay clergy pensions. During the 1980s there was intense dispute, some of it in Synod, some of it in the House of Commons, about the Church investing in companies who had large holdings in South Africa. Richard Harries, the Bishop of Oxford, himself a Commissioner, took the Commissioners to court in 1990 to clarify which areas it was proper for the Church to invest in and which it was not. He pointed out that already they did not invest in alcohol or tobacco, but that apart from that, anything seemed to be permissible. 'Hitherto the assumption has been that ethical considerations can be taken into account only if there is no overall financial loss ... in short ethics may be taken into account provided it does not lose the Commissioners a penny.'[3] The solution revolved around the status of the Commissioners: were they like a pension fund, or 'more akin to a charitable body'? If the latter, should they not be expected to show loyalty to the aims of the body they served? The court found against the bishop, deciding to regard the Commissioners' duties as more in the nature of a pension fund.

The Commissioners had had a chequered history in the field of ethics, from the bad old days (until the mid-1940s) when the Ecclesiastical Commissioners owned 500 acres in the borough of Paddington which, scandalously, housed poverty and prostitution, to later scandals in the 1980s when decisions to gentrify certain areas of London (Maida Vale, for example), led to a modernising of houses. This was swiftly followed by increases in rent which were beyond the means of those living there. The district eventually turned into a prime residential area, at great cost to poorer families who were forced to move out. 'In July 1985, three hundred from the Maida

Vale Estate lobbied the General Synod in protest at a decision by the Commissioners to sell five houses after the occupying families had been unable to buy them.'[4] However, it must be said that the Commissioners still own a large working-class estate in Maida Vale.

In the Hyde Park Estate hundreds of ordinary homes were demolished to make way for luxury apartments and houses, which effectively destroyed local community. Not all the Commissioners' actions were socially destructive. For example, they provided low-rent housing for working-class families in Walworth and Lambeth.

The Great Scandal

On 11 July 1992, the biggest scandal to date was uncovered to the general public in an article by the journalist John Plender in the *Financial Times*. Under the headline 'Unholy Saga of the Church's Missing Millions', Plender, as a result of a careful scrutiny of the Church Commissioners' annual reports and accounts, was able to show that the Commissioners had sustained huge losses in their property portfolio as a result of property speculation that had been grossly mismanaged. At the time it was thought that the loss amounted to £500 million. Later £600 and £800 million were mentioned. The *Financial Times'* article coincided with, and was designed to anticipate, the announcement of this embarrassing disaster by Archbishop Carey at the July meeting of General Synod in York.

Though a tremendous shock to most church people who had believed for years that the Church Commissioners were paragons of financial prudence, and exempt from the usual follies of humankind, church dealings had already, in fact, begun to be gossiped about by those in the City whose business it is to study the markets, and the word had been out for a while that the Church's financial affairs were being badly mismanaged.

Terry Lovell, in his masterly study of the Commissioners' fall from grace, recalls the kind of terror that shook the Church as the news broke – the fear of closures, of falls in stipends and a collapse of pensions, of parishes merging and of clergy numbers being substantially reduced.

As a response to the crisis, in October 1992 the Archbishops set up the Lambeth Group, an independent committee with seven members under the chairmanship of the Bishop of Chelmsford, John Waine, himself a Church Commissioner, to investigate what had happened. Oddly, apart from the chairman, the small committee included three Church Commissioners, as well as a member of the Central Board of Finance of the Church and two City businessmen.

Strangest of all, it included the financial consultants Coopers and Lybrand, who had themselves been advisers to the Commissioners. Not surprisingly, this choice of investigators was heavily criticised.

The First Estates Commissioner, Sir Douglas Lovelock, effectively company chairman in a corporate institution, was regarded, together with colleagues, as the architect of the disastrous policy of investment that had been pursued. He was certainly the most powerful person involved. Lovell says that his 'central power base' was the chairmanship of the Assets Committee, responsible for generating around 25 per cent of the Church's running costs of around £600 million, and that members of Synod had long resented the unquestionable authority of this Committee.

The Committee had extraordinary freedom of control over the Church of England's assets, an almost absolute power to manage and invest. Technically they were overseen by a Board of Governors composed of senior churchmen, but the committees which served this body, and the plethora of bureaucracy, led to an almost Byzantine complexity in an area which few people understood. Lovell writes of the 'almost supreme authority' of Lovelock in this situation. The ninety-five Church Commissioners met only once a year to agree (Lovell says 'to rubberstamp') annual reports and accounts. The Lambeth Group found 'reckless property investments, unethical conduct, massive borrowings of hundreds of millions of pounds, and a level of administrative incompetence'[5] which a Parliamentary enquiry was later to describe as 'unbelievable naïveté'.

Archbishop Carey, as Chairman of the Church Commissioners, was required to present himself before a Parliamentary Select Committee to answer questions, the first archbishop to whom such a thing had ever happened.

Finger in the Dyke
One of the most disturbing aspects of the whole incident was what happened when it was discovered that the Assets Committee, in a frantic attempt to put things right, had gone in for the unethical business of 'coupon trading' or 'dividend stripping', a practice which the Commissioners concealed for a time under the euphemism of 'temporary income', and refused to disclose. It worked by a process of 'purchasing fixed interest securities just before an interest payment is due to be received, and then, immediately after the receipt of the interest, selling the securities at a price inevitably reduced by the absence of the imminent receipt of interest'.[6] It is a method of using capital to purchase income that is possibly illegal, and could never form part of good financial practice.

In spite of the fact that Sir Michael Colman, Douglas Lovelock's successor, was deeply reluctant to do this, the bishops decided to continue the practice for the time being rather than face the alternatives. There were two possible alternatives – one, to make a general appeal to the Church to help make good the loss, to avoid the potential closing down of some clergy jobs (which might have worked if parishes felt they were about to lose their parish priest), or two, the Church Commissioners using capital to make loans to dioceses (on which they would pay interest) to provide money for stipends, while trying to raise levels of parochial giving, which seemed like a workable idea.

> The third possibility was to continue coupon trading. This was much the easiest alternative and to their great discredit the House of Bishops took the soft option and told the Church Commissioners that the Church could not find the extra money which would allow them to stop coupon trading . . . This costly and despicable practice continued until Parliament passed the Church of England Pensions Measure which enabled the Commissioners to spread their capital lawfully.[7]

Taming the Tiger

Not surprisingly one of the, quite proper, ambitions of the reforming Turnbull Commission had been to tame the tiger of the Church Commissioners. By the time the Commission met for the first time, much had been done to recoup the appalling losses of the recent past (though, as correspondents to the *Church Times* acidly pointed out, there was still a considerable loss of interest involved), and there had also been cost-cutting exercises.

What needed to be recognised, however, was that, apart from the intrinsic absurdity of the way the Church had been dealing with its finances, the Commissioners' task had, in recent years, become progressively more impossible to carry out. The Church needed more and more money to pay clergy, to counter inflation, and to set aside for pensions, and in addition to this mammoth task the Commissioners found themselves requested to finance building and other projects. In what, at least from one point of view, can be seen as loyalty to the institution they served, their efforts to increase their income became ever more Herculean, and this may have made it tempting to invest in more and more daring projects to reap large rewards, and to neglect the diversification which is usually thought to be the prudent method of investment. Maybe there was pride in answering the Church's insatiable need for money with ever larger profits. The resultant crash brought it about that the Commissioners were to be reduced in rank to the role of guardians and stewards of the Church's money, and the real decisions about investment should in future, the Turnbull Report suggested, be taken by a National Council (now known as the Archbishops' Council).[8] It also suggested that the number of Commissioners should be cut from ninety-five to fifteen. In the event they ended up with thirty-three.

All Change – the Clean Sweep

Court No. 3 – General Synod

General Synod is the outward and visible sign of the inward and invisible grace of democracy. In 1919 Parliament passed the Enabling Act which recognised the need both for the laity to play a larger part in decision-making, and for the Church of England to run its own ship at least more fully than it had done in the past. This included the chance to make its own mistakes, which it almost immediately began to do in the matter of the 1928 Prayer Book, as internal quarrels scuppered the chances of getting it approved by Parliament. Before Church Assembly archbishops and bishops had ruled the roost, with interference, sometimes considerable, from Parliament. A few blips apart, Church Assembly, a national forum which gave lay Christians a voice in the central structures of the Church, was a success, and, in the fullness of time, 1970, it blossomed into the more developed structure of General Synod. From now on, a three-tier system was established in the running of the Church – the House of Bishops, the House of Clergy and the House of Laity working and voting together. The House of Laity was elected at the grass roots, at deanery synod level, and a somewhat similar method applied to clergy, though with some input from clergy outside the local synod. The House of Bishops consisted of all the diocesan bishops, and nine suffragan bishops. Their function on Synod was, according to the Bridge Report on Synodical Government (1997), to be 'guardians of the worship and doctrine of the Church'.[1] The Church was, in a shorthand phrase, to be 'episcopally led and synodically governed' henceforward, as many of the daughter churches in the Commonwealth already were. There were ex-officio members on Synod – the three Church Estates Commissioners, the Chairman of the Central Board of Finance and others.

Until 1993, the getting on for six hundred members of General Synod met three times a year, twice in London at Church House and once at York. (Nowadays, to save expense, the Synod meets twice a year, once in London and once in York.) Synod was, and is, as much like a court as Lambeth – buzzing, a little claustrophobically, with its own absorbing and often self-referential business, and with a cheerful camaraderie, which, of course, encompasses gossip, rumours, scandals and squabbles. Or perhaps it is less like a court than it is like the House of Commons, with which, for want of another model, it has seemed to have a sort of 'copy-cat' relationship. It has committees, wire-pulling behind the scenes, and a voting system that works by members walking out of the chamber to register their votes (a dangerous process in situations when bishops and clergy fear their vote might land them in huge controversy). It 'promotes Measures' to do with the legislative business of the Church, which then go on to Parliament. Parliament no longer has power to amend what the Church has painstakingly decided, but can either reject a Measure or recommend it to go forward for Royal Assent. Synod also deals with liturgical and financial business, and discusses issues of importance in society. Although Synod's general deliberations can be fascinating and well-informed, it sometimes seemed to be pontificating from a rather lofty Christian stance, about issues and about lives of which it knows very little, and with a worrying lack of humility about the fact that no one much notices what it thinks anyway. (Unless it offends the propriety of the prim and prurient British press, i.e., shows itself lenient about sex before marriage, homosexuality or divorce, something which it is not prone to do very often.) Watching such debates I have often had a sense of big fish (or wannabe big fish) throwing their weight about in a small pond.

In most major debates I have sat through, Synod has predictably wheeled a handful of extraordinary diehards out of the closet (and I don't mean the gay closet – only fools, heroes and madmen emerge from that at Synod), the closet of those who had not noticed that the world has changed since 1914. Yet equally members could be, and frequently were, just, generous, funny, broad-minded, brave and intelligent. All in all, it probably represented pretty accurately the virtues and faults, strengths and weaknesses, of the Church of England.

A criticism of Church Assembly, which was again levelled at Synod, though in a somewhat modified form, was that the members were not 'typical' of the laity. The members were, as how could they fail to be, people who were not afraid of the sound of their own voices, who held views on religious matters, and who could abandon home and family for three days in the middle of the week to go to London or York. Inevitably they were, for the most part, middle-aged and middle-class. Many were women, a welcome addition, in my view, to a Church where male voices have predominated. It would, of course, have been wonderful if the Synod had included miners, factory workers, garment- and cardboard-box makers, cleaners and train drivers, but given the nature both of Church and society, this was never very likely. What Synod did do, admirably, was to bring intelligent and articulate lay voices to a central church discussion, and those who spend much time in church discussion, especially if they are lay people, soon learn that clergy and lay people often see issues very differently, and that both are needed to make up a whole.

Vive la différence!

I may be wrong, and it is not easy to produce clear evidence, but it has often seemed to me that the growing strength and independence of lay opinion has, in the past ten years or so, begun to be looked on askance by some bishops and clergy. Back in 1968 when it seemed prudent to involve lay people more closely, it was hard to envisage a theologically sophisticated laity – they were still the 'simple faithful' who must be protected from difficult and dangerous ideas like John Robinson's *Honest to God*. Indeed one still hear echoes of that kind of condescension in public utterances. I remember a Northern bishop at a debate about the ordination of women in the late 1980s telling Synod that 'his people' were not ready for it. My impression was that 'his people', or those at least who had thought about it at all, loved the idea (borne out by subsequent events), but that he himself could not quite get his head round it.

The workings of General Synod were, and are, underpinned by the permanent staff of Church House, a kind of civil service who prepare papers on important issues of relevance to the Church – mission, ecumenism, ministry, education, young people, liturgy, social issues, etc.. In the early days of Synod they had, I seem to remember, a somewhat amateurish feel. As time went on, the staff became much better qualified and skilled, becoming, I think it is fair to say, an exceptionally competent and useful body of men and women, who brought creativity and new ideas into the 'civil service' of the Church. This was partly because the Church was a good employer, and Church House had begun to acquire a reputation as a good place to work, to the extent that gifted people would accept a drop in salary in order to work there. The knock-on effect was that the work of its staff achieved a reputation outside the Church, and because many of them had worked in other organisations and institutions with resonance in the secular world they had vital contacts outside the Church, for example in the worlds of education, the trade unions, industry, employers' associations, etc. They were themselves regarded as credible in high places, and worthy of consultation by bodies outside the Church, a priceless asset. Many of them were lay people, of course, though there was a good sprinkling of clergy.

Synod and Church House staff together worked mainly in four key areas: Ministry (the selection, training, support and pay of ministers); Education (working with both church and state schools, at higher levels of education, in adult Christian formation, in youth work, and in work with children); Mission and Unity (concerns with Christian mission in Britain and abroad, ecumenical matters to do both with other Christian bodies and with other faiths); and Social Responsibility (concerned with the lives of all in society).

There was a two-way process of bringing about discussion of important matters at the highest levels of the Church. It was possible for church leaders to ask the Boards for advice and information in the areas they covered. It was equally possible for staff who worked for the Boards, working through their Chairmen, to promote discussion in Synod of matters which seemed to them to be important or urgent. They thus had a 'shop window' for thoughts and ideas. This was roughly how the Church came to discuss matters of importance to it. Questions might arise at the grass roots, at the deanery or diocesan synod level and work themselves up to a bishop or Church House department and become the focus of discussion. Questions might arise among the bishops and equally find their way into public discussion. There seemed a certain flexibility or movement of ideas in the system, even if the effect could be very wordy and time-consuming.

Belling the Cat
The misdoings of the Church Commissioners provided a very good reason for change in the Church: the tiger plainly needed to be tamed. The Archbishop and others saw a need for 'coherence' and 'transparency' in the Church, and while thought was being given to that and to the disciplining of the Church Commissioners, it was the perfect opportunity to look again at General Synod, and indeed the whole bureaucracy of the Church. In order to do this the Turnbull Commission – thirteen men, one woman, plus three male assessors – was appointed by the Archbishops in 1993 to review the organisation of the Church (the dioceses as well as the Church Commissioners and General Synod), and it reported two years later in the Report known as *Working as One Body* (henceforward just called *Turnbull* in these pages).[2] At around the same time another committee was

appointed (by the Standing Committee of General Synod) – six men, two women, plus three male assessors – to look at Synodical Government in the Church of England, and this was chaired by Lord Bridge of Harwich, who was also a member of the Turnbull Commission (henceforward just called *Bridge*). The Church of England was preparing for a thorough spring-clean.

How much previous intention was there behind the scenes to bell the cat of General Synod as well as to tame the tiger of the Church Commissioners? Certainly both *Turnbull* and *Bridge* seemed to have a puzzling compulsion to play down the very real achievements of General Synod and to speak of it in regretful tones. *Turnbull* speaks in a slightly sinister way about 'negative power'. The impression given is that 'right-thinking people' widely regarded Synod as a failure. But did they? Sometimes the Parliamentary style of Synod could be tedious, sometimes the revelation of prejudice, on a number of issues, could be spine-chilling, but I can also remember many fine speeches, well prepared, by people who knew what they were talking about. And even the most bigoted of them, and there were always one or two bigots on any Synod, at least reminded everyone that Synod was not a collection of saints. Synod had faults, very human ones, but to many of us it all seemed much better than a Church without lay input at the centre. Yet when the two seminal Reports of the 1990s came to be written, it was if the whole brave democratic enterprise had to be played down in order to justify changing the system radically.

When I interviewed Michael Turnbull, Bishop of Durham, and chairman of the Turnbull Commission, he said this of Synod:

> One of the disappointing things about General Synod is that whereas the original idea was that each bishop should bring his diocese and representatives to a national consultation – it was to be a meeting of the minds of the dioceses – what happened is that General Synod ended up as a confrontation of party caucuses. That's very evident from the way people sit – they don't sit in dioceses. You can see the black-suited gentleman, and the free-for-all evangelicals sitting together, and debate takes that sort of form instead of somebody standing up and saying, 'As we discussed this and prayed about it in Durham/Bath and Wells/Norwich . . .' It doesn't work like that. How it works is that the parties have met beforehand and they then confront each other. The General Synod has failed in that sense to be the gathering together of the Church of England from regions and it's become much more political.[3]

It is undeniable, of course, that there were party confrontations in

Synod, more especially, as one might imagine, when issues were involved that touched upon churchmanship itself, or upon the interpretation of the Bible – Anglican/Methodist reunion, homo-sexuality, and the ordination of women all come to mind as these sorts of issues – though I am far from clear how any of the recommendations made by the Commission will reduce that. And in any case, the conflicts uncovered are genuine and need to be confronted rather than hidden – this, presumably, is what being an 'open' Church would mean. What I find puzzling in Turnbull's critique of Synod, however, is that the House of Bishops was just as partisan as anyone else, in fact virtually every major Synod confronta-tion tended to be vigorously led or supported by a bishop (regardless of whether they were expressing the mind of their diocese). Bishop Graham Leonard led his troops relentlessly against Anglican/ Methodist reunion and the ordination of women. Far from the bishops gathering their dioceses about them in Synod, and encour-aging them to come to a united opinion, what I remember most vividly from sitting through many Synod debates, is the solid phalanx of purple-stocked bishops sitting down in the well of Church House, very much the separate 'House of Bishops'. If Synod failed, and (bar some problems which needed looking at, I don't believe it did), the House of Bishops are more implicated than most.

The Coming of Collegiality
In the 1990s, of course, bishops don't pursue pet causes so much. They vote, and even speak, with worrying unanimity, as one man, 'singing from the same song book', as Madeleine Bunting put it.[4] Since most of us know, from knowing bishops, that their views are not unanimous, this seems to be taking the new buzz word 'coher-ence' too far. Or that even more useful word (because it trails a sort of theological respectability along with it) 'collegiality' – borrowed clothes from the Roman Catholic Church which do not quite fit, since the Church of England is a very different organisation. Those who are interested in the deliberations of the Church want to know what the bishops are actually thinking, as individuals, not as an undifferentiated mass. We would hate to think that they have forgotten the art of disagreeing. This is, or was, the Church of England, not the Vatican. Or the Kremlin.

The Cat's Cradle
If *Turnbull* and *Bridge* were less than fair about Synod itself, they were damning about the Boards who underpin it, painting a picture of a muddle of committees duplicating work and wasting everybody's

time. 'There is a cat's cradle of autonomous or semi-autonomous bodies with distinctive, but sometimes overlapping functions which are a source of confusion and wasteful duplication' and 'much of the work of the national bodies is committee-bound'.[5]

'When we read *Turnbull* we at once denied this,' a member of the Church House staff told me.

> We said 'Our Committees work well. They are not reproducing effort and we are not dysfunctional.' We were told 'Well, *your* Committee is fine, actually, but some of the others are not so good.' It was flattering to be told that we were exempt from the general condemnation, though I know now that it was said to others too, but it tended to silence us. What we had done was challenge the current myth, the one that gave the red light for a change that a handful of people were determined to push through, and we had to be silenced.[6]

Who's in Charge Here?

The heart of the debate about change was, of course, actually about power – who had it and who wanted it. Leaving aside the Archbishop's determination to stand at the helm (and this only slowly became evident to those outside his immediate circle), what most people, including General Synod, wanted was to take power away from the Church Commissioners. 'It seems to me,' said the same member of the Church House staff, 'that because the Church Commissioners' errors were attributed to grey-faced bureaucracy, the Church House staff were lumped along with the bureaucrats who needed to have power taken away from them, and I think this will turn out to have been a serious mistake.'[7] It certainly made it easier for significant shifts of power to take place, and I believe that it was in the interest of this that Synod and the Church House staff were given such short shrift in *Turnbull* and *Bridge*.

Archbishops' Council

So drastic changes were set in train at both Millbank and at Church House. The main aim of *Turnbull* is essentially one of centralisation: 'The Church inescapably has to have a central machine . . . the centre can see – albeit imperfectly – the broad challenges which face the Church.'[8] It sounds neat, and possibly because there is little heart for exploring what the deeper reasons of Christian malaise may be, it is tempting to think that this busy solution must be the answer. Even if it were true that what ailed the Church was the lack of a central executive (and I think the problems may lie elsewhere), to implant new features in a long-established body which already has many evolved checks and balances in place is a risky undertaking; the danger is of the last state being worse than the first. Wesley Carr describes *Turnbull's* vision as 'corporate even curial', by which I think he means a managerial role that has moved on into a strongly authoritarian mode. 'It is unlikely that this will succeed, not least because of a gut antipathy to centralism.'[9]

The body which would have the task of putting everything into a 'single framework' was what *Turnbull* originally called the 'National Council', a committee to be led by the two Archbishops in order to gather the reins of decision-making in the Church into its hands. Various adjectives have been used to indicate the aim: the Church is to be 'coherent', 'open', 'attractive' and 'inclusive'. By the time the Council came into being in 1999, indeed long before, it had acquired a hierachical look and was called 'the Archbishops' Council'. Its primary function was help 'the Church to develop a clear sense of direction, of the opportunities presented to it and of its needs and priorities if it is better to fulfil its mission in the world'.[10] It abolished the old Standing Committee of Synod and largely assumed its functions, thus lifting a sizeable amount of power out of Synod's reach. It would assume the roles and functions of several other Synod bodies as well as that of the Church Commissioners (who would remain as trustees and asset managers). Within the single framework of the Council, policies and strategies would be developed, and all the executive bodies that serve the Church would 'interrelate' through it. Resources, including man- and woman-power, could be reviewed centrally, and dioceses could be supported and, if necessary, helped to co-ordinate their work.

Turnbull went on to recommend that once again there should be four key areas, though they were not the same ones as before. The four main concerns now, with consequently important officials leading them, would be ministry, mission, heritage and legal services, and finance. The officials, who would be nominated by the archbishops and approved by General Synod, would exercise responsibility for leadership in their particular areas. It is difficult not to see Education and Social Responsibility (in many ways the liveliest and most creative members of the old set-up) downgraded by this change. In future they would have to negotiate at the top level not with their own chairperson who was thoroughly versed in their work, but through other representatives who were 'standing in' for them.

A Diversion into Subsidiarity

A very important feature of *Turnbull* concerned parish life. While centralising the Church firmly with one hand, it was equally firmly decentralising it with the other. A key word for the second plan was 'subsidiarity', one borrowed, by both Conservative and Labour Governments, as well as now by the Church of England, from the Roman Catholic Church (Pope Pius XI's Encyclical *Quadragesimo Anno* of 1931).[11] In the Pope's view it had to do with handing responsibility down to the lower levels of the Church, and with larger and higher associations not 'arrogating' to themselves functions which could be performed efficiently by smaller and lower social groups. 'The social doctrine of subsidiarity holds that the higher body is subsidiary to the lower.'[12] A knowledgable Roman Catholic whom I consulted about how this worked in practice was a little cynical about the concept in use. 'It means making the grass roots financially responsible for all sorts of things, but on the other hand if they seem to be coming up with any ideas that the centre disapproves of, then they are slapped down in no time.' Something very like this has also happened in the political application of subsidiarity, with the Tory Government devolving many financial responsibilities to local authorities and then rate-capping them as they tried to raise more money, or the new Labour Government, at one stage, saying that it was a scandal that nurses were not paid more money but that it must be found out of the income of already hard-pressed Trusts and the National Health Service. What at first appears as a welcome devolution of power can quite quickly look like a cynical manoeuvre to pass the buck.

Money, Money, Money...

Whether or not this is fair, what it means in practice is that the parishes will have to work much harder to raise money, more of which in the past came from the diocese and from church investments. The hope is that the wealthier parts of the Church will help support the poorer parts.

The expectation that more money will be raised in the parishes is not in itself unreasonable. If anything, the Church of England, unlike its Roman Catholic and Free Church brethren, has suffered historically from 'featherbedding', the comfortable feeling that financially it was well provided for, which often in the past it was, and that there was little onus on parishioners to pay properly for the services they enjoyed from their church. As Professor Robin Gill put it, the Church suffered from 'the effects of unchallenged, open-ended subsidy. To put it bluntly, [it] has subsidized [its] own long-term decline.'[13]

184

Anyone who has had much experience of a parish church will have slowly become aware of quite wealthy members of the congregation who give the church next to nothing financially. Not to take financial responsibility, or to face the cost of what is being enjoyed, is to behave childishly and selfishly, and the new expectations offer a chance for parishes to grow up in this respect. People who 'own' their church in terms of taking responsibility for it, are more likely to have a general sense of commitment about the work and mission of the Church.

However, important as this is, it is not the whole answer. The Church of England has an unusually large share of historic churches and cathedrals to maintain, and the contribution from outside agencies is certainly not at all adequate to the task. In the case of parishes the cost of 'keeping the roof on', the steeple intact, the tower safe, the building dry and warm, the organ functioning and all the rest of it, can be so prohibitive that it permits churchgoers little energy for anything else. Then again some parishes are simply poor, with very few members of the congregation living above subsistence level. It is simply not practical to expect all parishioners to produce large sums of money to maintain their church, nor might it be an appropriate use of money which might more properly be spent on shoes, clothes, food and necessities of living. So that if the new system is to work at parish level, although being 'self-supporting' has a lot to be said for it, it will also need great acts of generosity between richer parishes towards poorer ones, either directly or by way of diocesan funds.

What's New, Pussy Cat?

If the bold tiger of the Church Commissioners needed taming, General Synod had to be controlled by something more like strategic stroking to make it into an amenable pussy cat. It is difficult for a large unwieldy body of many different shades of opinion to act shrewdly and concertedly, and memorably, at least once in the recent past, Synod had been led by the nose by the bishops into a project they had not thought through properly, and might not have voted for if they had. Church House staff were rather more experienced and acute, but among them, as among General Synod members, there was satisfaction at seeing the arrogant Church Commissioners cut down to size, a humiliation which was felt to be richly deserved. This perhaps proved a dangerous distraction from noticing how extensively the changes would affect themselves.

A careful reading of *Turnbull*, however, should have suggested to Synod members that they would be affected drastically. 'Most of the existing central bodies would disappear.'[14] That is, some important Committees on Synod would go, and the powers of staff in Church House would be curtailed. The ironic slant was that Synod would then be asked to vote for this. As one Synod member, Arthur Pollard, memorably put it, 'Will a turkey vote for Christmas?' The answer turned out to be an overwhelming 'You bet!', with only eleven clergy voting against, only twenty-seven of the laity, and, no big surprise, no bishops. A motion was passed for the turkey to have its neck wrung, that is to say for the Standing Committee of Synod to surrender its power. The Measure was accordingly passed to the Ecclesiastical Committee of Parliament and received the Royal Assent. The mills of the Church of England could start to grind.

In July 1998 a 'provisional' Report[15] was produced by the House of Bishops to show the changes were going to be implemented. It was written in 'management speak', a mixture of grandiosity and the inflated and slipshod prose that is born of committees, of writers who are, or who feel it safer to be, vague about what they are actually trying to say. 'The House of Bishops is considering its role of vision-building for the Archbishops' Council . . . to help the Council set its priorities and organisational objectives. The House sees this process as ongoing and iterative.'[16] (Remembering my schoolgirl Latin I decided 'iterative' must mean 'repeated', but I was still confused. Did it mean that the House will do the identical piece of work many times, or that there will be a succession of objectives, in which case I think the word they needed was 'continuous'? Visions are usually simpler affairs than this.) A sudden switch from management gobbledegook to pious ambition was anything but reassuring. 'Meeting in a spirit of worship, stillness and prayer to listen fervently to what the Spirit is saying to the Church, striving always to preserve the unity of the Spirit in the bond of peace, the Archbishops' Council aims to serve the Church and the nation.'[17]

In addition to these officials and others representing the House of Bishops and the clergy, there would be six 'appointed members' whom the Archbishops would select out of those who applied. The application form which was available to anyone who was 'a communicant member of the Church of England or another Church in communion with the Anglican Church' (a little odd this last), made it clear that what the Council was looking for was people making 'a significant contribution . . . in a field which would advance the Church's contribution to the wider community e.g. finance, strategic planning, etc. A proven track record of translating vision into strategy and delivery is the key. In addition the Appointed Members must possess a lively Christian faith and commitment to the Church of

England . . .' Plainly if your vision for contributing to the wider community happened to lie in the field of the arts, social work, health or education, your chances of being chosen were slim (though one teacher did make the committee). Money and strategy were thought to be what was needed to reinstate Christianity in these islands. Puzzlingly, at least to me, the form went on to describe the function of the Council as 'green field', a phrase I only understand in connection to housing development. Latin could not help this time. Virginal? Unexplored? Ecological? Maybe Church House Publishing should publish a glossary to translate Anglican Newspeak into the vernacular.

The Council Meets
Much was made of the first meeting of the Archbishops' Council at Lambeth Palace in the Green Room in January 1999, round a new oval table specially built for the occasion. The members consisted of nineteen people; ex officio there were Archbishops Carey and Hope; the two Prolocutors of Canterbury and York, Canons Hugh Wilcox and John Stanley; the chairman and vice-chairman of the General Synod, Drs Christina Baxter and Philip Giddings; and Sir Michael Colman, the First Church Estates Commissioner. The elected members of the Council were Bishops Turnbull (Durham), Gladwin (Guildford), both elected by the House of Bishops; the Provost of Derby, the Very Revd Michael Perham, and the Archdeacon of Northolt, the Venerable Pete Broadbent, elected by the House of Clergy; and Brian McHenry and Mrs Christina Rees, elected by the House of Laity. There were also six appointed members, chosen by the Archbishops from applications which members of the church-going public had been free to make (so long as they knew about finance and strategy). These included Michael Chamberlain, an accountant, David Lammy, a black barrister, Jayne Ozanne, a marketing consultant, Elizabeth Paver, a teacher, Stephen Bampfylde, the managing director of an executive search company, and Professor Peter Toyne, the Vice-Chancellor and chief executive of John Moores University in Liverpool. 'What we have now is a really exciting group of people and a dynamic vision of what is possible' said the Bishop of Durham. 'There is going to be change and it is going to be swift' said Mr Lammy. Others were a bit more modest. The Provost of Derby remarked less ambitiously that 'We'd be well advised to do [our] job quietly and privately and thoroughly . . . If we can create a council that enables the Church to be and to sound more confident, then that's very good.'[18]

Four committees were drawn up from the members – a 'business' committee, a 'church-and-world' committee, a 'finance' committee, an 'audit' committee, and a 'church heritage' forum.

At their second meeting, after 'team-building exercises', organised by one of the new member-experts (which I would have given a good deal to have witnessed), the Council 'commissioned research into how "consumers" viewed the Church' via focus groups in twenty dioceses.

> Jayne Ozanne, an appointed member of the Council and a key figure behind the Council's strategic planning, said on Wednesday that business principles would be an important element of the Council's approach. 'We believe business strategies can be applied to the Church – the skills you need to understand your consumers are the skills to use right across the board' she said . . . A national management expert, Professor John Adair, Professor of Leadership Management at Exeter University, was brought in to coach Council members in working together as a team.[19]

The way one receives such statements as this must depend on how much one trusts business and business ideas, and is prepared to make a shift to regard oneself and others as 'consumers' rather than 'worshippers'. Is this how anyone wants to be seen? What has happened, one wonders, to the Church's own considerable insight, and experience of people working together as teams, and why is it ceasing to use its own language of love, and its ethos of people mattering, in a way that persuasion and profit do not? Is the message a hidden one of the Church's loss of confidence in itself, and rather pathetically attempting to make this good by marketing ploys?

The Archbishops' Council is serviced by a Policy and Resources Co-ordinating Committee whose task is to 'develop a strategic overview', 'help to assess priorities', look at 'cross-border' issues and the ecumenical dimension, and take responsibility for an overall budget. This Committee comprises the Secretaries of the various Boards who meet with an Associate Secretary General.

So now what we have, apart from General Synod and the House of Bishops, are four main 'directors' under the Secretary General reporting to the Archbishops' Council: the Director of Ministry, the Director of Policy, the Director of Central Services and the Financial Secretary.

Alas for the Church and the World

Under the aegis of the Director of Policy, Richard Hopgood, a whole bunch of concerns with no particular similarity between them are bundled together in the area of what is broadly known as 'the Church and the World', including the Council for Christian Unity, the Board of Education, the Board of Mission, the Board of Social Responsibility, the Hospital Chaplaincies Council, and other concerns to do with church fabric. Whereas in the past each had had its own chairman with close knowledge of the work of its Board who could report directly to General Synod, now they are forced to work through a chairman with a much wider remit, stretching over all kinds of other things – indeed with an impossibly large responsibility, and very possibly no direct awareness of the work they are doing. Hopgood has an assistant in the person of Philip Giddings who, however, has a full-time job in addition to his work for the Church and the World. It seems impossible in these circumstances that, in the crucially important area of the Church and the World, communication can possibly be anything like as good as it has been in the past, and taken together with the enhanced emphasis on other internal matters, supremely finance and ministry, it suggests a turning inwards, despite all the official claims to the contrary.

The 'bundling' of the Church and the World section is a powerful argument against the draconian measures *Turnbull* took against the Synod Boards. Not all were treated in an equally cavalier way. The Ministry Division, for instance, has enjoyed both increased limelight and a greatly increased budget. The Communications Department, too, seems largely to have escaped the Synod holocaust. Money, clericalism and publicity – they have their importance, of course, but the emphasis of the 'new reformation' somehow does not warm the cockles of the heart.

Pismires and Others

Back to the inner court of Church House, the place where this turmoil of ideas, structural changes and new attitudes had to be digested. Dropping into Church House one day in the spring of 1999 to talk to some of the staff I found them coping slightly frantically with all this, and also with a switchboard revolution which temporarily had cut most of them off from the outside world (not an omen, they trusted), and extensive alterations and repainting which made actually getting on with their work quite difficult.

As we chatted about how Church House staff were seen and understood by the wider Church, one of the staff told me that she was dismayed when George Carey met with them on one occasion and remarked that he thought of them as 'pismires' toiling away unseen and underground to make the Church work. (He was referring to a poem by the American Trappist monk Thomas Merton which is called 'Bureaucrats and Diggers'. Whether or not the Archbishop knew it, Merton, who did not like bureaucrats, was almost certainly writing satirically.)

> Oh curse them not nor rail
> Upon nor arm against the mole.
> And do not lift your spear
> Against the poor pismire.

(The mole and the pismire together, Merton goes on to say, are ignorant of the glories of life above ground – 'the sound of Easter morning bell'. Yet in their lack of imagination they are, annoyingly, in this world's terms, more successful than the visionary and the creative.)

> These drizzling years
> Make laughing moles and prosperous pismires.[20]

The employee, a person as it happens of unusual imagination and creativity, was surely not alone among her contemporaries in not knowing what a pismire was. She was not very reassured when she looked it up. A pismire is a sort of ant or emmet. Presumably the archbishop was not aware that, because of its unfortunate odour, the pismire gave its name to piss. What worried her, however, was that this troglodytic image illustrated the gulf between Archbishop and Church House staff, suggesting the latter as a blindly toiling body of people, whereas she had thought that they were intelligent and clear-sighted and operating towards clearly envisaged ends. Despite the reputation of ants for industry, nobody really wants to be seen in such a faceless and obsessional light.

Vision and Mission: Yes, but Whose Vision and Which Mission?
All of the material preparing for the changes talked a lot about vision and mission. There are different 'visions' in the Church, and different ideas of what 'mission' involves, and the differences need to be unpacked. Ironically both words have acquired an additional meaning because the secular world of management has borrowed them from the churches. In business-speak, 'vision' is the 'short version' (easily memorable) of the overall intention of an organi-

sation, and 'mission' its more detailed aims of what it now intends to do. In church statements in the old days there was a useful ambiguity about the word 'mission', which concealed the fact that, to some people, it meant something much more boldly vigorous ('proactive' as the managers say) than it did to others.

The implication of *Turnbull* is that a more efficient and better managed church would attract 'the punters'. For others, however, there is a crudity in this kind of 'strategy' which is offensive, since they believe it quickly declines into what is vulgarly called 'bums-on-seats' thinking. There is a very real dilemma here. If the numbers involved in the Church continue to decline there will be no organisation left with which to do anything at all. A bold, determined, caring initiative does seem a very tempting idea, rather as Coggan's Call to the Nation seemed to him in 1975, or the Decade of Evangelism did to the Archbishops in 1988. Certainly more is being staked on this 'new Reformation' in the Church than was staked on the other 'mission' movements, and certainly the striking success of evangelical and charismatic churches in increasing numbers points to this approach.

If it achieves nothing else, it temporarily relieves the anxiety of those who lead the Church with a sense that it is 'on the move'. The danger is that 'the changes' may be little more than a diversionary tactic, a palliative drug, a Prozac which leaves the underlying problems untouched, when what is needed is to look much more profoundly and honestly into the reasons for decline (something *Turnbull* barely attempted at any depth), and to recognise that whatever the role of the Church in the future the chances are that it will be a very different one from what it was in the past. The Church has 'come down in the world' like an aristocrat in a revolution. In twentieth-century terms, it finds itself in a buyers', not a sellers', market, forced to shift for itself in a way for which little in its past prepares it. It is no longer for the Christians to dictate terms, but rather to see how and where they fit in to a world that no longer gives them a prime place.

Maybe, instead of hurrying into new initiatives, what was needed was a process both of grieving and of 'sitting with' the unpalatable facts, indeed I do not believe the Church can escape these processes on the way to refinding itself.

I had just written these words when a report emerged of the first six months work of the Archbishops' Council.[21] Plainly a good deal of work had gone into the task of 'melding' the disparate elements in the Council in that time, but now they were ready to produce their 'vision' – for themselves, presumably, since 'vision' for the Church, according to *Turnbull,* is the task of the House of Bishops. The Council's vision is that the Church shall be

> United – growing together in the love of God
> Confident – living and proclaiming the good news of Jesus Christ
> Outward-looking – sharing in the mission of God in the world;
>   working for God's justice and peace for all.

It is impossible to be against any of these objectives, any more than it is possible to be for adultery, but do they really touch the kind of problem that the Church has? What if we are actually *not* united or confident, nor all that sure if we trust Christians of some other shades of opinion, or quite certain what it is that we believe? Are we being asked simply to pretend to be so? And if so, what is that likely to achieve? Maybe our record of justice within our own organisation is not so wonderful to commend us all that much to others – talk to the women priests, the gays, the ethnic minorities in the Church?

The *Church Times,* reviewing the Report, complained of

> the language of New Management: relentlessly optimistic regardless of whether circumstances warrant it. Such optimism is more likely to achieve results than the grim pessimism it is attempting to replace. But somewhere in between is the need to admit to the Church's inadequacies as well as its strengths. The Council is more likely to carry the rest of the Church with it if it begins to use a more recognisable language, one that matches the reality of life in so many of our parishes.[22]

The Very Reverend David Edwards, who served on the Turnbull Commission, remarked in a letter to the *Church Times* the following week that it troubled him that there was nothing in the mission statement about truth, study and revision.

> What seems to be missing is any emphasis on the fact that a Church whose committed membership has declined very steeply in the century now closing, needs to think very seriously about the truth of what is taught either about Christianity itself or about the application of Christian insights to the world's problems. A Decade of Thinking would be a good idea.[23]

Nothing, one feels, could be further from the intention of an anxious Church than a period of silence and reflection.

Pismire's-Eye View

It is not surprising that Church House staff, caught all along in the blast of the winds of change, were not impressed. A group of staff working for the Church Commissioners, the Central Board of Finance, Lambeth Palace and the Pensions Board were subjected to a staff survey by the Surveys and Audits Consultants of the the Industrial Society. The Industrial Society studied the way they had learned about the process. They noted that staff had tended to be 'informed by paper', 'thus denying people the opportunity to ask questions and contribute their own views, and that this has not always been written in the most accessible language'.[24]

Quote: 'We get regular bulletins but they could be written in German for all I can understand them.' 'We've already used up a couple of rain forests on *Turnbull*, but no one reads it. It's so turgid that you just throw it away.[25]

This is bad enough, but the survey reveals more worrying trends than this, of a staff anxious and somewhat depressed, and having small faith in the effectiveness of what was being undertaken at some cost to themselves. The major worry seemed to be about loss of job satisfaction. 'The very high levels of job satisfaction and commitment which people feel for their current roles and to their current organisations', say the authors of the Survey,

> mean that they are perhaps more concerned about the impact of change than might otherwise have been the case. People tend to have a good understanding of the objectives and purpose of their present employer, and are very supportive of the goals they are working towards – they have yet to gain any real confidence that the new Church body will enhance that in any way or produce any tangible benefits for their organisation or for them as individuals ... Survey results generally indicate a relatively undemanding workforce which derives satisfaction from interesting work, friendly colleagues and a commitment to its organisation's purpose rather than being driven by career aspirations or greater financial reward.[26]

The inquiry showed that this mainly happy and satisfied staff had felt very worried about the changes, 25 per cent believing that they would be greatly affected, 39 per cent that they would be affected to some extent and 30 per cent seeing few or no changes on the horizon.

Those least worried were those who worked at Lambeth Palace. 'It won't make any difference to us at all.'[27] Those most worried were those at the highest level, that of Assistant Secretary and above.

A comment that recurred was that the whole thing had been

precipitated by the financial difficulties of the Church Commissioners and that the extensive restructuring was therefore taking a sledgehammer to crack a nut.

> I believe that the concept of the Archbishops' Council and Unified Staff Capability is a misguided and belated response to a problem which has now been rectified. I also believe it will be an expensive folly which may well have a detrimental effect on staff pay and conditions and may lead to decisions on such matters being taken on political grounds.[28]

> Turnbull is a kneejerk reaction to investment problems.[29]

There was a note of paranoia: 'It's not difficult to find out what's happening, but it's what's *really* happening. Will they come out with some big announcement that contradicts all previous communications?'[30] The view of 37 per cent was that the restructuring had not been well handled. One person said: 'The change process has been interminably long, poorly led and managed and its integrity is now doubtful.'[31]

Only about 15 per cent thought the changes would achieve their objective, and even at senior level more people disagreed than agreed that the objectives of restructuring would be achieved.

> The Turnbull Report was entitled 'Working as one Body'. The intention was clear but seems to have been lost . . . Some areas of work in the different bodies have no clear overlap but are pushed together.[32]

> The original concept was right and good. Disparate groups should come together. What we've actually done is move the furniture around. There's no encouragement that we'll work as one body.[33]

> The expectation is that the Archbishops' Council will cost less than current structures. We know that it will cost more.[34]

The part of the Survey designed to discover whether the staff believed the restructuring would achieve its objectives showed that a number of senior staff – Principals, Senior Principals and Assistant Secretaries – were in the 'doubting' category. Those who were hopeful of success were the Lambeth and Bishopthorpe staff and the Maintenance section.

The overall fear is that the new organisation will not serve the Church better than it has been served in the past, and the working body will feel 'amorphous'. 'I don't want the organisation to lose its ability to treat people as individuals and allow them to exercise their individuality' one respondent says sadly.[35]

Part of the problem is what the compilers of the Survey call 'a clash of cultures'.

> The fact that it is a Church body is much less important than the fact that it is a charity. We don't want 'God bothering' brought into the workplace. The concern is that this might happen.

> There are cultural changes. The Commissioners are now concentrating more on money/budget, staff are secondary. People are not valued, you're an item in the budget.

> We're thinking that this can't work. We're a commercial organisation making money. There's a big division between the non-religious and the religious.

> *Turnbull* will change things because there will be more layers – we will be more remote from Synod.

> The new structure puts in another layer between us and the Synod. It will make it more difficult.[36]

Only 2 per cent thought that job security would improve, in fact the only ways most people thought their working lives would be substantially better would be in 'access to IT', and in opportunities for social and sporting activities. Only .07 per cent thought that professionalism would be improved and .03 per cent were hopeful of career opportunities. 'Caring' commitments, working environment, prospects for pay, speed of decision-making, a sense of identity, were all expected to deteriorate, with job security being placed at the bottom of the list.

After criticising the lack of effective communication with staff, the Survey goes on: 'Despite all the reassurances that have been issued with regard to job security and terms of employment, people are still worried about these issues.'[37]

Staff morale, in fact, had taken a beating in a number of departments. 'One member of my staff', wrote someone from the Church Commissioners, 'tells me he cannot sleep for worrying about his future, another finds it hard to concentrate on work because of his concern and a third is actively looking for other employment.'[38]

The Ramshackle Wall

It is, of course, difficult to know whether the reactions of staff revealed in the Survey are simply a result of the fear that 'restructuring' inspires in most employees or whether they are symptomatic of a damaging change in working practices; perhaps a bit of both. In certain respects – in a valiant effort to avoid redundancies, for example – the restructuring has behaved admirably in human terms, though it is difficult to see how, in the long run, redundancies can be avoided.

I decided to make some enquiries among people personally known to me on the Church House staff. Their comments were not identical to those in the Survey – they were made at a later date – but they were similar in tone. One of the things upon which those I talked to agreed about was that they had been consulted in the course of the process, but they could see little sign that what they had said had influenced the final result. They felt that what they had said had either not been heard or had been ignored.

> What I feel is that Synod is losing its teeth. People who want to influence what is happening will not work through us but will go straight to the Archbishops' Council. There are signs already of this happening, as well as initiatives that have come directly from the Archbishop duplicating, or competing with, work we are already doing. The reasons behind all this change do not feel like *our* reasons, I mean ones we can own for ourselves. The pushing together of different kinds of work that may have little in common, for example. It seems ironical to us that just at the point where the big companies – ICI, BT and many others – are working hard at decentralisation and getting rid of 'stepped hierarchy' in favour of what they call 'a flat hierarchy', in which workers carry more responsibility themselves, the Church is going the opposite way. This is American management style as it was understood in the 1970s.[39]

I asked why the speaker thought it was happening.

> It's partly a desire for tidiness, and tidiness is not always the best way to run things. Bishop Tom Butler told a story on *Thought for the Day* that has stuck in my mind in this respect, though I am not sure what it was that he had in mind at the time. He described how his garden, which backs on to a field full of sheep, had a ramshackle wall that looked a mess, but which actually kept the sheep out of his garden. Wanting a neat appearance he had the

rickety wall removed and a new, tidy one put in its place. Suddenly the sheep, finding that the wall was safe to jump upon, started using it to enter his garden.[40]

This speaker felt that 'a ramshackle wall' had been been a very good analogy for the Church of England, and that a misguided attempt at tidying it could damage it badly. S/he also said that the whole exercise felt as if 'a trick had been played on Synod'.

Another very experienced member of Church House staff with valuable experience gained outside it, said:

> What I feel more and more in working for the Church is 'muffled'. It is becoming less and less possible to suggest ideas with any sense that they are being heard, and this will not help towards creative working. Instead of having our own Chairman to report to we now have to make suggestions to someone who often knows nothing of our work, who then passes them on to the Archbishops' Council in whatever form feels appropriate to him. Plainly suggestions may die the death if the Archbishops don't happen to like them. This is very different from a system in which a Chairman who thoroughly understood the work in hand could pass a suggestion directly to the Standing Committee who could then float it for discussion on General Synod. We have now handed the Archbishops and their Council the right of absolute veto on ideas which no one else may ever learn anything about.[41]

The 'Dumbing Down' of the Church
A priest, whom I will call Fr Jones, not on the staff at Church House, though closely identified with it, and with a considerable first-hand knowledge of management in a secular organisation, also spoke critically to me of the changes. (He did not ask me not to give his name, but he is still employed by the Church, and in a period where dissent, however loyal, is not welcomed, I felt hesitant about doing so.)

'There is a basic error in the whole plan, which is the idea that the Church needs to be "run". The Church has got on without being "run" for centuries.' In management terms he felt that there was a serious flaw in the arrangements, what he described as a 'management nightmare'.

> What we are putting into place now is a double line of authority – Church House staff having two bosses and no longer sure who they are answerable to – line management bifurcating at personnel level. What happens then is that one level plays off against another.

This comes, of course, at a time when there is considerable authoritarianism in public life – governments telling us whether we may eat beef on the bone, or whether single mothers should give their children up for adoption – and it is difficult not to feel that the Church is adopting a similar authoritarian style.

There is a fiction that something non-authoritarian is happening i.e. subsidiarity, which is supposed to be a handing of responsibility to the grass roots, but this tends in practice to mean a handing down of financial responsibility in particular, while reserving the right to interfere if people do not agree with the diktats of the centre.[42]

What seems to be emerging is an obsession with controlling everyone and everything. Fr Jones again:

What we are increasingly getting is a Church in which nothing can happen unless it is 'authorised'. Clergy, who used to have a special kind of freedom in their work (which admittedly they could, and sometimes did, abuse) now have to toe an increasingly prescriptive line. Everything is ticketed and targeted, in a pathetic imitation of what happened in secular management twenty or more years ago. It adds up to a 'dumbing down' of the Church.[43]

Fr Jones was also distressed by the 'bums-on-seats' tendency, the 'need' to get as many people as possible to church, which he regarded as exploitative, however much disguised by talk of mission.

The Church is there to *serve* people – there is far too little about servant theology in *Turnbull* – not get them into church buildings for its own ends. If they come, that is wonderful, that is *gift*, not a matter for triumph. In my own working-class parish we found that if we carefully worked out what the needs of people were, we could (just) find the resources to serve them. This did in fact bring people to church, but the emphasis was service, on what we could do for them. I hear very little of that in the present dialogue. In any case the 'bums-on-seats' method doesn't work. People sense the falsity of it. They're not stupid.[44]

Finally he spoke of the 'fear' among clergy.

It's like Cranmer's England. Those who speak up, who disagree, may find themselves marked and in a sense doomed. They won't lose their jobs, but they may never be offered new ones – hence the sight of excellent clergy stuck for years in jobs which do not fully extend them and which, after a time, frustrate them.[45]

It was this last comment which caused me not to give this informant's name.

It would be good to feel with the Archbishop and the Turnbull Report that the Church was set on a new and inspiring course which would halt decline and make the whole system run much more happily. Criticisms of the changes by some of those most heavily involved in them, and straws in the wind – style, language – already evident are not reassuring. The danger is that in choosing to be 'run' (and of course, the process went through the proper channels) the Church has made itself vulnerable, it would seem in perpetuity, to the personalities, party angles, flaws of judgment and idiosyncrasies of any particular archbishops who happen to be in power. As with Tom Butler's ramshackle wall, some of us may much prefer the democratic muddle of General Synod to the oligarchic tidiness of the Archbishops' Council. The system could only work if the archbishops were able to be completely dispassionate about issues in the Church which, very naturally, they are not.

It looks more and more as if serious damage may have been done to a system that actually worked quite well. Of course, the premise behind *Turnbull* is that it did not work well, and that this is what accounts for the 'loss of morale' and other failures of the Church, but my fear is that this is a projection – there is a need for a scapegoat, and it is Synod, the latecomer with its preponderance of laity, that has been chosen to be it.

All We like Sheep (may) have Gone Astray
It would be easier to trust the whole plan if it showed a less clone-like tendency to follow the management style of the business world. But the Church is not a business and its priorities should be rather different. To think otherwise may be to kill the very thing that makes the Church worthwhile and attracts people to it.

The obvious person to turn to with some of these uncertainties was the Secretary-General, the senior executive of General Synod, Philip Mawer, and I went to interview him in his office at Church House.[46] He was patently sincere in his convictions that the new structures would work well, and quite frank, I thought, about where some of the problems might lie.

Interview with Philip Mawer, the Secretary-General of the General Synod
I began by asking Philip Mawer about the continued geographical separation of the staffs of Lambeth and Church House, something which *Turnbull* decided to leave as it was, while keeping it under

review for the future. Was there, in fact, an overlap between the functions of the two bodies?

> There are areas of shared interest, but I think the main distinction between the staff at Lambeth Palace, and the staff here at Church House, is that those at Lambeth Palace are, as it were, a cabinet, a body that works in support of one person, and this, of course, is concerned with the Archbishop's role not only in relation to the Church of England but in relation to the rest of the Anglican Communion. So far as the Church of England is concerned there are certainly areas of shared interest between the two. For example, clearly the Archbishop is very interested in mission and evangelism and this has led to a number of initiatives coming out of Lambeth which have been very much the Archbishop's baby e.g. Springboard, so that it has required us to be very clear about who was doing what.

Did the Church House staff find that difficult?

> I suspect no more than the Lambeth Palace staff do. It's a challenge in terms of the co-ordination of the various interests, and the message that I've tried to get across both to staff here and at Lambeth Palace, is that the staff here are as much the Archbishop's staff, wanting to work for him and in support of his priorities, as are those more immediately around him.
>
> One of the objects of the *Turnbull* reforms was to try to get us to realise, more fully than we had perhaps hitherto, the areas of shared interest, and to try to get the two groups to work more deliberately closely together. And we're still trying to work away at that. I think there always will be a certain gap. There's a physical gap, because we work on two sides of the river, and there's a mental distance too. This is because the staff at Lambeth are concerned with the totality of a personal ministry, the Archbishop's, whereas here at Church House, people are concerned rather more with the Synodical and related life of the Church of England at a national level. And of course there's a massive overlap, but we're approaching sometimes the same issues from slightly different angles. At a working level there are close relationships, for example in the area of ecumenical relations, or in the area of public affairs, and so on. And this is a necessity if we're to be successful in supporting the Archbishop in his ministry.

Did the staffs, or anyway the staff of Church House, always see their role in the past as placing so much emphasis on support of the Archbishop?

I'm not sure whether they did or not. I only had a brief period of working here when Archbishop Runcie was in office. But I think that what we're aiming at is a relationship; in any organisation you'd be looking for a relationship with the person who is seen by the world as being in charge of it. It's part of our task to convince the Archbishop that we're working in ways that go to tackle the big issues that he's concerned about, and to be sure on the other hand that he understands the nature of the work that's done in Church House and the aspirations of the people who work here.

The new methods of working had clearly shifted some responsibilities. Policies were to be made now by the Archbishops' Council. Where had they been made before? What had been taken away from Synod?

It is complicated, and your question reveals the scope for potential misunderstanding about it. First, certain responsibilities of the former Standing Committee and the Central Board of Finance have been transferred to the Archbishops' Council. Others to do with the management of the business of the Synod have become the responsibility of a new Business Committee of the Synod; they've not been given to the Council.

The second thing: 'What has been taken away from Synod?' Something given to the Archbishops' Council has not necessarily, in fact, been taken away from the Synod. After all, a majority of the Council is on the Synod, well, they're all on the Synod, but a majority are elected by the Synod. Then, they're all answerable to the Synod. Finally, in order to be able to do anything they need Synodical approval . . . well, *anything* is an exaggeration, but to do anything of significance, they're going to need Synodical approval either to the policy itself, or to the means of resourcing it, or to both. So to look at the changes as if Synod has lost out and the Council has gained all the power, and the Archbishop's position has been improved and strengthened thereby, is, I think, to misunderstand what is, inevitably, given the nature of the Church of England, a more complex scene than that.

And the third point I'd like to make out of your question is about what policies the Council are going to make of the kind which other people made in the past.

One of the main reasons for having a Council was that in large areas of activity no one was previously responsible for making a coherent and comprehensive policy. Either because bits of responsibility, e.g. in the area of ministry, were shared with the Church Commissioners, some with ABM [Advisory Board of Ministry] and so on, nobody had an overview. Or because there wasn't a body in the Standing Committee of the Synod which was capable, or which saw it as part of its task, to step back and say where are the challenges facing the Church? How are we going to respond to them, take advantage of them, use them? And in that context develop a policy? There is a key difference about the Council from the old Standing Committee which is not that it has more power, because it doesn't at the end of the day, since it's dependent on the Synod as I've described. The difference is that there is an expectation at the end of the day that, if there is an issue confronting the Church, it's the Council's responsibility, not necessarily to do something about it itself, but to make sure that somebody is doing something about it. There is now somewhere where the buck stops in that sense.

MF. You are saying that previously there were various groups in Church House working away at ministry, theological education or whatever it was, but there wasn't a central intelligence saying 'How does this fit into the overall picture?'

Yes, there was no one whose business it was to say, as they looked at the problems and challenges facing the Church, 'Given our limited resources of people and money, where should we be putting our effort? What are the really important things to tackle and what are the less important things to tackle at this particular time?' Well, the Council in its first six months has tried to identify some areas to which it is necessary to pay priority attention. But it's also going to try to engage the Synod and the House of Bishops in dialogue about whether it's chosen the right ones, how it should go about tackling them, etc. And I think that is the style that the Council's going to try to develop – not dictating. If it tries to dictate, people will just cock a snook at it!

MF. I am not sure anyone had imagined the Council dictating exactly. What seems to me potentially more worrying is that it is a relatively small group of people with whatever their particular limitations happen to be, with the consequent danger of their seeing the Church through whatever their particular set of blinkers happen to be. You see them taking things back to Synod and therefore recruiting a wider range of opinions? What I'm not clear about is, if they propose something really firmly, is Synod in a position to oppose it if they don't like it?

Well, the proof of the pudding will be when that happens. I think there are at least two safeguards. One is the Synodical control one which you've mentioned, which I believe will be real. And the second is that of course the Council itself is designed so as to try to produce a representative cross-section of people.

MF. But do you think it succeeds in that? For instance, there isn't anyone from the health service, there aren't any people from a social work background, or the arts, and there seems to be a heavy emphasis on business and marketing. I'm not saying business shouldn't be on the Council, of course, but it seems to be weighted in their direction.

Well, you've got to work within the limitations that you're given, and nineteen places, of which ten are elected and three are appointed, that leaves six appointed places. So within those six you've got to try to strike an awful lot of balances – men/women, ethnic background, etc. – And, yes, there are areas of knowledge that are not represented on the Council, but I suspect that's true of any body that's sized so as to be capable of some reasonable interaction. I certainly don't think it could be claimed that the previous Standing Committee was a model of representativeness in that sense. There is a danger, of course, with any group that's limited in size, that you will miss out particularly important sections, but I think you've just got to try to build in the checks and balances to avoid that happening. We've got a number of those in place, including also access to a wide range of expert advice, and I hope that we'll be successful in avoiding difficulty.

MF. At such an early stage, it's a question of wait and see?

Yes, and it's going to take quite some time. The Council's only been going for less than six months at the moment. It's very early days, and it's taken quite an effort to weld people coming from quite different backgrounds with their very varied knowledge and experience of the work of the Church in its national bodies, into a coherent whole, and bring them up to a certain common level of understanding of their responsibilities. One of my concerns is to try to balance the levels of expectations that there are around about the Council with the reality of the Council's situation, because one wants it to make a difference, otherwise why have it? On the other hand, one wants to be realistic about what it can and should try to achieve. I think at the moment the world (in this case Synod), is not quite clear what it should try to expect from the Council – there's a balance to be maintained in terms of expectations and deliverability . . . It's not just a question of what is it realistic to expect the Council to deliver, it's what should the Council be expected to deliver.

MF.   So it's a question of learning on the job? How often does the Council get together?

At the moment it's meeting roughly monthly, but there won't be a meeting in August for example. But my guess is that the frequency of meeting will slacken off a little. And frankly I would rather have it meeting slightly less frequently and spending more time when it is meeting on focusing on important issues, than meeting often and having lots of dribs and drabs.

They usually meet for the inside of a day, but there are two longer meetings during the annual cycle in April and September when they meet residentially for twenty-four hours, or slightly longer over a forty-eight-hour period. So they'll come together at lunchtime and perhaps depart at tea-time on the following day. During the daily meetings, the meetings tend to begin at 11 and finish about 4 p.m. That's partly dictated by getting people to London and those sorts of considerations. It doesn't give you a lot of time if you want to tackle some quite tricky issues in depth. There's a lot of just getting people up to speed at the moment.

MF.   How does the Council relate to the House of Bishops?

I think the House of Bishops, like a good many other parts of the Church, is in two minds about the Council. On the one hand it wants the Council to succeed, because I don't think bishops were particularly confident of the previous process. They could see the problems with the previous arrangement which I don't need to rehearse now. On the other hand, they are concerned about the implications of an active Council in an episcopally led Church. I think, curiously, although for twenty-eight years we had a Standing Committee of the Synod, we have never resolved there the question of the relationship between the House of Bishops and the Synod. In fact I think it is one of the tensions with which the Church of England has to live. And it's a tension actually with which all Anglican churches have to live, and we've got our particular set of institutions for managing it. The Council has now entered that tension, is another element in that tension – the tension between the Synod and the House of Bishops.

I think the House is unclear at the moment about what an active Council might mean for its role in terms of leadership in the Church. My personal view is that the House doesn't have too much to worry about on that score provided that it engages with the Council. If it stands back and just lets the Council get on with it, then there is a danger the Council won't understand what is properly the House's responsibility, it will start playing on their turf, and it'll fail to engage their support, interest, and commitment in what it's trying to do. If the House actively engages with the Council, at the level of specifics – programmes of work, things the Council is doing – then I think it's got a real chance of influencing how it develops. But if it stands back, as I think it tended to do in the early stages of Synodical government, from all I understand, then I think there is a problem. So I hope that the two will engage in continuing dialogue with one another, and work to ensure that that happens.

MF. Are the bishops fearful that something is being taken away from them?

I think that some bishops are concerned about that. In the Council you have a body that contains bishops but also, critically, laity and clergy, which is assuming, and expected to assume, a leadership role in the Church which hitherto the bishops have felt was pretty much their own prerogative. As I say that, I'm conscious of stating the position more sharply than a number of the bishops might want to put it. But I'm doing so in order to give clarity to the situation. I think there are two elements which cause them concern: one is the leadership question, the impact on episcopal leadership; the second is the question of the scope for diocesan autonomy. This has underlaid quite a lot of reaction to the Council.

They are properly concerned about these things. If they can be clear that the work they do is valued, and that if it is to be changed or modified they themselves are part of the process of deciding what is to be changed or modified or not done in the future, then I think anxiety may lessen. Some bishops feel concern about what the Council may mean for the House of Bishops' relationship with the archbishops. If the archbishops find in the Council a very supportive body, with its clergy and lay representatives, what, some bishops wonder, will it do to bishops' particular relationship to the archbishops? I think that they're entirely off-beam in that worry, but it is a worry which some people have articulated.

There is a real debate to be had within the Church about the extent to which we should emphasise diocesan autonomy, or the extent to which we should, on the other hand, be looking to develop national policies in certain areas. This is a tension between the national and the local which many organisations are having to face. The contemporary world is both more global and more international in its outlook, and at the same time more locally focused. So the second concern of the bishops is about whether, as a result of the Council, a whole series of national policies are going to be developed which, in some way, might confine and limit the extent of diocesan autonomy. Hence there's a very strong demand from them for subsidiarity – a vogue concept.

MF. What about the Church House staff and the Council – how are they going to get along together? One or two Church House staff I've talked to are obviously quite anxious about the whole set-up, and its implications for their own work.

There's great nervousness among staff, though not all staff, perhaps because it took a long time to become clear precisely what was going to be implemented. It took three and a half years more or less, and during that period we went through a very predictable fluctuation in staff attitudes. In the beginning they were really quite positive, then we went into a period where everything went quiet – the debate began to be conducted within the political stratosphere, so they naturally became switched off. Towards the end of the period there were a number of compromises, changes and amendments made. Looked at objectively these were right and proper. I mean, if you're going to consult about proposals, you expect to have to change them. But a number of staff saw the changes as compromising in the worst sense of the word, and modifying and moving away from the original idea/concept of *Turnbull*. So there was some disillusionment. We have now got a considerable challenge in terms of building up a mutually confident relationship between staff and Council. I don't think that it's an insuperable challenge, one we can't meet. The staff are naturally concerned about their own employment because that is a factor that everyone is concerned about, but I don't think that is what primarily motivates them. What primarily motivates them is the success of their work, and I think this will make them capable of achieving a rapport with the Council.

In a way that's the immediate challenge. In the first six months of the Council's life we've inevitably had to focus quite a lot of energy in getting the Council itself coalescing as a group, and being clear about what it's about. In the coming period, a lot of effort is going to be, and will have to be rightly devoted to getting Council and staff together to face up to these questions.

Board members too, because they're the other critical factor – the group of members of Synod and other outside experts, who are associated with particular areas of work. The Council is faced with really quite considerable pressures. On the one hand, to continue doing existing work which certainly will have its champions; any piece of work has its champions throughout the Church. There only has to be a whiff of a suggestion in Synod that we might not do something in the future that we've done in the past and immediately a lobby appears! On the other hand, dioceses and parishes are worried about how much it's all costing, and are reasonably saying well, hang on, do you need to do all this? Should the priorities change just at this moment? One of the challenges of the Council will be to try to work with the staff to find ways of addressing those kinds of question. Which should not be seen as destabilising, unsettling and all the rest of it, but of allowing the hard questions to be asked.

MF. Is the new system going to be more expensive than the old one?

No, it shouldn't be, the Council should not cost more in total than the work that preceded it, since it hasn't employed more staff. It's meeting more often than the Standing Committee did, but at least one of the sub-committees of the old Standing Committee isn't meeting now, so rolling the two together it costs about the same. Our object is to try to make sure that it doesn't cost any more, and beyond that to make sure that, over time, it costs less in real terms.

MF. Are the Board's priorities going to be the same as the Council's priorities?

That's the next critical step I'm engaged in. The first report from the Council to the Synod has indicated twelve areas that it thinks it might need to focus on. It's trying to come down a funnel, if you like, with a narrowing neck, and it's trying to say to itself and the Synod, what are the things that we really need to be focusing on? This is an invitation to the Synod and the House of Bishops, to say whether they think the priorities are right and to try to help the Council to narrow them even further. I would rather that the Council does fewer things well than trying to do too much. One of the Church's problems is that because we can see the case for doing work across a whole range, we tend to be shotgun in our approach rather than more focused. We tend to try to pick off a lot of targets at once.

MF. It's encouraging when you get one right, of course?

Yes, it begins to establish a mood of confidence and competence. So I'd rather that we managed to select a few. And, will they be the same as Church House's? Well, in the next six months, and through a process of dialogue, our objective is to try to get Council members and staff and members of Boards talking together about the priorities – are they the right ones? If they are, how could we go about them? So we build up an integrated view about what the priorities are. That's the current challenge.

MF.   If you can do that, you'll probably be home and dry, won't you?

Being a realist we'll get, I hope, 90 per cent of the way. What, of course, is also clear is that there will be great areas of the Council's activities which are essentially reactive. There are always ongoing bits of executive work, or you're reacting to events like briefing bishops for the debates in the House of Lords, or whatever. That's got to be done anyway. So long as we have bishops in the House of Lords, someone will need to brief them. You need a certain resource to be able to do that. There's not a lot of argument in that kind of area about whether you need to do the work or not.

MF.   I can see that one of the advantages of the Council is that they can see certain priorities and initiate ideas. How does anyone else – a Synod member, a member of Church House staff, for example – who sees something that needs doing, set about the process of getting it debated, or anyway considered?

I think there's a lot of scope within the Church to get things on the agenda. One way in which it's regularly done by Synod members is to promote private members' motions in the Synod. That certainly influences agendas. Another is through questions at Synod; they focus areas of concern. Another is through the endless flow of correspondence that comes in. People do influence events by writing, by complaining, by putting questions forward, whether they are Synod members or not. As far as staff are concerned, one of the good things that most staff would say about working in Church House is the degree of autonomy that they have, the capacity that they have to actually mould a job in the direction that they'd like to mould it.

MF.   My concern was whether, under the new system, it will be equally easy to advance the insights learned on the job?

It shouldn't be any more difficult, and it might be easier in that in the Council there will a body that's competent to pick the issue up. I mean, the old Standing Committee, which I don't wish to knock, was essentially a mini-Synod, and the bottom line was that at least some people tended to be on it to stop things happening that they didn't want happening in the Synodical context. In its better moments it got beyond that, and became more positive. In the Council I hope that balance between negative and positive, if you like, has been reversed. Of course, to the extent that we're able to make it representative, there will be differences within it, and people won't be able to hold a common view, and thank heaven for that. On the other hand, where they are of a common view, or where they can see that there's an issue to be dealt with, it's much more its responsibility and recognised as such, to pick an idea up and say, yes, that is something we ought to be dealing with. So in that sense I hope it will be easier.

15

Statistics, Spin and Management

He uses statistics as a drunken man uses lamp-posts – for support rather than illumination. (Andrew Lang)

Under the moulting wing of Mother Church . . . (George Orwell)

There is no doubt that worries about diminishing numbers of those who use the Church, or appear to find it of value, have been important in helping to precipitate extensive change. Quoting the sociologist Grace Davie that we belong to an age of 'believing not belonging' (that there are many who have religious or Christian sympathies but who do not want to join the Church), though it is food for thought, does little to console. Church worries are not in themselves exaggerated – some of the figures would give any organisation proper grounds for concern, though one of the (doomed) ways in which the Church has tried to deal with them is by keeping quiet about them.

A welcome exception is *Youth a Part: Young People and the Church,* a report on youth published for the General Synod Board of Education in 1996, which says that 'the total Sunday attendance at Anglican Churches amongst 14- to 17-year-olds is 60,739', a drop of 34.9 per cent since 1987.[1] It does not take very advanced arithmetic to see that, if the same rate continues to apply, there may be no young people at all in the Church in twenty years time. The report goes on to say that this does not just apply to church services – a similar drop has also been observed in church organisations. Reasons given by young people are ones of boredom, lack of interest, distaste for others taking part, and poor facilities and organisation. These problems might theoretically be fairly easy to rectify, but it is difficult not to suspect that they might be part of a much bigger problem, to do both with the general secularisation of our society, and perhaps with the Church's own loss of self-esteem and vitality.

The decline in numbers spreads throughout the other age ranges, though not so dramatically, and all this towards the end of the Decade of Evangelism which was supposed to help set things right. Betty Saunders, in her interesting, but rather determinedly upbeat, account of the Church, says 'Twenty-two people in a thousand will be in Church of England churches on Sunday, a total of about 1,090,400 out of a population of 40 million: a few more than will be going to football on Saturday.'[2] (If she was referring to adults, the figure is now more like nineteen in a thousand.) To see the Church as marginally more successful as a crowd-puller than football in a society where football often seems the major focus of commitment and devotion *is* a cheering idea. This diminution into a sect, however – as it might be a sect of opera-lovers, badminton players, or bird-fanciers, is not how the Church has traditionally seen its task; rather it regarded itself as omnipresent and universal in its meaning. It would seem that it must either lower its ambition, or admit that it is not keeping up.

The second idea might be valuable because it breaks the habit of denial, the 'public relations' insistence that all is well, and thereby offers the opportunity of 'working through' the inevitable depression, and moving on with deepened understanding to a more realistic grasp of the problem. There is little sign that this is happening. The tendency is to search for the 'quick fix', a hope that some secular trick will catch the fancy of people young or old – 'pumping Indie' in the hallowed precincts of St Paul's Cathedral, importing 'business methods' and the language of consumerism on to the Archbishops' Council, inflating the very modest numerical successes of the Church here and there, and even suppressing evidences of decline. No harm in trying these things, I suppose, though they may devalue the currency of what the Church says about itself, which may in turn become a problem, but they do seem to have 'lost the plot', the quintessential Anglican style of doing things.

Spinning the News
An interesting correspondence about this took place in the Roman Catholic weekly the *Tablet* in January 1999. The doyen of religious columnists, Clifford Longley, writing about 'spin doctoring', the art of trying to improve one's image by correcting what is felt to be a skewed picture of it presented by the media, says 'Sadly, even the Churches are being seduced by these black arts.' And he went on to suggest that journalists were unhappy with the style of the Reverend Dr William Beaver, the Church of England's Director of Communications (as the spin-doctor-in-chief is called), and his

211

determination that they should write 'what he wants them to write about'. Longley feels concern about this – that a sense of truth is being lost. If the price for this is for the churches to be badmouthed, he says, then so be it – it is the job of Christians to be 'a sign of contradiction'.[3]

William Beaver replied to this criticism by denying spin-doctoring,[4] saying that it was, after all, his responsibility 'to represent the efforts of literally millions whose labours and prayers make up a considerably more confident Church of England than for many years'. He cites the difficulty of his task, by describing how when, previously, he had tried to interest a journalist in 'another annual rise' in the number of ordinations, he had not wanted to know, indeed had remarked cynically that 'the Church of England getting its act together isn't news'.

Clifford Longley was unconvinced.

> The primary responsibility of an honest press officer is to openness and to the truth, good, bad or indifferent, not the suppression of facts or the 'talking up' of a particular trend. I believe the Church of England made a fundamental mistake in its press relations when it decided in principle some time ago that its approach had to become much more aggressive. Dr Beaver says he was disappointed by the media response when he tried to put out a story about an annual rise in ordinations. Yet he withheld publication of the annual church attendance figures for the Church of England, which rumour says showed a drop below the million mark for the first time, because they did not fit the image he was trying to create. That is why the press won't listen.[5]

In a further response William Beaver claimed that the former statistic the Church of England used to indicate 'Usual Sunday Attendance' was 'a rather clumsy financial tool which the press looked on as the sole indicator of Anglican worldly well-being' and that this was why it had vanished from Church publications.[6]

I think Clifford Longley's point stands – the Church is much more niggardly with depressing figures than it used to be. *Church Statistics* are still published,[7] but alongside them is a free 'summary of current statistics', the one most people are likely to read, a pamphlet the size of an A4 sheet, which is very selective indeed.[8]

Everything You Are Allowed to Know
It begins with anodyne 'good news' about the numbers of dioceses, parishes, church schools and colleges, and church links with other churches here and overseas. Nothing very startling there. Then,

under the heading 'The Nation's Church', it tells us that in 1994 there were 86,000 weddings in Church of England churches – a third of all weddings. In 1996 189,000 people were baptised and 43,000 confirmed. 1,290,000 people were on electoral rolls in the same year. On Easter Day 1,242,000 people took communion and 1,344,000 on Christmas Day.[9]

This might suggest, is clearly intended to suggest, that a lot of people are using and valuing the Church, and a million *is* quite a lot of people, though only a small percentage of a population of 40 million (figures for England, not the United Kingdom). But the figures cannot be adequately 'read' unless one can compare them with earlier sets of figures. For example, in 1984, ten years before the 'new' figure, there were 111,248 marriages, as I discover from an old set of church statistics on my shelves. In 1993 there were 91,214. If we go back two years before the official baptism figures to 1994 the total number of baptisms was 203,480 and this was itself a small drop on the figure for 1993. The Electoral Roll figures (the figures of those who sign up for church membership) in 1994 was 1,478,500 (actually a slight increase over 1993). (To be fair, there was a general revision of Rolls in 1996, which always results in some pruning of those who have left or died but have got left on the lists, so this figure may not be a very significant one.) Easter Day communicants in 1994 were 1,299,700 and Christmas Day communicants 1,487,800 – revealing a small drop by 1996 in the Easter figures and a rather large one at Christmas over the two year period. The new sheet illustrates just three sets of statistics by graph – the numbers of those recommended for ordained ministry, the amount parishes are contributing to stipends, and the amount given by parishioners in 'covenanted planning', all modest successes.

The pamphlet ends up at the old saluting base. 'The Church of England is a dynamic community of men, women, children and young people who in their lives and work are the body of Christ.'[10] Well not *that* dynamic – a dwindling body, in fact, with fingers and toes dropping off here and there. To set against the mathematics of decline suggestions that everyone does not go to church at once, or that giving is rising modestly, seems to be a desperate reaching for a meaning that so far is just not there. Two swallows don't make a summer. A more comprehensive set of figures does appear in *The Church of England Yearbook* but, true to the Church's present bashfulness, it is equally coy about church attendance there.

This 'talking up', as Clifford Longley calls it, is, in the true sense of that now much-misused word, pathetic, not least because it does not deceive those the Church would like most to deceive – that is to

213

say, the press. It may, I suppose, pull the wool over the eyes of the ordinary churchgoer, though those with any real commitment to their churches know, at least in less affluent parishes, what a struggle it is to make ends meet, as well as to attract people to church. But if keeping the truth from the press means also being economical with it with the ordinary churchgoer than something has already gone very wrong. Economy with the truth does nothing to encourage a realistic assessment of the dangers nor does it give a clear message of what is needed from ordinary lay people – apart from money – to help it to survive, if that is what the laity want it to do. A hush-hush policy, in which only the 'grown-ups' are allowed to know the bad news, infantilises us all.

The Reason Why
It is possible to know all this, however, and still feel a lot of sympathy for the reasons behind it. As the Secretary-General, Philip Mawer, remarked in interview, 'It is sickening to know that there are some very good things going on in the Church, but find ourselves stereotyped by the press as a failing institution nevetheless.'[11] I wonder whether the Church does not exaggerate the power and importance of the press, including how much the population believes what they read in it, and whether it would not do better to give up trying to seduce it, an action which so easily produces the opposite effect from that intended. Why not simply say, 'Things are difficult, but we are working on it'? Why not just work away behind the scenes trying to make everything better (as it *is* energetically doing, of course) and let the press look more and more foolish if and when people's experience varies from what is being printed in the papers? The Church may not welcome the idea but it could learn here from the experience of the Movement for the Ordination of Women. The pioneers in the 1970s and early 1980s suffered a good deal from press ridicule – 'bosomy women in T-shirts', 'butch women in boiler-suits', 'aggressive', 'strident', 'Nazi fellow-travellers in jack boots' (the *Daily Mail*), etc., but as time went on and the case was increasingly seen to be put by normal women (and men), this ludicrous carica-turing began to make the press look much sillier than those advocating women priests, and almost overnight the press changed its tune. The truth won out, not by way of any huge publicity machine or 'spin', still less by suppression of relevant facts, but by dogged 'carrying on', pleasant spokeswomen, one of whom was finally described in the *Evening Standard* as 'a classy filly', and painstaking dialogue and 'education' at every possible level. Nothing is so effective as the truth, as Christians should not need reminding.

So Who Are the Christians?

Luckily, for those of us who like to look facts in the face, there is an independent publication *Religious Trends*,[12] which publishes a much more extensive and less tendentious set of figures about churchgoing and religion than the Church of England. Its proprietor, Peter Brierley, told me that he believes that the churches need much more information about available facts if they are to make effective decisions.[13] He begins from a different standpoint from the Communications Department and the Statistics Unit of the Church, the very useful one of looking at Christianity in general in Britain, and also of looking at the growth of other religions, often in relation to immigration.

Religious Trends shows that, in the United Kingdom in 1995, around 65 per cent of the population were Christian, or thought themselves to be so, using the traditional yardstick of trinitarian theology, which includes all the mainstream churches. Of the rest of the population 28 per cent described themselves as non-religious and 7 per cent belonged to other religions, which includes the figures for non-trinitarian Christians. *Religious Trends* uses two diagrams to describe the shades of religious devotion, one for 1980 and one for 1990. Both diagrams use a large circle which contains at the centre two overlapping circles. The space (D) between the outer circle and the two inner circles represents 'notional Christians', those who accede somewhat vaguely to Christian ideas but have no kind of church commitment. Those in the left-hand inner circle (A) are those who attend a place of worship at least once a month. Those in the right-hand inner circle (C) are church members who don't go to church because of age, infirmity, or for some other reason – what *Religious Trends* describes as 'nominal' Christians in contrast to 'notional' ones. Those in the section where the two inner circles overlap (B) are those who attend regularly and belong to a local church. In 1980 there were 47 per cent in the unattached 'notional' D category, 3 per cent in the 'once a month' A group, 9 per cent in the 'nominal' C group and 8 per cent in the overlapping B group who could be said to wholly belong. In the 1990 diagram, in contrast, 50 per cent of the population have joined the D category and become 'notional', 1 per cent belong to the A category of occasional church going, 5 per cent are members of the C 'nominal' group and 9 per cent are fully practising.[14]

The ten-year shift of a 1 per cent rise in the number of fully committed and practising Christians, together with the penumbra of vaguely wannabe Christians, though not brilliant news of the kind Dr Beaver would illustrate with a graph, might, perhaps, be taken as evidence of an interesting switch in public attitudes. It would seem that there is still good feeling abroad about Christianity – see the numbers of nominal and notional Christians – but fewer people are interested in 'the name without the game', lip-service to a Church they no longer attend. People are less inclined to go because it is 'the thing' – indeed at present it is not 'the thing', and this might be registered as a stroke for honesty, or at least an absence of hypocrisy. On the other hand, there is this modest increase in those who are fully committed. This is, of course, a statistic of Christian attitudes in general, and is not specific to the Church of England, but it seems to indicate something potentially important.

Apart from this small straw in the wind, statistics about the Church of England, or indeed about the churches in general, are not encouraging. In the twenty years between 1980 and 2000 the Church of England suffered a 27 per cent decline in church membership. The Roman Catholic Church suffered a similar decline in the same period in mass attendance. Methodists, Baptists and others suffered decline too, though in all the churches, it must be said, there have been significant successes in certain churches and particular enterprises. The only institutional church which has continued to grow has been the Orthodox Church – Greek and Russian – where demand for churches exceeds supply, mainly because of immigration from Orthodox countries.

There is a rather touching footnote to all this, which is that people questioned about how much they go to church, give figures which, if true, would add up to twice those given by the churches. I suppose there could be different interpretations of this. My suggestion is that it indicates a wistfulness to belong; it can be seen as a kind of statement about the person people wish to be, as the unread books on bookshelves (of those who still read books) may say something about a fantasy self. It is a secret revelation which seems worth noting, though not in order to organise some kind of power-play around it. It would be useful if it promoted a sober study of what it is that has gone wrong if many people long to be part of the Christian enterprise, yet cannot actually bring themselves to do so.

An interesting set of comparisons for the Church of England is the way numbers are increasing or declining in different kinds of churchmanship. I wonder if it is possible to be quite so clear as *Religious Trends* manages to be about where divisions occur. I am not clear, for instance, about the difference, within a Church of England context, between 'Anglo-Catholics' and 'Catholics'; and 'Broad' for the liberal wing of the Church has a rather old-fashioned feel. 'Catholics', the largest group, estimated to number about a million by the year 2000 are declining the fastest, but what demands notice is that charismatic Evangelicals, still one of the smaller groups in the Church, are growing rapidly – by around 6,000 every five years. Evangelical Christians, according to the nomenclature of *Religious Trends*, are also growing and moving up towards the half million mark. These last two groups are undeniably success stories numerically, and more power to their elbow.

Numbers of parishioners, or of people using the church are not, of course, simply evidence of the loss of interest in Christian belief or of the Church's failure to stimulate it; they have a direct effect on the finances of the Church. Further big losses in the numbers of churchgoers could drive some dioceses towards bankruptcy.

Clearly the Church feels that its hopeful news at the moment is in the number of men and women being being accepted as ordinands – people training to be clergy. In a church where clergy play such an important role as they do in the Church of England numbers of clergy are important. There has been a slow fall in the number of stipendiary clergy (as opposed to NSMs, i.e. non-stipendiary clergy), with women priests helping to make up in numbers the loss of men. In 1980 there were 11,053 ordained men. In 1995 there were 9,440 men and 820 women – actually rather encouraging figures in terms of sheer numbers.

When do People Go to Church?

It was, I think I am right in saying, Peter Brierley who first pointed out that those closely allied with the Church may number many more than collected figures let it appear – and it is this observation that has been seized upon by the Church as an excuse for not publishing churchgoing figures until 'more research has been carried out'. Brierley suggested that whereas modern churchgoing patterns *do* often involve people going regularly, that no longer means weekly, as it once did, but maybe fortnightly or monthly, itself an indication of changing social patterns. I have myself noticed that whereas the total number of attenders at my parish church is about the same almost every Sunday – 30 to 40 people – this group is drawn from a much wider pool of people who attend regularly but not every week. Brierley quotes the kind of reasons people give for coming to church less frequently than once a week:

> It's the only day we can get to see my mother because it takes us three hours to get there.

> I work on Sundays.

We have a caravan at X and we like to spend summer weekends there.

My son plays football on a Sunday and he likes me to go and watch him.[15]

These are all indications that Christians are now living in a secular society (one that makes it difficult or impossible for them to preserve Sunday as a day dedicated to religious observance), and that work, family and living patterns have all changed radically since the Second World War. The tendency in family life for both parents to work outside the home also imposes extra burdens in terms of getting household chores done, as does the widespread habit of DIY. There are also many opportunities for Sunday entertainment, hobbies, and weekends away, etc. that were not once available. The Church can do little more than attract and persuade people to church.

T. S. Eliot once addressed the subject in minatory tones reminiscent of an Old Testament prophet:

> I journeyed to the suburbs, and there I was told:
> We toil for six days, on the seventh we must motor
> To Hindhead or Maidenhead.
> If the weather is foul we stay at home and read the papers . . .
> And the Church does not seem to be wanted . . .
> And now you live dispersed on ribbon roads,
> And no man knows or cares who is his neighbour . . .
> But all dash to and fro in motor cars . . .[16]

There is truth in this, of course, but the lordly tone recalls that of middle-class Victorian Christians who could not understand why the much put-upon labourers of their day did not wish to come to church in their very few hours of liberty. No doubt, from the relative ease of Faber and Faber, and European holidays at a time when most working people never got further than Brighton or Southend, it was difficult to understand why those who worked, as he admits, six days a week, might prefer motor cars, if they could get them (as George Carey's parents could not) and a trip to the country, to the fine prose of Cranmer. As for knowing one's neighbour, somehow one cannot see Old Possum dropping in for a cup of sugar or taking in the odd parcel, something many working people did then and do now. Perhaps superiority – about social habits, money, education and sex – has got to go if the Church is ever again to be seen as a welcoming place, rather than one where people are judged and found wanting.

But also a place where people do not feel used, manipulated, pushed around as so many already feel in the work places where 'managerialism' has taken over. In the last few years a number of senior clergy have taken management courses, and have returned full of the jargon – 'the product', 'line management', 'performance indicators', 'pew counts' etc. In October 1997, the *Guardian* described an archdeacon from Leeds, the Venerable John Oliver, who was studying at the Leeds Business School (£4,130), where he would take an Institute of Directors' Diploma in company direction.[17] He would learn 'business strategy', 'organisation culture and strategic management' and 'devise change strategies and generate strategic options'. He was enthusiastic about getting 'real guidance in man [sic] management'. Trying to be fair, I thought well, maybe a little organisation never did anyone any harm, but then I read what Bishop John Sentamu said about managerialism a few lines further on and caught the full drift of what this new movement is all about. 'We've got a product to sell which is the love of God. If you are in the business of communicating a product, you've got to do it well. In the future the best parish priest will be the best organiser.' Thinking of good parish priests I had known, some of whom had been good organisers and some had not, I thanked my lucky stars that what they had made me, and others, feel, was that they actually cared about us as individuals, not as pawns in some pew-filling plan. They 'sold' the love of God all right, but entirely unselfconsciously, and only because they gave their own love freely and uncalculatingly. We were not their 'target', their sales statistic, or their consumers. I thought the bishop's statement came as near to blasphemy as I had ever heard any bishop utter (and that is saying a good deal).

I was glad to see that Professor Richard Roberts of Lancaster University called this development the 'McDonaldisation of the Church'. 'Managerialism is about pursuing objectives with minimum cost and getting value for money. It's a form of political economy which leads to the commodification of every part of people's lives and this can become extraordinarily intrusive.' He might have added that it primes people to fit submissively and unquestioningly into global capitalism. But he made it admirably if depressingly clear, that, from here on, the real Christians are going to have to be dissidents in the system.

Bright the Vision: Ways of Thinking about the Church

Churchgoing figures hold steady one year, so there is excitement that the tide has begun to turn, and people feel there is no need to do anything differently – churches will start to fill again of their own accord. Then, the following year, churchgoing figures are down again. It is not too difficult to see how decline becomes a way of life. That is just how things are. (Robin Gill[1])

It is becoming something of a practice, almost a sport, for people (well, clergy mostly) to make analyses of the Church, and suggest ways to correct its various problems. In a review in the *Church Times* in February 1999 of yet another book on the subject, *A Church for the 21st Century*,[2] David Edwards suggested wisely that part of the problem may be the Church's absorption 'in the problems of organising its own ... life'. Self-consciousness becomes its own handicap. But it is a universal tendency to obsess about issues which are unresolved, and the future pattern of the Church has, so far, barely begun to take shape.

Turnbull's plan of a 'coherent' and 'transparent' Church grouped around the Archbishops' Council, is the design on the drawing-board at the moment, and it is gradually getting off the drawing-board and out into the dioceses and parishes. This plan is for a 'slimmed-down' but also a 'managed' Church, much of the money coming, not as hitherto, from the investments of the past, via the Church Commissioners, but out of the pockets of churchgoers. 'Subsidiarity' is the smart word here, yet, confusingly, it is combined with increased centralisation and additional hierarchy. Which must at least invite us to ask the question whether 'subsidiarity' is a device for appearing democratic while actually maintaining tight controls about what people are allowed to do at the grass roots. The two other best-known users of 'subsidiarity', the Roman Catholic Church (who invented it), and New Labour, are not necessarily reassuring examples.

If he/she who pays the piper calls the tune, however, 'those who do contribute . . . are likely to want an ever more significant say in the running of the church, at parish, diocesan and national levels'.[3] I see little sign of general awareness of this possibility in Church statements – the assumption, and it is one that is very typical of the Church of England, is that the laity will be as traditionally docile as they have been in the past. Subsidiarity may have some shocks in store. Already there are signs of parishes refusing to pay quotas when they disagree with diocesan actions, though this development, so far, tends to be clergy-led, used as a political instrument to bludgeon the Church into agreement on vexed issues such as women priests and homosexuality.

However, the full working out of these ideas is in the far distance. What is evident at the moment is the clear intention of the present Archbishop (and *Turnbull* is very much his baby) to set in train a wholesale return to the Church. This is seen very much in terms of 'conversion', and the success of the evangelical and charismatic churches who take, as it were a 'hard' view of being a Christian (a requirement of both religious experience and commitment, not just a drifting into church), certainly lends credence to the idea that this could work. At least with some people.

Yet by no means all members of the Church of England are likely to see the way forward in terms of wholesale evangelism. Whether or not the idea is likely, they might have reservations about what might get lost or hidden beneath a mass movement that ignored the doubts and uncertainties of present day England. Forget the methods of the past. What form should Christianity take *now*, they might ask? It is our task to find our own authentic voice, not mimic that of some former 'age of faith'.

Having said that, it is vital to address the *fact* of decline. No philosophical, theological or psychological talk will replace the question of 'What are we actually going to *do*?' and *Turnbull* is a bold and painstaking attempt at an answer. Those who believe it inadequate have to show that they too have put serious thought and effort into a way if not forward, then at least *through*.

One Man's Vision

Robin Gill, already mentioned above, has made the attempt, which *Turnbull* does not, to analyse in depth the reason for widespread decline in churchgoing. In his most significant book, *The Myth of the*

Empty Church[4] he examines a number of the 'myths' (in the sense of untruths or quasi-truths) that surround the whole subject of church-going decline as defined by the fact of empty, or half empty, churches. His researches and thinking on the subject open up new ways of looking at the phenomenon. He shows that the decline started much longer ago than most people think, at least as long ago as 1900. One of the factors that brought about half empty churches was an over-enthusiasm for building churches which had the effect of fragmenting congregations. There was sometimes a spirit of rivalry over this, as between Methodists and Anglicans vying for members, or between Methodist groups of different persuasion, who divided the available churchgoers between them. The Roman Catholic Church, in contrast to the other mainstream churches, had relatively few churches for the numbers they served, which presented the encouraging sight of full churches for mass. The Church of England, on the other hand, being generously subsidised, found it possible to maintain too many churches and to pay too many people to service too few Christians. Very small congregations present a depressing sight to casual churchgoers, and also do not usually contain the energy and variety of gifts needed to make a church buzz. If nothing succeeds like success, nothing fails like failure. What is fresh and thought-provoking about Gill is the recognition that structural problems unwittingly hastened the decline of the churches, at least as much as other things that have been blamed – cars, television, the growth of Sunday and community activities of various kinds.

Another very interesting theme which Gill touches upon rather than explains is the effect of secularisation. Many writers, including myself, have cited the growing secularisation of our society as an element of key importance in the decline in churchgoing. But Gill asks the pertinent question 'Why is that the United States of America, apparently just as secularised as Europe, has such a large churchgoing population?' He does not have an answer, and neither, as far as I know, does anyone else.

What seems the bedrock of his research is the fact that, in England, what kept the Church going as long as it did, was the children of families which were already Christian. This handing on of the baton of the faith concealed the fact that it was not reaching out particularly successfully to those outside the fold, so that as, in our own time, the children fall away, there is no new blood to bring the necessary vitality to the Church. Precious money and resources, Gill feels, got poured into the maintenance of the status quo, and not enough into mission, nor was there sufficient recognition of the kinds of clergy who were good at bringing people in to the Church. 'Financial and deployment subsidies should be seen as the seed-corn to promote mission,' he says.[5] On the other hand he does not seem all that sanguine about 'church planting', or about evangelical gains, seeing both of them as simply removing worshippers from other churches, and thus indirectly adding to the empty churches which themselves precipitate decline.

Gill did not leave the matter there. In the year after *The Myth of the Empty Church* he published *A Vision for Growth*, a study of what makes churches grow, and what stops them, emptiness apart.

He begins his study of churchgoing and the lack of it with an encouraging emphasis on need and longing. 'People need to worship . . . worship needs people.'[6] To Gill worship is a natural activity which our society has somehow lost touch with or forgotten how to do, and which he believes is connected to values. The effect of people getting together to worship God seems, he notes, to produce a kind of social glue – certainly in the community as a whole, the proportion of churchgoers, or at least notional Christian believers (in Brierley's terms) who play an active role in trying to make life better for others, as their belief actually requires them to do, is surprisingly large. 'The strongest finding suggests that the person who is most likely to be involved in voluntary work, of one kind or another, is both a believer and a churchgoer.'[7] This may be 'do-gooding', but it does good. It would be possible to show, if anyone had a mind to do it, that specific groups of people, near and far, are measurably better off for the efforts of a small community with ideas about loving its neighbour. This is not to say that others who are not Christians do not do good, and do not feel concern for others – plainly they do. It does seem to be useful, however, to have an organisation that is in place, which makes the whole exercise very much easier and less formal than the social services, and whose members feel an imperative to try to do good things for others.

Gill suggests that the Christian imperative for 'loving one's neighbour as oneself' emerges from 'worship', the activity now partly lost to many of us. In worship the primary direction is towards loving God – prayers, psalms, hymns, sermon, ritual, holy communion are about turning away from the obsession with oneself and reorientating oneself into a bigger landscape, which then places others in a different, less competitive light.

The real heart and guts of the Christian religion (and this perhaps is something on which all Christians might agree) is about a God being encountered in worship and also within everyday life and relationships, suffering and joy. Some believers might say that they were not sure a lot of the time whether they had much sense of God (others would claim a different experience), but that occasionally, and sometimes crucially, they have, or have had in the past, such a sense, and that this was the pivot on which everything else to do with faith turned. It made it possible to put up with much else – disappointment with the Church, with life, with fear, sickness, death, but it also brought a special quality of joy. The central mystery, with the life and death of Jesus pointing towards its heart, is seen as the truth, however imperfectly understood, a truth around which other truths in life may be arranged.

Gill sums up his simple doctrine. 'For the whole of the twentieth century, empty churches have been sending out an unambiguous signal. It is simply this: religion is failing, churches are on the way out, churchgoing is a thing of the past, secularism of the future.'[8]

He sets out his stall of what, in his view, will change the prognosis. He begins by saying, unarguably, that 'the primary motivation for church growth is theological – the conviction that worshipping God in Christ is the most distinctive thing that Christians can do'.[9] What he calls his 'most important precept' is the realisation that 'most people change churchgoing habits when something else is changing in their lives'.[10] I take this to mean that newcomers are most likely to join the Church at points of growth or need. These might arise as a result of marriage, the birth of a child, some startling success, or it might be as a result of bereavement, an acute disappointment, being made redundant, marriage breakdown, illness, psychological breakdown, failure or disgrace. Clergy *are* often turned to in all these situations – as also at weddings, baptisms, funerals and, more informally, on hospital and home visits. When people are happy there is often a longing to open themselves to God, and equally when life is hard there is a hope that religion may carry them through. So that *response* to these heightened times of sensitivity, not just from clergy but from all church people, would seem to be natural and caring, an invitation and a welcoming that is a mile away from the 'bums-on-seats' attitude.

Liturgy, the church services themselves, are another area Gill recommends for study. Whatever a church does it will not please everybody – 'your or my ritual is always someone else's superstition'[11] – but it needs to be accessible to newcomers, pleasing to ear and eye and intelligence, and, given the widespread ignorance of Christian ideas, at least somewhat educational. Gill urges charity in not condemning forms of worship which may not be up one's own street. Talking of overcoming his own doubts of charismatic worship, he says 'I am beginning to get used to the arm waving and tongues. It is not everyone's taste, but then neither are Bach, vestments and incense.'[12] We need charity in worship, as in all else.

Education is Gill's next necessity – religious education for children which they very probably will not now receive anywhere else, and education for adults in the form of active prayer and study groups. The decline not just in Christian belief, but in basic knowledge of what the religion that framed our culture was about, has accelerated rapidly within a generation, Gill points out, as Christian instruction has been removed from schools, and as the Sunday Schools have themselves declined.

Some sense of real responsibility for the finances of the Church is also important for the congregation if they are to make a proper contribution. He believes strongly in the importance of congregations taking a responsible attitude to finances. In the past, money seemed to come miraculously to Anglican congregations, some of it because wealthy landowners or industrialists either thought religion would be good for the lower classes, or because they saw it as a form of soul-saving. Gill describes the huge boom among all the denominations at Barrow-in-Furness in the 1880s. Not to be outdone by the burgeoning Free Church growth, the Anglicans opened four large churches on the same day. Each church cost £6,000, of which the Duke of Devonshire paid half, and the Duke of Buccleuch, and the shareholders in Furness Railway and Barrow Steelworks, provided most of the rest. 'Only a sixteenth of the total cost of the four churches was raised directly from local churchgoers.'[13] This was in striking contrast to the local chapels where most of the money was raised by the chapel-goers themselves. 'The Church of England' has been 'suffering for many years from the effects of unchallenged, open-ended subsidy. To put it bluntly, they have subsidized their own long-term decline.'[14] This is a difficult background for members of the Church of England to grow out of, and one of the good things about *Turnbull* is that it insists that they must do so.

Lay ministry or shared ministry with churches in other denominations may also help to eke out stretched budgets, and might well bring considerable benefits of its own. Gill is critical of the way stipendiary ministry has made churchgoers dependent on their minister, and prevented the growth of a strong laity who fully understand the theological, liturgical and even executive implications of everything that is done in their church. Certainly the growth of extra-ecclesial groups – feminist and gay, in particular – revealed both how timid lay people were, initially, in composing liturgy or in leading services, and then how much confidence and joy they gained as they realised they could do it, and discovered that it deepened their understanding considerably. 'I suddenly saw what the eucharist was about for the first time,' a woman at the St Hilda Community, a lively Christian feminist group, told me. Childish dependency on 'the Vicar' is not the way forward for the Church, but much thought will need to go into training clergy to a somewhat different expectation of their role. Among the changes that Gill sees as vital in a changing Church are the laity supplying gifts and functions to supplement those of the clergy (there is some of that going on already), and the laity being freed to ask difficult questions about any aspect of church life (of which, I suspect, there is very little going on). 'One of the most disturbing and challenging discoveries is that stipendiary ministry can sometimes impede the ministry of a congregation.'[15]

Church communities thrive on a mixture of executive ability, financial expertise, aesthetic sensitivity and skill, particularly in the areas of music, drama and artistic ability, and teaching ability, particularly in the area of work with the young. Few congregations of less than fifty have the human resources to generate interest, though even one or two exceptionally able people can make a huge difference. The legacy of this is that the sense of community which is what attracts people to belong to a church is harder to achieve, and clergy become overworked in trying to fill the gaps. In the country, in particular, clergy may find themselves 'looking after' three or more churches. Surveys suggest that clergy with two or more congregations begin to lose vital contact with members.

Gill maps out a plan for church growth by *analysis* – the mapping of points of strength and weakness; *planning* – the drawing up of a careful plan setting attainable objectives; *responsibility* – identifying ways in which churchgoers may be encouraged to take responsibility for new growth; *development* – identifying new opportunities for growth; and *testing* – having set the other parts of the plan in motion, testing to make sure that the growth is being attained.

He talks, I think very effectively, of the need for a sense of *ownership* in a congregation. 'The modern concept of ownership suggests that all members of an organization have a real role in decision making and feel responsible for the decisions once made.' It follows from this that congregations will play a very big, even a decisive, part in choosing their incumbent.

Gill's conclusion is typically low-key and modest. 'If a particular plan does not produce growth, then admit as much, and try another plan. Keep trying, keep being honest, and keep testing. That is how dynamic bodies grow, even in difficult times.'[16]

Meeting between Archbishop Geoffrey Fisher
and Cardinal John Heenan, c. 1960. 'I have seen the future ...'

The Coronation of Her Majesty the Queen in Westminster Abbey, June 1953.

CND. Canon John Collins and others marching from Aldermaston, 1959.

Archbishop Michael Ramsey, 1974.

Fr Trevor Huddleston of Sophiatown.

Archbishop Robert Runcie in 1981. The first media Archbishop.

Archbishop Robert Runcie after signing the agreement
with Pope John Paul II, 1989.

Terry Waite, just released after five years of being
a hostage in Lebanon, January 1987.

Archbishop-Designate George Carey
greeting Cardinal Basil at General Synod in November 1990.

Archbishop George Carey addressing
the Evangelical Alliance in December 1996.

Campaigning for women priests outside Church House at General Synod,
September 1989.

Campaigning for women priests outside St Paul's Cathedral, September 1991.

Meeting of Cost of Conscience (clergy opposed to the
ordination of women) at Church House in 1990.

Women ordained to the priesthood at St Paul's Cathedral, April 1994.

© J. M. Rosenthal

'Shame'. A group of women and men protest at General Synod at the passing of the Act of Synod in November 1993.

© Steve Mayes/Church Times

Outrage demonstrates at a meeting of the Courage Trust (a group claiming a 'cure' for homosexuality) at St Andrew's, Chorleywood.

Living with Conflict

Another interesting study of the prospects of the Church is *Say One for Me: The Church of England in the next Decade* (1992) a collection of essays edited by Wesley Carr. It is sharply focused on the Church of England as Gill's work is not (though an Anglican himself, and shrewd about the Church of England, Gill is usually addressing Christian churches in general), and begins from asking the most fundamental question of all: 'Is there a future for the Church of England?' It works, as I believe the most helpful analyses must, from a sense of the way the Church has been strongly determined by its history. The painful and violent legacy of this has often been skilfully ignored or airbrushed into something more appealing, but this has not helped 'Divisions, which have hitherto been mainly contained, are now becoming so critical that a consensus can no longer be sustained. The old familiar splits persist, such as those discerned between Catholic and Reformed (Evangelical). The two wings, however, seem to unite in the face of another grouping – "the liberal establishment".'[17]

Carr thinks the synodical system not merely demonstrated, but aggravated, and brought into greater prominence, differences which, formerly, were handled in 'more discreet ways'. He also suggests that the differences now stretch back behind Synod and into the parishes. Writing just before the vote which brought about women's ordination to the priesthood, he remarked gloomily, but somewhat prophetically, that the differences 'might not be contained much longer'. They were, we know now, but at the dangerously high price of the Act of Synod, which in a sense did not contain them at all but simply postponed a resolution, at some cost to the women and to the authority of diocesan bishops. 'There is a perennial question about how much conflict should be borne and how much it can be sustained without the membership of the institution declining into a debilitated quarrelsome few.'[18] This is a sober, almost Lenten, estimation.

Carr goes on to say, however, that the vitality of the Church has been, to a large degree, 'generated through conflict' – 'it has never been united in any obvious sense'. A kind of ecclesiastical Balkans, the Church of England has found itself forced by its tumultuous history to live with conflict. Up till now it has found a way for people of different shades of Christian belief to live together, often with surprising good humour, while placing their emphasis variously on tradition, ritual, the Bible, the Spirit, reason. Will the habit last?

Carr is no lover of synodical government. For him, the answer (in 1992) was to put everything back into the hands of the bishops. 'There is, for instance, a major problem as to whether this sort of church can sustain – or should attempt to sustain – a synodical form of Government and whether this is appropriate to an episcopally ordered church . . . If the synodical system diminishes, or even attempts to remove, the influence of the episcopate, then what sort of church is left?'[19]

I am not clear in what way, before 1992, Carr felt that 'the influence of the episcopate' was undermined or removed, or indeed what was so damaging about the Synod. What has happened, via *Turnbull*, in my view, is that the role of General Synod, or those who work for it in Church House, has been somewhat lessened by the creation of the Archbishops' Council. Very possibly, by the same token, the role of the bishops has also lessened. This may or may not be because of specific changes in the way business is conducted – it is too soon to be quite clear about that – but rather because of a change of focus, the 'bishop-in-Synod' as the lever of Anglican government having lost ground to the 'cabinet', the Archbishops' Council.

Carr paints an attractive picture of what the Church of England has it in it to be at its best, when, he suggests, it follows the *via media*. Elevating tolerance as a virtue, walking in the footsteps of Jewel, Hooker, Andrewes, Maurice, Gore, Temple and Ramsey, he describes the Church as having evolved a method which 'gives priority to God and the unknowability of faith'. 'First there is thoughtfulness, a gently sceptical attitude towards certainties which other Christians may display. The second mark is holiness, a sense that in the end all that matters is a sense of the presence of God, which is usually found in public worship . . .'[20] Carr sees the task of the priest as an interpretative one – 'to interpret people's experience of life in relation to God, thus putting them into a divine perspective'.[21] This interpretative task operates within the framework of the parochial system. This is part of what he calls the 'incarnational' style of the Church.

Another contributor to Carr's book, Bernice Martin, a sociologist at London University, makes a telling point about meaning. All human beings, she claims, need a sense of meaning in their lives – not necessarily religious, but it needs to be a meaning that makes life feel coherent. And societies frequently, if not invariably, show a bias towards looking for religious meaning, 'a powerful and recurrent desire for a transcendent reference'.[22] For four hundred years the Church of England was the main provider of that frame of reference in much of British society. It provided 'the clearest, most systematically articulated and authoritative source of overarching meaning'.[23] She suggests, quite hesitantly, that the Church may be 'steadily losing its role as holder (of meaning)', or articulator of overarching meaning. A powerful case can be made, for example, for considering the new mass media as serious rivals in the business of offering meaning in modern society. Yet, she continues, 'the readiness with which people still reach for the church . . . to plug gaps in meaning and celebrate identity suggests that at least an important residue of the role remains in place'.[24] This suggests that now, the new millennium, may be a turning-point in the Church's history ('the tide', as Hamlet put it, 'which taken at the flood leads on to greater things'), or alternatively it may be the moment in which the Church sinks beneath the waves of controversy and misunderstanding of its potential.

Robin Gill and the contributors to Wesley Carr's symposium favour the sober style of the medical consultant. One may not trust their expertise or their prejudices at every point, but the bedside manner is reassuringly quiet. Mark Stibbe, in contrast, in *O Brave New Church: Rescuing the Addictive Culture* (1995) believes he is bringing 'the gift of prophecy' to his task. He believes that the task of the Church is 'culture watching', the sort of thing Ezekiel did when he was told by God that he was 'a watchman for the house of Israel'. What Stibbe has learned from his observation point on the outside, is that the whole culture is rotten with addiction – sex, drink, drugs, shopping, even churchgoing, you name it – anything people enjoy they are addicted to. Of course, one cannot totally reject his thesis – there are social problems in this area and they cause great suffering both to those who are addicted and those who have to live with them – but in his readiness to fit us all into his thesis of universal addiction he seems guilty of serious distortion. It smacks of the old evangelist's trick of dramatising a situation almost out of recognition, as well as of pumping up guilt. It is what sociologists nowadays call 'moral panic', the selecting of a distressing feature of society and then encouraging the belief that it is much more prevalent than it is.

Those who are not particularly in the grip of addiction – and that seems to cover most people I know – must wonder in which direction to go in order to repent. Give up tea, perhaps. Stibbe would feel that the answer to those suffering from addiction would be to go to a charismatic evangelical church, and of course, that might be of help to some people. But addiction needs a much wider social remit in which he is not remotely interested – he seems indifferent to the fact that some 17 per cent of the population are officially below the poverty level, something which can make a 'quick fix' – a fag, a drink, a gamble – very inviting.

Finding and Refounding

Much as I admire Robin Gill's helpful pragmatism and Wesley Carr's clear analyses, I find myself returning to the guru who is not an Anglican, but who says things that I believe the Church of England badly needs to hear. This is Gerald Arbuckle, who has written a series of thoughtful books, papers and articles studying decline in the Roman Catholic Church (where the pain has been acute, since until the 1960s it was enjoying impressive growth), and placing the problem in a wider context than any Anglican I know of. He began by looking first at religious communities (he is himself a member of a religious community). Being relatively smaller than the rest of the Roman Catholic Church, and more vulnerable to change, these communities underwent the painful awareness of decline first, with all the difficult emotions this threw up.

What he learned was the need to face and grieve for what was lost, but also to accept that, whatever came next, it would not be in quite the same form. Acceptance paved the way for new possibilities, new ways of doing things, for listening to people – the 'loyal dissenters', as he calls them, who had 'different', ideas. Refusal on the other hand, in the form of pretence or group-denial, the insistence that everything must go on as usual in the same old way, meant that everyone got stuck in what he calls 'restorationism', a desperate and probably hopeless desire to restore the status quo. Cultures, in Arbuckle's view, have life-cycles just as individual lives do. It is as vain to try to return to an earlier stage, as it is vain for the elderly to try to pretend they are young. The only option any of us have, suicide apart, is to 'go on'.

He believes that there are ways of transformation, paths to a deep conversion, but they come by way of believers sharing their faith and their doubts genuinely with one another, facing outwards towards the culture of which they are a part, having fun together. But the grieving comes first.[25]

The Radical Option

Canon Vincent Strudwick, a Tutor at Kellogg College, Oxford, and a teacher of theology at an Oxford theological college, wrote a letter to *The Times* just after the summer meeting of General Synod at York in 1999. A speaker had claimed that, at this time of crisis for the Church, people were talking very loosely about belief and that this was dangerous. The suggestion was that the heresy canons should be re-examined and tightened up to bring dissident voices into line. Strudwick was appalled at this suggestion and wrote a letter protesting. I asked him to say a bit more to me about his thoughts on this subject.[26]

> I didn't think anyone was about to be burned at the stake, but it seemed to me that the thinking was part of a general movement in which bishops, each in his diocese, seemed to be getting rather alarmed about exploratory theology. At a time of crisis a kind of *laager* mentality can obtain in the Church, where you put up the doctrinal walls and you put up the bureaucratic walls. You retreat into a defensive *laager*. I perceive that as something that is happening to us. I understand why it happens. Authoritarianism and centralisation are what tends to happen in a time of crisis, but I think it is entirely the wrong reaction.
>
> I can see some of the reasons for the *Turnbull* changes and the Archbishops' Council and all that, but I think it detracts from the splendid plurality of the Church of England, and all those balances that have developed in the past, like, for instance, between patron and bishop. I'm not arguing necessarily for patronage, but what happens is that the authority of the bishop gets increased and there aren't the checks and balances in place that historically were there. Modernisation occurs without the checks and balances. I got about twelve letters strongly supportive of my letter to *The Times*, a number of them from senior colleagues, three or four letters against (two of them from Orthodox Christians!), and the usual six loony letters.
>
> I do think there is a crisis in the Church, but that this involves us in an opportunity which a spirit of drawing back will inhibit. In 1980 Anthony Russell, the present Bishop of Dorchester, wrote a book called *The Clerical Profession*, and in it he suggested three ways of possible change for the Church of England. One is *tradition*, trying to keep everything the same – nothing must change. Another is the *adaptionist approach*, which tries to keep the Church the same but allows for cultural change to affect it. You adapt it piecemeal, as and when. Local ordained ministry, for example. Your basic concept is still the stipendiary ministry in the parish, but you allow for changes to meet the needs of the day. Lay ministry? The ordination of women? Yes, of course, but under the umbrella with which we're all familiar. I guess I was an adaptionist for years, though not necessarily consciously.
>
> Russell's third alternative was the radical Church of the future in which you look very carefully at what the purpose of the structures is, and are prepared to change the structures radically, not just adapt them, in a new cultural situation. I find that in my old age I have embraced the *radical approach*. We are in deep crisis now, with the Church in decline on almost all fronts. We've seen the gradual decline in church attendance, the decline in ordina-

tions, in confirmations, and now in baptisms and weddings in church. The Church as an expression of community, a liturgical sign and rumour of hope in the community, is such for fewer and fewer people.

From the 1960s the decline accelerated and we saw the Church adapt – things like the ASB, non-stipendiary ministry – all those things. But now in the 1990s I think we are seeing a much sharper decline and a detachment from the institution. There used to be many who had a nodding acquaintance with the Church. When I was Rector of Fittleworth in Sussex there were lots of people in the village who never came to church but on a gift day they would come up and talk to the Rector. Or they would say 'Rector, come round and have a glass of whisky and talk about God!' My perception is that there are fewer such encounters.

In every great phase of change during the 2000 years of the Church there has been a reintegration and representation of gospel with culture, which has produced new forms of institution and new ways of expressing the faith. That is how the whole thing has worked. In the first stage there was a Jewish sect which was taken by Paul and others into a Greek cultural context. It got taken over by them and so the concepts and the way of making Church was very different from that little isolated group in Jerusalem. You then got the Greek period ending with the crisis of the collapse of the Roman Empire, and the Church which, until then, had been very provisional, as it waited for the Second Coming, then became a Church which knew it had got to survive in a very hard world. Augustine wrote *The City of God* which is about a way of being as a Christian. There was what became known as the Dark Ages, and the Church surviving that. Little isolated bubbles of Christian living – the Benedictine houses – the libraries, the culture, the leisure, the structure, the hierarchy, a sort of harking back to the Roman family. All of it a preserving of the tradition, the heritage in a time of change, and passing them on until, in, say, the eleventh century, you got a redrawing of theology which reflected a new economic and political environment of feudalism – the writing of Anselm. Society affects the way you do Christian teaching. The whole tradition of the medieval Church which springs from Augustine and Anselm flowers through those next five hundred years and helps to create the kind of society that we've got.

My thesis is that the creativity happened because of the retrieval of the tradition and allowing this to integrate with the new structures of society to form new Church and new teaching out of the old, always with the guardians, the door-keepers, saying 'This is the same really.'

We seem to be in the middle again of another big change – at least since the nineteenth century. Durkheim said in 1912 that we were in the middle of an upheaval, and it is a very slow process of gestation. It is difficult to work out how long any of the former transitions took. As secularism grows in Western Europe (over against the flowering of Christianity in the Southern hemisphere), my fear is that Christian groups will withdraw into the model of a previous culture, put up the walls, put up the boundaries, and become little cultural bubbles, like the Amish sect in America. In the twenty-second century Christians will become people you go and look at on your day off to see how quaint they are! This was the thinking behind my letter to *The Times*. My feeling is that the Church as an institution has to understand the culture in which it finds itself and be integrated with it. It's where the laity are 90 per cent of the time.

'Stablish'd It Fast by a Changeless Decree'

What is 'Establishment'? The report of the Chadwick Commission (1970) defined it rather economically as 'the laws which apply to the Church of England and not to the other Churches'. The Church of England had an 'authorised' status, especially after the Elizabethan Settlement, and again after the Act of Uniformity of 1662, that was not permitted to others; with that went a number of privileges and responsibilities. Leaders like Richard Hooker, one of the great theoreticians of the Church of England, had a vision of it as coterminous with all Christian people in England. It was an impossible ideal, of course, though there was a generous and creative impulse behind it, and a conviction that the unity of the Catholic Church might be captured at home, but in practice it could only be brought about by compulsion. The modern idea that people cannot be compelled to religion had not fully arrived, but those who held other convictions resisted as best they could. They suffered severe sanctions for their intransigence, and their history, in the case of both Roman Catholics and Nonconformists, is one that reveals great heroism. The worst sanctions against Roman Catholics, Nonconformists and Jews – in particular concerning politics and education – were lifted around a hundred and thirty years ago, though handicaps still remained.

Despite the belated recognition that not everyone could be compelled, and that the Church of England was not coterminous with Christianity in England, the Church of England, for good and ill, continued to retain its 'special relationship' to monarch and Parliament; crowning the monarch, having seats in the House of Lords, subject to the power-plays and variable understanding of Parliament in the matter of legislation (a Parliament that became increasingly less Anglican as time went on).

Nowadays the gap between the aspirations of the Church and the comprehension and involvement of MPs grows ever wider. Those who attended the debate on the ordination of women in the House of Commons in 1993 were treated to the laughable spectacle of, on the one hand, the Revd Ian Paisley explaining why the Church of England should not ordain women, and, on the other, the almost equally absurd phenomenon of a clutch of willing women Labour MPs, with only the dimmest understanding of how the Church worked, explaining why they should. Fortunately, for the subjects of the legislation, a number of Conservative MPs, who were practising Anglicans, were very much in favour of women priests and spoke to considerable effect. A number of MPs, including Tony Wedgwood Benn (who also spoke in favour to considerable effect) and a Jewish MP, said that they did not think the House was the right place for the discussion. This was hardly a convincing piece of lawmaking.

'The dilemma, some might argue the tragedy, of the Church of England, has been the *damnosa hereditas* of an Establishment which had been historically inevitable and fruitful too but was now making less and less clear sense' writes the Roman Catholic historian Adrian Hastings,[1] rather charitably all things considered. He quotes Charles Gore asking Archbishop Lang crossly in 1912, 'How *can* you go on believing in an Established Church?'[2] The unspoken answer was that it was too awkward not to; as it has remained. Almost everyone, then and now, has shrunk from the Herculean task of dismantling the special relationship. Archbishops who had floated the idea earlier in their careers backed away from it once they were in office – for example, William Temple and Robert Runcie. George Carey is quoted earlier in this book, saying, I am sure with perfect truth, that neither of the Governments he has known has shown any great desire to bring disestablishment about.

All the same the Church of England has chafed from time to time at the restrictions of its status. Parliament, an effectively lay body, despite its twenty-six bishops in the House of Lords, has either made or approved major decisions concerning the Church, most notoriously rejecting the Revised Prayer Book (twice) in the 1920s. The Church has obtained important concessions about decisions since then, but the women's ordination debate did reveal the impracticality of MPs debating issues on which not more than a handful of them have much real understanding.

Not all Anglicans have seemed to mind 'the chains' of Establishment. Bishop Hensley Henson (1863–1947) saw the Church of England as a body for which 'every Englishman has responsibility' – he dreamed, somewhat as Hooker had done, of a national Church.

The powerful Anglo-Catholic group descended from the Tractarians, whose great horror was a Church controlled by the state, on the other hand, wanted the Church to be 'master in its own house'. It was, as Hastings points out, an odd and ironic inversion of Catholic view of 'church', which tends to be an inclusivist and semi-established one. 'It was the old-fashioned Protestant who really stood for the medieval "Catholic" view of the inclusive Church, and the Anglo-Catholic who argued for the "Protestant" view of a Church distinguished by the explicit faith and commitment of its members.'[3] Christians do have a proper allegiance to governments under which they live, but, as a number of tyrannies have demonstrated, there is also an allegiance to a truth that may go beyond that of the state, a devotion that has cost many their lives.

What is unarguable is the way the Church of England, living alongside the power of the monarchy and Government, has remained bathed in the glow of their influence. Sometimes the Church itself influenced government decisions, or helped sway an important vote, sometimes its influence was negligible, but it was never far from the seat of power. Bishops, and many other clergy, of course, came from the same bands of families, went to the same schools, attended the same universities, as those who ran the country, and a glance at the pages of Trollope shows just what a comfortable niche this oligarchic group was to fill. The novels of Edwardian and even Georgian England were full of the Us and Them feeling – Us being the gentlemen, public school and often Oxbridge educated, the members of exclusive clubs, and Them, the ticks, the yobbos, or what John Galsworthy, who had a social conscience, liked to call 'decent little snipe'. The awareness of how much was held in common across all the corridors of power naturally helped to promote the mutual seduction of Church and state, something from which the other churches were largely excluded, though there were some aristocratic Roman Catholics who could 'pass' because they were 'gentlemen'. Methodists, however wealthy, did not usually make it to the enclosure – the association with the working class was too strong. Some very rich Jews, however, did.

In the course of time the Church gradually removed itself from the most pressing dependency of the relationship with Parliament. Four Commissions, in 1916, 1935, 1952 and 1970, helped the task of liberation along somewhat. The first of them, the Selborne Commission, was a response to a rising demand for a new relationship between Church and state. The Life and Liberty Movement masterminded by William Temple and Dick Sheppard had called upon Parliament to give the Church its freedom. What it got was a limited freedom in the form of the Enabling Act of 1919 which introduced lay participation in the government of the Church and gave the Church the right to introduce its own Measures. The second (Cecil) Commission of 1935 performed a sort of 'mopping-up' operation after the Prayer Book crisis of the 1920s, and the third (Moberly) seeming to be amiably in favour of change.

These all took a fairly gentle stance, perhaps at heart wanting only modification and not root and branch change. The last, however, the Chadwick Commission of 1970, revealed some real resentment of Establishment (among its Anglo-Catholic members). After that a quietness on the subject seemed to set in. Exhaustion? A conspiracy of silence? Hard to say, but it is a silence that is the easier to live with since the Church does enjoy new freedoms, and maybe everyone, not just Anglicans, is a little apprehensive of more extensive change. Better the devil you know . . .

The most important of the new freedoms was the right, first of Church Assembly, then of General Synod, to propose Measures to Parliament on matters of importance to it, which Parliament might either ratify or turn down. Nowadays, it is unlikely that it would turn down a strongly desired Church Measure in the way it turned down the introduction of the Revised Prayer Book in the late 1920s (which the Church then went on to use extensively!). Indeed the Worship and Doctrine Measure of 1974 devolved most of the power to alter liturgy to General Synod. (Such measures as the Enabling Act and the Worship and Doctrine Measure can, indeed, be seen as a gradual disestablishing, unrecognised as such.)

The present focus of resentment against 'Establishment', however, has to do with the appointment of bishops (see Chapter 18). There is increasing exasperation at the idea of the prime minister (any prime minister) appointing bishops, who may not be the people the Church itself believes it needs, and resentment of the present method is all the greater because it works in such a secretive way.

And yet the Church still has, and enjoys, privileges. Of course, it does not defend them, at least publicly, in terms of power, but in terms of service, as 'being there for everyone', 'on call' when parishioners need help, or require a baptism, marriage or funeral. But there is a disingenuousness about this. Presumably Roman Catholics, Methodists and Baptists do not turn away the needy just because they are not the Established Church?

Bishop Colin Buchanan, in 1994, wrote a rather brave book,[4] putting up a lone fight for disestablishment (and some strong arguments) in which virtually no leading church figure joined him. In his book he points out that the formerly established Churches of

Ireland and Wales, when disestablished, did not suddenly abandon concern for the people who lived in their parishes, but continued to perform very much the function they had performed when established. Nor have they come, in any sense, to see themselves as sects rather than mainline religious bodies, as critics of disestablishment often assert could happen.

The argument of service to others, of being there for everyone, of at least keeping up an element of pretence that people and Church are somehow coterminous, is the respectable 'front argument' against disestablishment. (The trouble with the Church of England, Bishop Buchanan remarks in conversation, is that it lives in a fantasy world.) The other argument has to do with being 'an influence', 'a Christian presence' in our largely secular society.

Behind the scenes people are prepared to be more honest. I remember a 'group' which met to discuss Establishment within the context of a liberal church conference I attended a year or two back, all of us Anglicans with the exception of one Methodist minister.

'We'd be fools to give up Establishment,' one priest remarked. 'If something works, don't fix it.' It sounded alarmingly like the unwritten text of many crude but popular beliefs about race, gender and class. ('We are the lucky ones – let's keep it that way.') The Methodist minister, I noticed, did not return for the second meeting of the group.

Colin Buchanan did not think it was lucky to be an Established Church – he felt that such privileges as there were were outweighed by the disadvantages, the chains, as he called them. His book looked hopefully to the Turnbull Commission (sitting at the time he wrote his book) to tackle the issue of Establishment. It did not do so. In interview at the beginning of 1997, Michael Turnbull said to me that there did not seem to be a pressing interest in the subject at present, which at the time did seem to be the case.

Since *Turnbull*, the Labour Government's desire to reform the House of Lords has skated over the topic of disestablishment. In the early days of the New Labour government kites were flown. The Christian Socialist Movement produced a disestablishment pamphlet which described Establishment as a 'political and religious anachronism', but was quickly put down by the Second Church Estates Commissioner, Stuart Bell (himself an apparatchik of Establishment, of course), who managed to imply that the Prime Minister shared his enthusiasm for Establishment.

In the short term, the bishops are to keep all twenty-six of their traditional seats. The Archbishop of Canterbury (see interview above, pp. 158–67) points out that, at present, it is common for the leaders

238

of other churches in this country to ask the Anglican bishops to make their points for them (a heartening sign of how far ecumenism has come), and that he himself would welcome being joined by other church leaders as 'lords spiritual'. This would have quite a different feel from making the same people ordinary peers as, for example, the Chief Rabbi is already. No plans appear to have been made to set leaders of other faiths – Hindu and Muslim in particular – in positions of spiritual honour and respect, which seems a pity. What is always needed in inter-church as well as in inter-faith relations is generosity, going two miles, as the Gospel puts it, out of goodwill and before one is somehow compelled, and although this is not strictly in the hands of the Church it would be good to think they were pushing the Government to more religious inclusiveness.

There are signs that the Roman Catholic Church is looking for some such recognition. A problem for them is that their canon law explicitly forbids clerics from assuming 'public office whenever it means sharing in the exercise of civil power' (canon 285.3), and Cardinal Hume is known to have refused a seat in the House of Lords. As recently as spring 1999 a meeting of the Catholic bishops of England and Wales still felt that they would be unable to sit in the Lords. Later in 1999, however, they made a submission to the Royal Commission on Lords reform saying that, subject to the approval of the Holy See, they would like seats to be offered to Catholic bishops. (They envisage a dispensation from the Vatican.) The Catholic weekly the *Tablet*, plainly uneasy about the plan, asks 'For whom would they be speaking? The theological answer must be the international college of bishops with the Pope at its head. That is certainly not what the Royal Commission has in mind.'[5] Please God, nothing again will ever revive the old British terror of 'popery', but if anything could do it, such a cadre of bishops might.

The reform of the Lords apart, there seems a kind of bewilderment in the Church about Establishment, as if no one quite knows what to do next. Certainly wholesale disestablishment would be an extraordinarily complicated manoeuvre which would unpick a good deal of the fabric of our society, so that it needs the most careful study. Some caution does seem desirable, though not as a mask for pure self-interest.

Colin Buchanan suggests that disestablishment is happening piecemeal anyway, though he thinks that it would be better for it to happen in a conscious controlled way. 'It is my strong conviction that in the course of changes' (in the relation of Church to society) 'even a weakening establishment has crossed a watershed from the conceivably defensible to the self-evidently harmful.'[6] There was a time,

239

he suggests, not so long ago, when it was possible to make a case for the idea that the majority of people in this country, however loosely attached to the Church, liked to see themselves as C of E. He calls this 'folk religion' and suggests that between the 1950s when there were still strong relics of this, and the present day, this fringe of the Church has largely fallen away. It has left a mood of goodwill behind it, and a willingness to use the Church for occasions like baptisms and weddings, but it does not represent any real commitment.

It is impossible not to agree. Like many regular churchgoers I observe many baptisms at my parish church in which large family parties arrive with a baby for baptism, are welcomed warmly and given the best service we can provide during which parents and godparents take immensely serious Christian vows. They then disappear and are never seen again. Whatever was going on, it was not an act of commitment to the Church. We are dealing, gently and kindly, with the last traces of folk religion in this country, but we may be signing a death warrant to our own claims to be taken seriously.

One of the few people to engage actively with the issue of Establishment on the 'pro' side is John Moses, now Dean of St Paul's, at the time he wrote, Provost of Chelmsford.[7] He takes a diametrically opposite view to Colin Buchanan. He is a 'folk religion' man, and although he acknowledges the huge falling away of support for the Church, he nevertheless believes in the almost mystical ethos of the Church of England as by law established.

> The institution is essentially inclusive. It is a comprehensive, all-embracing institution. The dividing line between church and community is not always clearly drawn. There is implicit in [the Church's] pastoral strategy a strong sense of the incarnation, because the institution is rooted in the life of the world ... The church as an institution embraces, or attempts to embrace, everyone and everything.[8]

Dean Moses thinks the Church should simply carry on, Established, continuing to 'exercise its ministry in ways that are serviceable, accessible, evocative, worthy of respect and tolerant', showing by this that it continues to see itself as 'part of the life of society'.

An equally revealing statement about Establishment was written by Frank Field when, as a member of the Working Party on Senior Church Appointments of the Standing Committee of General Synod which reported in 1992, he produced a minority report disagreeing strongly with his colleagues. The rest of the Working Party were proposing reforms, for example in the matter of appointing suffragan bishops, which reduced the role of the Crown. A key idea, which might seem very reasonable to most people, whether Christian or not, was that the majority of places on any advisory committee which was to appoint senior clergy should go to those active in the Church – not *every* place, you understand, but the majority. Frank Field would have none of it. He claimed this suggestion meant that the Working Party saw the Church of England as a 'sect' and he explained why he thought so. Their

> approach ignores what the Church of England has meant to the English nation, and the response of ordinary citizens over the centuries. On the basis of attendance we have rarely been a church-going nation. Despite the penalties, large numbers refused to attend church even in medieval times. Failure to accept a set liturgical diet cannot be equated with disbelief.[9]

Field believes that the largish penumbra that *Religious Trends*[10] describe as 'notional Christians' – those who have a vague wish to be associated – actually *are* the Church of England, and goes on to have a sideswipe at clergymen who make difficulties about baptising the children of people who know nothing whatever about the Church. They 'erect barriers betweent the Church and the nation, but ensure that fewer and fewer people understand what the Christian message is about. Unless the Church radically changes its approach we may now be living with the last generation which understands anything about the Christian message.'[11] While it is difficult to disagree with the last statement, it is surely naïve to believe that this is due to a handful of clergy who refuse to baptise the babies of unbelieving parents, or the deliberations of the unfortunate Working Party, or, as Field goes on to say, the difficulties of understanding Christian language.

But he insists that by identifying with the Church with 'activists' – those who are actually involved and committed – the Working Party were making of the Church of England a sect. Maybe sects are in the eye of the beholder, but it is very difficult to imagine that any decision about how bishops are chosen is likely to bring one more person to church or make one more person stay away.

Reading both Field and Moses, I found myself thinking of people I have known with broken love affairs who simply refused to recognise that a relationship that has meant a lot to them is over as far as the other person is concerned. Hoping against hope, they battle on, convinced that the other person *will* come round and succumb to their faithfulness in the end. Unfortunately this usually does not happen – the psychology of the situation is all wrong. Worse, it becomes a refusal to recognise the freedom of the other to make their own choice. It is, of course, perfectly possible that people in this country may one day begin to see the churches differently, but the way to achieve this may not be to keep appealing to the past, and to a supposed former relationship, but to make a break and start, as it were, from scratch. The danger, as Buchanan points out, is of living in fantasyland, and a rather perverse fantasyland at that, the fantasy of those who are convinced their passion is returned when there is not the slightest indication of it.

Other churches in this country, not established, seem to be facing an almost identical crisis to that of the Church of England. I find it interesting that neither Moses nor Buchanan seems to take their feelings very seriously. What must it be like to be part of a church which, in the case of the Roman Catholic Church, and a number of the Free Churches, historically suffered real hardships and sometimes active persecution, and to continue to live alongside the Church of England, who once supported the persecution, and to observe it still having a 'special relationship' with the state? It is very easy for Anglicans to fail to consider how the issue of Establishment feels to members of other Christian churches – the extraordinary situation in which the Church of England is treated as No. 1 Church, like the wife of a polygamous mandarin, and the rest as concubines of inferior status. I am amazed at the good humour with which they put up with it, but it strikes me as an unnecessarily humiliating position, and one that is inconsistent with the Church of England's claims to promote ecumenism.

A leader in the *Tablet* in January 1998 said this:

The Church of England's contribution to the life of the nation has been definitive. But no modern society, devising its constitution anew, would want to give one particular Christian denomination the special duties and privileges that establishment status has conferred. It is often said that other denominations and faiths in England now support Anglican establishment because it has become benign and serves as a bulwark against total secularisation. There is much truth in this. Cardinal Hume has made it clear that he does not consider establishment to be a threat, nor its removal a priority, though he added that disestablishment would become a necessity for ecumenism . . . Nevertheless, establishment surely cannot go on as it is . . . Disestablishment elsewhere than in England has not brought the adverse consequences that some English Anglicans envisage. The experience in Wales 75 years ago suggests the Church of England could draw energy from a new sense of freedom and maturity. Nowhere else in the Anglican world has the severing of previous legal ties between Church and State subsequently been viewed as a mistake.

In a multifaith pluralist society, the continued special status of one particular Church risks contradicting the principle that the machinery of State, its head, chief executive, government and legislature, must represent and serve all citizens equally. The Church of England is fully able to confront such a challenge to modernise – if it wants to.[12]

The clear message of this article is that the sensitive and loving action would be for Anglicans to go one mile towards their fellow Christians. It seems ironic that, in defence of Establishment, there is so much talk of a relationship with 'the people' of this country (which begins to look more and more far-fetched), yet in the matter of caring about the very real relationship enjoyed with practising fellow Christians, the Church of England is so unfeelingly cavalier.

This is bad enough, but one does not have to dig very deep to discover just how bitter was the sense of rejection by the Methodist Church when the Anglican/Methodist Reunion scheme collapsed in 1972. A minister who took a leading part in that scheme and had high hopes for it, recently described at a meeting the immense damage the collapse did to the morale and self-esteem of the Methodist Church, as it voted itself out of existence in order to join the Church of England and then had to put itself back together again, a dislocation from which it took years to recover. It was clear that his own, very remarkable ministry, had been deeply scarred by the whole experience and it was impossible, as an Anglican listening to him, not to feel pain and shame at what had happened in our name.

So what next? A word I have heard bandied about in the course of attending conferences and talking to interested parties is 're-establishment'. I am not quite sure what this means; perhaps it is an attempt to recognise publicly the centrality of Christian influence in our history and culture in a way that would allow all practising Christians to feel equally valued, but equally an attempt which would not make people of other faiths feel downgraded or threatened. If this allowed a role for the Church of England not of privilege but of leadership as *primus inter pares,* but gave proper weight to the influence of the other churches, that would seem a fitting and realistic expression of how things are, or should be, in the relation of Christian bodies to one another. I would myself hope that this included a role for the Crown, though not in the meaningless way of rubber-stamping the appointment of bishops.

In England, partly as a result of a historical accident, the monarchy has borne and continues to bear an extraordinary weight of meaning, as if central to the identity of a people. If this meaning were to be expressed in a Christian ceremony of Coronation, one in which all the mainstream churches took part, but which gave recognition to the many subjects of a future monarch who are not likely to be Christian, this (though of course it would not please everybody) might speak, in as united a voice as our community and country are capable of, about the centrality of sacrifice and commitment.

18

In the Purple

Bishops are one of the distinctive marks of the Church of England, a sign of its link with the early traditions of Christianity, and of its refusal to go 'all the way' with the Reforming tendency that wished to dismantle every trace of Catholicism. To this day the Church regards the episcopacy as 'unnegotiable' when, for instance, it is having talks about reunion with the Methodists. In a society that is less and less hierarchical, the Church has this fixed pattern of episcopacy, derived from the Greek word *episkope*, which means 'oversight'.

'Oversight' sounds a little threatening, as in the word 'overseer' but the tradition is that the oversight is that of a shepherd for his flock, and this is the reason that part of a bishop's insignia is a shepherd's crook. Biblically, the shepherd is devoted to his sheep, is prepared to lay down his life for them if necessary, as in some parts of the world archbishops and bishops have had to do. This has not recently been the fate of bishops in this country, though some lost their lives in the Reformation itself, and some later suffered imprisonment.

St Augustine said of being a bishop, 'I am a bishop for you, I am a Christian like you.' Using this as his text in his inaugural sermon Cardinal Basil Hume, speaking of his experience of being a bishop in the Roman Catholic Church, said that he did not see it as 'a position of honour', but rather 'a function' within the Church. 'It is a function of leadership, but of a leadership that is different. It is characterised by service and devotion. A bishop ought not to impose himself on others. Rather, he should seek to draw out from others what is best in them. He should not stifle but release spiritual energies. He should not attempt to regiment others . . .'[1]

The two archbishops, or chief bishops, of the Church of England, of Canterbury and York, have the title of Primate – Primate of All England and Primate of England respectively. Old rivalries clung to the original distinctions but are no longer of importance; the two archbishops, who doubtless disagree sometimes in private, nowadays tend to show a united face to the world. Although each of them presides over their province of Canterbury or York, they do not in practice have superior authority over the bishops; they are expected to act with them in some form of consensus. Archbishops meet with the House of Bishops to discuss church business, and usually a common agreement is arrived at. Bishops tell me that one way this can happen is for the archbishops, on occasion, to ask bishops not to handle certain 'hot potatoes' at that particular time. The bishops usually go along with this.

Forty-Three Shepherds
Episcopacy, as we have seen, is one of the keys to the Church of England, along with creed and Scripture. England is divided up into forty-three dioceses, (forty-four if you count the diocese of Europe), thirty in the Province of Canterbury and fourteen in the Province of York, each of these territorial units presided over by a diocesan bishop, whose 'see' it is. He is usually helped by one or more 'suffragan' bishops. There were suffragan bishops in late medieval times, but they disappeared until they were revived in 1870. In recent times some have been made responsible for a particular geographical area of a diocese. There are now more than sixty suffragans. There are also 'assistant bishops', retired bishops who help out in a part-time capacity. At one end, as it were, of the bishop's job, he administers the diocese, and with the aid of the bishop's council and the diocesan synod, makes decisions on its behalf. At the other, the end that primarily concerns the parish, the bishop ordains clergy, plays a key role in their appointments, inducts and installs clergy into parish jobs, carries out confirmations and sometimes appears for special occasions – the dedication of a church, say. Behind the scenes the bishops are responsible, with the help of the archdeacons, for organising and disciplining clergy, and also for supporting and encouraging them.

Bishops' Move
Turnbull saw the bishops as the key to future developments in the Church after the Archbishops' Council itself. 'We believe the House of Bishops should in future play a more sharply focused and purposeful role among the national institutions of the Church.'[2] Two bishops would be elected by their peers to the Council and they, 'together with any other episcopal members of the Council would ensure (in consultation with the House of Bishops' Standing

Committee) that the House developed, at regular intervals, an articulated vision for the direction of the Church of England. The General Synod would debate the vision and the House of Bishops would be informed by its views.'[3] It seems a rather partial and proxy arrangement for vision. A bit like Milton's view of Adam and Eve – 'He for God only, she for God in him'. Bodily images are, of course, appropriately Christian, since the Church is often referred to as 'the Body of Christ'. If the bishops have reserved the metaphor of the eyes and brains I wonder what that leaves for the rest of us. Something lower down in the body, I imagine. It would be lovely if the bishops did have an exciting vision, of course, but most of them seem too busy for the quiet and reflection that vision usually requires. And in any case, the Archbishops' Council seems to think that vision is its prerogative.

The service for the ordination of bishops in the Alternative Service Book says that 'a bishop is called to lead in serving and caring for the people of God and to work with them in the oversight of the Church. As a chief pastor he shares with his fellow bishops a special responsibility to maintain and further the unity of the Church, to uphold its discipline, and to guard its faith.'[4] Among other duties he is to 'know his people and be known by them' and to 'ordain and send new ministers'. The new bishop has to swear that he feels called to do these things, to accept the faith and discipline of the Church, to live as a good Christian and pastor, and to 'promote unity, peace and love among Christian people and to be a faithful witness'. He is being ordained again, this time into a higher order. The archbishop asks the consent of the congregation to do this, and they give their consent.

At the most solemn moment of the ordination service the archbishop and other bishops lay their hands on the bishop-elect, calling down the Holy Spirit upon him to enable him to carry out his difficult task. He is then presented with a Bible: 'Here are words of eternal life.' Different groups in the Church see the moment of ordination in different ways. For many it is simply a calling down of the Holy Spirit. For others, particularly since the Oxford Movement for whom it was a vital issue, it is a sign of a succession right down from St Peter – the Apostolic Succession – a special 'touch' or grace that is passed on and is a sign that the bishop is the genuine article. It seems a little tenuous within the Church of England, though it gave rise in a previous era to a famous joke about the way the idea of Apostolic Succession gave credence to an unpopular bishop since he 'must be descended from Judas Iscariot'.

Scholars point out that bishops have had different functions at

247

different stages of church history. In the early Church a bishop was not much more than a pastor. As the centuries rolled on, however, there were many different kinds of bishop. There were grand prelates who were also consummate politicians, there were prince-bishops who lived as stylishly as any aristocrat, there were greedy bishops who robbed the poor and grew fat on their suffering like the Bishop of Hereford who was famously humiliated by Robin Hood, there were Trollopian bishops, with and without wives like Mrs Proudie, and there were ordinary decent bishops who tried to get on with the task of caring for the clergy and people for whom they were responsible.

The Church of England has numbered some immensely distinguished men among its bishops – scholars, pastors, mystics, holy men – whose legend, as in the case of Michael Ramsay, George Bell and William Temple, lives on and acquires, as legends do, encrustations which may or may not describe what actually happened, but catch *en passant* the spirit of a great soul. My favourite story is of George Bell, an enthusiastic connoisseur of wine, entertaining some junior clergy to a meal at his house. He went round the table, filling their glasses, until one of them, who objected to alcohol on moral grounds, put his hand over his glass and said 'No, thank you, my Lord. I would sooner commit adultery.'

'So would we all,' the bishop is said to have replied, 'but drink your wine!'

Bishops have contained among their number not only very gifted people, but also very eccentric people (sometimes the two were one and the same, of course). It would be good to believe that both gifted and eccentric people would continue to be offered jobs as bishops and would feel like accepting them. In the conformist mood of the millennium Church that looks less likely than ever before.

Yet there is life, energy, intelligence and courage to be found among the present crop of bishops. The courage with which Richard Harries, Bishop of Oxford, took on the might of the Church Commissioners in 1990, questioning whether their investment in certain businesses and regimes fitted the moral beliefs of the Church, gives hope of a less timid interpretation of the bishop's role – it was boat-rocking of the highest order. With a similar capacity for insisting on a global, not merely domestic, conscience, Peter Selby, Bishop of Worcester, has written on the subject of debt and the harm we do with our thoughtless consumerism.[5] Bishop Colin Buchanan criticising Establishment also encourages serious questioning of the identity and mission of the Church.[6]

Bishop's Function

As the consecration service itself shows, bishops are often seen as having a rather different role from mere pastoral 'oversight'. What we expect of bishops is that they should watch over the doctrinal and liturgical inheritance of the Church, advising and warning if they think the Church as a whole is wandering too far from this, holding to this central truth while others may wander off into the wilderness – into marketing, as it were, or an obsession with finance, or bitter party disputes. A difficulty is that not so many bishops these days seem more than modestly au fait with theology – many outside their ranks know as much theology or more, though it is, of course, open to the House of Bishops to co-opt theologians to their meetings and they do, in fact, do this. Post-*Turnbull*, the growing, and worrying, expectation seems to be that bishops exchange the pastoral and spiritual aspects of their job for becoming 'managers', those who 'employ' clergy rather than lead them out into new pastures. One theologically inclined bishop, Stephen Sykes, has recently exchanged his episcopal job to return to teaching.

It is difficult to see how a modern bishop could be either a deep theological or philosophical thinker, or even a profoundly spiritual person, so essential is space, reflective time, and reading, for thought and prayer, and so prevalent is the culture of 'busyness' in the Church. I once attended a conference of newly consecrated bishops, 'baby bishops' as they are sometimes called, as a speaker, and found that part of the training they were being offered had to do with helping them with the stress of the endless demands and the overwhelming correspondence of their job. Bishops are hugely in demand and their diaries are booked up for months ahead. Apart from the House of Lords, for the twenty-six bishops who have seats there, and the residential meetings of the House of Bishops twice a year, there is General Synod twice a year, committees of the Church on which a number of bishops sit and on which they are expected to play a key part, confirmations, inductions of clergy, preaching in their own cathedral and elsewhere, pastoral visits to parish churches, interviews with clergy, interviews with lay people, council meetings in their own diocese, committees connected with good works, working trips abroad, and being pursued for 'soundbites' by the press. Not to mention entertaining, spending time with family and friends, and attempting to pursue the private interests and hobbies which help keep the rest of us sane. It is not surprising that the conference I attended gave the baby bishops information about how to recognise stress in themselves, and advised them how to act upon its sinister signals.

This does make it seem that the job can now only be done by those who are natural organisers, and it is worrying to think of the degree to which this must exclude visionaries, dreamers and muddlers-through, who might have other gifts to bring to the role. Obsessionals rule, OK? At least for as long as they don't crack up under the strain. As a job the bishop's does not seem enviable (though some do enjoy it), and I have known a number of promising clergy who have refused pointblank to take on episcopal duties. This degradation of the job in terms of pressure, therefore, affects the quality of at least some of the people who are prepared to take it on. I was surprised that *Turnbull* seemed so little interested in the problems associated with this.

Where Do Bishops Come from?
Anglicans often amuse themselves by trying to draw up a blueprint of a bishop, if only to spot those among their number who are likely to end up in that role. The quintessential bishop is tall, handsome, athletic, has plentiful silver hair, a fine singing and speaking voice, and a confident manner. He is public school/grammar school and Oxbridge-educated. His six foot something is augmented at ceremonies with a mitre, which makes him preternaturally tall, like a beautiful alien who has come down from his own immaculate planet to set lesser beings on a path of righteousness. Of course, not all bishops are really like this, but a surprising number bear some resemblance to it, particularly in the matter of height, perhaps because a number of them at least until recently inherited an upper-class physique. (Maybe this is a prejudice on my part – I am open to the possibility – but the mere fact that this stereotype of a bishop as physically bigger and better-looking than most of the rest of us is lodged so firmly in my mind does in itself seem somewhat significant.)

Watching and listening to a number of bishops during Synod debates I have sometimes had a sharp insight that their privileges were a handicap – that they cut them off from understanding what life is like for most people. I am not writing of their privileges of office, but the privilege of, in some cases, being of 'good family', more usually nowadays of being clever boys who have done well in a good education system, who have been admired and applauded throughout that system and through most of their lives. Sometimes they have been good-looking, charming and athletic boys too, and have never felt a need to develop abilities that went much beyond this auspicious beginning. Their combination of gifts and their undentable confidence make them a natural choice for the Church as leaders. How could they (with rare exceptions like the present Archbishop) imagine what it could be like to be poor, to be brought up in a tough neighbourhood, to have very little choice in life, to be deprived of the education which could have bettered your life, to be a battered wife, a woman who longed to be a priest but was not permitted to be one, or a kid on the streets? There comes a point at which privilege is a drawback, since it cuts you off from the simplicities, what June Osborne calls 'the roughage', of ordinary life. Talking of the way the House of Bishops disseminated their ideas to others, she found them inept and gauche. She complained that they did not 'know how to function except within [their] own grouping. They talk about a hospitable Church, but they need to look at the way they operate. They are dysfunctional as a group of people, and some of that I do put down to the fact that they haven't got any women among them.'[7] Certainly on the subject of women, and of sexuality of various kinds, their ability to open their mouths to put their feet in them seems striking, though they never seem to learn from (or even notice) their mistakes. From outside, their narcissism appears to be impregnable.

Height and good looks apart, bishops do seem hedged about with grandeur, from the chic of their purple stocks and the splendour of their ceremonial robes to the rather lovely houses in which some of them live, the kind that only tycoons otherwise inhabit. Not all, admittedly. One bishop of my acquaintance lives in the ugliest and least convenient house I can imagine, with the delightful and eminently suitable house of former bishops in tantalising view through the drawing-room window. One of the perks the Church of England does sometimes offer to bishops and senior clerics, however, is a stunning historical house. Much history is tied up in the bricks and mortar of these places – for instance, in the extraordinary house of the Bishop of Durham at Bishop Auckland, the canonries of Westminster in Little Cloister, or at Wells, or Canterbury, or Salisbury, or the ancient and very beautiful, thirteenth-century prior's lodging, later used by Charles II as a hunting lodge, which is the Dean's house at Winchester. The houses may not be convenient, but they are often enchanting. How does anyone live in them and still remember what life is like for the vast majority of people? I don't know.

Money is not implicated in the same way. In terms of stipend bishops are not coining it in, though occasional outbursts in the press from hostile journalists like to imply this. A suffragan bishop earns £23,790 (at the time of writing, though these figures only obtain until the year 2000). A diocesan bishop earns £28,930. They have official expenses on top of this, and some money towards secretarial help, and a chauffeur/gardener. (The chauffeur idea sticks in some people's gullets, inevitably – it does seem rather grand – but if one needs to travel a great deal, as bishops do, it seems useful not to wear oneself out with driving, or having to find a parking space, and it must be convenient to be able to mull over a sermon, a talk, or a committee agenda, in the car on the way to an appointment. Or to be able to fall asleep on the way home.) An official review, the Mellows' review of bishops' remuneration, is in hand and will shortly report, with an emphasis on giving bishops the resources they need to do their job effectively.

Three bishops, Canterbury (£53,370), York (£46,760) and London (£43,580), break into a different stipend bracket. Compared to salaries in the rest of society, these sums are not stupendous for the responsibilities carried, however much the rest of us might wish we earned that much.

Another form of episcopal chic is the abbreviated Latinate signature – 'Richard Londin . . .', 'David Ebor . . .', 'George Cantuar . . .', peculiar to archbishops and diocesan bishops in ancient dioceses with Roman associations. Other diocesans become known by their Christian name and the name of their diocese. I notice that at least one of the Provincial Episcopal Visitors affects the Latinate signature. The Latin title, with its identification with a place and its history, seems to me a great deal more appealing than another way of referring to a bishop, one of which I have no recollection before the last twenty years or so. It is a habit of speaking about a bishop in conversation by his title and Christian name – Bishop Tom, Bishop Jim, Bishop Timothy – the same man not so many years ago would have been known as Bishop Butler, Bishop Thompson, or Bishop Stevens. I fear what it indicates is a willed intimacy, a pretence that bishop, clergy and laity are on much closer terms than in fact they are. It is not very convincing.

There is a certain mystery about the path that clergy tread on the way to becoming bishops. In the old days class and education undoubtedly played a primary role (hence, I suspect, my fixed stereotype); nowadays that is much less true. At the risk of traducing the system, I suggest that increasingly now they are found among the ranks of those who are personable, good speakers, have shown themselves efficient as pastors (or less often, as scholars), have a nice way with the outside world, and are not known to have what church officials regard as bees in their bonnets (excessive pacifism, feminist sympathies, too great a concern for homosexuals or any tendency to criticise the current 'line'). Embarrassment must be avoided at all costs. Whereas not so many years ago, awkward bishops (judged by rather narrow church standards) seemed a natural part of the Anglican scene, nowadays they are rare beasts, unless, of course, they break out once they are safely within the episcopal ranks. This change is a great loss, and indicates the growing inability of the Church to live with dissent.

Fudge and Focus

Perhaps the coming of General Synod helped the bishops to harden into more of a conglomerate than they had been before. Over and against organised groups of clergy and laity they became conscious of themselves as 'the House of Bishops'. Two worrying trends developed from that. The first appeared during the long struggle in the Church over women's ordination. Bishops appealed to by those, men and women, seeking change, used to say 'I am a focus of unity' – a plea that they could not take any stand at all in case they distressed one side or the other. Some sense that a bishop listens carefully and lovingly to all sides and does not shoot his mouth off without thinking about the implications of what he is saying is, of course, important, but a refusal to declare a position on an important issue begins, after a while, to seem merely lily-livered, evoking the classic picture of a supine bishop 'sitting on the fence with both ears to the ground'. The *Church Times* in July 1999 had a brief interview with Michael Langrish, about to become Bishop of Exeter.

'Nobody can put me in a box. I am an Evangelical Catholic.' The article goes on: 'His theology is both sacramental and strongly biblical: he ordains women, but has an understanding of why some object; and he voted for the Lambeth resolution on homosexuality while deploring any tinge of homophobia.'[8] The very model of a collegial bishop, indeed, Bunyan's Mr Facing Both Ways. Come back, Graham Leonard, all is forgiven.

In his classic book *BeLonging*[9] Peter Selby makes the overall point that the Church is constantly tempted to be 'tribal': to confine membership to those of whom it approves, rather than 'adoptive': welcoming as sons and daughters all who are drawn to it. Within this context he discussed the problem about bishops being foci of unity. 'The concept of the focus of unity is also capable of exploitation under the impulse of tribal self-defence.'[10] (In the case of women's ordination the dominant tribe being the tribe of men.) 'The desire to unite quickly becomes the desire to stay together at all costs, and the wish to pursue a ministry of reconciliation degenerates, often unnoticed, into a fudging of issues and the extinguishing of dissent.'[11] This was written and published before the Act of Synod of 1993 but prophetically it caught the mood exactly.

Close to the device of 'focus of unity' is the idea, borrowed by the bishops from the Roman Catholic Church, of 'collegiality'. Collegiality emerged as a key word at Vatican II, a sign of an important reform which emphasised that the Pope must not act unilaterally, but only in collaboration with the other bishops. The hope and intention was that this idea of collaboration would filter down to lower levels of the Catholic Church. In recent years it does not look as if this hope has been realised.

As borrowed by the Church of England, however, a church with a very different system of government, and with different ideas about 'authority' and 'democracy', the word has come to have quite another connotation. It appears to mean that the whole body of the House of Bishops tends to vote alike, however much bishops are known to differ individually in beliefs and ideas.

Peter Selby suggests that the *raison d'être* is that it is felt that this is

the only way in which the unity of the whole Church can be safeguarded.

Here again we have a concept of immense spiritual significance and at the same time full of immense danger. It witnesses to the essential corporateness of the Christian enterprise and the fundamentally shared nature of Christian ministry. When, as is so in my case, you have spent nearly your whole ministry working as part of a team, and are now engaged actively in encouraging others to see ministry in that way, it is especially hard to be critical about collegiality as an idea.

Yet it is vital to be critical about it, and particularly about its capacity to serve what I have called an ethnic rather than an ecclesial identity for the Church.[12]

The joining of ranks can mean that no faintly threatening idea or person ever gets near the citadel of the Church. Since Selby wrote the book it could be argued that the Archbishops' Council has protected the citadel more firmly than ever.

In Selby's words, collegiality 'can endanger the possibility of dissent'.

What does it have to say about issues and situations which are bound to drive people into separate and opposing positions? At such points it tends all too quickly to lead either to an oppressive demand for loyalty come what may, or an empty form of anonymous pluralism, of the 'some think this . . . some think that' variety, in which the struggle over the issue is simply given up.[13]

Again Selby touched with uncanny precision on events which would occur two years later.

It must be said, however, in fairness to the Church, that later in the same decade Peter Selby was appointed a diocesan bishop – at Worcester – so a spokesman exists in the House of Bishops to remind them that Christians are about adoption and not tribalism.

The Hollow Crown

A persistent talking-point in recent years has been the way bishops are appointed, this being where at present the shoe of Establishment pinches. A medium-sized move away from the traditional method was made in 1976. Up till that time the Crown appointed bishops solely on the advice of the prime minister, and though in practice there was consultation with the Church behind the scenes, it took no official part in the process. A Motion was carried by General Synod in 1974 which affirmed that the decisive voice in the appointment of diocesan bishops should be that of the Church, that a small body, 'representative of the vacant diocese and of the wider Church, should choose a suitable person' and submit the name to the Sovereign, and asked the Standing Committee of Synod to look into the implications of this.

This bold claim for freedom was received with some sympathy by the Prime Minister of the day, James Callaghan, who nevertheless felt that the state 'could not divest itself from a concern with these appointments to the established Church'. He proposed a compromise – that the prime minister should still advise the Queen in the matter and 'retain a real element of choice', but he was prepared to accept the principle of a 'small committee' which would draw up a short list of two names which might be given in order of preference. 'The Prime Minister would retain the right to recommend the second name, or to ask the committee for a further name or names.' It cannot be said that, over the course of years, this has pleased or satisfied the Church. There is profound dislike of the secrecy of the whole process, with candidates not even aware that they are being considered, and the relevant information being processed through the Prime Minister's appointments secretary, who may, very naturally, have his own prejudices. This could scarcely be more at odds with modern views about 'open appointments' at all levels of society. Rumour abounds about prime ministers insisting on their own choices – for example, Tony Blair and the Liverpool appointment, or Mrs Thatcher and the Canterbury appointment, in which it is often claimed that she chose Archbishop Carey partly, at least, out of dislike for another candidate. Since the Committee is sworn to silence about the choice, no hard evidence is available, and it is a situation in which suspicion is rife. It seems ludicrous that the Church cannot be trusted to choose its own officials.

A later Working Party (1992) published a review of the methods of appointing suffragan bishops, deans, provosts, archdeacons and residentiary canons, which repeated all the previous arguments about secrecy, openness and the problems surrounding appointments.

The most interesting thing about it was the minority dissenting report by Mr Frank Field MP. He began by reiterating the conclusions of the Working Party about the need for change. 'The present system – operating as it does in secret, dependent upon the old boy network, with candidates unaware even that they are being considered and the views of the interesting parties channelled through a single person to the Prime Minister – may have been acceptable in Trollope's time.'[14]

Agreeing at many points with his colleagues, Frank Field is troubled by the conclusion of the Working Party that the existing system of the Patronage secretary should go, though the monarch's very limited role should be kept as a kind of façade. As an Establishment man Frank Field was very worried by this – he could not bear the idea of the monarch taking a reduced role – his arguments make a very interesting study of the way a thoroughgoing supporter of Establishment, himself a devout churchman, thinks. He will not contemplate even this small degree of separation from the state.

Recently another working party has been set up to review the working of the Crown Appointments' system, reflecting current concern and anger about it in the Church.

Speaking up for the Churchwardens

Frank Field's worries seem a far cry from the kind of Church most of us know about, yet just occasionally a little bit of state interference can offer a useful intervention. In the spring of 1999 Parliament interfered to balk a Synodical Measure which would allow bishops to deprive a churchwarden of his or her function apparently at will and to appoint a substitute of his own choosing in their place. It was not clear what had made such a Measure seem desirable – a 'trawl' of churches and churchwardens seemed unable to uncover any scandal which would justify such a draconian step, and it looks as if the idea was due to the Church's current preoccupation with 'control'. Mercifully, it was stopped in its tracks.

Bishops Aloft

There are four among the present bishops who represent a rather different kind of function from what has been described up till now, one that has never been practised before in the Church. In order to accommodate those clergy who felt unable to go along with the ordination of women after General Synod passed the Measure for the Ordination of Women Priests in 1992, the House of Bishops proposed that 'diocesan bishops . . . shall from time to time nominate from within their region one or more bishops who are opposed' (to women priests). Called 'Provincial Episcopal Visitors', or, more popularly, 'flying bishops', their task was to offer 'extended pastoral care and sacramental ministry' to those opposed, as well as 'act as spokesman and adviser' for them. Forward in Faith, the movement that sprang up to defend those opposed to women priests, claimed that bishops who ordained women were in 'impaired communion' with those who did not. A man properly consecrated bishop of a diocese, therefore, who ordained a candidate for the priesthood, might not be deemed acceptable to this school of thought, if he had previously touched (ordained, in this context) a woman priest. Those who favoured women's ordination claimed that this was a break with a Catholic order (in fact, a more radical break than ordaining women), since the authority of the bishop has always been paramount in the Church of England and in the history of Christian tradition. They felt that what was being pioneered here was a 'doctrine of taint' (hands that touched women being somehow contaminated), something that those opposed to women priests have continued to deny, though not very convincingly. Three bishops were immediately consecrated to the purpose of this extra-mural function.

An article by an area dean, Lesley Bentley, in a book of essays called *Act of Synod – Act of Folly* (1998)[15] pointed out that whereas the flying bishop plan had originally been seen as one designed in compassion and courtesy to help clergy who felt alienated by the decision, but who might become reconciled in time, it was plainly not seen in this light by Forward in Faith.

> *Forward in Faith* is widely seen, not as protecting an existing constituency, but as promoting an increase. The fulltime Director of *Forward in Faith* (Stephen Parkinson) makes it clear . . . that the intention is to boost the numbers of priests opposing the ordination of women to the priesthood. The very existence of PEVs conveys the same message. If we appoint a bishop on one particular aspect of his ministry and it is that aspect that he is seen to work most within, then we must expect a certain attempt to pull others

in the direction he has been appointed to defend. The question must be then asked, how far is this likely to promote unity?[16]

She goes on to suggest that far from bringing about unity, what is happening is 'the increasing isolation of those opposed to the ordination of women'. Subsequent letters in *The Times*[17] have questioned the usefulness of the continued practice of having flying bishops, and suggested that the PEVs should move back into the 'normal structures' of the Church.

Now, two widely differing views of the Act of Synod are held in the Church. There are those who say with pride that it reflects the capacity of the Church to contain division, and shows charity and compassion, and those who say that, apart from damaging catholicity, it shows a lack of imagination about the impact it has on women priests, and less directly, on all women who have to witness it. There are now, after all, more than two thousand ordained women priests, some thirteen hundred of them working very effectively within the church structures. They are obviously here to stay. In order to protect itself the Church claims exemption from the Sex Discrimination Act of 1975, but an ecclesiastical lawyer, Lynne Leeder, is not at all sure that, if an appeal was made in Europe, the Church would be permitted such an exemption.[18]

The present situation pleases nobody except those, rarely personally affected, who want to use it as an example of Christian charity. There are growing pleas from the disaffected for a 'Third Province' or a 'Free Province', that is to say a para-church for those who cannot accept women, for which, they hope, the Church of England would provide resources.

The Act of Synod of 1993 placed a rod in pickle for the Church of England in general and for its architects, the bishops, in particular, and it is very difficult to see how to move forward from the appalling muddle it created. Prudence, though not necessarily in the form of timidity, should now be the watchword. As the bishop said to the actress.

Lesser Fry

Beneath a bishop are two archdeacons who preside over a large number of parishes. I learn from Paul Welsby's useful *How the Church of England Works*[19] that the archdeacon is thought of us *oculus episcopi*, the eye of the bishop – less, one hopes, a spy than one who looks sympathetically on the work of the parishes and reports it faithfully. In addition to some important duties connected with ordination, installation of incumbents and discipline of clergy, the archdeacon is also responsible the fabric and contents of churches within his archdeaconry. At the time of writing two women have so far been appointed as archdeacon, Judith Rose to Tunbridge Wells and Joy Tetley to Worcester.

Below the archdeaconry is the rural deanery, a small group of parishes presided over by the rural dean (sometimes in an urban setting known nowadays as the 'urban', 'area' or 'borough' dean). The rural dean is himself a parish priest. Like the archdeacon, the rural dean holds a title with an ancient ring to it which disappeared and was revived, in the early nineteenth century in this case, and he or she is a part of the chain of communication which runs between parish and bishop. Rural deans hold clergy chapters, known as 'deanery chapters', in which matters of common concern are discussed. The rural dean is also the chairman of Deanery Synod, a forum of clergy and laity which exists to promote the work and life of the Church by discussion of common concerns and problems and by building a sense of intimacy with other local churches. It can act as a reference point on behalf of Diocesan Synod, and may in turn send resolutions for debate to Diocesan Synod. It elects members for General Synod.

The Bridge Report[20] was unhappy about Deanery Synod in ways that will be familiar to Christians at the grass roots. People already busy serving their own parishes were unwilling to devote further time to meetings; it often felt as if the clergy, who met regularly at chapters outside the synod, controlled what happened at Deanery Synod, and tended, in any case, to be better informed and possibly more articulate on issues than lay members.

The answer the Bridge Report came up with was an odd one, a bit of a non sequitur from its criticisms. It was to demote the deanery synod by taking it out of the synodical structure altogether, a move which seemed likely to accomplish little beyond diminishing the status of the deanery synod, and therefore probably finishing it off altogether. A more useful idea might be to show that the deanery synod might assume more power rather than less.

19

The Poor Parson

But Cristes lore, and his apostels twelve
he taughte; but first he folwed it himselve.
(Chaucer, Prologue to *The Canterbury Tales*)

The basic building blocks in the ecclesiastical pyramid are the laity
and the parson/minister/pastor/vicar/rector/curate or priest
(choice of one or another of these words can say a great deal about
the beliefs of the person who utters them). Chaucer was perhaps the
first writer in the English language to draw a full-length portrait of
the good parson. Gentle, dutiful, caring for his 'people', not
constantly running off to the city in search of adventure or preferment, not preaching anything he is not prepared to practise, he
shines out from the pages of the Prologue with a lovely light. As
Chaucer suggests, he was, above all, a good example, and saw it as
his task to be one – 'If gold ruste, what shall iren do?' Most of us who
know the Church at all well have met his, and more recently, her,
like, and been enriched by the gold. There is a longing, inside and
outside the Church, to find this caring, loving person who will devote
himself or herself to the task. There are still a surprisingly large
number of them about in spite of more modern, and more mechan-
ical images of priesthood.

George Herbert, in his brief time at Bemerton in Wiltshire before
death claimed him, embodied this legend of the good priest.
Although an aristocrat and a courtier by background as well as a fine
poet, his 'imitation of Christ' involved regarding others as his
brothers and sisters, and the legend as told by Izaak Walton includes
the story of his taking off his coat to help a carrier whose horse had
fallen and whose cart had got stuck in the mud. Herbert had been
on his way to a musical evening, and arrived looking so unusually
dirty and dishevelled (he was usually rather neat and fastidious),
that his companions remarked on it and he was obliged to explain

what he had been doing. Some were shocked that he, a gentleman, should so demean himself, but Herbert insisted that he felt he had been privileged to have the opportunity. 'And now' he said, eager to change the subject, 'shall we tune our instruments?'

So deeply ingrained is his example in the Anglican canon that the radical paper of the 1970s, *New Christian,* used to talk in shorthand of 'the George Herbert syndrome'. There was a note of satire in their references. While admiring Herbert, I think they felt that there might be other ways of being a good priest, and we should not be confined in this particular tradition.

The point about Herbert was that he was a gentleman, living out his Christian love by his goodness to 'his flock', and that was admirable. But the old days of *de haut en bas* are gone, and what moved me most in my researches was the sense of clergy standing alongside local people in all kinds of situations. Sometimes it was in an area where poverty, violence and unemployment seemed endemic, sometimes in a more salubrious neighbourhood which did not, however, lack its own problems and suffering. Everywhere I was impressed at the commitment, the devotion, the willingness to work for years on modest pay (or in some cases no pay at all – literally working for love) and with very little recognition. Clergy are some of the unsung heroes and heroines of our time, without whom social problems and human despair in this country would be infinitely worse. Some have to endure the loneliness of working in parishes where the response is almost non-existent, and they pay a terrible price for the sense of failure this can induce. Many of them continue to be a remarkable image of Christian love.

Clergy come in many shapes and forms including, nowadays, the female shape, and endowed with every shade of temperament and ability. Their historical contribution to British society has been remarkable, not merely in the running of the Church, but in the field of learning – botany, biology, astronomy, psychology and the arts. Two names that stand out are those of John Flamsteed, a priest but also a very distinguished Astronomer Royal under Charles II, or Charles Lyell, whose work as a botanist inspired Charles Darwin's evolutionary discoveries. The Church of England has, in its time, been proud of the learned men who took orders in the Church – men who had studied languages, history, classics and theology. Few future Archbishops of Canterbury will probably have a First in Greats as Archbishop Fisher did, and few parochial clergy now seem to be privately making scientific discoveries, but in the past few years I have met a number of clergy who are practising actors, poets, historians, novelists, composers, singers, instrumental players, painters and potters. I remember reading of one who was a world expert on snowdrops, and clergy always seem to feature in any press correspondence about steam trains, with which they apparently have an affinity.

The question must be whether, in the direction in which the Church is moving, it will have room for those gifted creatively, as opposed to good at organisation, and whether it will not miss a great deal if it loses them, men and women, who have a vision of life that goes beyond efficiency, targets and goals. Creativity takes time, not merely to produce the 'finished object', whatever that may be, but in an apparently fruitless period which leads up to the act of creation, what the Trappist Thomas Merton called 'trifling and vegetating'.

The mind often only produces its jewels when it apparently lies at peace. Far from Satan finding work for the idle, it is often in idleness, quietness, silence, relative calm, that the Spirit speaks. An ideal of 'busyness' not only destroys this, but plays into the warped fantasy of a society obsessed with money-making and consumerism.

Is there a recurring stereotype in clergy as I see, or imagine I see, among the bishops? What has often struck me among clergy, seen both in church and in their leisure moments, is their ability as performers – as actors, singers, speakers, tellers of stories, preachers. It is possible, of course, that those who like to perform in public are attracted to a career where they have this opportunity, and also that long exposure to public platforms makes for more confidence in public situations than most of us have – a bit like the extraordinary facility with words enjoyed by politicians. But clergy, I suggest, are more akin to the actor than the politician, and it is worth remembering the close links between stage and Church: that the theatre grew from the Church in the way described by Eamon Duffy in *The Stripping of the Altars*, and down the Anglican generations it has not been at all infrequent for actors and priests to emerge from the same families.

Certain traits appear in both (though the Church has never been at pains to point this out) a pleasure in dressing up, in ritualistic (staged) events, in touching upon the great events of life in an 'as if' mode ('as if' Hamlet is a real person as he struggles with his dilemma, 'as if' we are actually standing at the cross on Good Friday, or in the Easter garden on Easter morning), as well as encouraging others to meditate in depth about what life is about.

In other cultures – for example, Aboriginal culture – some of the priestly tasks would be performed by the shaman, and those of us who care for ritual and find it a powerful religious vehicle at times find ourselves seeing the clergy in a shamanic role. I believe that it may be important for clergy to be much more conscious of this, both to avoid identifying unconsciously with the archetype themselves, with the consequent danger of developing a power-complex, but also as a way of understanding and harnessing the power of the shaman in a creative way. To do this, however, the Church needs to overcome its fear and horror both of homosexuality and of transsexuality. Shamans of many different cultures nearly always have some transsexual ritual in their training, as if there is a recognition that at the deeper levels of human experience there is a need to have experienced, either in fact or imagination, a dual sexuality, to recognise and welcome both male and female within. (A similar capacity is sometimes noticeable in great writers, Shakespeare and Tolstoy being obvious examples.) This is where the healing of many human wounds takes place. Some clergy who can do this will be heterosexuals who are conscious of their feminine side, some will be homosexuals; the Church has been hugely enriched by male clergy with both of these aspects, and will doubtless be enriched by women in a similar way. Clergy who can only be 'macho' or 'ultra feminine' are not likely to be much use in their job, since they can only identify with half the human race.

Priests have a particular significance at the threshold places in human lives – birth, marriage and death. They have the privilege to be with people at moments of great joy and hope, and, if they have the psychological strength, at moments of great suffering, as people face death, bereavement or other human tragedies. They are privy to more intimate secrets than most of the rest of us – to sorrow, terror, suicide, violence, shame, disgrace, despair – and, unlike the therapist or the surgeon who works in and is protected by a clinical setting, the priest often meets with people in their own homes or in the street.

To be the loving witness of great distress asks an enormous amount of any human being, and requires inner resources to be able to survive it, yet there is no doubt in my mind that this kind of 'standing by' the suffering of others is one of the redemptive actions in a world of shocking and otherwise hopeless violence, a remaining at the cross of Jesus, and a holding to it, until the unimaginable moment of resurrection at last arrives. (Of course, not only priests do this work, but their job and vision makes them particularly accessible to such a use, and it is itself part of their vocation.) Sometimes priests in recent years have themselves become the victim of violence.

At its best the job of the priest is a vocation – that is to say, a job to which people feel themselves called. People with other forms of vocation, which seem to them of value, can feel very irritated at clerical assumptions (more than actual statements) that their vocation is somehow superior to all others. This can be very evident at ordinations, which seem sometimes to have almost the nature of a wedding about them.

'I can't bear the way they think they're so special' said a doctor friend of mine, herself with a very strong sense of vocation. The truth is, of course, that we are all of us 'chosen', all of us equally 'special'; to be the person that we are with the gifts that we have in God's purpose is what is required of a Christian – there is no higher or lower, better or worse. A sense of inferiority, I believe, is what makes some clergy cling so hard to their own specialness. The specialness can only be in the doing, not in the vocation itself.

The Making of a Priest
The process of becoming a priest in the Church of England is not a particularly quick one. It involves the individual being recommended at a local level, by someone who believes that they have a vocation, to a Diocesan Director of Ordinands. They will need to have enough education to complete the training course, reasonable health, and the sponsorship of their bishop. (Educational attainments are not what they were. Some 57 per cent of clergy now do not have a degree.) They then attend a residential conference which decides whether to recommend that they should proceed. If they are recommended they will then embark upon a period of training, the length of which depends somewhat upon their previous education and experience, but it quite often takes a couple of years either on the campus of a theological college, or in a non-residential course. After some very drastic pruning in recent years, there are now eleven theological colleges in England. Geographically they are quite well placed, in locations as far apart as Durham, Oxford (three of them), Cambridge (two of them), Birmingham, Yorkshire, London and Bristol. Fifteen local schemes to train for ordination are recognised by the House of Bishops and these are widely distributed over the country, and in addition there are a number of regional courses working in the same area.

Vincent Strudwick, who teaches theology at Oxford University, and also at St Stephen's House theological college, has reservations about the intellectual training of clergy.

> One of the things that really disturbs me is that in the theological colleges and courses they are becoming more and more geared to doing systematic theology, and learning to enhance pastoral skills, which is fine, but at the expense of opportunity for reflective

understanding both of the nature of our Church and of the culture in which we live. I think ordinands need to learn historical theology – the formation of the Church of England, the fact that we have an ecclesiology that is different from that of Rome, and that it is informed by people like Jewel and Hooker . . . I think they need to get to grips with the ideas of Hooker and Andrewes.

At St Stephen's House they weren't doing an Anglican ecclesiology. When I suggested it, they said 'What is Anglican ecclesiology?' Now they allow me four lectures and I do a short lecture course on Anglican ecclesiology. The guys and girls light up with this stuff, because it's new to them. They contrast it with post-Tridentine ecclesiology, and see how the Roman Church is shaped differently from us in our concept of bishops, in our concept of authority, in the way authority is exercised in the parish, the *sensus fidelium*, etc. All the ideas that come out of Hooker, and the Anglican sense of relationship with the community, which is different from that of the Middle Ages, I believe.

Everyone who runs courses says there's no time, we can't fit anything else in. But I think that a reflective understanding of the way theology develops in different cultures and milieux, and in our history and our geography, is vitally important.[1]

Those whose complete their training course, and are approved by their superiors, are ordained as deacons in a solemn ceremony involving the bishop, and sent to work, usually in a parish. Then, after a year, they are ordained priest. They continue training in post for several years in what is called Post Ordination Training, colloquially known as 'potty-training'. As curates or assistant clergy they have the chance to gain experience both of preaching and conducting services, as well as for caring pastorally for people. The job to which they are ordained is an unusual one, demanding a wide range of skills, from public speaking, to singing, to counselling, to administration, to (ideally) a strong liturgical and aesthetic sense, to an effective religious faith and an ability to articulate it.

Mrs Cranmer's Box

Theological colleges have changed in a generation or so almost out of recognition. Humphrey Carpenter's life of Robert Runcie describes the life of students at Cuddesdon in the early 1960s when Runcie was Principal – a degree less monastic than it had been during the reign of his predecessor Edward Knapp-Fisher, when wives and girlfriends had to live more than two and a half miles away from the college, but nevertheless austere with an austerity that weighed harder upon the wives and girlfriends than it did on the men themselves. For example, all meals had to be eaten by students in college. The state of mind of wives who, like the wife of the Principal herself, spent their days caring for tiny children in isolation and craved adult conversation and company, scarcely bears thinking about. It was a modern equivalent of 'Mrs Cranmer's box', the alleged travelling method of Cranmer's wife, who was not really supposed to exist at all, between archiepiscopal houses.

By chance I visited Cuddesdon in 1961, invited by a church body to write something about the modern church and how clergy were trained, and I was surprised to discover that I was the first woman to be allowed to sleep at the college. I learn from Adrian Hastings' *History of English Christianity* that when the Council of William Temple's Life and Liberty Movement decided to meet and hold a retreat at Cuddesdon in 1917, the Principal would not allow Maude Royden, the only woman member, to sleep there. It would be good to be able to report that Temple and the other men decided on the spot to leave as a bunch, but they did not do so. Maude Royden resigned from the Council and they accepted her resignation and continued with their meeting. All these illustrations speak more eloquently of male fantasies about women than about anything else – of the curious belief (or hope) that women are so sexually voracious that it is not safe to spend a night under the same roof with them, or that it may be more 'spiritual' not to spend time with a woman, even if the woman concerned is your own wife.

Nowadays at Cuddesdon, and every other college except Mirfield, women and men train alongside each other, and husbands, wives and children often live on campus or nearby. This is very different from the ethos of thirty years or so ago when (male) clergy were seen as quasi-monks, and their wives, if they had them, were not supposed to intrude on their privileged calm. The effect of this upon family life was overlooked, and many clergy wives were left with a permanent sense of grievance, not simply about the way training took their husbands away from them (which was, after all, only for a limited period), but at the way it set a pattern that the job was always was to be more important than family commitments. One clergy wife I know told me how much she minded that it took her husband twenty-four hours to make it to her hospital bedside after the birth of their first baby.

Training Old and New

The old training was based on the idea that you should be single while it was going on, and if you were not, then you had to live as if you were. It expected a university background, preferably Oxbridge, before the theological training began, which necessarily produced a large cultural gap between priest and many of the people he served. I remember how astonished I was as a child at the 'Oxford accents' of the clergy who presided in our local church, and how wickedly my sister and I used to imitate them. I had never heard anyone who talked like that before. In the course of my lifetime too we have seen the priesthood cease to be the preserve of 'gentlemen' or those who would or could pass as such (something which grammar schools did its best to help its pupils to do). The new part-time courses, the first of which was started by John Robinson when he was Bishop of Woolwich, worked on very different assumptions of who and what a priest should be. From the end of the Second World War the class gap was, in any case, gradually closing. Grammar school boys and others joined the priesthood. In the postwar years there was the shock of hearing clergy who did not speak with public school accents – now it is more of a surprise if they do. From the 1950s too there was a new clerical phenomenon, that of retired men training for the priesthood. The first person I knew to do so was the churchwarden of the church I attended in my twenties, a civil servant in his late forties, who went on to become a curate. In 1987 women became deacons and could thus become curates. In 1994 they were finally ordained as priests.

In the 1950s there was still money to pay extra clergy. In the past twenty years financial shortage has divided the ministry into three ranks: the stipendiary, the non-stipendiary and the ordained local ministry, though only sixteen dioceses so far have the last. The original expectation about NSMs (non stipendiary ministers) was that they would be priests working in secular occupations outside the structure of the Church. It has not worked out like that. Some non-stipendiary clergy are comfortably pensioned people living off the money saved by them and their employer in their previous employment. Obviously they are a very useful resource for the Church. Other priests are non-stipendiary because they want to do the work, and no stipend is made available to them even if they would wish for it. Where both a husband and wife are priests, for example, the wife has a reduced and often non-existent stipend, a real injustice that causes understandable bitterness, since it is an exploitation of goodwill. In a society where it is now the norm for wives to work, and where most clergy couples both bring in an income, the ordained wives of clergy are deprived of a proper return for their services, which can do little to make the marriage feel good. 'The present position is a scandal' writes a (male) priest in the *Church Times*.

Men whose wives are teachers, professionals in many fields – even hospital consultants earning up to £100,000 a year – are never asked to become NSMs and serve on a house-for-duty basis. Yet almost every woman in this diocese (Peterborough) whose husband's resources make a significant contribution to living expenses can expect no offer of a stipendiary post after their first curacy . . . I can bring to mind only four women who are enjoying a stipendiary second ministry. All the rest give their skills and talents on a non-stipendiary basis. They are rarely considered for preferment, and this has been a means whereby the old boy network has been retained.[2]

Credence is inadvertently given to this point of view by the preface of the *Church of England Yearbook* published in January 1999, in which Canon Hugh Wilcox called for a review of current clergy pay, stating that the stipendiary ministry was being 'subsidised by working spouses'.[3] But what of the couples where one of them works 'for free' for the Church? His comments were given point by the fact that the Guildford diocese (one of the wealthier dioceses) had recently broken ranks with the other dioceses by putting up its stipends beyond the agreed rate (even taking regional variations of cost into account). Average stipends for incumbents (vicars and rectors) over the country as a whole range between £14,600 and £15,510, with the value of provided housing estimated at about £7,820 p.a. A letter in the *Church Times,* however, from a parish priest in Newport Pagnell, the Reverend Maurice Stanton-Saringer, saw it rather differently.

The national average income in April 1998, the last date for which figures are available, was £19,561. The average clergy stipend is about £15,250. In addition most clergy receive expenses of a minimum of £1,000, and in many instances twice that figure or more. Our housing is virtually free, with tax allowances on part of our fuel, garden-maintenance and cleaning costs . . . The housing package, including council tax and water rates, themselves worth about £1,200, is estimated to be worth £7,820. That makes our remuneration worth about £24,000. I find it hard to believe that a package worth considerably more than the average wage is hard to live on in reasonable comfort. The Commissioners guarantee to help retiring clergy find suitable housing, which I know from visiting the retired priests around here is more than adequate, with a full service pension worth about £12,000, in addition to the State pension.[4]

He adds wryly, 'Perhaps we should add the subject of personal financial management to the curriculum in theological colleges.'

A subsequent response to this discussion in the *Church Times* raised the interesting question of whether the Church would not do better to give up the whole 'tied cottage' approach to the housing of clergy, thus cutting down substantially on the work of the Church Commissioners but also giving clergy a chance to save, as so many others do nowadays, by investing in bricks and mortar.

The concept of OLMs (Ordained Local Ministers) is that, as in the earliest history of the Church, particular congregations should call out suitable people from among them to receive training as ministers. The training is quite an imaginative one, some of it specific to the OLMs, some of it shared with lay readers, and some with the wider ministry courses. There seems a great deal to be said for priests with local knowledge, and already known by a congregation, as opposed to clergy arriving at a job with virtually no link at all with a church. The risk must always be of their being treated as second- or third-class priests.

Perhaps a growing danger in the Church is of financial shortage placing heavy responsibilities on individuals who may not have the training, the experience or the support needed to handle them.

A contentious affair is security in the clerical job. After serving as a curate many priests, in the past, obtained a 'living' with what was known as the 'parson's freehold'. This device, devised at an earlier period of history when shifting political allegiances could make the parish priest vulnerable, offered great, indeed almost absolute security of tenure, unless there was some serious moral breach or dereliction of duty. It is now gradually disappearing, although about two-thirds of clergy still have it. A recently retired priest told me that in his previous job he had 'six livings'. 'Now the bishop has put a priest-in-charge in every one of them.' There was much to be said against the 'parson's freehold', as any church that has ever had to put up with a plainly hopeless rector or vicar will tell you, yet short-term contracts, the new habit, seem not to give the decent security human beings need in a job, particularly if they are to found a family. What is wrong with a system in which it is assumed that men and women will continue in their job as long as seems appropriate to the parties concerned, but which offers some legal method of despatching those who cannot do the job satisfactorily? Most of us, before the managerial revolution made people quickly expendable, worked in such jobs. It is not good for the Church that clergy plainly feel much less secure than they did; in the Church, as elsewhere, stretched resources make people fearful and paranoid. A working party on clergy discipline, *Under Authority*, was published in 1996 (known as *Hawker*) and a draft Measure which emerged from it is still undergoing a revision process.

It is a sign of the times that some fifteen hundred clergy and church workers have joined a trade union, the Manufacturing, Science and Finance Union, and numbers have increased rapidly. Chris Ball, the secretary of MSF Clergy and Church Workers, says 'Bishops have immense power. A few take an "I'm the king of the castle" approach. In some particularly difficult cases, they have not even been willing to meet to discuss important issues.'[5] The Church has been able to take a relaxed attitude to work obligations in the past by claiming that the Church is not an employer – the clergy are not employees – a rather dubious manoeuvre that impresses nobody.

Issues that concern the MSF at the moment are clergy stipends, clergy discipline, and the abusive treatment of women clergy alleged by the Revd Judy Lynas, who published a report on the subject.

Church officials deny the problem the MSF sees. 'I have no evidence of bishops treating people in a seriously inappropriate way,' says the Ven. Gordon Kuhrt,[6] Director of Ministry, and certainly few glaring examples have recently come to light. What is in evidence is the anxiety clergy are feeling as the balance of power between bishops and clergy shifts significantly in the bishop's direction, especially as the bishops have financial and legal resources available to them which are beyond clergy means. In this, as in other areas of its life, the Church needs to address the underlying feelings, not simply insist that all is well.

Nowadays, after two or three years as a curate, a man or woman becomes available for other jobs. Some of these are outside parochial ministry – clergy work as chaplains in schools, hospitals, prisons and industry. Those who stay within the parish structure may become a priest-in-charge or vicar who is part of a team on a short-term contract.

Whatever the incidental worries or stresses of being a priest, *Explaining and Forecasting Job Satisfaction* (1999), a report by researchers at the University of Bath, showed an extremely high level of job satisfaction among clergy. 'Their level of satisfaction is described as "abnormally high", given salaries which the report acknowledges to be very low in absolute terms for a professional group . . . For the clergy, low material wants and expectations, as it were, "go with the job" and entrance to the clergy is conditional upon their accepting them.' Of clergy surveyed 72 per cent were 'positively satisfied'. Even long hours were cheerfully accepted – clergy complained 'less than fire officers, prison warders or pharmicists'![7]

A Sample

I decided to sample a number of churches in different geographical locations, interviewing the vicar, priest-in-charge or rector and attending a Sunday service, where that was possible. The result was a series of surprises – my prejudices about churchmanship different from my own were never fully borne out by what was going on. I was delighted at what good things seemed to be happening and how stimulated and encouraged I felt, as a loyal member of the Church of England, to see that this was the case.

Yes, there are 'sink' churches just as there are sink schools where nothing goes right, particularly in areas where social conditions are very hard, or where the Church has been failing for years. Clergy working in such situations need massive input – financial and human – to survive, and possibly, if they have young children, should not be there at all since the family may find itself victimised. A recent *Church Times* news report described how the black adopted child of a white vicar in South London was victimised and had his spirit broken by racism in the neighbourhood.

It should not be beyond the capacity of the Church to inspire teams of young men and women to go and work for a few years at a time on the sink estates and neighbourhoods and help restore new hope to communities terrified by violence and demoralised by vandalism. This would seem to marry well with the excellent 'regeneration' work of the Church Urban Fund. In such situations, to establish a base of safety and human decency is the only conceivable way that faith is ever going to reach the agenda. Most of the churches described below are not in that situation, though one or two come near to it. I have concentrated on churches that 'work', rather than churches that fail.

20

A Handful of Parishes

Holy Trinity, Brompton, London

I visited Holy Trinity on a fine spring evening. In the avenue of trees that runs up to the entrance of the church from the Brompton Road there were several young couples, hand in hand, en route for HTB (as it is known) and its five o'clock evening service. (It also has a 7.30 evening service as well as two morning services.) Although I was very early, hymn singing was already in full swing, with a band and singers, and the words of hymns indicated on an overhead projector. The congregation struck me as decidedly well-to-do, with many young people in early adulthood. In a large congregation I noted only one black face.

The service was briefly introduced by the Vicar, Sandy Millar, wearing a sweater and trousers and no clerical collar. There was then a very long hymn-singing session with repetitive choruses – the hymns seemed to me to mount in emotional intensity. This was followed by a long sermon by a lay man who, Sandy Millar told me later, was Vice-Chairman of Warburg's. It must have had a biblical text but what stuck in my mind afterwards was the novel by John Grisham that he mentioned at the beginning. There was then 'the Blessing' – the calling down of the Spirit, which has become known as 'the Toronto Blessing' – because the phenomenon came to new prominence at the Airport Vineyard Church in Toronto in January 1994. The community prayed and those who wanted healing were asked to come forward. Those who did were 'supported' by members of the congregation who went up and stood beside them.

I had heard of the strange occurrences that went on at Holy Trinity – people rolling on the floor, clucking or barking, but nothing of that kind occurred, though a few people shook a little and one cried. Sandy Millar then said that he believed someone in the church had a bad headache, and that if they would come forward hands would be laid on them. Three people did come forward and had hands laid on them.

To my surprise there was no Bible reading and no public intercession.

Talking to Sandy Millar afterwards I asked what happened to people who had experiences which touched a deep place in them while at Holy Trinity. He said that the church had many visitors, and no long-term work could be done with those unless they asked for it. He saw 'long-term healing' as taking place 'within the fellowship of the Church' and for this reason Holy Trinity placed a lot of emphasis on small groups and structures. Some visitors, in any case, simply wanted the anonymity of prayer and ministry.

Sandy Millar has been part of Holy Trinity for a very long time. He was first a member of the congregation, then on the PCC, then was ordained and came back to Holy Trinity as curate in 1976, and finally became Vicar in 1980. The 'signs of renewal', as he puts it, began to appear in 1977–8. 'It was nothing to do with me, but I was here to see it.'

Millar remembers how much emptier the church was in earlier days.

> We are in the shadow of Imperial College, you know, and I used to see these young things come in the west door, look around, and they were just mystified at the whole thing because they've never been brought up in the Church. When I came here we had 1662 sung mattins with a choir, and believe it or not, I actually love that. But the fact is that very few people do.
>
> The thing is there is a new hunger for freshness and freedom in liturgy and it's everywhere. In the past year we've been to Australia and New Zealand, right across America, to South Africa, Norway, Sweden, all over the place . . . Ireland – I did five conferences over there. The same phenomenon is happening in all these places and it's totally uncoordinated – it's a movement of the Spirit. Another part of that is the desire to meet in small groups. And another thing that's happening in nearly every denomination across the board is a renewed interest in spiritual gifts. People want to be taught about that sort of thing – they want to understand about supernatural activities. If they don't get that in the Church – the activity of the Spirit – they'll go somewhere else, where they're interested in ouija boards, spiritualism and that sort of thing.

I asked whether this led to a danger of people coming to church because they wanted to 'see something happen'.

I quite agree, and I would resist that. I never let photographs be taken – it panders to a desire to see something odd and it can get exaggerated, and frighten people. But I do think what people want today is to experience God and that is a New Testament thing – as we read in the Acts of the Apostles about when the Spirit fell on people. There was always something going on and they were filled with the Spirit or someone was healed – it's an exciting thing. A woman came up to me at Spring Harvest about three weeks ago – there was a word of knowledge for couples trying to conceive – and she told me how she had driven her son and daughter-in-law to the front on a similar earlier occasion because they had been trying in vain for a baby for years. Ten months later her granddaughter was born, and she said 'I'm so grateful to God'.

Things like that happen every day. There is, I think, a new sense of expectation, and it coincides with a generation that craves experience – the whole of the New Age movement depends on experience, though I do not believe all those experiences, if any, are healthy. But the desire for experience is there. What we've noticed on Alpha courses is that you get at least two sorts of people – you get the ones who are really interested in head knowledge – the teaching – they want to know the facts about the Bible, Jesus, etc. And then you get those who just want to know God loves them. The second group love the weekend on the Holy Spirit, and the others find it a little harder. The coming together of the two, I think, head and heart, as we would say the desire to be committed and involved, is what makes the Christian faith.

I asked whether what we might be looking at was an unconscious or half-conscious revolt against the rationalism of a scientific age, with its lack of sympathy for emotion. Sandy Millar said that it seemed to him within the Church there were three important emphases: the message, the model and the market.

The trouble I believe with the Church of England is that, as the market is distancing itself increasingly from us we have been forced to change either the message or the model. When we try to change the message, I think it's a total failure, because what the market hopes to hear is that somebody really does believe in something, they don't want to be persuaded that because the Church actually no longer believes, they needn't believe either. What I think we have to do is alter the model. Which is why I unashamedly want to make it something which is acceptable to the market. Now the market is getting younger and younger and we have to try to bridge the gap. This is where Alpha is so key because it brings the Church within reach of people.

The frustrating thing for most churches is that there is a hunger out there, but people are not interested in the Church. That's frustrating because the Church feels that it has a lot to offer but the public don't. People want what the Church has to offer but they can't get at it. Alpha is trying to make it accessible in fifteen sessions – over twelve weeks – and this is a chance to bridge the gap. If we want to bring people in, and I think we do.

I asked about the criticisms of Holy Trinity, Brompton I had read in the Church press. What did Sandy Millar think that was due to? Envy from clergy with half-empty churches perhaps?

I don't really know. Every conference we run here is full, and a lot of the people there are Anglican clergy. So I find it sad that the church press, which is just as commercial as the *Sun* really, has a go at us. That's why we publish our own newspaper.

There had been a major Church report about unemployment just before I talked to Sandy Millar and I asked him where Holy Trinity stood on social issues that were responsible for huge human distress.

The Church of England has been responsible for much unemployment itself in recent years – they've cut and cut clergy all over the place, and then they whinge about unemployment. The Church of England has got assets of billions which is said to be set aside for the pensions of the clergy. I don't think the Church should be criticising the Government all the time – the purpose of the established Church is to help the Government, at least in the circumstances which prevail in this country – not under a Nazi government or something like that. I was very grateful for the example of Maurice Wood when he was a bishop in the House of Lords. He was always there not lecturing them but giving little booklets and offering to pray with them and help them . . . Godly men built the Brompton Hospital with private money – Christian men. Now all I hear is 'the government ought to do it . . . they're not doing enough . . . it's a disgrace – a scandal.' It surprises me that the government doesn't say 'Well you're the Church – you do it. You're sitting on a lot of money.' Lecturing the government from an Olympian height makes us look facile – the bishops are always doing it – offering easy solutions to things that politicans on both sides have pored for hours over. When did the Church start talking about abortion as an issue – the wholesale murder of endless babies? Do we say that unemployment comes higher than that in our priorities?

I suggested that these things were connected, that poverty aggravated all such problems.

'We probably should do more. But I want to get them saved – I want to get Mr Blair saved.'

'What does being saved mean?'

'Converted to the Christian faith.'

St Paul's, Highfield, Hemel Hempstead, Hertfordshire

St Paul's is in a countrified district of not very pretty housing and, before unemployment hit the district, many of its inhabitants had worked in semi-skilled trades in factories, particularly at British Aerospace and Rolls Royce. The church is within the team parish of Hemel Hempstead in the diocese of St Albans.

Peggy Jackson, the Team Vicar, answered an advertisement for a team vicar in 1990 – she had just done a three-year curacy in the Derby diocese – and arrived on 29 August, the date of the beheading of John the Baptist, a fact that was later to feel something like an omen.

> There were difficulties. This was before the Measure so that I was still a deacon, of course, and it was by no means as obvious or automatic that women could be Team Vicars as it is now. There had been a full-time Vicar of St Paul's, but in order to help Highfield meet its quota, things had been rearranged and I was coming as two-thirds Vicar and one-third adult education co-ordinator, which worried the congregation for a start: 'Which days are we going to see you?' they asked. But more of a problem than that was that I refused to be appointed as curate – I felt I had passed that stage – yet the diocesan lawyers said, 'Well, you can't be a Team Vicar – you're not a priest.' In the end, after all sorts of consultations with Church House, I was appointed as a 'member of the team'. All this debate made the congregation really wary, and one person who represented a few others appointed a solicitor to prove that I could not be legally appointed because the team constitution said that there should be a Team Vicar at Highfield. In fact, that didn't stand, because it is at the bishop's discretion whether there is or is not a Team Vicar at Highfield.
>
> At one stage in the debate it was suggested that the non-stipendiary priest who would have to celebrate here, since I was not allowed to, would be called the Vicar and I would be called the Curate, just to make everything safe and legal. I would do the work and he would serve the eucharist! Well, I wouldn't have taken the job on that basis, and a number of men put their jobs on the line for me and said 'no way'. The team clergy wanted me – they were ready to fight the battle for women. There were seven of us altogether. The Team Rector was very supportive and so was the suffragan bishop.

Once I was here it was fine, of course. Most members of the congregation were very supportive. In the second six months a trickle of people started coming who said, 'Well, I was a bit wary at first, but then . . .' So after about a year there was no problem.

St Paul's has seventy names on its electoral roll, and can expect about fifty people in church on a Sunday. Soon after Peggy arrived, British Aerospace and Rolls Royce closed their local factories and there was a lot of pain.

People had bought houses in the Thatcher years and they were now being repossessed. After that there were never many people in the congregation in permanent work. I think of Highfield as a place with the right number of trees but inside people's homes there's trouble and pain. In terms of statistics it's a very deprived area – overcrowding, sickness, single parent families, special needs children, no jobs – poverty, in fact.

MF. So what brings your congregation to church?

Neighbours – people get to know a neighbour who comes. Sometimes a need for safety and respectability – there are some who are escaping their untidy lives. When the next crisis comes they go away again and come back when they've tidied it up – 'Now we've got remarried and settled into a house we'll go to church again.' Some come when there's been too much suffering. Some come back – older folks, often after many years outside – they've come back because they've found the Church has changed, or maybe they just give it another go. I think people try it out every five or ten years or so (this is only my gut feeling, you understand), and if it's OK they'll stay for a bit.
    You know, there's a wistfulness in many people's attitude to the Church; those outside are always listening, listening to what's going on in it. The husbands listen to what happens to the wives and kids in church. For each person who comes there are five or six listening through them to what's going on, and asking what does the Church think about this nowadays, and if I came in the door what would they say to me? There's a lot of that. Because of it I changed the baptism policy to morning baptisms, which brought in a lot of enquiries about baptisms.
    Baptisms are jolly hard work, and sometimes it's awful if you get a church full of friends and visitors who don't quite get what it's about, but then you are getting a church full of visitors who actually see something of the church at work. And of the fifty or so who come a few are actually interested.
    We found ourselves coining a phrase early on: 'Passing through

277

is OK!' So we've tried to stop groaning or feeling inadequate because the baptism families don't come back – our being there for them *is* the vision. And it's worth noting that every single one of our Sunday School – usually between twelve and twenty kids – came in through a baptism! In one case too we had a Mum who had three baptisms of her children in our church and the third time she stayed, starting coming to church, was confirmed, and went on to run the Mums' and Tots' Sunday School.

I have a simple belief that the way to get more people is to acquire more of them, not fewer. At one time there was talk of cutting parade services – since we had not got many kids it was thought we might as well cut down. I resisted that and we had some rather imaginative youth services and because it had been a very traditional church people noticed this.

Peggy regards herself as a 'liberal Catholic'. 'But "liberal" is a dirty word now, isn't it? A pity, because it's a good word. A "modern Catholic" then.' She finally became Team Vicar in July 1994, three months after she was ordained priest.

In 1992 I wasn't even sure how people at Highfield would take the vote in favour of women priests, which speaks volumes in itself. But by the time of my ordination people had got really used to the idea, and we had had six months of planning for it. I was ordained on a Saturday afternoon so the Sunday morning was the first eucharist, and it was just unbelievably wonderful, for the congregation as much as for me, I believe. Having been through so much they just walked tall. We danced at that Eucharist – that was the first time we had had a circle dance in the church here – and there were men in tears. Men came to the door in the week following and said, 'I cried, I wanted you to know that I cried when we danced at your service.'

Two other women joining the team later on moved Peggy a great deal. 'It transformed the place for me. The first time Sally celebrated, I was all over the place – I was in tears, it seemed like proof that the whole thing had been real.'

Peggy became a Christian after a personal crisis and was confirmed in 1983. 'I don't worry about whether I believe things or not, what I discovered when I was in the pits was that God *is* there.' Two years after confirmation Peggy became an ordinand and started training at Cuddesdon. The change in her working life was financially sacrificial. She was a qualified chartered accountant, and her salary dropped to less than half of what it had been. 'The only thing I ever cried about was that I never got the company car which I would have got if I'd left six months later than I did! I'd always wanted a company car . . .'

On another level she suffered from the doubt and conflict about her ministry that was so much in evidence when she first came to Highfield.

> I coped at the time, yes, of course. I remember near the end of my interview a sinking feeling inside me, and saying to myself 'I can't do this' and then a little voice inside, saying 'Well, yes, you can.' It was either do it or knuckle under to the system and become a curate just so that the problems would not have to be faced by the Church. So I coped at the beginning, but a lot of emotion got tucked away – that's what you do when you are just trying to cope – and I notice that I've been feeling the distress of that quite recently when it's been safe to feel it.

Peggy notes that she missed out on the 'Christian feminist' phase of the struggle for women's ordination – it was not where she was psychologically at the time and she is still working through the ideas that that movement threw up.

> I was in college before I learned about inclusive and exclusive language. I found that when I knew that other women were coming to the team I was worried at what it would feel like not to be the only woman. I think I both wanted and resented the others – I thought they might be better at the things that I was the best at. But it didn't work out like that. In the team meetings, it was just staggering how wonderful it felt to be understood. It made me realise the degree to which I hadn't felt understood before. This is not peculiar to the Church – it was a problem I sometimes had with male colleagues in my accountancy days. I would say something, as it were in a light vein, and be taken too literally. I couldn't then say 'But I didn't mean that!', but a woman would never have thought I meant it anyway. It must be something in the body language, or the way one says it, or throws away a line, or the giggle afterwards.
>
> It seems to me that there are two languages – a men's language and a women's language. Men must have a collective knowledge which they tap into with little key words or phrases or something like that, because in the same way that is what women do with each other. As I say this I am aware that you understand me, whereas if a man were sitting here he might not. Talking to you I get the feedback which tells me that you understand me, but also I know that you will have had the same experience of not being understood in all-male gatherings. And I know that men won't know, cannot imagine, what that feels like.

Gender feels to me like a primal grouping – the gender experience of being a different body.

I asked her to say more about this.

Well, I love the way men bluff. I'm enormously impressed by it. It's because they need to – it's how they get things done. And sometimes they have to bully their way out because they've bluffed the wrong way. But they're still standing at the end of it and able to go on, whereas women would have been caught out and demolished, totally disabled.

I asked Peggy what the implications of this were. If the Church is dominated by men, and it is, and they need bluffing as their technique, how can anyone trust what is said?

Religion covers the fact that we have the most terrifying doubts – it is itself the cover up of the doubt. I often think that the most significant moment of the liturgy is the silence at the end of the eucharistic prayer. During which you think 'Do I actually mean what I say? Do I actually believe it? Has anything happened here?' There is something there in that silence, and it is as if the whole liturgy is a great protective layer around it.

I asked whether, if one asked the individual members of a congregation what they believed, there would be any sort of consensus of why they were there. Is there a vibrant core of belief?
'Of course there is.'
'But where is it?'

Well, I'm not sure it's in the Church really! There's a deep spiritual core in most of the people I meet, lots of whom don't come near a church building particularly. People come to church for other reasons besides spiritual need, but in church they find that there is a common reaching towards the vibrant core; the Church stands for this, and so in a perverse way it kind of works. Church stands for this thing that we do not know how to name and those out there won't say. The Church plays the social game of providing room and space and company and all the rest of it which makes it possible for people to be intimately associated with one another which can create the conditions for spiritual growth.

I suggest that the Church, the great container of spiritual truth in Europe and some other parts of the world, may feel too tight for us now – we may be potbound.

I think of it in terms of lifting off a lid. I really think it's safe to lift the lid off and open the doors and take the walls down and turn the church into a tent or a car park! Because there is a God. I don't/can't live at the point of knowing that the whole time. On the day when I don't believe anything at all, somebody else in the building does and the message is still there with someone to hold it. God is not dependent on my believing every week, let alone being good or something. It doesn't stop being true if I stop believing.

There was one final, rather gnomic, thing that Peggy Jackson said which is down on the tape of our interview. I'm not sure what it means, but I like the sound of it.

If you're moving you can change direction. If you're not moving, you can't remember which way you're facing.

Peggy Jackson is now Rector of Mortlake.

St Michael's and All Angels, Hackney

St Michael's is a modern church, consecrated for worship in 1961, to replace a church on the other side of London Fields (the local open space) which was badly damaged during the war. It is more or less square with an altar almost central to the church. There is a gallery, and some interesting wall paintings by John Hayward.

I attended a baptism service, which was incorporated into a eucharist, and was struck by the racial diversity of the congregation, a fairly equal mix, so far as I could judge, of Africans, Afro-Caribbeans and whites. There were two choirs, one robed one, which sang the more conventional church music, and one composed largely, though not exclusively, of Nigerians, who sang in a style I found tremendously exciting. I am still haunted by the memory of them singing 'Let the blessing of the Lord come down'.

Later, when I talked to the Vicar, Alan Everett, I asked if it was correct to describe him as a 'liberal Catholic' and he said that it was.

' "Liberal", of course, is a term of abuse now in the Church, which is nonsense. If you believe that the Bible is open to interpretation, you are a liberal. If not, you are a fundamentalist. It's a clear choice. I would have thought that the Anglican affirmation of Scripture, tradition and reason – intellectual integrity – would make us all liberals.'

Alan Everett came to St Michael's, Hackney in 1994, after a break working for his DPhil. I asked him what attracted him to the job and he said it was partly because of the East End location and also because the particular church appealed to him.

Looking at the people here, it's a very diverse congregation, multi-cultural, but also quite diverse in class terms. The housing is diverse. Some parishes in Hackney are almost unremittingly deprived, whereas this parish has an interesting mixture, which I found attractive. There are four or five streets of up-market terraced housing, but most of the parish consists of Council and Housing Association accommodation.

Apart from their value in themselves, middle-class parishioners help to raise the money you need to keep going. You do depend on a minority of the congregation to give a large proportion of the total income. The churches round here which are really struggling tend to be small parishes in extremely deprived areas – it's almost impossible to see how churches in that situation can survive without a heavy central subsidy. Also a middle-class balance provides some useful professional skills. So just from a purely practical point of view I could see that this was a situation which would work, that would work dynamically, which I believe it has and does. There was also the advantage that the church is a modern building, so that I knew we weren't going to be stuck with a huge building project. In terms of the local geography I was glad that London Fields was just a few minutes walk away.

Sister Helen, a priest from the Society of St Margaret, joined me after about six months as a colleague. We have worked really hard at the liturgy, trying to make something that felt more coherent to us, and we also put a lot of effort into the sermons. Informality and reverence, that's what we aim for. The eucharist is celebrated reverently, and we value silence, which means leaving time for the noise to die down! I try hard to choose hymns that people know and will sing, and I have spoken about the need to sing hymns with gusto. About half the monthly all-age services have become eucharists. There are no suitable Anglican children's eucharists, so we adapted a Roman Catholic mass. We found that the best way to do this service was to gather people in a circle around the altar, or, if there were too many for this, all the way round the church. Which meant that people who had come along to sit back and watch the clergy perform now found that they were participants. Some people left at that stage. But it was an exciting thing to do, a really marvellous thing to do, and more people started coming. We also started giving children agape bread that we had blessed. We felt that it was quite clear that it wasn't what the adults were receiving, but something especially for them. We've been doing that for three or four years now and those services seem to me to have a lot of depth.

Once people had had a chance to experience the changes we

conducted a worship questionnaire to find out what they thought
about them ... what sort of things they liked singing, what sort of
things they liked to see, at both the main services and the children's
services. What most people wanted from hymns was a combination
of old and new. So we bought copies of *Hymns Old and New*, after
battling on for ages with *Ancient and Modern*, and it has definitely
gave a boost to the singing. We had a hymn suggestion box.

In terms of the eucharist itself there is not really all that much
room for manoeuvre – it's a question of style and approach. There
are small things which can make people feel differently about what
is happening. Even the way people come up to the communion
rail.

The other major innovation in terms of the other three Sundays
of the month is the singing group. We'd had a robed choir which
was gradually running out of steam because people couldn't make
the rehearsals on a regular basis, so the PCC agreed to assemble a
robed choir, or a choir after that model, for special services five or
six times a year, often with some quite intensive rehearsal before-
hand. We found a lot more people wanted to be involved in that,
perhaps for Easter or Christmas or whatever. That left a gap Sunday
by Sunday. About a year and a half ago I started asking some of the
Nigerians if they would like to sing some of the choruses they sing
in Nigeria and they said they would. I put that to the PCC and they
said they were happy to see how it went, and it's gone from strength
to strength. It's interesting, the singers are not just Nigerians now.
One or two white people join in, and West Indians as well. The
choruses have a buoyant, affirmative, joyful quality, full of a sense
of the spirit.

Alan Everett contrasted this joy in the present with the greater
melancholy of much West Indian music, which he often heard at
funerals, with its emphasis on looking ahead out of this vale of
suffering and tears, but which he also feels expresses a rich spirituality, often based on suffering and anticipation of the world to
come. 'Some of my most powerful experiences here have been at
West Indian funerals.'

The conversation moved on to what the Church was trying to
achieve in terms of relationship.

The question is whether the Church aims to give people the
opportunity for relationships which they wouldn't otherwise have
– a rather nice given, which you can then enjoy – or whether you
want to try and push it a bit further. If you start trying to push it a
bit further, then you find yourself reaching for a theology of
liberation. Despite the fact that this is an established church you

may end up providing an environment which destabilises social relations!

All Saints' Church, Old Penshaw, Houghton-le-Spring, Tyne and Wear

The parish of Penshaw includes the village of Old Penshaw and a number of estates. It feels somewhere between a town and a village, known for the strange Doric memorial perched above it on a steep hillside. It has had three histories – a farming community, a mining community and a stone-quarrying community, the latter two industries, which have largely shaped Penshaw, now handing the country back to the remaining farmers. The Rector, Keith Walker, says:

The effect of the closure of the mining industry in Penshaw was dramatic, and many people who were part of the old mining community are now unemployed, retired, or living on fixed incomes here. A lot of the houses just down the street are mining cottages, and this house we're sitting in belonged to one of the managers of the mine. And a bit further away you will find quarrymen's cottages in little hamlets nearby. The mines in Penshaw have been closed for a long time now, since back in the 1960s, which means that Penshaw has looked in other directions to see what people could do. We have got a lot of elderly people here, but on the new estates there are pockets where people commute.

I believe we now have about 30 per cent unemployment. Although we are not classed as an urban priority area, we still have a lot of the problems you find there. In one part of the parish, when I first came, one of the churchwardens said to me, as we were driving round, 'This is an area where you never park your car, and where you'll find children running around with no shoes on!'

There is Old Penshaw, which used to be very much a village with the blacksmith and miner's cottages – now it has new bungalows and farmhouses which have been renovated and a riding school. And, of course, there is the church in the middle of the village. [The church is a stone Victorian building with an Anglo-Catholic tradition.]

Last year we celebrated 250 years of the church in Penshaw, and we purposely aimed it at church and community. We had a week of celebrations – we put on shows, concerts – they were free – we felt we wanted to give something back to the community. People round here are very good at supporting the Church. Well, when I say supporting the Church, they'll come to anything like that and support it that way. Last year at the village fair we got two thousand people. People dressed up in seventeenth-century dress – all the pubs joined in, and some of them roasted a pig. We try to put the emphasis on church and community – bringing people together – and it works – people actually know me. It feels as if there's a trust between Church and community, and it's getting stronger. I am pleased about that. They see the Church as something that has always been there. The mines have gone, but the Church has remained.

At the eight o'clock you'll get twenty to twenty-five, at the ten o'clock an average of eighty maybe, depending on what's going on (last Sunday there was a baptism and there were a hundred and fifty people), at Evensong you get twenty-five. We have a choir at two of those services. If we have a three o'clock baptism with five babies, we have anything up to three hundred people in church. Baptisms are very popular round here. It's folklore, maybe, but it's a connection with the good news, to let people see that they're part of the Church and community together. It has paid off, actually. That's where the support comes from. People feel that they're not rejected. That they can come to the Rector and have their baby baptised, even if they don't come to church regularly. When we don't place too many restraints on people, then we find them coming to church – the children coming to Sunday School and the parents coming too.

We have a lot of social activities, again with an emphasis on Church and community. And there's an active Council of Churches – predominantly Roman Catholic and Church of England now in Penshaw – the chapels are gone. We have a small Salvation Army chapel though. We all work together. This year we're having a Horticultural Show which the churches are organising, with entries for all ages. Tomorrow night we've got a Chinese evening – two chefs are coming to cook a Chinese meal, and over sixty people are booked to come. But it won't be just church people who come. Events like that bring people along to the church in a safe situation while they see if they like the feel of it.

When I first came to look at Penshaw, a priest who had been my first Rector said to me 'Penshaw's not for you. Too inward-looking and too quiet.' So I said 'Well, we'll have to change it!' And we have. It *was* very quiet. The walls of the Rectory garden in those days seemed like the boundary. We had to move out of that. We are now involved at every level – deanery level, diocesan level. We've got a lay visiting team of about fifteen people, and it's growing. I felt that the parish had been written off, and no parish should be written off like that – they've all got potential.

My wife and children have also been very involved, though my wife has a career of her own, and people have liked the family element here. Our house was used as a meeting place before we got the hall built. I think people see that we are committed, and if they think you're committed, they'll commit themselves. I love this parish, and I would do anything for them.

St Chad's, Wood End, Coventry

St Chad's, Wood End, is a large and rather bleak Basil Spence church in the centre of a very large postwar council estate on the north-east edge of Coventry, which in the 1950s attracted workers, car workers in particular, from different parts of Britain. In those days it was a 'mixed' population with some professional people, but they moved out, leaving a working population which gradually became an unemployed population. Wood End is probably the poorest area of the city, with 50 to 60 per cent unemployed. Of the people 83 per cent have no income except state benefits, and 97 per cent of all the primary school children are eligible for free school meals. It is an area of great poverty and a good deal of crime. There is a con-tinuity among families who have remained at Wood End since the 1950s – some have as many as three hundred relatives around the place!

Nerissa Jones came to work there in 1992 just after there had been fighting in the streets of Wood End, as in a number of other similar places – Blackbird Leys, Sunderland etc. Nerissa, with grown up children, and now with grandchildren, had a late vocation, had trained at Cuddesdon, and then had worked as a curate at St Botolph's, Aldgate. She came up to look at St Chad's, which a number of other clergy had turned down, and decided, improbably you might think, that this was the place for her.

Nerissa is a small, delicately built woman (she was once a dancer) married to a retired Army officer, David, and they both speak with unmistakably upper-class accents. 'It doesn't matter,' Nerissa says. 'The children think it very funny, and do imitations of me, but they imagine everyone in the south talks like I do.' Just before she came to live and work at St Chad's she told the woman in the shop across the road from the church that she was soon going to be the Vicar, and received the reply, 'I hope they don't do to you what they did to the last one.'

'What did they do to the last one?' I asked.

They just made his life a bloody misery. He had liked it here at first and been much loved and liked, but then he had a lot to do with setting up a Credit Union and that made a certain family of loan sharks very angry. It was awful. They watched him, and broke in and robbed him every time he went out. Once they threw an enormous bit of paving stone through the window. Not surprisingly, the situation eventually got him down and he was quite ill for a time.

Apart from the physical and psychological dangers of the job there were technical difficulties about appointing Nerissa.

It was a Crown Appointment, and the Crown Office said they must find a priest, and I wasn't a priest, of course, because this was 1992 and women could not yet be ordained as priests. I was terribly disappointed. In the end because no one else wanted to come, the bishop suspended the living so they could appoint me anyway.

By then it rather looked as if it was curtains for the church here. The Vicarage was boarded up. The hall too. It had been completely smashed. Some youths got in, stole or smashed everything, what they didn't smash they shat on, broke all the windows. The one bit of income the church had had was £3,000 a year for renting out the hall to the playgroup, so that was gone too. The church garden was a mess, and it all looked as though the tide had gone out for the church, though both the bishop and the congregation were still trying to keep it going. The congregation were marvellous. The Sunday morning after the Saturday night when the hall was smashed people went out after church, boarded it up, and wrote in huge black letters – Love, Peace, Hope. What they said was 'We thought we'd get our graffiti up first!'

I remember the bishop asking me what I was going to do here. It felt quite a strange question because I didn't have any idea really except to come, to get the boards off the house and make the place look lived in, mow the grass, take the rubbish out of the church yard . . .

The hall has now been rebuilt, and the garden around the church is cared for.

I asked Nerissa whether she had been scared when she started work at St Chad's, but apart from telling me how she had got a burglar acquaintance to advise her on security, and how she insisted that the diocese must install all the devices he suggested, she seemed not very much interested in this question.

Perhaps I should be more frightened. I haven't been physically attacked here, though I was a few times at St Botolph's. I've been threatened – that people would 'get' me – but I feel very supported by the community. I sense that though it would be acceptable to break into my house, to hurt me would be an unpopular act.

Anyway, I'm not scared, and they know I'm not scared. I've chased people off from robbing things.

I suggest that hers would be an impossible job for a vicar with a young family.

Quite right. Horses for courses. I wouldn't think it would be a very easy job if you had no companion either. So you either want to do it when you're young before you have a family, or at least with very little babies, or you could do it with two women living here or two men. Not with children, though – you see too many sacrificed clergy children. Luckily David and I had our children while I was young, I'm still perfectly active, and tough enough.

David, who had worked as a Director of Oxfam after retirement from the Army, plays a very active part in Nerissa's enterprises.

'I think some of the boys think I was in the SAS,' he says. 'I let them believe it.'

Nerissa and David live in a modern house with a garden beside the church. The area under the stairs is piled with tins of food and clothes.

'If people have to buy an anorak or a pair of shoes for their kids they don't have enough money to manage until the next giro,' she explains simply.

'So why did you come?'

To make sense of my belief. If you really believe that God is love and that Jesus came into the world for the sake of the oppressed and the downtrodden, then this is a place where the Church ought to be. Not from the point of view of trying to get people to see everything like I do, because there are people here with very profound religious understandings who wouldn't set foot in a church at all. But I think that the Church – the group of Christians who are here – should be demonstrating what it's all about . . . I find it heartbreaking how awful it is for people here – nothing beautiful happens, really. Damn it – people die here ten years earlier than they do on the other side of the city. When I first came here I thought, 'Why am I burying so many people of my own age and just above?' and then there was a survey which showed the differential in the ages at which poorer people died. It's a result of misery, I think, the end result of poverty. That bit is extraordinarily sad, but in other ways I don't feel saddened at all. I feel invigorated by the marvellous way that people manage to hang on. It tells you something of the essential strength and often great goodness of human beings.

'So what did you do when you first came?'

Talked endlessly to people. There's no point in doing anything until you've done that. I just talked and listened to people for the first three months. And then we had the first parish conference. What we had realised by then is that there are eight and a half thousand people in the three housing estates in the parish, and three thousand of them are under fifteen. Most of them have no hope of any work, no hope of anything – just giving an address here would put most employers off. And they turn into criminals unless they're looked after in some way. The only hope for this place is to do something about them.

St Chad's has around fifty on its electoral roll.

The thing about our electoral roll is that you expect to see all the people on it in the course of a month. We usually get about thirty-six to forty on an average Sunday.

'What brings them?'

All the things that bring people to church, I think. Everything from absolutely altruistic love of God – and the feeling that this is how you express it in a community – to companionship, friendliness ...

It happened to be Palm Sunday on the weekend I visited St Chad's, and they were having their monthly 'informal' service which is specially designed to be accessible to newcomers. Nerissa stands in the 'Catholic' tradition, though I am not sure I could have guessed it from this service which paraphrased the eucharistic prayer and used hymns from the Evangelical tradition very effectively. Part of the intercession stuck in my mind: 'Christ Jesus, look upon us all in St Chad's Parish, in Wood End, Henley Green and Manor House; keep our kindness alive.' St Chad's did feel like a place of kindness, and of safety in a dangerous world. The first hymn went 'Lord, the light of your love is shining,/In the midst of the darkness shining,/Jesus, light of the world, shine upon us.'

The service sheet (for Holy Week) included 'washing the feet of anyone who wants it done' on Maundy Thursday, a Good Friday procession, a communal cleaning and polishing of the church, flower arranging, and tidying of the garden on Holy Saturday. There were two Faith and Bible Study groups during the week, and a midweek eucharist with shared lunch.

There was also the Homework Club, started by Nerissa for children who needed to do their schoolwork in a quiet space, the Saturday Club, for quite young children – 'they do things like playing Snakes and Ladders and Ludo with older members of the congregation – something many of them have never done' – and a teenage activities group which includes swimming, trips, camping and other things.

At the back of the church was a board where people can write out a prayer request and pin it to the board. The requests were deeply moving – about illness, relationships, children, work.

To spend much time with Nerissa and her husband is to hear hair-raising and wonderful stories. One is about the football club Nerissa started for teenagers which started playing local teams. One day, at a home game, the other team began to win and to annoy one of the home players, who disappeared on his motorbike and came back wielding a baseball bat with which he attacked the opposing players.

'What did you do?'

'I ran after him and took the bat off him.'

'How on earth did you manage to do that?'

'They don't expect someone of my age to be able to run so fast or to move so quickly!'

Another much more terrible story is of the four-year-old whose father stabbed his mother one morning. The little boy tried to get the knife out, but failing to do so went next door to get help. The woman was dead. Nerissa sat with the child all afternoon as he tried to deal with his emotions by drawing and talking.

Part of the problem at Wood End was that so many children were excluded from school and therefore roamed the streets with nothing to do except get into trouble. Houses left empty were ransacked and burned. A number of young adults have never worked but make money dealing drugs, which introduces a criminal element into the place. Nerissa had a plan to set up a schoolroom for the excluded children in the church hall, but the education authorities turned her down. Something to do with cubic air space.

St Denys, St Dennis, near St Austell, Cornwall

Approaching St Dennis by car the eye is astonished and, in my case, entranced, by the huge heaps of china clay waste which turn a harsh but beautiful farming environment into a surreal moon landscape.

The little church of St Denys (after the French saint) is medieval in origin and lies in the embrace of an old Iron Age hill fort. No one is quite sure why there was a church in such a remote spot – until the late nineteenth century there were only one or two farms near to it – and it is sometimes suggested that it was provided for people on hunting expeditions, or for tin-streamers working on the nearby Goss Moor.

A rebuilding of the church in 1847, when large beams were put in, made it seem less like a parish church than a chapel. In the 1860s the china clay industry brought workers from other parts of Cornwall, and from beyond the county, and a village of around two thousand people was established close to the existing church. Cornwall at that time was very remote from the rest of England.

'Even the time down here was different,' says the priest-in-charge, Tim Russ. 'Clocks in Cornwall were then twenty minutes behind those in the rest of the country – sunset comes twenty minutes later here than in London.'

St Dennis, like so much of Cornwall, had a strongly Methodist constituency, with a ration of Methodists to Anglicans of five to one. To this day there are four chapels locally, three of them in the village.

St Denys was badly burned in 1985, so badly that only the walls and tower remained. It was deliberately set fire to by a prisoner, allowed home on compassionate leave because his mother was dying of cancer. In a fit of rage against God he set fire to the church, and the church burned so fast that he only escaped with his own life because the firemen arrived promptly.

'The church had been very dark with a screen and stained glass windows. The new church opened in 1987 had a very different feel.'

Tim Russ, the whole of whose previous ministry had been in London, came to St Dennis in 1992. The parish was in a melancholy mood. Asked to fill in a form in preparation for the arrival of a new priest, the question 'What hope do you see for the parish?' was answered with the dispirited reply 'No hope'.

Seven years later the church feels happy and at ease with itself, with a congregation of around forty on a Sunday, and sixty-five on the electoral roll. 'We tend to see all of the sixty-five in the space of a month.'

Tim has an assistant priest, a non-stipendiary minister, Jan Salter.

I found the churchyard particularly moving with Cornish surnames, still to be found in the village, constantly recurring – Varcoe, Vercoe, Griggs and Benedetto (an oddly foreign-sounding name which is relatively common locally). The churchyard, like so many churchyards in Britain, is also a significant conservation area. While I was visiting, a botanist discovered a meadow saxifrage there, unique in Cornwall.

'The level of the churchyard has risen became of all the people buried there, so that the earth is up to the windows. I like the feeling of the dead surrounding the church.' Tim went on to describe the difficulty of digging graves in that part of Cornwall, where the ground is mostly granite. 'They often had to use dynamite to open up the ground.'

I suggested this said something about the hardness of the country where it was not even possible to dig a hole in the ground without difficulty.

'We've tried to echo that idea in the liturgy. We use an advent candle stand made out of china clay, and we have another candlestick made out of granite which is what china clay comes out of.'

St. Dennis is not a prosperous village – there is 22–25 per cent unemployment as against 4.5 per cent in other parts of Cornwall and 2.8 per cent in Devon. But it felt a warm and friendly place.

Even the Anglican/Methodist divide is bridged at times – for example on Remembrance Sunday when both churches worship together.

In addition to his work at St Dennis, Tim Russ has also worked for the Truro diocese in the field of education. Until recently his job was to promote local ministry, to encourage the selection of OLMs, as they are called, that is, 'ordained local ministers', from church communities. This has worked well in Cornwall, with some fifteen being ordained in the last three years.

'I like the idea of Cornish people serving other Cornish people. It seems odd to me now that I only met one or two people in this village before I came to work here.'

'Sarf London'

I thought it would be interesting to focus on a group of churches in one area with a mixed population, south-east London, which is well known to me, and one diocese, Rochester.

St Michael and All Angels, Birkbeck, Beckenham

St Michael's is an Anglo-Catholic church in a suburban area neither very poor nor very rich. A tin hut was put up on the Birkbeck Estate in Beckenham in 1877, the church having moved away from the local Holy Trinity parish when its building plans became dominated by a wealthy Evangelical patron, Mr Peek (of Peek Frean fame) who went on to finance Holy Trinity Church, Beckenham (see below). In 1899 the foundation stone was laid of the first permanent St Michael's, and it has just celebrated its centenary. St Michael's was consecrated in 1906, completed in 1935, and destroyed by bombs in 1944. The church carried on its worshipping life in the church hall for twelve years, and then in 1956 the present church was built.

'People say that of its age it's a very good church,' Fr Fayers said.

It is a good church, I found, in which to worship – a long, low building with a kind of Franciscan simplicity of design, and the statues, stations of the cross, baptistery, all, to my eye at least, in very pleasing taste.

St Michael's is a Forward in Faith parish, as I could tell immediately from the pew notices. The day I went to mass there was a baptism, and there was virtually a full church, with a number of young couples. The service was easy to hear, follow and understand, and very welcoming. Later, when Fr Fayers told me of another priest (Fr David Diamond) whose motto in church was said to be a song from *Oliver*, 'Consider yourself at home, consider yourself one of the family', I thought it would have done equally well for St Michael's.

Originally St Michael's served an artisan congregation. In recent years Fr Fayers has noticed a gradual move away from an all-white congregation to one which now includes Afro-Caribbeans, Africans and people from the Indian subcontinent. Now, because houses in south London are relatively cheap, the congregation has many 'first-time buyers', living in this long thin parish, bordering on Penge and South Norwood.

'The frustration with our kind of young mobile membership is that they move on so fast,' says Fr Fayers.

> No sooner have they arrived, than they're off. And then you have to start all over again. We have a lot of people who are 'on the edge' of the Church, and will perhaps come once a month – that's how it is now in many churches, of course – so there are quite a lot of people who are happy to associate themselves with St Michael's but who, if I were to say, 'You've got to come every Sunday', would run away! So you just have to be glad that they come at all. We want to give them a religious experience, but one that they can feel at ease with.
>
> Our problem as a parish is that we are technically Beckenham – we *are* Beckenham – but we don't quite fit in because we don't have the money of Beckenham, on the one hand, but we don't get the sympathy of 'poor Penge' on the other. We miss out in all kinds of ways. I served my title in St Paul's, Deptford, and in a clear inner-city parish like that, there's a great deal of sympathy for the various kinds of problem, and a wanting to pour resources into the Church, which an area like this doesn't attract.
>
> But we have quite a few people who leave to go elsewhere in the country, or to more leafy parts, and my hope is that what we have tried to give them here creates a strong sense of the faith that they can take and develop elsewhere.

The size of St Michael's Sunday congregation for Mass is variable.

> On the first Sunday in the month, for the Family Mass we might sometimes get one hundred and fifty people, and then, on a bad Sunday, there might be just fifty or sixty. I would say that, with children, it averages at between seventy and ninety. There are ninety-eight on the electoral roll.

The church has over two dozen lesson-readers and intercession-leaders, a similar number of altar servers, six people who administer at holy communion, including, for the first time, two women. Recently ten or so other important tasks at St Michael's have all found volunteers to do them.

Fr Fayers has the air of a man who really loves what he does. He remembers with pleasure a chance conversation that brought him to his ministry at St Michael's.

> I was coming to the end of my time at Deptford and thinking about a move, and a priest I met who knew this said 'Do you know anything about St Michael's, Beckenham?' Which I didn't. I had an interview with the patrons in 1987 – the Society of the Maintenance of the Faith and the Bishop of Rochester – and they offered me the job. The interview was on 4 August 1987 – I've never forgotten the date, especially as it is the Feast of the Curé d'Ars, which seemed like a true sign!

I asked Fr Fayers how he saw his work.

> What for me comes out of the word 'Catholic', are words like 'whole', 'inclusive' – universal in tradition. Whole means that there is a ministry to the whole person, obviously, and this means a sacramental ministry, trying to listen, to give time to people, being able to affirm them and their value. It means also having a wider vision of what it means to be a Christian other than just a parochial one – I'm here really to help people to see that they belong to something bigger than themselves, bigger than this parish, bigger even than the Church of England – the Holy Catholic Church. And to help them have a sense of oneness with the world beyond. I would place a particular value on the communion of saints, and that's why, in our baptistery, we have our book of remembrance in which we list all the people who have died from the church. We have our shrines and our opportunities to light candles, and I've always been very impressed at the number of people who do go and light candles and the ease with which they pray for the dead. Inclusiveness makes me feel that I should

welcome everybody who comes through the door who shows the slightest bit of interest, and show them that we're actually pleased to see them, whoever they are, whatever their background, irrespective of race, gender, sexuality or tradition.

It all has to be put into a context, and I feel that I am here to teach and to preach and to help people to grow through study, and it's been a great joy to me that more people have come along to study, wanting to know more. And I stand within a tradition, of course. I'm here to teach the Church's faith, and it's a timeless faith. I think it's very good for an island race like ours to remember that the Scriptures didn't drop from heaven in the form of the King James Bible, and that our faith is one received and passed on – and it didn't start in England, it started overseas and was brought to us. It's the sense of the handing on that's important.

And part of the sacramentalising of life is for Christians to be able to enjoy being together, to be able to show people that yes, we do love one another, and yes, we do care and support one another, but we can also have a lot of fun together. Within the Catholic tradition pilgrimage is important, and parties, socialising, having a good time. It's saying that what God has given us is fundamentally good.

One of the things that helped to firm up where I stand is when I was talking to an Evangelical priest and he was saying that in his view human beings were fundamentally evil but touched with some measure of goodness. I said, 'Well, I disagree. I think that human beings are fundamentally good, but flawed.'

Despite the fact that most churchgoers at St Michael's, as elsewhere, do not attend every Sunday in the old style, the church has enjoyed some impressive signs of growth.

The people we have had contacts with through baptisms and through pastoral contact over the years have responded, and that's been very good to see. After a mission by Fr Augustine Hoey in 1992, the church, eighteen months later, had the highest number of confirmation candidates for fifty years. Then two years ago we had our highest number of Easter communicants for sixty years. And throughout the decade we have had the highest number of Easter communicants since the war. With all the talk of decline, I find this very encouraging. It shows that the Church of England is not ended – there are signs of healthy growth.

I wondered how Fr Fayers felt about the huge diversity of religious expression in the Church.

I think one of those unique contributions the Church of England can make to the universal Church is being able to contain within it such a diversity. Sometimes that's maddening, infuriating, because you can't say to somebody who is leaving your parish church, 'Go to your new parish church and you will find what you find here.' That's the disadvantage. There can be a contradiction in terms of the things you have taught about sacraments or about the Mass. But there is also the sense of being able to contain a diversity of tradition with a mutual acceptance. It has a distinctive contribution to make to the universal Church.

I asked why, after several hundred years, the diversity was still so strong. Was it something about human psychology, or the English temperament?

I wonder whether there is an English, or British, trait, not wanting to too closely define, a pragmatic aspect of our nature. Once you begin to define things too closely and say, 'This is the only way it can be done', it kicks against the temperament. You can be in a tradition but if you push it too hard a lot of people begin to think, 'This is getting too extreme' and may back off. Though it also seems to be true that the British temperament itself is changing – the expression of grief at the funeral of the Princess of Wales was more like something you would see in a Latin country. For me it seemed like a sacramentalising process – lighting candles, putting down flowers, setting up shrines, weeping, expressing grief instead of keeping it all inside. This can be shallow and many British people will resist it, but the fact that it happened at all is an indication of change.

Christ Church, Anerley

Christ Church, Anerley, is a charismatic evangelical church set in Anerley and Penge, a suburb of south-east London. The district has a mixed population, both in terms of class and race. There is a good deal of unemployment and poverty, in Penge particularly, but also some middle-class professionals attracted by reasonable house prices and excellent rail connections to central London. There is a sizeable Asian and Afro-Caribbean community and also a refugee community.

Christ Church, at their Sunday morning service, has a good mix of all these groups. There were about one hundred and twenty people present at the 'family service' I went to, a smattering of adolescents, quite a lot of young adults, a number of couples with young children, and a good many middle-aged to elderly women. It was an impressive congregation in terms of numbers, and in how mixed it was in both race and age, the sort that many churches would give their eye teeth for. I was greeted warmly at the door by a 'pastoral assistant' who wanted to know whether I would like her to sit with me in church or to sit alone. I opted to sit alone because I thought this would be less distracting than having a companion, and she accepted this decision cheerfully.

The modern church building is built on a mound. (They are now in the process of excavating rooms beneath the mound to extend their activities.) It has bare brick walls and timber inside, and I kept getting the fantasy that I was worshipping in a small barn – the church is functional rather than beautiful. There are huge embroidered banners high up round the walls saying 'Over Death Victorious', 'Celebrate his love', 'Sin conquered', and 'We belong to him'.

The altar is obscured by the reading/speaking desk for most of the service – only when communion starts is this desk wheeled away and the altar fully visible. They have communion twice a month, on second and fourth Sundays.

Hymns were being sung before the service started. There was a 'worship band' with two girl singers, two electric guitars, a trumpet and a keyboard, and an overhead projector showing the words of the hymns. When they stopped a few minutes before the service the congregation was incredibly noisy – I could hear two women behind me discussing an operation in some detail. When the Vicar, Mike Porter, wanted to start the service he had to call rather desperately for quiet.

Mike introduced the service. A young-looking fifty-four-year-old, he wore a sports coat and a turquoise shirt with a dog collar which he had put on between greeting me at the door and starting the service. He wore no vestments and, communion apart, took little part in the service. Lay people, men and women, were impressively in evidence, reading, interceding, preaching, and doing it extraordinarily well. People held up their arms and swayed gently a good deal during the hymns till we got to the more rhythmic ones where some, not all, clapped; some people seemed rather to be pointing upwards – to God or heaven presumably. The words seemed banal – 'Jesus is the best', 'I love him because he died on the cross'. There were a lot of repetitive choruses, rather too many for my taste, of pleasant singable tunes. There was something very peaceful and relaxed about the singing.

Holy communion was a very much truncated ASB rite, with the First Eucharistic Prayer heavily cut. While people were going up to receive, the two women behind me were discussing a legal problem about selling a flat. After communion the children left the church to go to their various Sunday groups, and there was intercession – with

297

very real feeling for the victims of an appalling earthquake in the preceding week – and a 'Bible study' sermon by Roger, the lay reader, that took half an hour, and made very effective use of a popular TV programme.

The best moment of the service came for me near to the end when a young woman just across the aisle suddenly began to sing in a very beautiful voice. I could not understand the words, and realised that either she was singing in a foreign language, or this must be 'singing in tongues' (I so much wanted it to be the latter that I could scarcely believe it was.) But it *was* singing in tongues, and I was transfixed by the purity of it, an extraordinarily poetic moment in a liturgy which otherwise felt to me rather utilitarian. When she had finished, Mike said that usually 'tongues' were followed by a 'response' which provided something of an interpretation. The response came in the form of another woman singing about praising God. The worship, followed by coffee, altogether took about two hours. For a number of the congregation it took longer than that. They had met in the room below the church an hour before the service began to pray for the service and for the people who would attend it.

A week or two later I attended by invitation one unit of the Alpha Course at Christ Church. It began with the famous meal, in this case shared with the 'Beta Course' who met the same evening, members of an earlier Alpha Course who wanted to continue the pattern of beginning the evening with a meal. I sat at the Beta table with the Vicar's wife, Chris. The Beta members were young adults. The boy beside me told me he had come because his girlfriend had talked him into it.

'But then I really enjoyed it. They were very open, you could bring up anything and they didn't mind.'

People round the table spoke of a day they had all recently attended when many had 'received the Spirit'.

There were eight of us, all women, on the Alpha course. One of the members, who turned out to be my favourite, offered me her Alpha manual.

'I always drop off to sleep in this bit anyway!'

I glanced down the unit headings – 'Who is Jesus?', 'Why did Jesus die?', 'How does God guide us?', 'Does God heal today?' The Alpha Course, I learned later in the evening, is based on Nicky Gumbel's book *Questions of Life*.

The particular unit of the course we were doing was about 'evangelism' and 'witness'. Roger, who led the course, took as his text 'We have found the Messiah. Come and you will see' from St John's

Gospel. The basic message was that no one could really live unless they were in relationship with Jesus, and that therefore it was important to bring as many others as possible to this relationship. Roger had good stories and anecdotes, in particular one about an adolescent boy not interested in very much except girls who, because he was taken to a prayer meeting one night, grew up to become Billy Graham.

'We cannot all be evangelists,' Roger said (i.e. as Billy Graham is), 'but we are all called to be witnesses.'

After about an hour there was a break for coffee, and then we settled down to a discussion group led by a man, and there was a bit of male/female joshing. He got the conversation going by asking how, if they were going to be converted, they would want to be approached. The youngest there, still a schoolgirl, said that she would want someone to make friends with her first. She later said that she thought it important to play the Christian message very coolly, to leave the other person curious and wanting to know more.

My favourite participant (I am afraid because she was the most dissident and also was the funniest) said that what would be important would be that the Christian was as 'normal' as possible. 'Some Christians are so weird!' There was a moment's silence after this before conversation picked up and went on. She later described how her aunt, who had given her and her sister a wonderful time as children, taking them to the pictures and up to London, then got converted and never took them anywhere again!

There was more discussion about how to make the Christian message attractive. I wanted to ask the schoolgirl whether there was a difference in making friends with someone because you really liked them, or making friends with them because you wanted to convert them, but thought it inappropriate to intervene. No one brought that up, though one or two people came near to it. The danger of wanting to convert someone for reasons of power, or to bolster one's own beliefs, did not come up. During the evening, I learned, members of the congregation were downstairs praying for us.

What struck me as I talked to church members was what a warm social life buzzed around the church, and how attractive this must be to young adults in particular, with their need to find friends and partners as they study, or as they set out on the first stages of their career. There seemed a huge amount of energy around Christ Church, and a very impressive teaching structure ranging from young children through to grown-ups, with Alpha and house groups. One of the ways in which this energy showed itself was in the huge amounts of money raised from a not particularly rich congregation. Another way was in the social concern, particularly in helping refugees with whom Christ Church was particularly concerned.

Before the Alpha evening I had been to talk to Mike Porter, a friendly unassuming man with whom I felt an immediate rapport. He told me how, like many schoolboys in his youth, he had belonged to the Crusader movement, and how at eleven he had 'given his life to the Lord'. But the real turning-point in his life, the 'coming to Christ', had been at the Billy Graham Crusade of 1966. Mike worked in the Bank of England, married another evangelical, Chris, and decided to become ordained. He trained at Trinity College, Bristol. In the early 1970s, influenced by Colin Urquhart's book *When the Spirit Comes*, and by Michael Harpur, he became increasingly interested in charismatic theology, with its distinctive features of 'baptism in the Spirit' and 'waiting upon God', of 'tongues', prophecy and interpretation. Mike admitted that this could lead to unpredictable and chaotic effects at times but added, 'Better the mess of the nursery than the order of the graveyard!'

Mike was a curate in Corby, in a new town in which the steel works had closed down. He went from there to Rainham, near Romford, in Essex for twelve years, most of them as Team Vicar. This led to the most painful episode of his working life, in which irreconcilable differences sprang up within his church, and a large group left. Mike seemed very real, very human, as he described this event of unhealed conflict, something that most of us have struggled with at one time or another.

In 1995 he came to Anerley, a mixed and, as he put it, 'not-leafy' suburb. The congregation includes teachers, professionals of various kinds and a psychotherapist, and has people from Zaire, Kenya and the Afro-Caribbean islands. Mike presides, rather self-effacingly, over a buzzing Christian community.

I said that one thing that often bothered me about Christian communities was the way everyone was so nice – too good to be true, really. What happened to their feelings of anger? Mike surprised me a little by saying how much he agreed, and that this was particularly true for vicars who were supposed to be nice to everyone all the time. He had learned the hard way that the price of too much niceness could be depression, and he was working on it.

Holy Trinity, Beckenham
Holy Trinity, Beckenham, despite its title, is not in Beckenham, an affluent and leafy London suburb that was once part of Kent, but is in Penge, a much poorer and more downtown suburb of south-east

London. (There are historical reasons for this discrepancy, of course, but they are too boring to go into.) In 1993, as described at the beginning of this book, Holy Trinity was burned out as the result of an arson attack. Other churches in the area suffered a similar fate.

The year after the fire, Tony Rutherford was appointed as Vicar, and he chose the church out of four offered to him by the Archdeacon because he liked the idea of a church 'beginning again'. One of the things which particularly appealed to him was the way that Holy Trinity, before the fire, had seen itself as very much part of the local community – it had called itself a 'church centre' even in those days, and had encouraged local groups such as a playgroup to use the premises. One of the things that Tony, an ex-Baptist, likes about being an Anglican is the attitude of 'being there' for the community and not just for those who come habitually to church.

'I've often felt more like a Projects Manager than a Vicar,' Tony says. Certainly in the period after the congregation moved back to the renovated church, a degree of general exhaustion set in, and the church seemed to mark time for a bit as Vicar and people recouped energy. But that could only be a temporary remission, as Holy Trinity needed to rebuild its congregation, many of whom had disappeared during the long period of being without a church. There were about thirty 'regulars' who had met regularly at a local junior school and they returned to resume their liturgical and social life in the restored church of Holy Trinity in Lennard Road in 1997. This is not quite enough to make a congregation feel thriving and lively – and a year or two later the financial difficulties of a small congregation began to be felt. In 1999, by which time the congregation was beginning to pick up, the church had to face the fact that it could easily become bankrupt, and valiant money-making attempts were put successfully into practice. The church was helped in this by the work of a very energetic non-stipendiary priest – Nicholas Lang – who took on the planning of this initiative. Holy Trinity also has a gifted lay reader, Jill Blackshaw, who helps conduct services. The church is generally 'pro' women priests.

Holy Trinity is a 'broad' church. It sticks carefully to the Alternative Service Book, except at its monthly All Age services, which are written specially with newcomers and young people in mind; it regards holy communion as at the centre of its worship, its clergy wear surplice and stole in church, but not chasubles or copes. It is flexible about using any traditional ritual which feels effective – ashes placed on the head on Ash Wednesday, a washing of the feet on Maundy Thursday, lighting the Easter Candle on Holy Saturday night, a Midnight Mass at Christmas. There are Bible study classes,

301

Sunday Time – a very lively form of Sunday School for children and young people – a lunch for the elderly on Wednesdays, coffee mornings for those living alone.

'I like the feeling of being "broad",' Tony says, 'of holding the two wings of the Church together, because sometimes I feel as if the wings are taking over the centre. I believe the broad tradition has a wider and more general appeal. It is not so extreme.' He pauses. 'I seem to be getting into a rather birdlike metaphor. I'd like to think we could help the Church to fly.'

Tony specially enjoys encounters with people on the edge of the Church – couples about to be married, couples bringing a baby for baptism, people he meets at funerals. He likes 'walking the streets' of the parish, talking to people on a casual basis. He would like to be seen by his parish as an 'enabler', one who stands back and encourages others in their own initiatives.

Christ Church, Beckenham

Evangelical churches often seem to be called Christ Church – I suppose because the name is not as 'Romish' as a saint's name, though many evangelical churches do have saints' names, of course. Christ Church, Beckenham, according to Fr Fayers, was originally built in order to oppose the 'papalism' of the group of Anglo-Catholic churches, of which Fr Fayers' church was one, grouped around St George's, Beckenham. It stands just off Beckenham High Street, with church buildings which abut the street, and when it has developed current plans it should have a face on the High Street itself. It is a conservative evangelical church, or as its Vicar, Nick Wynne-Jones puts it, a classic evangelical church.

A visit to it on a Sunday is impressive. It is a large church built in the traditional format of a distant altar, a large chancel with choir stalls, a pulpit, and then a nave with pews on both sides. There were perhaps two hundred people there on the Sunday on which I went. (There are 461 people on the Electoral Roll). There was a striking sense of affluence – of prosperous Middle England at prayer. There were many young parents with children.

The clergy did not wear robes, and the service was introduced by a lay man with the words 'We should remember that God loves each one of us, and that he is looking forward to our service this morning.' (This gave me an irresistible picture of God, having finished his Sunday bacon and eggs, rubbing his hands in anticipation of being adored.) I was struck by the fact that no cross seemed in evidence – in the centre of the altar was a very beautiful arrangement of lilies.

The hymns were mainly from the new evangelical school – Graham

Kendrick, Kingsway Publications, etc. and were sung lustily. The preacher for the day was Robert de Berry, from a missionary organisation that works in Africa. First he showed slides of Rwanda and talked extremely movingly of the Church's attempts to bring healing and reconciliation in the desperate situation after the genocide – I have never heard a better description of the state of mind that makes it possible for people, in this case the Hutu, to slaughter others. He introduced a retired couple who had decided to go and work in Rwanda. He then preached on the theme of St Peter eating the 'unclean' animals as commanded by God to do. The sermon was part of a planned series of sermons. There was no communion, since that only happens once or twice a month. This was 'Morning Service' though fairly loosely following the ASB. When the service was over members of the congregation made a point of speaking to me in an easy and natural way and offered me coffee.

Christ Church has two curates, Simon Dowdy and Marian Raikes.

What feels very impressive is the thoughtful planning and work behind every detail. Alongside the Sunday morning service there is a crèche, and teaching for children from three to eighteen, suitably divided up according to age. There are some seventy young people active in the church. There is a boys' choir and a girls' choir, and a band. On Tuesdays there is a 'Meeting Point' for 'ladies'(!), with Bible study, discussion, prayer, etc., either at 10.30 a.m. (with creche) or at 2.30 p.m., which seems to exclude working women. There is also a Parent and Baby Club, a Parent and Toddlers' Club, a Singing Group and a Coffee morning on Fridays. Wednesday night is 'Church night' – an hour of worship, Bible teaching, and prayer which alternates with house groups in people's homes.

In a nicely printed pamphlet intended to welcome newcomers Christ Church Beckenham lays its cards on the table. It says 'Our mission is to share the love of Jesus Christ in word and deed, so that people become His followers to the glory of God.'

Nick Wynne-Jones tells me that Christ Church owes part of its present success to a history of vital clergy and a lively congregation; he particularly mentions Guy King who, in the 1940s, laid down a solid foundation for the later success of the church – as he put it, 'teaching the Bible Sunday by Sunday'. Wynne-Jones places emphasis on the supremacy of the Bible, and of the importance of making its teaching known. He also believes in the importance of 'the ministry of every member'. Everyone is expected to play a part – in welcoming newcomers, in attending functions, in helping with organisation, in helping fund initiatives.

Holy Joe's, the Bag o'Nails, Buckingham Palace Road
While this informal church does not consist of a parish in the way
that the other churches described above do, it nevertheless stands in
for the many other informal churches, of different brands of
churchmanship, which feed those who feel too uneasy to step inside
the formal structures. They perform a useful function in fostering
people's interest in religion, and sometimes in bridging the way for
individuals into the formal Church. It would be good to see the
churches befriending these 'outsiders' – as a few of them already do.

Dave Tomlinson grew up in the Brethren, and in the 1970s, as a
result of experiencing 'the baptism of the Spirit', was asked to leave
them, since his church thought this event was 'pentecostal emotional-
ism'. He left, and became involved in the early house church
movement, which was later known as 'the New Churches'. He worked
for twenty years in the New Churches. In the late 1980s he and his
wife Pat felt that it was time for a change. They were acutely aware of
how many people 'were on the edges of evangelical and charismatic
churches or had fallen off the edge altogether'. At the Greenbelt
Arts Festival, and elsewhere, Tomlinson became aware of just how
enormous were the numbers of people who no longer attended a
church but still had faith. This had the effect on the Tomlinsons of
rethinking what 'church' might be, and they set up what they called
'Holy Joe's', first at a pub in Clapham, now in one near Victoria, The
Bag o'Nails. In the last few years Tomlinson has become ordained in
the Church of England.

I went along to one of the Holy Joe meetings at The Bag o'Nails,
which was held in a private room. It was a Bible study, looking at the
book of Jonah, which it did with some imaginative reconstruction. It
was a very young gathering – everyone except myself, a friend who
came with me, and the Tomlinson couple, looked as if they were
under thirty. People brought drinks in from the bar, and could smoke
if they wished. Towards the end of the two-hour meeting there was
some introduction of personal problems. At the next meeting the
group was due to have a discussion about physics. In addition to
Holy Joe's, Dave now holds communion services twice a month at a
church off the Caledonian Road in Holloway.

21

Cathedrals – Popular Icons

Unlike parish churches, cathedrals seem to be enjoying a boom, though it is one which makes considerable demands on their resources, financial and otherwise. There are forty-two cathedrals in England, a number of them of great antiquity and beauty, and they draw huge numbers of visitors – for the history, the music, the architecture, for worship, in pilgrimage, or simply for something to do on a visit to London, or on a wet afternoon in the country. *Heritage and Renewal* (1994), the Report of an Archbishops' Commission on Cathedrals (henceforward referred to as *Howe*), had a rather poetic way of describing them as 'having been conceived or adorned as great canopies over the bones of saints, as stone reliquaries on an enormous scale'.[1]

The origin of cathedrals in the pre-medieval and medieval phase of Christianity in England was as a place where 'the bishop maintained his household . . . and where there was, among other buildings, a church which contained his teaching-chair or cathedra'.[2] It quite often also provided a school, which meant that the Church ran some of the first schools in the country. Rather movingly, cathedral architecture incorporates features from many sacred cultures, not all of them Christian – Herod's Temple at Jerusalem, temples to the Greek gods in the Middle East (some of which actually became Christian cathedrals), and Roman basilicas, which were conceived as meeting halls rather than houses for a god. The great holy space of Hagia Sophia in Constantinople haunted future builders. Less consciously, probably, the pagan idea of a sacred avenue leading up to an altar also affected them.

In England cathedrals came into being as urban phenomena, with small churches more slowly springing up in the countryside to offer a Christian presence. Some cathedrals, under the monastic influence of Archbishop Lanfranc of Bec, came to be administered by monks – Benedictines or, in one case (Carlisle) Austin friars, while others were run by 'secular canons' – men who led a common life but had not taken religious vows. Gradually bishops became less integral to the cathedral system, and because of this deans and chapters gradually assumed control of cathedrals and its pastoral functions.

Howe suggests that a certain unease has existed ever since between bishops of dioceses and cathedral clergy. There is still a feeling that a bishop belongs with a cathedral, that it is his 'seat', yet there are anecdotes of bishops who are unwelcome within 'their' cathedrals. *Howe* discusses the possibility of bishops taking over the function of dean and chapter as a way of integrating cathedral and diocese, but rejects the idea, partly because bishops have too much else to do. The Report is very much in favour of bishops continuing to be identified with cathedrals, however, and particularly of their attending their own cathedral regularly, as preacher or celebrant.

I invited June Osborne, Canon Treasurer of Salisbury Cathedral, to tell me something of her own experience in a cathedral setting. She commented first on the size of Salisbury's regular congregation – excluding summer visitors they can expect about six hundred people at the 10 a.m. Sunday eucharist. (Which means, of course, though she did not say this, that support, both financial and personal, which might be given to local churches, may be getting siphoned off into the cathedral. Of course, it is also possible that if some of the worshippers did not attend the cathedral they might not go elsewhere to church – see the interview with Trevor Beeson below.)

June Osborne notes that a cathedral congregation do not 'own' the cathedral in the way a parochial congregation own their church; neither the building nor the institutional life belongs to them in the same way. The 'effectiveness' of cathedral life is, for her, primarily about something different. It is about

> overlapping networks of interests which we have to protect – civic ones, city and county, diocesan ones, voluntary agencies, interest groups like Amnesty International, visitors who come to see a heritage site whom we're constantly trying to making into pilgrims . . . the effectiveness of the cathedral is very much about how much it keeps its doors open but at the same time invites people into experiences. In a sense it's very easy in a building like this because there's an instantaneous experience of awe and majesty and just aesthetic pleasure. There's a unity about the whole thing.[3]

> I often think it's a very intoxicating place but it's also toxic – I think cathedrals are. This is to do with power. At a popular level

Susan Howatch's novels describe that very toxic power. The work that Hugh Dickinson did as Dean trying to build a common life, a life of consensual values around the Chapter, was hugely important because what it tried to address was the handling of power. I'm very conscious of how easy it is between a magnificent building, history and statutory authority, and a huge enterprise to run, for relationships to go adrift, as they have in some places where it has received a lot of publicity. This is why building a strong common life in the Chapter is so important.

There's enormous power vested in the mixture of a heritage building and history. I have an eleventh-century job description – there have been nine hundred years of Canon Treasurers before me. To a woman it's particularly interesting inhabiting a role which people give honour and prestige to, because whatever they make of the gender issue they cannot get away from the fact that my office – my stall in the cathedral – and my duties and responsibilities, carry authority.[4]

One of the problems *Howe* highlighted was the problem that untrained clergy could, on a cathedral staff, find themselves responsible for the disposal of immense sums of money. Their answer was that such powers should be ceded to lay people. June Osborne does not entirely agree.

In addition to the normal budget for the cathedral I have a major repair programme for Salisbury which is in total about £15 million. Visitors from Washington Cathedral who were here last week were absolutely horrified that the governance of a building and institution like this was left in the hands of clergy!

... I came here from a parochial appointment where for more than ten years I had been doing negotiations with English Heritage and so I knew a little bit about the way funding works. But I wasn't appointed on the basis of that expertise, and I'm learning on the job which I find hugely complex and fascinating. In a way, you know, I could make a case for clergy taking roles like mine. In the case of the fabric of Salisbury Cathedral, there's lots of different tiers. You've got technicians – works department or consultants – working on things like medieval glazing or paintwork or whatever it may be, who have to make their sort of judgments, you've got budget controls done by accountants, and you have to make policy decisions as a team. But in the end the spiritual dimension, the liturgical dimension, is an experience of the building I think needs to be judged by people who have theological skills ... So long as you have competent lay people working alongside, having somebody who doesn't think they know everything is a very good check and balance. I'm not at all afraid to say to my architect 'I've

307

no idea how you've come to these figures – can you show me again?'[5]

Suppose, I asked, a Canon Treasurer did start to get things seriously wrong?

There is a kind of check in the system which is our corporateness – the four clergy on the Chapter which includes the Dean, who govern the cathedral, and then the Chapter Clerk and the Chairman of the Finance Advisory Group which form an executive. What is important is that the Dean, who chairs the meetings of the Chapter, does not let us get too cosy with one another. He has to create an ethos where things can be questioned between us, and this can happen without resentment. Often the questions are a way of saying to one another, 'Are you under too much pressure?' but it could equally be, 'Do you think you have got this right?' And quite often there are issues between us where we are not pleased by what we have to say to one another. But I keep coming back to the idea that it's not just about executive responsibility, it's about *common life*, the values we share. If you are going to tell each other the truth you have to do it in a context of firm relationships. It's like a marriage – if you are going to say hard things to each other you have also to be affirmative – seven good things for every hard thing!

One other thing – *role* is important in cathedrals in a way that it is not in parishes. This is because a cathedral is an institution and you are working with a team of skilled people and it needs to be professional, not on the basis of relationships, as it may be with a group of volunteers in a parish.[6]

A recent book by Trevor Beeson, who was a Canon of Westminster for eleven years, before becoming Dean of Winchester, was *Window on Westminster: A Canon's Diary 1976–1987* (SCM Press, 1998). His Westminster book describes a different institution from Salisbury Cathedral within the same genre – that of Westminster Abbey. The Abbey has a national rather than a local and diocesan role: the crowning of the monarch, royal weddings and funerals, diplomatic and military occasions, all take place there. It has close links with Parliament. It has royal tombs and memorials to many famous people as well as the grave of the Unknown Warrior.

Westminster Abbey is not technically a cathedral: it is a 'Royal Peculiar', an institution directly under the jurisdiction of the Queen and therefore independent of the Church itself and of episcopal control, but this distinction apart, it shares the concerns and problems common to cathedrals.

Beeson describes the four or five religious services a day held in the Abbey, led by its magnificent choir, services which quite often attracted very large numbers of people. There was, and is, an attempt to reach out to more casual visitors by way of hourly acts of prayer, sermons, lectures, educational activities and music.

But Beeson is clear-eyed about the fact that many visitors never penetrate the inner meaning of the Abbey, at least as Christians understand it.

> A large number of visitors belong to the post-Christian element in the Western world, and some are surprised to discover that the building is still used for religious purposes. It is necessary therefore to maintain a delicate balance between the sacred and the secular; thus intense forms of sacerdotalism are always likely to be out of place. The Abbey is more of a frontier post than it is a religious enclave.[7]

(A priest known to me who sometimes assists in St Paul's Cathedral on a Sunday told me how some communicants clearly have no idea what it is that is about to happen, as they make their way to the altar, and they look quickly round to observe 'the form'. Several have been seen to slip the host into a pocket. One asked if he could buy some wafers – he would like to put one in his scrapbook at home.)

Keeping a 'frontier post' like Westminster Abbey or St Paul's running entails a large staff – around two hundred people in the case of Westminster. The administration of an institution such as the Abbey, with its priceless memorials and fabric, and its endless public exposure, places great strain on the four canons at the heart of it. Nowhere else, perhaps, with the exception of St Paul's, is the sense of the Church as 'Established' so inescapable, and this is strengthened by the fact that one of the canons is the Chaplain to the House of Commons.

A problem is that the role of canons, until very recently, was so different. In living memory, being appointed to a canonry (for life), was to be given the chance to concentrate on writing books and preaching in a congenial setting, usually with a nice house thrown in. It was not unlike being a don at Oxford or Cambridge (though that role is also changing under financial pressure). As Beeson's book shows, a modern canon may find himself working so hard in the service of the Cathedral or Abbey that his health begins to collapse under the pressure.

In London, the two great centres of Christian history are the victims of their own success, so overwhelmed with tourists that, despite their best endeavours, and chapels set aside for quiet prayer, they tend to drive away those in search of tranquillity. Yet they badly need the money tourists bring with them to pay their way, and a year in which there is a falling off of tourists – because of a fear of terrorist activity, for instance – becomes a serious setback. The maintaining of ancient fabric, and keeping very old buildings in good condition, is horrendously expensive.

A few years ago there was a scandal which arose when Hereford Cathedral decided to sell one of its precious treasures, the *Mappa Mundi*, for the reason that they needed the money it would bring. In almost every cathedral the need for money has brought about all kinds of 'initiatives' – cafeterias, shops and necessary tourist adjuncts such as public lavatories – an era later than the period when stately homes began to do the same thing. There is now, since government has started to provide funding for particular projects in cathedrals, some useful financial support, though this does not affect the overall running costs. Government only supplies money, via English Heritage, for the restoration and conservation of buildings. External contributions do, however, highlight the importance of the 'accountability' of cathedral staffs: if public money is to be given, then clear and professional standards of dealing with it have to be maintained.

It was for these and other reasons (for example, the scandal of infighting among Dean and Canons at Lincoln Cathedral) that in 1992 the Archbishops set up the *Heritage and Renewal* Commission under the chairmanship of Lady Howe of Aberavon. There were eighteen men and two women, including the chair, on the Commission. (Not counting the secretaries who were, inevitably, women.)

Lady Howe, in the Preface to the Report, comments on 'the immensely impressive service willingly given in so many ways by a host of volunteers, including the substantial contribution of cathedral Friends'.[8] (It seems all the more of a pity that the Friends, guides, custodians, vergers, sellers of refreshments and religious bric-à-brac who greet one in cathedrals, many of them women, were not represented on the Commission. Quite apart from the many women who nowadays have professional expertise – in accountancy, architecture, conservation, education, sculpture etc. It makes you wonder how hard the archbishops looked for candidates.)

As June Osborne observed of Salisbury, many cathedrals nowadays have large worshipping congregations who, in effect, use the cathedral as their parish church. Trevor Beeson, recently retired as Dean of Winchester at the time when I interviewed him, spoke of cathedrals as 'flourishing more than at any time in their history'.

Both Trevor Beeson and Hugh Dickinson, the former Dean of Salisbury, mentioned to me a conviction that a number of worshippers prefer the relatively impersonal nature of cathedral worship.

> Quite a lot of people (worshippers at the cathedral) are refugees from parish life. Sometimes they just don't want to be involved in the running of it, and a certain number are on the edges of faith in one way or another. The cathedral feels like neutral territory and no one is going to get hold of you. There is no commitment. You can just attend on your own terms, anonymously.[9]

> On the whole people who like the parish church and are committed to it don't like cathedral worship, by and large. The other thing cathedrals can offer is quality of worship, preaching, and often of music. Intelligent and sensitive people sometimes find parish churches very difficult because of the poor quality of what is offered. The level of preaching can be appalling. People can feel insulted at what is offered to them.
> There are also people who go to cathedrals who have quite heavy responsibilities in the community and they just need feeding in some sort of way. They have no more to give locally.[10]

Cathedrals are not about 'signing on the dotted line', as often happens in the parish, i.e. coming regularly, getting confirmed, getting on the Electoral Roll or the PCC, helping with practical tasks around the place. But they have an important educational role – they attract quite large numbers of people, some of them high-powered in the community, to theological and other similar courses.

Howe no more than hints at the anonymity of cathedral life. It is positive about the future of cathedrals, and indeed about the vitality and imaginative energy shown by them in the present. They are undoubtedly one of the Church's great success stories, though they illustrate rather neatly what a two-edged thing success often is in Christian terms, with too much popularity stifling the quiet, simple aspects of a faith that was never really suited to those who wanted power and mega-bucks. It suggests that those who work in less popular areas of the Church are luckier than they often feel. But Hugh Dickinson's attempt at Salisbury to bring a vast enterprise back to the nub of the matter – the common life of a handful of canons, which might then provide a stable centre – is heartening to think about.

Either because of the special opportunities offered by cathedrals at the present time, or because of the quality of the men chosen (we have had no women deans as yet), deans and their chapters, when they are not at daggers drawn, seem quite often to offer creative work within 'the canopies erected over the bones of the saints'. I was interested in how deans came to be chosen for their demanding, but fruitful role. Hugh Dickinson described to me how he had come to be Dean of Salisbury.[11]

He had just spent nine years as parish priest at St Michael's, in the St Albans diocese, where he had been extraordinarily happy – 'a church full of creative and talented people who just wanted an opportunity to go ahead' – and knew that he had one last job ahead of him.

At an earlier point in his life there had been murmurings about making him a bishop, but by this time he knew that the one thing he did not want was to be made a bishop.

> I was then offered another deanery which I knew would not work for me. I talked to one or two people who said, 'Don't touch it.' And (which is ironic because of the way things turned out) I could see that it involved fundraising and I did not want to do that. Then about eighteen months later the Salisbury job appeared. When Jean opened the envelope she said, 'Oh, not Barchester!'
>
> We went down and looked at it. It was lovely spring weather and it looked enchanting. We actually asked ourselves 'Are we being seduced?' It was also made clear to me by a prime minister's secretary that if I said no to this I wouldn't be offered anything else! So we went, in 1986. In some ways I felt that I and the job fitted. I'm a practical person. We had to raise seven and a half million and it was a terrible slog. When I went there I had said to the bishop and the people who appointed me 'I am not a fundraiser. If you want a fundraiser don't appoint me!' What they had asked for was a parish priest, which was something that I felt I could offer. But, of course, it turned out differently from that. This was before English Heritage came in to offer help. I spent a lot of my ten years at Salisbury lobbying ministers. I used to go to London quite frequently and spend hours waiting to see this minister or that minister. I started the Association of English Cathedrals because I realised that if we didn't stand together we were going to be picked off one by one. A number of the senior deans were unbelievable hostile to the whole idea, because they wanted to run their own ships. Wesley Carr and I were regarded as the *enfants terribles* and we were sent away to produce a proposal. It seemed to me that if we did not present a common face to the Government we weren't going to achieve anything. I got a total sum of what all the cathedrals would need in terms of finance over the next quinquennium and it was something in the region of

£128 million. We went to the Government and said this is the deficit that is coming up. The cathedrals represent a very important face of both the nation and the Church and have an important symbolic function in our society, often at a deep, unconscious level. I believe that you need these great big sacred spaces for the community whether individuals are Christian or not.

Forms of Divine Worship

We exist in order to glorify God . . . The importance of worship is about our very being. Worship is also about the Church's mission: it is often described as its shop window; it is where much of the teaching, pastoral and social life is focused. But worship matters above all because it is the response of the Church to God . . . We are called to live as the body of Christ in the communion of the Holy Spirit, and that is embodied in the regular gathering of the church for worship.[1]

Reading this statement by Gordon Jeanes reminds me of the finding of Peter Brierley's *Research* that more people claim to be churchgoers than actually appear to be so. It's as if, even to postmodern man and woman, there is a longing, that is not quite a compulsion, to be part of a praying community, somewhat as one might have a longing to sing with other people (and the two things are not so very far apart), but know of nowhere where one felt able to do that. Both are about having to 'tune' with others. With churchgoing, as with singing, there is a dread of being 'out of tune', of being made to feel foolish. Yet 'being a churchgoer' is an idea that seems to partially attract people, even if they do not actually get to church. Perhaps the churches that have been most successful in encouraging others to join them are those which understand something of the fear, diffidence and hope, and make provision for this – in making a service easy to follow, for example. I have been amazed at how hard some regular churchgoers find it to recognise this. Because they know their way around the Prayer Book, they find it difficult to imagine the awkwardness of those who have never held one in their hands before.

'Those who sit beside them can help them!' somebody remarked impatiently at a church known to me, and went on to snort with rage at the suggestion that an adult might find this a rather humiliating process, and would feel better about the whole experience if they could find their own way through it. And why not? Why must it often be such an arcane process, whipping backwards and forwards through pages of text, everyone's head buried in the book, and to that degree less a part of the community in which they are worshipping?

My own reading is that there is a 'wistfulness' that surrounds the Church, with many seeking a way in who cannot quite work out how to do it. As Peggy Jackson noted in Hertfordshire, 'Those outside the Church are always listening, watching what's going on inside it.' Being received with coldness or indifference when people do get themselves to church, moral superiority, false ingratiation, discrimination against women, hints of fanaticism or rejection – all are noted down and used in evidence. On the other side of the equation, it is not easy being a shy English Christian trying to welcome newcomers into a church! The tendency just to talk to one's own mates, not to try to cross the bridge to newcomers, if one is not a natural extrovert, is strong, and churches need to keep on reminding their regulars to make the effort to introduce themselves and pass the time of day. The rewards are out of all proportion to the effort. There are marvellous conversations to be had with newcomers over coffee after a service.

I have also noted the delight of my non-churchgoing friends who, when happening, out of loyalty to friends or family, to darken church doors for a baptism, confirmation, wedding or funeral, have found the occasion, against their expectations, intelligible, warm and friendly, and the clergy who conducted the rite human and approachable. Times without number I have heard people say, 'You know, I think I might start going.' They may or may not do anything about this, but the inner movement, and the recognition that there is something there to be valued and enjoyed, is worth noting.

Worship is very often the meeting place between the Church and the secular world, both privately and publicly. It has to be accepted in advance that not everyone will be pleased, whatever happens. The marriage of Prince Edward and Sophie Rhys-Jones at St George's, Windsor, in 1999, brought letters in the press saying on the one hand that the service was formal, dour and old-fashioned, and on the other that it showed the Church of England in a dignified and attractive light. (It was, in any case, the form of service the couple had selected.) Correspondents seemed to be divided equally between those who wanted tradition and those who wanted innovation.

One argument against all kinds of innovation in ordinary Church of England services has been that, just as Roman Catholics in the pre-Vatican II days could enter any Catholic church in the world and recognise the Latin words that accompanied the form of service, so the Church of England, on its smaller scale, could claim a uniformity in the common use of the Book of Common Prayer. (That both Roman and Anglican services could be heavy and dull – what a critic of the latest royal marriage described as 'dour' – was also true, of course. Uniformity could be an excuse for dreariness where clergy lacked imagination or were too lazy to prepare their contribution adequately. Equally, there were ways of saying the mass or conducting an Anglican liturgy that could have a profound effect on the congregation.)

For contemporary worshippers Gordon Jeanes draws the tradition/innovation line slightly differently. He suggests that still firmly embedded even in the secular mind are words and phrases associated with liturgy 'I name this child . . .', 'for better for worse, for richer for poorer, in sickness and in health, till death do us part', 'I declare this couple man and wife', ' earth to earth, ashes to ashes, dust to dust', as well as the traditional words of the Lord's Prayer. There are also known and loved bits of the Bible like the Twenty-Third Psalm, or others, often with a strongly poetic content, that are easy to follow and enjoy, as well as cherished hymns remembered from childhood. What very occasional visitors to church want, Jeanes suggests, is to hear the words that they know being spoken in the context of what they recognise as a rite of passage. With regular churchgoers, on the other hand, if they are not to get bored, the diet of regular Sunday services at least needs to range more widely – over other psalms, prayers, readings, hymns – though they too like elements of the familiar and use them as 'hooks' to hold them to their earlier practice of their faith.

Holding Things Together

Bishop David Stancliffe, the Chairman of the Liturgical Commission, suggests that all liturgy is about 'holding past, present and future together'.[2] This does strike me as a precious function but it is one which must be performed nowadays within a postmodern world which has scant respect for history and seems interested in nothing not set firmly in the present. Like Stancliffe, I do not think that this is a reason for Christians to give up the powerful links with the past, however – with the tradition of our worshipping ancestors, as well as Jesus, the figure who is both history and archetype. The gospel itself, the awareness of 'the cloud of witnesses', that is, the long tradition of saints, martyrs and ordinary worshipping Christians down the centuries, seems to me a powerful handle of wisdom and sanity which the Church must hold on to even if others have lost sight of it.

Yet history must not become our graveyard. The Church of England began, after all, as 'a vernacular church', one which aimed to be 'understanded of the people', and sixteenth-century prose is opaque to probably the majority of modern worshippers. Jeanes comments on the 'unnaturalness' of the way the Church of England got frozen around the 1662 Book of Common Prayer. The Book had great virtues of language and theology, and is still a priceless treasure, but there was and is no overwhelming reason that no other form of liturgy can take its place. Cranmer was by no means so hard and fast. His 1549 Prayer Book yielded to the 1552 Prayer Book designed to hold disagreement more effectively, and given the chance, he might have continued to adapt and develop. The 1662 Book of the Restoration, like, to a lesser extent, its predecessors, was part of a peace process, as we would say, a kind of Good Friday agreement intended to force or persuade warring factions to live in harmony. No wonder it took so long – centuries – before there were moves to change it. The modest changes turned down by Parliament in 1927 and 1928 (which the archbishops were later to state could be used anyway!) brought about changes which reflected more modern ideas, like, for example, addressing the deceased at a funeral by name. (Though this was, of course, an ancient idea which the Church of England gave up at the Reformation.)

Alternative
The Alternative Service Book of 1980, though it was adopted very quickly on a scale no one had quite expected, managed to rub a good many people up the wrong way. It used 'exclusive' gender language just as this had come under heavy scrutiny (for some perverse reason it was the last piece of work undertaken by the Liturgical Commission that insisted on this). It was more abstract and conceptual than what went before it, and the language was often heavy and drab. I shall never forget the horror of the first ASB wedding I attended. Yet with its own kind of courage, it did pave the way both for liturgical change and for very necessary discussion which has gone on ever since, the intensity of which shows the vitality of the Church in promising ways. Changes are fiercely debated – six new eucharistic prayers have recently been turned down for general use by General Synod.

Yet the fact that it was possible to change what was said in church gave the green light for much more variation than there had been in the past, and sometimes it seemed almost what a feminist group I was part of once called 'Knit your own church'. At the moment, in

317

addition to some Anglo-Catholic and Evangelical deviations which have a long tradition of breaking canonical rules, there are an almost endless number of liturgical menus – truncated eucharists, family services (in which almost anything may, and does, happen), mattins, the ASB mixed with bits of experimental *Common Worship*, parish communions, sung communions, the Book of Common Prayer communions, charismatic services which are often very spontaneous, conservative Evangelical morning prayer with overhead projectors and long sermons, and so on. These liturgical experiments can be wonderful, dire, or something in between, depending on the skills of those designing them. In towns and cities, Jeanes points out, the competition for worshippers between different Anglican churches has a considerable effect. It may, of course, raise the standard of preaching and liturgy. Or instead, like too many channels on the television, it may reduce everything to a mindless pap. In the country, on the other hand, worshippers may be stuck with whatever the Rector lays on.

The Core of Worship

'What is going to be left that is distinctively Anglican in this welter of experiment, and should the Church be trying to insist on some uniformity?' I asked David Stancliffe. He, like the Archbishop, does not seem too worried about the variety. What matters, he says, is that certain core features remain with all the different presentations. Speaking out of an impressive record of experimenting with liturgy, he says that he believes four elements are vital:

1. A sense at the beginning of a service of a gathering of the community. 'People come to worship as a number of individuals with fragmentary grasps and scattered identities. Any gathering rite at the start of the service has two functions: i. to draw people into a single community; ii. to tune them in so that they can attend to, or engage with, the liturgy of the word.'
2. Engaging with the Word. 'The gathered community is invited to set its story and experience alongside the story of what God has done for his people, and in particular what God has done for his people in Christ. The interweaving of experiences allows cross-fertilisation and illumination. That's what the sermon should be about and it should shape the way the community prays.'
3. The experience of transformation. There is the opportunity of a moment of transformation. 'This may be a sacramental trans-action, an opportunity for penitence or healing, or even something so apparently simple as standing in a November

churchyard among the falling leaves, listening to the Last Post.'
4. Sending out. 'Worship is incomplete if it does not lead to the community which has been informed and transformed engaging with the community among whom it ministers to share that transforming vision, and to make things happen. It is bogus to celebrate the Eucharist and create community in church, but not to express that on Monday by taking a responsible part in – for example – Christian Aid Week. The concluding prayer in the Eucharist – 'Send us out in the power of your Spirit to live and work . . .' makes this clear; and this is the moment for the one crucial notice which is delivered by the deacon in church, and not merely printed on the weekly sheet before the congregation is told to "Go in peace to love and serve the Lord".'

Variety, even following such principles, is a new *theoretical* concept for the Church of England, though as the Archbishop pointed out, in practice there has been considerable variation for many years. Will a new freedom lead to liturgical chaos with no two churches doing anything remotely like each other? Probably not. Probably the 'churchmanship' that rules each parish will prescribe style – 'happy-clappy', pseudo-Roman, or Series 2-type worship. It is an interesting development, however, at a time when the Church seems otherwise so keen on tightening, regularising, authorising and centralising. Perhaps it is simply a recognition that this is going on and will continue to do so until, or if, a more consensual form of worship is arrived at.

A Liturgical Experiment

I must declare an interest in liturgical experiment. As part of a Christian feminist group, the St Hilda Community, which was founded in 1987 to invite visiting women priests from abroad to celebrate communion for the group (as a way of showing that we valued women's orders, even though the Church of England had not yet recognised them), I found myself studying liturgy in a depth I had not considered before. The group began by using the ASB, but almost at once found it, and its forms, inadequate for the particular community we were establishing. We were much more informal. To start with we were a group of eighteen men and women, though we rapidly increased to a size that many churches would envy, and we wished for much more 'input' from our congregation than most churches would value.

Because we met in a round chapel it seemed natural for us to sit in a circle, which had the interesting result that it made no one more

319

important, no more of a 'leader', than anyone else. It seemed natural for anyone and everyone to take part in the readings – we simply moved around the circle taking it in turns – and for readings to be discussed afterwards, sometimes critically. We soon found that this discussion was more fruitful for us than a sermon. Comments, even jokes, seemed an ordinary part of our liturgy. Intercessions were made by members of the group coming forward, lighting a candle and naming their concern. Communion was passed round the group from one member to the next. A collection of money was made to cover our simple expenses. Once or twice we gave it, discreetly, to a member of the congregation who needed money badly. Occasionally, we responded to a request and laid hands as a group on a member who was sick – in one case a few weeks before his death.

Quite early on members took it in turns to 'manage' the worship, to make sure that a liturgy had been prepared, and wine, bread, candles provided – the bread usually baked specially by one of our members. (Everyone who came, and we had many visitors from all over the country and abroad, was a member for an evening.) Reluctant, even terrified, to start with, each of us in turn found that thinking about worship in advance gave us a much deeper understanding of what liturgy existed to do, how it worked, or failed to work, in terms of making people feel involved. One after another, people started writing prayers, in somewhat the same spirit as they baked bread. The cooks were variable – some superb prayers were written for us by Janet Morley, for instance – but their primary concern was to produce material which met the needs of *that* community, as a cook might tailor her efforts to the taste of a family. The use both of female imagery for God, and gender-free language, came very naturally. We wrote so much material that later we published two prayer books, both of which sold extremely well by religious publishing standards, and we were to hear our prayers used frequently at conferences and in churches.

I notice that this kind of private exploration is usually deplored in books about liturgy – nearly always written by male clergy – and I think this is to fail to notice what is achieved by it. In an adult lifetime in the Church I had been taught almost nothing about the history, form and purpose of liturgy – laity, in my experience, are not expected to be interested – but in a few months in the St Hilda Community I had started thinking about it in depth, and I think this was true for many others. Much that we did, and do, at St Hilda's would not be appropriate in a wider setting – that was part of the point, that we had evolved a flexible form of service better suited to a smaller number of people. Nowadays St Hilda's meets, and prays, around a dinner table at which we both eat and pray together, as it seems likely they did in the early Church.

For me, and for others, St Hilda's did not negate what went on in church – a number of our members were clergy, and many of the other worshippers were to return from St Hilda's to regular church worship, which all of us had temporarily abandoned as a form of protest. Several of the group went on to become ordained. All in all we were little threat to the institutional Church (though it didn't always see it that way!), but we needed, at a period when the Church was giving women a hard time, the enrichment that the smaller group had given us. I imagine that many gay and black groups are still in that situation.

It seemed too that we also needed a different, more 'hands-on' experience of liturgy than most parish churches felt able to offer – for me, at least, despite our inadequacies as a group, St Hilda's was the most profound experience of a community at prayer that I have yet experienced. The liturgies had a warmth and vitality that I must confess not to have experienced since.

Initiation

If there is one place where warmth is of particular value in the Church it is at baptisms. The typical parish baptism is not, as it might have been in the early Church, a young adult who had undergone conversion, but a baby, often beautifully dressed, being brought by its parents, and a party of family and friends, to be 'christened'.

Controversy has raged in the Church between two poles – the pole of 'open baptism', in which a church is prepared to baptise all comers, and 'discrimination', in which the parents are required to be churchgoers, or at any rate to undergo careful preparation. I feel sympathy with both groups. I can see, as Peggy Jackson brought out so well, what an opportunity baptism is to welcome people to church who would never otherwise come – parents, and often a large party of friends, are exposed to the Church and its ideas, and sometimes, now and then, the experience *takes*. This view of baptism fits well with the Church of England's ambition to see itself as a 'people's' church – there for everyone who comes.

Heartwarming as it is to welcome the family and their baby, though, parents and godparents are required to make exceedingly important promises. In the case of ASB promises these were relatively modest (as compared, say, to 1662). *Common Worship* is much more ambitious and requires them to say 'I submit to Christ', a promise I have found distressing to hear forced upon parents and godparents in my own church to the point where I try not to attend baptisms any more. Either those making this declaration do not understand what they are saying (though they are supposed to have been prepared in advance) or they do not take it seriously. At any rate the vast majority of such parents are never seen in church again.

What they actually want, it seems to me, is not to 'submit to Christ' (in itself a promise with slightly worrying undertones), but to 'associate' their child with the Church – they like the 'feel' of that – to dress the baby up and have a marvellous party to which all their friends come. In order to achieve this they will say whatever is required of them, would indeed, in the unfamiliar world of the Church, say almost anything, but they are not for a moment seriously taking on Christian commitment and I think it is immoral of my own, and other churches to insist on a form of words that is, quite simply, a lie. It is not, as in the marriage service, that people may make vows that they find in practice they cannot manage to keep. Most people fully understand in theory what marriage entails. In the case of baptismal families there is, for the most part, no real intention of keeping the vows, even if, which seems doubtful, they understand what is being required. The fault is not theirs, but that of the Church which makes them jump through this particular hoop, but I wonder how much the process cheapens public respect for the Church.

Speak of the Devil
There are other follies in the new *Common Worship* baptism, not least the resurrection of 'the Devil' – not an expression much 'understanded of the people' nowadays, however well they understand the reality of evil. Even less than the ASB Baptism service it fails to meet people 'where they are'.

Surely it would be better and more honest neither to turn people away, nor to force important and unwanted promises upon them, which simply devalue the currency of religious language. (An adult who truly wishes to 'take on Christ' has only the same debased language in which to promise a serious commitment.) Since what people come seeking is what they call 'christening' – a naming of the child and an association with Christ and the Church, why not give them simply that, and keep the major promises for those for whom they are a discovery of a richer life?

I see from studying *Christian Initiation: a Policy for the Church of England*[3] that there are those who recall the wholesale baptism of pagans, both in this country in the early years of Christianity, and in other countries such as Africa, and think this, in our own newly pagan situation, might be the way forward. I can think of nothing more shameful or more foolish than to show this kind of contempt for the intelligence and integrity of lay people – it is precisely because the present policy often masks this kind of contempt under a style of welcoming everybody that it is so shocking. People need to come to see the Church as a beacon of truth-telling, whose yea is yea and whose nay is nay, not as two-faced and self-serving as a political party. Worship is, after all, as this chapter began by saying, about glorifying God.

The Church Performance

Liturgy is, of course, amongst other things, a form of education for worshippers, what David Stancliffe calls 'a performance tradition'.

> There is the effect of this in the transformed lives of countless Christians over the centuries. Week by week in the celebration of the Eucharist on Sundays, year by year in the celebration of the two cycles which celebrate incarnation and redemption around the birth and the death and resurrection of Jesus . . . and lifetime by lifetime as new Christians enter this chain of celebration in baptism and so continue to reinvigorate, hand on and live out the embodied life of Christ in a way that both creates it afresh in each age and culture, and sustains its members through achievement and disaster, this pattern is repeated.[4]

It is a noble undertaking, an exercise in being human as well as in worshipping God.

23

Belief: The Longest Journey

Tis myst'ry all! Th'Immortal dies:
Who can explore his strange design?
(Charles Wesley)

We rest our hearts, we focus our lives in persons, in causes, in
ideals or institutions that have great worth to us. We attach our
affections to those persons, institutions, causes or things that
promise to give worth and meaning to our lives. A centre of value
in your life or mine is something that calls forth love and devotion
and therefore exerts ordering power on the rest of our lives and
our attachments. Family can be one such profound centre of value
in our lives. Success and one's career can be important centres of
value. One's nation or an ideological creed can be of life-centring
importance. Money, power, influence and sexuality can all be
idolatrous centres of value in our lives. For some persons and
groups religious institutions constitute dominant centres of
value . . . Of course, from a religious standpoint, God is meant to
be the supreme centre of value in our lives. (James W. Fowler,
'Implications for Church, Education and Society' in *Stages of Faith
and Development*, SCM Press, 1992)

The history of the Church of England contains many paths by which
the Immortal's 'strange design' has been explored, and the road still
stretches before us. I begin by describing the well-trodden paths
which derive most directly from earlier explorers, but which still
strongly influence church people today, and then go on to struggle
with a few of the new, indeed revolutionary, theories about what the
Christian life may be about that some writers and thinkers are
offering us.

The Road Much Travelled

An interesting user of the exploration image is an Anglo-Catholic writer, Ross Thompson, whose booklet in a series published by Affirming Catholicism is called *Is there an Anglican Way? Scripture, Church and Reason. New Approaches to an Old Triad.*[1] Borrowing the method of the adventure computer game Thompson imagines what the great adventure game of the Anglican Church might look like on the screen. 'The path ahead leads through a dark, narrow defile,' says the rubric. 'What now?'

> As they survey the scene before them the travellers are divided. Some think the group should press on, others think the main path is that faint-looking one that climbs up the side of the rocks, avoiding the dangerous river in the heart of the defile, while yet others begin to think that the group has been coming the wrong way for quite some time, and needs to turn round and troop back to safer territory and better trodden paths.
>
> Determining the right path ought to be easy, but unfortunately does not prove so. Some have taken out their compasses and are busy taking bearings. They have brand new, up-to-date, precision models which, they insist, are completely sufficient for the task, so they refuse even a glance at the 2,000-year-old maps over which others are busy poring. The map people, meanwhile, regard these new-fangled devices as dangerous, unreliable innovations, and urge that the maps, old as they are, contain all things necessary to finding the way. A third party proposes that in cases of dispute like this, the leader should arbitrate . . . He does not need maps and compasses and other artificial aids; if only everyone would accept the cumulative weight of experience he represents, all would be well. But to the others, this view seems to give too much weight to human authority. The dispute rages on, as daylight fades . . .[2]

There are further intractable problems – the maps have no key to the symbols, so there is no general agreement about what they mean, or what those who follow them may encounter. The 'compass people' suggest using their modern devices to see what the maps refer to on the ground, but this does not go down well with the 'map people'. 'The map-folk distintegrate into a melee of warring map-factions, each battling for their own interpretation of the map. It is nearly dark now and the party finally takes a vote, in which it is decided to press on down the defile.'[3] The majority, including some of all three groups, and the leader, do this; others go off in search of another leader. Some of the 'map-folk' urge people to 'repent and turn back'.

It does not take great perspicacity to interpret Ross Thompson's

Anglican allegory. He sums up the picture.

> The map-folk are the Evangelicals who look to the Bible, the
> compass-folk are the Liberals who look to the guiding light of
> reason and up-to-date insight – something we each possess but
> need to polish and bring up to date – while the leader-folk are the
> Catholics who look for consensus and continuity among the faithful
> of the Church, and in case of dispute, resort to magisterial
> authority.[4]

The 'defile' for the purpose of this story, is the ordination of women,
though, as the author says, it could equally be other vexed issues –
sexual morality, lay presidency, liturgical reform . . . 'The trickle going
back to well-trodden ways is of course Forward in Faith, the hecklers
on the high ground are Reform.[5]

The Trialogue of the Deaf

It is a story with a moral. 'The real sadness of the story is that
between them the explorers have everything they need to find the
way . . . we are blessed with a balance of the tools we need.'[6] The
balance is the old Anglican triad, claimed since Hooker, of Scripture,
reason and tradition, each of unique and precious value. Our
problem is to learn the art of using the three together. Thompson
quotes the Roman Catholic writer Aidan Nichols, who speaks of the
ongoing Anglican conflict as a 'trialogue of the deaf'.

Perhaps it is imagination, but the deafness, and the insistence of
each on its claims, seems to have grown more acute than some of us
with long memories can ever remember in the Church of England.
Not more acute than it sometimes was in bygone years, of course. It
is a surprise, in an age when theology is no longer accorded the
academic importance it once enjoyed, that, within the organisation,
though certainly not outside it, it now seems to matter so much.
There are particular reasons for this. Some would blame General
Synod and the way the parties within it bodied forth particular sets
of belief. Many, not without some justice, would blame the whole
ordination of women dispute. I am not saying that it should not have
taken place – on the contrary – but it certainly brought to the fore
once again old disagreements which had grumbled along in the
background, and which, in relatively recent times (since, say, the
abortive attempt at reunion with the Methodists) had started to sink
into incoherent murmurings. Many of us who were in favour of the
ordination of women believe that the Act of Synod of 1993, intended
to encourage unity, backfired badly and encouraged disunity. The

issue of homosexuality – how far we truly welcome homosexuals into our churches and whether we are prepared to ordain them – also hardens opinions into party caucuses, with Reform, the Evangelical extremist group, breathing fire and threats like Apollyon, if the Church contemplates doing openly what it has done quietly for centuries – ordaining people known to be homosexual, many of whom have given sterling service to the Church.

I'll Take the High Road and You'll Take the Low Road

The basic Anglican division, as befits our complex history, is the old one of high and low church, which encompasses the twin poles of Anglicanism – Catholicism and Evangelicalism. Between them, and arguably the most suited to the temperament of a moderate and undemonstrative people, is the Broad or Liberal church, the *via media* which some think quintessentially Anglican. The comment of a vicar, Tony Rutherford, quoted above, as preferring to be 'Broad' because it 'held the wings of the Church together', I found a haunting one, not least because, as he immediately noticed after he had said it, it gave the subject a birdlike lightness, an ability to take off and fly.

The Catholic wing of the Church, with some derivation from the old 'high church' divines, but more from the impulse of the Oxford Movement, which metamorphosed into Anglo-Catholicism, has placed most emphasis on tradition, on continuity with the Church of the Apostles, and with the Roman Catholic Church, from which *ecclesia anglicana* suffered a parting of the ways under Henry VIII. The Anglo-Catholic movement rediscovered, to the huge benefit of the Church of England, the sense of ritual, of emphasis on the sacraments, of richness in liturgy – colour, music, light – of delight in the saints and the colourful history of Christianity. Also perhaps at least a rudimentary sense of the closeness of the dead that Eamon Duffy suggests was lost in the English Reformation. If one wanted to add a twentieth-century gloss to the movement, one might say that it knew how to reach and touch the 'unconscious', 'the archetypes', the central Christian myth (in the sense of a core story, not of an untruth). In short it offered ways to touch the depths of faith that did not depend purely on the intellect, that were available to everyone regardless of learning or knowledge. Its grasp of the aesthetic of faith lent it, it seems to me, a flexibility in living it out, a humour, a gaiety, a depth of learning, an ability to live with contradiction, that is often attractive and fun to be alongside.

If Anglo-Catholicism offered a way by which any, however childlike, might grasp religious faith, it also had a parental, authoritarian nature. It had, and has, an ambiguous relationship to the Pope and the Roman Catholic Church (ambiguous in the sense that it continues to see a return to the Roman Church as the most desirable outcome while giving allegiance to a church whose orders are not recognised by Rome; it was this ambiguity which made so many so suspicious of the Anglo-Catholics and their supposed 'popery' in the nineteenth and early twentieth century). It is authoritarian too at a more domestic level, with 'Father' being the arbiter in parish matters, in so far as the democratic slant of the Church of England allows it. It lacks, so it seems to me, a will for the grown-up participation of the laity (there are, of course, actual churches which are marvellous exceptions to this, often because they happen to have a very forceful and articulate laity), and though some liberal elements of the Catholic wing have tried hard, there is still a sense of women, in or out of the priesthood, as being vaguely suspect. It is an open secret that the Catholic wing has been the home of many male priests of homosexual orientation, some of them actually celibate, some purporting to be so, and some bravely living openly with partners. At times and in places this has made women feel like intruders in a male conservation area, even more than they sometimes feel in the Church as a whole, and I believe this needs to be recognised, exactly as the hurt and exclusion of all homosexual people needs to be adequately comprehended and healed by the Church itself.

Along with its authoritarian side the Catholic wing has often been energetically radical in politics, with a sacrificial and often very successful ministry to the poor, finding its expression in Christian Socialism. St John Groser, Norry McCurry, Kenneth Leech, David Randall, and back, long before them, to a magnificent tradition of 'slum priests', the line stretches. Such costly devotion inspires respect. One of the best known 'Catholics' of the last quarter century was Fr Trevor Huddleston, one of the fathers from the Community of the Resurrection at Mirfield, who worked with such distinction in the slums of Sophiatown, and was a significant opponent of apartheid.

In the late nineteenth and early twentieth century the Catholic wing was often at odds with the Church of England about its rituals and this grumbled on in complaints by other sections of the Church against Catholics who insisted on using the Roman missal. Catholic intransigence sank the Anglican–Methodist unity movement, inflicting great hurt on the Methodist Church in the process, but this was only a rehearsal for the great battle to come over the ordination of women. The 'hard' Catholic line, led by Graham Leonard, Bishop of London, was that the Church of England had no right to move in such a fundamental matter, and that, if it did not wish to endanger church unity in perpetuity, it should wait for both the Roman Catholic Church and the Orthodox Churches to make the same move, something which seemed likely to take a very long time. There was also the argument that women, being physically different from Christ, could not be the 'icon' of Christ at the altar which Catholic priests believed themselves to be. The Catholic group, joined by some Evangelicals in General Synod, worked extremely hard to defeat every motion designed to bring about women's ordination. In the teeth of such opposition it was remarkable that the project ever got off the ground, and a sign of how many in the Church of England actually wanted it, and did not intend to be balked.

A New Look for Catholicism

Slowly a more liberal Catholic group emerged, which for a variety of reasons, came out in favour of women's ordination. Affirming Catholicism came into being in 1990. Unlike the 'hard line' school of Graham Leonard they were prepared to proceed up Ross Thompson's 'defile' in the fading light, though their official reasons for existing have nothing specific to do with women priests but are about promoting 'theological thinking about the contemporary implications of Catholic faith and order'.

Their President, Dr Rachel Waterhouse, told me that 'Affirming Catholicism believed in a Catholic Apostolic Church which runs itself by Synodical government, and when that Synod decides something we accept the decision. If you have Synodical government I cannot understand how some people can refuse to accept the decisions of the Synod.'[7]

She saw Affirming Catholicism as in the main an educational organisation, and felt that what was desperately missing in the Church was proper instruction for the laity, and very possibly the clergy too.

> There's nothing easier than to get people to fall in behind some populist idea. It's much more difficult to get them to think through their faith, and work out what it actually means. And I think that's true at every level. It always annoys me when clergy stand up and say, 'Well *my* congregation would never understand this.' Usually people would perfectly well understand if only it was properly explained to them. I think too that we could expect more of children and young people in helping them to understand – they want to join the adult world and a really good Sunday School can help them to do that.[8]

I asked Rachel Waterhouse if she felt any hesitation about *what* should be taught either to adults or children, whether she felt that there was often a considerable gap about what people found themselves saying in church and what they privately believed. She said that she thought David Jenkins had been a very good influence in forcing people to look at their beliefs. Was not the rage that people like Jenkins and Don Cupitt seemed to produce among some clergy and laity very significant? Were people angry because these two touched sore spots?

'I think a number of people who do come to church nowadays are seeking a prop. And they don't want any criticism of the prop, in case they feel unsure of themselves again.'[9]

So was the role of Affirming Catholicism gently to remove the prop?

'I would see us trying to encourage people who don't actually need a prop, but who want to understand, want to grow.'[10]

Did she see any difficulty about the language and doctrines of the Church? Were we in danger of making people say things that they either did not understand or did not in their hearts necessarily believe?

> We carry the weight of this tremendous scholarship, theology, practice that has gone on over the centuries which is built on top of the fairly straightforward, simple gospel story. Christianity has, in a sense, been taken over by the clergy. Nowadays one of the really big changes is that whereas in the past the clergy were the educated class mixing with the upper- and middle-class educated people, now the laity are educated too, they have their share of PhDs, some of them in theology. But it is terribly difficult to break down the old clergy assumptions. Many clergy are just totally imbued with the idea that the laity don't know, or that they are a threat.[11]

June Osborne was also interested in the way clergy experienced laity as a 'threat'. What she sought was 'a *porous* Church, living unafraid of the world beyond its boundaries, in fact actually communicating with humility because it saw itself as a learning community. Everyone else is having to cope with changes – the Church is just one more partner in learning.'[12] Another important relationship was between 'the middle ground and the extremities of the Church'.

> I have put quite a lot of my own energies into the hope that Catholic theology and Catholic liturgy will recover from its crazy negative spiral over the ordination of women, because I think Anglicanism cannot be without being Catholic in some way. It's almost as if what happened to Anglo-Catholicism is that it became Protestant – it got itself into a state of reaction, and there is

nothing more Protestant than the feeling of being against things. In my view Affirming Catholicism, in its turn, has missed its step somewhat, from being issue-orientated, but at least it got the issue right – it's about affirming the middle ground without being liberal (I am not a liberal); the emphasis is on affirming.[13]

I mention the 'anti-woman' feel of Anglo-Catholicism, and June Osborne knows what I mean at once and produces the interesting image of Anglo-Catholicism having been like a beautiful flower, a poppy, but then there was the opium, the toxicity.

Trickling
Opposition to women's ordination caused another group of 'Catholics', those whom Ross Thompson depicts as 'the trickle going back to well-trodden ways', to form two organisations to back the 'hard' Catholic line. The first of these was Cost of Conscience, which organised rallies and raised funds to try to block women's ordination altogether, and then Forward in Faith, a body to link those opposed to women priests, and to try to continue the struggle against them within a Church that supposedly had already made up its mind to ordain women. These formidable bodies have appeared to be well resourced financially.

After the Act of Synod in 1993 Forward in Faith had three effective symbols of their disagreement – the Provincial Episcopal Visitors or 'flying bishops'; the Act itself had established the dubious principle that those who are unhappy with their bishop do not have to remain in communion with him. Forward in Faith publish a regular news-letter, *New Directions* (people play naughty word games with the title), which has a wounded, uncomprehending air about it, as if everyone is out of step but the authors.

We Blossom and Flourish like Leaves on a Tree
The Evangelical wing of the Church could scarcely be more different. Unlike the Catholic and Broad sections which are taking a bad beating in terms of numbers loss, the Evangelicals are in a state of boom which shows little sign of busting. To spend much time around Evangelicals is to feel oneself caught up into a mood of cheerfulness, vigour, enterprise, hope – it is a bit like going out with a likeable puppy, which not only jumps all over you and licks your face, but travels five times the distance you are travelling out of sheer *joie de vivre* and exuberance. They are a living reminder of something that, in the elaborations of Christianity, is easily forgotten, that Christ-ianity was and is about 'belief' (catching the idea as people around

331

Jesus did) and 'repentance' (turning – from one kind of life, which may have been destructive, like that of a prostitute or a drug addict, or, more prosaically, simply respectable, that of a decent householder – towards an entirely different understanding, a life set in the perspective of the love of God).

The Evangelicals are Thompson's 'map-folk', firmly recalling you to 'Scripture' at regular intervals. They feel very directly descended from the Reformers. They are plain people, with little interest, it seems to me, in the aesthetic of worship. Where the Evangelicals worship in modern churches these are functional to a degree. Where older churches have been adapted to new styles of worship, and the barn-like look is absent, overhead projectors ruthlessly interrupt the lines of the building and the intentions of the architect. A table, which will be wheeled out later as an altar, may be bundled away behind a reading stand or a 'worship band'. The words of some of the hymns are as banal as those of pop songs. The eucharist, if used, may be shamelessly and awkwardly truncated. Neither the eyes nor the ears are indulged. It is as if beauty is deliberately evaded. No feng shui for the Evangelicals!

Yet within these brutal spaces some rather marvellous services take place. Partly it is the sheer numbers of the congregation. (Yes, I know numbers are not everything, but the whole thing does feel a likelier enterprise with two hundred people than it often does with a bare thirty or less.) Partly it is the wholeheartedness and emotion with which the (sometimes rather dreadful) hymns are sung. Partly it is that those who intercede for others pray as if they meant it. Partly it is that the laity, in virtually every Evangelical church I have visited, recognise that it is for *them* to make visitors welcome, to labour in the vineyard, to cough up the money for new enterprises, and to take the beliefs on for themselves. And Evangelical clergy give power to the laity generously and enthusiastically. And the preaching, though I can weary of its length, is meticulously prepared and often very good indeed. What deserves, and gets, success in the Evangelical churches, is sheer hard work and the spirit of enthusiasm. Energetic beehives make an awful lot of honey.

It used to be said that Evangelical churches were only interested in converting people, but had little concern with the social gospel, and in a very interesting essay about Evangelicalism in *The Post-Evangelical Debate*[14] Michael Saward, who has remained an Evangelical, describes how in 1960 he and another curate had to persuade their Rector to support Christian Aid Week – the Rector believed that it 'was nothing to do with the Gospel'.[15] Saward's point is that Evangelicalism has moved fast and far since then, and is now effectively showing social concern in many spheres. I suspect it would be difficult now to find a vicar who thought like Saward's old Rector.

What struck me about the success of a number of Evangelical churches is that they have successfully tuned into pop culture – and since this is what the majority of people of this country listen to and read in a secular context, it is not surprisingly a form of church where they feel at home. In a Church which has rarely reached the working-class nerve or understood the common touch since it shook off the dust of Rome, it could be that the Evangelicals have stumbled on, and then worked hard over, the secret – a tabloid Christianity that manages simultaneously to be genuinely caring. I think it would be a pity if the envy of those who belong to other forms of churchmanship stopped them from recognising the genuineness of the achievement.

The Evangelical church offers a simple and simplified teaching which anyone can grasp. A close study of the Bible, a strong emphasis on the crucifixion as being related to the individual's sins, an emphasis in being in some special relationship with Jesus that is reached by a conversion experience, the importance of witnessing to one's belief and so converting others, a strict moral sense – all of these, together with a warm, social climate, are of the essence. The Evangelicals seem to have been among the first to grasp that the present generation, unlike previous generations, were and are in total ignorance of Christian teaching. Logical and determined, they stepped in with Alpha and other forms of teaching.

The Club of the Reformed

An interesting thing about Evangelicals is the looseness of their attachment to the Church of England, in contrast to their powerful attachments, via the Evangelical Alliance, with other Reformed churches. What rarely gets put into words is that they do not believe that the other sections of the Church of England are the real thing. Other sections seem to be less interested in mission, conversion and the 'substitutionary sacrifice of Jesus' and detailed exposition of the Bible, and, to conservative Evangelicals at least, this makes them suspect, not of the tribe that knows Joseph. To spend much time around Evangelicals is to get the message that one is not saved at all, a difficult basis, in its confident one-upmanship, to carry on a continuing Christian conversation.

But the inner world of Evangelicals appears to be a very exciting one. Some of their books describe fierce internal disputes about theology within their private culture – which the rest of the Church of England neither knows nor cares about. Within individual churches one senses an enormously warm and containing atmosphere, with so much work to be done that the outside world seems a bit remote. Armies of keen Christians are making coffee, serving meals, organising Alpha, playing and singing, arriving early at church to pray before the service starts, or praying while the Alpha meeting is going on, organising or going to house church meetings, doing good works. When, I found myself wondering, do they get round to tennis or bowls, an ordinary choir, a garden club, a rambling society, Townswomen's Guild, Rotary, etc. – some place where they rub shoulders with non-believers? Does everything have to be christianised?

Maybe it does. Maybe if the longing is to convert everyone 'to the saving power of Jesus' as they say, it is impossible to spend too much time with other Christians doing Christian things. I wonder why the idea of this, or any other, Christian para-culture fills me with such a feeling of claustrophobia?

The New Evangelicals

Evangelicals have, in recent memory, undergone some extraordinary changes which have somehow placed them just where, I suspect, they want to be, at the edge of mission and change, with a strong sense of themselves as a body whose time has come. They have, as people say nowadays, reinvented themselves. Once thought to be rather prim about things like drinking alcohol, going to the cinema, reading non-Christian writers, or non-Evangelical theologians and biblical scholars, Evangelicals have become broader, more daring, more ready to face their critics. Without losing their original principles they have battled with themselves and one another to find a way to achieve what was most important to them, the very substance of their existence, the chance to 'spread the gospel', or 'bring people to the Lord Jesus'. It is impossible to listen to this without recalling the vigour and zest of the early Church, and along with the vigour and zest go many things that were part of that first development – preaching, in particular, and in some areas of the Evangelical church, experiences of 'the Spirit', speaking or singing 'in tongues', and healing. What is impossible to deny is the extraordinary outpouring of energy going on at the moment in the Evangelical churches.

For many reasons it works – it succeeds in making full, vibrant churches. It is easy to come up with 'psychological' reasons for this of a slightly reductionist kind. In a world of terrible uncertainties people feel comforted by a 'simple' message – nothing complicated about the Evangelical word about salvation, Jesus, sex before marriage, homosexuality, abortion or much else. In a society where, almost unnoticed by the churches as whole, suddenly a generation had grown up ignorant of all things Christian, Alpha straightforwardly set out to instruct and inform. In a society of great loneliness, the Evangelical community offered a warm society, shared food, recognition, affirmation, a way to go that satisfied religious longing.

There is what feels like a very genuine movement within the Evangelical movement as a whole, successful because people have acted imaginatively and courageously on the insights they had. They have much to teach the rest of the Church, if they can bring themselves to talk, really talk, to it, and forgo superiority, if they bring themselves not to badmouth Liberals or despise the trimmings of the Catholics. But where issues are not simple, but complex, it seems to leave some of the deeper levels of human experience untouched.

The Student Scene
On the student scene, according to press reports, Evangelical Christianity is very big indeed. In September 1999, the *Guardian* reported their huge success at the University of Durham, with the Evangelical Christian Union now the biggest university society, with getting on for five hundred members. A pop band which is very much the local rage, Coastal Dune sings songs about being drawn by the cross of Jesus, of dying in order to live. 'Every song carries an overt religious message.'[16] A new generation of students arrives at university with almost no pre-knowledge of Christianity, and hears the message of Coastal Dune for the first time. Even more significant, perhaps, they are the children of parents of the sex, drugs and rock-'n'-roll generation, and it is the contention of the writer of the piece, Jonathan Margolis, that Christianity may be becoming the 'symptom of youthful rebellion, a novel counter-culture for students'. Prayer groups, dinner parties where religion is the main topic, and solemn discussions about the meaning of sex in the pub are all major student activities. Alcohol, sex and drugs do not feature much in these young people's lives.

One student, hitherto a churchgoer, expresses her dismay at what she believes is going on, in what she describes as 'in your face' religion. 'It very soon became obvious that it was not only evangelical, but very orthodox and fundamentalist, with elements of racism, sexism and homophobia.'[17] What is striking is the conservative interpretation of the Bible, with a narrow view of morals that ignores, for example, consumerism and does not prevent these students from moving to take well-paid jobs with vast multi-national conglomerates with little moral concern for the parts of the world they exploit.

'The prospect of a flood of hardline religious zealots emerging from Britain's universities is certainly one to ponder,'[18] Margolis concludes. The danger of a growing fundamentalism here, especially if it becomes politically useful, as it now is to politicians in America, is a scaring one.

To those who see the Christian religion like this, other Christians are simply wrong-headed, which makes dialogue difficult. It is hard to talk to those who know you are wrong.

Pharisees and Publicans

Dave Tomlinson who comes from an Evangelical background and now would call himself a post-Evangelical uses to great effect the gospel story of the Pharisee in *Post-Evangelicals*.[19] The Pharisee thanks God that he not like the crude Publican, who gets his prayers all wrong. In Tomlinson's version it is the Evangelical who thanks God that he is not as other men, even that miserable Liberal bishop over there.

What Next?

So will the Evangelicals dominate the Church of England? Betty Saunders reported the Evangelical Canon Michael Saward as describing a kind of 'destruct' effect that emerged whenever Evangelicals got near power. 'They'll blow it again. They always have.'[20] Numbers, he explained, are not the same thing as power. 'The moment they get near a position of power they disintegrate. Somehow they don't know how to handle power, because they assume that power means corruption.'[21] He uses the example of an incident in the nineteenth century when, requested by Palmerston to nominate bishops, Shaftesbury, a keen Evangelical, helped nineteen godly Evangelicals into power. Simple godliness, says Betty Saunders, 'perhaps a desirable quality in a bishop even now, was not enough on its own without the back-up of a harder edge and the capacity to lead, direct and inspire'.[22] The evangelical bishops of the nineteenth century failed to take advantage of their opportunity.

Another problem that Saward pinpointed for her was the detachment or indeed hostility of many younger Evangelicals from the Church of England, a bad starting place for a takeover. 'Younger Evangelicals have grown up into a student world of renewal-style worship, very relaxed, no robes at all: that sort of thing. They're at odds with the institution that pays them.'[23] Saward felt that Evangelicals were too unpopular in the Church as a whole to get the promotions that would make them influential, yet he commented, surely correctly, as the Lambeth Conference of 1998 in many ways underlined, 'If you look at world Christianity en masse, Anglican Evangelicals are dead centre, at the pivot point, though no one spots it, or says so.'[24]

Saward points out that there are those who are Anglicans first and Evangelicals second (a group in which he counts himself), and those who are Evangelicals first and Anglicans second – quite an important difference.

Reformed or Reform?
The most extreme form of Evangelicalism at present is Reform, a body which began by opposing the ordination of women, on the grounds that women could not hold positions of authority, but once that issue was largely lost, moved on to the issue of ordaining, or rather not ordaining, homosexual clergy. It has a brutal, blackmailing approach, threatening to withdraw parishes from the Church, or to refuse to pay funds into the diocesan system, and until such bluff is called will succeed, as Forward in Faith has succeeded, in holding the Church to ransom. Reform does not seem to be much loved by fellow Evangelicals, though some Anglo-Catholics have joined it, as some Evangelicals have joined Forward in Faith. It is reminiscent of what W. R. Matthews called 'the unholy alliance between the extreme Protestants and the extreme Anglo-Catholics'[25] over the attempts of the Church to update the Prayer Book in 1927. This cabal wrecked the majority wishes of the Church, 'the former because they feared the Mass and the latter because they feared they might be prevented from saying the Latin Mass in their churches'.[26] Such alliances, based not on shared principle but on expediency, seem rather ignoble.

Liberal Liberties
The Liberals, in particular during the 1980s and on into the 1990s, have been the group that both Catholic and Evangelical wings of the Church have loved to feel superior to – the publicans whom the Pharisee feels free to despise. The Catholics see the Liberals as taking dangerous liberties with tradition, exalting reason, or common sense, or the latest secular humanist enthusiasm, above doctrinal faith and credal statements. The Evangelicals see the Liberals as taking unpardonable liberties with the Bible and not being zealous in evangelism, of being 'too intellectual' or 'too modernist'. For the heavy mob on either the Catholic or the Evangelical side a little ritual beating and execration of the Liberals is a routine warming-up exercise.

Fortunately Liberals tend to have a bouncy quality about them, an almost unshakable confidence. They have, after all, seen a good

337

many promising Christians forsake their Evangelical origins from time to time and end up as Liberals, and many Catholics have Liberal tendencies anyway; in fact I was struck by how often the words 'liberal Catholic' came up in conversations with those I interviewed. Perhaps the Liberals are sustained by a profound belief that the Church of England, no matter what tangents it shoots off at from time to time, is a centrist body, reflecting the moderate character of the British. The solemnities and romantic aspects of Catholicism, the excitements of Evangelical conversion, and its unyielding moral tone, the extraordinary adventure of 'being slain in the Spirit', important as they may be, never permanently replace the Church of England's bias towards an essential ordinariness, a lack of extreme in religion. And then again the group with the compasses – in Ross Thompson's allegory – know that compasses really do work rather well.

Bishop John Saxbee, a leading and unashamed exponent of Liberalism, sees its presence within and without the Church of England. 'Within mainstream Christianity [there is] a significant body of believers whose approach to Christian believing, belonging and behaving is essentially liberal in style and substance.'[27]

He leads a lively group of Liberals, including a number of younger theologians, who see the distinctive Liberal contribution not as a vacuous tolerance (though Liberals are not always tolerant of non-Liberals), but as a dynamic interaction with the culture of the society in which the Church finds itself. It can neither withdraw into a solely sacramental religion, nor one which forms a para-culture which it hopes to persuade everyone to join. It wants to expose itself to the ideas, the art, the politics of its period, finding Christ within that where it can.

A Way of Being in the World

Martyn Percy, Director of the Lincoln Theological Institute for the Study of Religion and Society, suggests that Liberals should not think of themselves as a 'party' within the Church, but rather a genre of thinking – 'a particular way of being in the world which seeks truth and the common good in the face of a complex and fast-changing environment'.[28] It may be a journey of questions and some ambiguities, just because truth itself is complex and ambiguous, yet he sees it as 'a critique of the world in a prophetic sense yet also a befriender of it.'[29] 'One of the tasks of the Church is to find its place in society in such a way that the status, order and functioning of society is raised and maintained.'[30]

Percy does not see the Church as doing this successfully at present.

The danger is that the Church becomes a club, with an ageing membership which is essentially devoted to maintaining buildings and the ideas of a bygone age. The debate on homosexuality in the Church typifies this within Anglicanism. We stand apart from society with a poorly argued rubric and are in danger of holding policies for clergy that are at odds with the European Court of Human Rights. Ironically we cling to this with almost no regard for the public cost of such a position – indeed we are still a body exempt from sexual discrimination legislation, to our great shame.[31]

Saxbee is ready to admit that 'evangelism' may be a kind of Achilles' heel for the Liberal group, since there is a complacency, or a delicacy, in its approach to the consciences of others, which seems to inhibit proselytising. Yet it may simply be that this is to misunderstand where the Liberals are coming from. Saxbee sees the liberal thrust as one of making the Christian faith intelligible and credible, a faith that will satisfy intelligent, questioning and honest minds from one generation to the next. Yet this must be more than 'intellectual', since human beings are more than simply thinking creatures, and need to be reached on other levels of being, the parts, as Saxbee says, 'that liberalism has often failed to reach'. His desire is to do this both among those who already think of themselves as Christians and those who cannot yet bring themselves to be part of the Church.

Statistics show the Liberals, like the Catholics, losing ground in terms of numbers, unlike the Evangelicals. But it is interesting that the Liberal group, the Modern Churchpeople's Union, which suffered an eclipse in the recent past, now has a fast rising number of members, the majority of them Anglican, with a strong feeling of life and energy around its annual Conference, which enjoys an average attendance of ninety or so people.

Stimulating the Church of England
Richard Truss, its Chairman, the Vicar of St John's, Waterloo, Dean of Lambeth, and Chaplain of the National Theatre, began his Christian life as an Evangelical, but moved on to become a Liberal. Although, as he remarks, for a good many years now 'Liberal' has been a dirty word, the Modern Churchpeople's Union has been unashamedly Liberal throughout that time. 'The purpose of the Union,' he says, 'which celebrated its centenary in 1988, is to try to stimulate the Church of England, which is often quite a moribund body, to take on board the age it lives in, the ideas that are prevalent, and not to be fearful of what is being thought round about it.'[32]

The MCU reached its peak in the 1930s, and then suffered a slow decline as some of its leading members grew old and died. Henry Major, Charles Raven, W. R. Matthews and Edward Carpenter were some of the more famous Liberals. Now the Union seems to be regenerating.

'Who joins?' I asked.

> I think a lot of people who are seeking, clergy whose bookshelves I hope are still up to date many years after ordination or since they left university, those today who are perhaps somewhat disenchanted with the Church, but who are counterbalanced by those who are very much at the centre of things. I think that has been a healthy balance – people with one foot very much outside and one foot very much inside, and they meet up at our Conferences and stimulate one another.[33]

Truss thinks that the Union has benefited from the reaction to the hard Conservative (political) line of the 1980s which has made people again prepared to think about things like community, and change being perhaps a good thing, and the Church not being there as a burrow to hide in, but an influence which may be a catalyst in communities.

> The other reason, of course, is the ordination of women which we supported, and because we were there and supported it, I think a number of people found us and joined us. That connection has been good for us. It brought in a lot of people, some of them women priests.[34]

Truss likes the word 'liberal' because he feels that it stands for both progress and breadth, which he feels that the Church at its best embodies. He thinks that societies in the Church are useful in giving Christians a place beyond their own parishes and their diocesan structures where they can think and discuss and find companionship of ideas, 'find their identity', as he puts it.

Is There a Meeting Place?
Is it ever going to be possible for these different groups within the Church to get along together, not as competitors and rivals, but as friends, with admiration and respect for the gifts that others have? Some, it must be said, show no wish to do this, but it strikes me that there are those in all the major groups within the Church who are both capable of this and who have a desire to do it. John Saxbee has an extraordinarily haunting image of this.

The New Music

He has a great admiration for the nineteenth-century American composer Charles Ives. Ives was the son of a small-town bandmaster in Danbury, Connecticut, and a whim of his father was to set two bands marching towards each other from opposite sides of the town, each playing a different tune. Townspeople covered their ears at the cacophony when the two bands finally met and passed each other, but the young Ives, with the ear of a supremely talented musician, loved this moment, and could hear a new tune being created as the bands played away at their separate scores. What is the tune that we are missing in the Church of England by our mutual suspicion and our failure to come together? Another priest I talked to had a more mundane version of this – his struggle, when listening to Mozart in the sitting-room, to endure the thumping bass of his daughter's pop music being played in a bedroom above!

The Family Secret

It seems to me that the Church of England finds it easier and more rewarding to be ecumenical with Roman Catholics, Orthodox Christians and Methodists than to try to build bridges, however tenuous, within the different branches of its own family. Catholics, Liberals and Evangelicals are nervous of one another, afraid on the one hand of compromising their own beliefs, but on the other afraid of snubs and of the ultimate British dread, embarrassment. It is as if the fallings-out of the sixteenth and seventeenth century live on, like a dark family secret, unexamined and unhealed, the children and children's children not even remembering quite what it is all about; yet preserving the old antipathy, not without some pride in their own tradition, as the Orangemen of Drumcree still take pride in the arrogance of the annual march down the Garvaghy Road.

Perhaps the time has come for pride to be abandoned, and Liberal, Catholic and Evangelical to reach out to one another to learn and discuss, a rapprochement which I was pleased to see that the Archbishop of Canterbury would like to see come about. To get to that point we have all got to admit to our own prejudices, to be open to new kinds of learning, and to stop being driven by fear, the fear of losing something we value. I believe that if this could happen at a parochial level, with comings and goings between local churches of different kinds of churchmanship, we should be immeasurably strengthened. Perhaps we should hear the harmonies heard by Charles Ives.

Before this kind of thing really gets going, however, it seems to me that we must get down to basics with the men and women in the pew.

Of the people who attend conferences that support one kind of churchmanship or another, the majority are clergy, or people studying theology, or, at the very least, people used to bandying around the sort of argument that occurs in theology. What do people in the pew think or understand about theological ideas?

Alpha and other instruction groups do, of course, offer information about Christian beliefs and practices, and this has its value, particularly for a younger generation who have arrived at church almost totally ignorant of Christian background. But what of those who have been going to church for years, and, by the same token, have had a long experience of life? Is it instruction they need, or the opportunity to examine the faith problems which arise in the course of trying to make sense of belief in the context of work, family and social life? I do not think that attending the liturgy week by week produces this opportunity.

Some time ago my Vicar gave an 'interactive' sermon on the subject of prayer and asked people in the congregation why they prayed and what they felt about it. Most people talked enthusiastically about praying; no one admitted to any difficulties with it.

It might be that what we have in south-east London is a congregation of precocious spirituality with most individuals in constant conversation with God. Or it may be that, being polite, they did not want to offend the Vicar and played along with what they thought were his expectations. It is not for me to judge, but I was sorry that nothing more 'heartfelt' seemed to emerge from the Vicar's invitation. What we did not have, it seemed to me, what most congregations do not have, is a religious culture in which questioning feels natural. Just before this service, a friend who was a curate in the East End of London had told me how, in response to one or two private conversations with parishioners, he had advertised an evening at his house to talk about 'doubts and uncertainties', and had been amazed at the numbers that showed up. He had unwittingly opened the door to a real longing in the congregation, the chance to 'open up' about their religious problems. My suspicion is that many lay people are very unsure about things they find themselves saying in church, may imagine that such problems are peculiar to themselves or may feel guilty about the large statements and promises of the liturgy. Not all can live with this silence. Instead of going to church, they may feel more 'honest' if they stay away, like one of my children, unsure of her religious beliefs, who would have liked a church wedding, but 'I don't think it would be honest. I don't want to feel I am *using* the Church.'

Clergy often seem surprisingly uninterested in the doubts and hesitations people have about faith, or maybe they are afraid of opening a kind of Pandora's box. The laity pick up the message that their doubts are not wanted and obligingly keep quiet about them, but then they are not given the chance to grow through them into a greater religious maturity. There are all sorts of reasons for going to church – finding it soothing, liking to sing hymns and carols, because one's parents went, or one needs the company, or because it is a structure which is useful to society; but none of these are as satisfying as they might be if the central purpose of it all – to love and worship God – is lost in a fog of falsity, anxiety or pretence.

The kind of certainty that the Archbishop felt helped to bring about the success of Evangelicalism in getting people to church, can also work against bringing in those who may not wish, or be able, to swallow down doubts about the Virgin Birth or the Resurrection. This kind of seeker feels rather different if they know that doubts are allowed, and it is all right to express them freely and talk them through.

In the course of working on this book I asked a secretary to transcribe some notes I had made on *A Vision to Pursue*, a book by the theologian Keith Ward, who not only talked about the authenticity of Eastern religions and the way he thought Christianity ought to relate to them, but also the huge changes in our understanding of the Bible brought about by biblical criticism. He questioned whether it is possible for Christians to go on thinking of Jesus as 'the Second Person of the Trinity', not least because it is unlikely that Jesus thought of himself in those terms. The secretary returned the book to me in a state of what I might call 'theological excitement' and talked the issues over with me at length with the greatest interest. I think it had not occurred to her before that there were people who did not find such questions frightening. For her, religion had suddenly come alive. Ward's book was bigger and more exciting than the nervous beliefs being peddled by the Church.

A recent report prepared by a Working Group of the Board of Education on the subject of the laity was called *Called to New Life: The World of Lay Discipleship*.[35] What the report strongly suggested was that many lay people were not encouraged in the church context to talk in depth either about their faith itself, or about the way it impinged on their daily life. A number of them complained that it felt useless to try to talk about their work situation either to clergy or to fellow Christians. 'Clergy feel threatened about being involved in a ministry in which they by definition are not the experts. In the workplace issues of their congregation members, they are "lay", and most clergy sadly cannot cope with being in that "weak" position.'[36]

One man quoted in the Report worked in middle management and had a longing to speak to the congregation:

> There is so much that I learn from my work that could relate to the worship and teaching in the church. I put this idea to the PCC and several people were really enthusiastic about it. The Vicar said he would take the idea to the Ministry Team. Almost a year went by and I heard nothing, so I asked the Vicar about it. He said that it had been discussed by the team members – the Readers especially were not happy about someone who had not studied theology preaching in the main service on a Sunday . . . He then asked me if I considered whether God was calling me to be a Reader! I was very disappointed.[37]

What a tragic waste to deny this man's insights to the congregation, to refuse him the adult status of contributing theological ideas, as well as the chance to unite his working and worshipping life!

Other complaints were that sermons and intercessions which touched on the working world often seemed directed exclusively to family life, and to 'caring' professions – education, health service and emergency services – rather than to the profit-making businesses in which many people actually worked; that professional work seemed more 'highlighted' than 'trades', shop-floor workers, etc.; that women were usually pictured in domestic and family roles, or in the lowlier jobs, never in management; that 'mission' was thought of in terms of homes, schools, hospitals – not usually in terms of factories, garages, farms or offices.

What I found worrying about the interviews in this Report was that although it was obvious that lay people had noticed very acutely the ways in which they felt left out and uncared for, it did not appear in most cases that they had spoken up and objected until specifically questioned for the purposes of the Report. This seemed an extraordinarily significant fact (though not apparently of great interest to those who compiled the Report). There is a long habit of passivity among Anglican laity, a sense of an inability to change things, as if they are young children at home with Daddy or Mummy Vicar, not grown-up people with the power to alter what offends them. Yet they notice and are wounded by their impotence and the sense of neglect. What is it about Anglican church culture which promotes this kind of ineffectualness?

I want to argue that a kind of general healing is called for in the Church – the building of bridges across rifts – and this is important not only between one kind of churchmanship and another, but also between clergy and laity. The word for this healing is 'dialogue', a word that means we talk to one another not as parent and child, or *de haut en bas* from a superior theological position, but as equals, each of us truly open to the possibility of listening and learning, not just waiting for the other to stop talking so that we can plunge in. For the Church to 'work', to come alive, requires that each of us bring our doubts and certainties with us, our unique experience of the world, our experience as workers, as married people or single, as men or women, parents or children, working or unemployed, rich or poor, heterosexual or homosexual, healthy or sick, successful (in the world's terms), or unsuccessful.

As it happens I have stolen the word 'dialogue' from the theologian George Pattison, whose work interests me very much. 'Thinking about God' he says 'is not the business of technicians (i.e. theologians), but a matter of dialogue between embodied, living voices.'[38] A Cambridge academic, Pattison begins from describing the way in which the role of theology itself has changed. Once, in medieval times, it was 'the Queen of Sciences', the ultimate arbiter of knowledge. A whole variety of ideas toppled Her Majesty from her throne – Enlightenment philosophy, Darwin, Marx, Nietzsche, Freud, the horrors of the First World War, the Holocaust, the atomic bomb, science and technology, critical theologians and religiously pluralistic societies.

Because of its interest in 'final truths', its preoccupation with 'ultimate concerns' and the 'big picture', the temptation of theology is to speak from 'above the battle', to give an 'overview', 'to define itself in such a way as to make claims that seem to impact upon every field of human knowledge', to feel that it is entitled to the 'last word'. At one time it felt it had the right to interfere with the findings of science, as it did with cosmology and evolution, though it is difficult to imagine contemporary theologians either having the power or wishing to do that.

If I have understood Pattison correctly he is saying that theology, with its claims to an 'all-encompassing and unsurpassable overview of the whole field of human knowledge and behaviour', overvalued itself. Theologians had no direct line to God, no skills that are not shared by other workers in the humanities, possessed no 'deeper wisdom' of its own that gives it the right to be somehow 'special'. 'If he is not to be convicted of special pleading or of belonging to the intellectual equivalent of a holy huddle, the theologian must take his place on the common ground of intellectual learning, teaching and research.'[39]

Pattison quietly undermines all the favourite grounds for a 'special' status – Catholic, Protestant, revelationary, mystical and other – he favours theologians being down there getting messed up in the general hurly-burly. Or if there is a special status for Christianity (and I would want to argue that in some senses there is, though not in such a way as to deny the truth of others' beliefs) he puts his finger on what the problem is.

> To the extent that the uniqueness and untranslatability of the Christian story is emphasized, I am inclined to believe the former, but then, if that is correct, such theologies are going to have to face a series of simple yet devastating questions that they characteristically avoid, questions like these: What is it that is going to make someone who is not already living 'within' this story choose to do so? Wherein does its superiority lie? Why is it to be preferred above all others? . . . I am being asked to believe that this story is in some way a statement of or a response to the way things really are in the world, or the way human beings really are, and because of the unique importance that he attaches to this story in shaping his life choices, I am in fact being asked to believe that this story (and no other) provides access to the really real. It is not just more real than live role-playing; it is that story than which no realler story can be told.[40]

Pattison goes on to say that neither philosophy nor theology can actually answer the basic question, which is what 'Being' is, not at least in the same demonstrable way that contemporary science can show us what works, what can be predicted and what can be manipulated. In contrast to scientific certainty, 'all interpretations of the meaning of life, the world and the universe seem to be left hanging in an ontological void . . . We cannot even begin to answer the eternal questions: what is true, what is it all for . . . what does it all mean?'[41]

He goes on to make the point that the outcome of all this doubt is not necessarily nihilism. What he thinks might emerge from it is a new style. He contrasts what has often been the Christian method of 'monologue' – one way of seeing and discussing something – with 'dialogue', an interactive method. When monologists confront one another the result is often 'a static and sterile stand-off'. Dialogists, on the other hand 'will be able to speak to one another fruitfully, and with some excitement, without necessarily reaching agreement. Each may nurture the hope of winning the other round, but will also recognise that there are many useful things to achieve in terms of clarification and understanding that fall short of out-and-out victory.'[42] He goes on to make the point that, despite the way the Bible has often been used in a monologic way 'it would not be hard to argue that the biblical text itself, because of the kind of text it is, welcomes a dialogical reading'.[43]

Pattison is asking for a radically new method of theological discussion (now that theology has abdicated or been deposed as the Queen of Sciences).

> We must be prepared to . . . argue our case and enter into dialogue. We can only do that, however, on the condition that we acknowledge the possibility that the line between truth and error does not lie between one and another church, one and another period of history, one and another theology, or one and another individual, but runs through the middle of all these. Whatever good reason we have for holding our view, we have to concede that others may have at least some good reason for holding to their contrary view.[44]

Pattison's rejection of the role of the theologian in a world now shaped definitively by secularism could not be more different from 'radical orthodoxy', another way of talking about theology to emerge from Cambridge, one difficult for non-theologians to follow and perhaps designed to be so. 'Radical orthodoxy' has large ambitions. In an article written by three supporters of this school, John Milbank, Catherine Pickstock and Graham Ward, there is a note of indignation about the fact that for several centuries secularism has been 'defining and constructing the world'. They are going to put a stop to that. In a world which the writers believe is imploding as a result of 'its own lack of values and lack of meaning', one which 'promotes a materialism which is soulless, aggressive, nonchalant and nihilistic', they complain that the 'theological is either discredited or turned into a harmless leisure-time activity of private commitment'.[45] Along with a contempt for the modern (postmodern) world goes a curious tetchiness of written style, as if the writers are almost too exasperated for words. A review of their latest anthology in the *Times Literary Supplement* by a fellow-theologian complained that the essays in the book showed insufficient knowledge of, and interest in, the work of other scholars working in relevant fields. And although it evoked 'the Church' as an important feature in its picture of the world, it seemed oddly uninterested in the current problems of this institution – it seemed to be more a concept than a vulnerable entity.

'Radical orthodoxy' seeks to reclaim the world by situating its concerns and activities within a theological framework. It is, I think it is fair to say, nostalgic for the supposed unity and sense of meaning of pre-modern religion and society, what it calls 'a richer and more

347

coherent Christianity that was gradually lost sight of after the late Middle Ages'.[46] It is committed to credal Christianity and its 'patristic matrix'. Not surprisingly, while it claims to transcend 'confessional boundaries', its 'feel' is more Catholic than Protestant, though more high Anglican, so far as I can judge, than Roman Catholic.

It aims at a return to patristic and medieval roots, 'and especially to the Augustinian vision of all knowledge as divine illumination'. It sets out to deploy this 'recovered vision' systematically to criticise modern society, culture, politics, art, science and philosophy with an unprecedented boldness. Finally it wants to 'rethink the tradition'. Plainly, it does not lack either energy or confidence. The introductory article is called 'the turn of radical orthodoxy', a slightly odd title, as if theology was a ride on a roundabout.

I was puzzled by the suggestion that puritanism, in its erotic and other forms, is all the fault of secularism, rather than something much more deeply rooted in the human psyche, Christian and otherwise. This feels a difficult contention to substantiate. And I wonder how seriously we are to take their desire to turn the clock back to the late Middle Ages (to a time when clocks were very primitive indeed and kept dubious time). Is 'radical orthodoxy' a kind of Oxford Movement arising in Cambridge, with Milbank, Pickstock and Ward and a penumbra of others firing off tracts?

It is possible to share some of the concerns of 'radical orthodoxy' – the loss of a sense of meaning in art, for instance, or sadness at the degradation of sexuality – without feeling that the cure they recommend is either possible or, in the forms they prescribe, desirable.

What is simply amazing is that any group at the beginning of the twenty-first century can boldly (their word) make plans to redraw all the maps in favour of Christianity in so comprehensive and inclusive a manner. It feels a bit like the old chestnut of 'the conversion of England in this generation'. Is it a kind of mad hubris like a lunatic believing she is Queen of England, or does 'radical orthodoxy' know something nobody else knows (as if the lunatic knew perfectly well that she had been kidnapped from Buckingham Palace in infancy and actually was the rightful sovereign)? Watch this space.

Feminist theology shares some of 'radical orthodoxy's' sense that there is something unique about the present time that requires a unique response, what one feminist has called 'a historical juncture within western religious consciousness', though 'radical orthodoxy' shows little sign of being interested in feminism or vice versa.

The 'historical juncture' is due to the fact that, plainly, in the second half of the twentieth century women have discovered a very new way of seeing themselves, and of living their lives. This must be set against a body, the Church, or a group of bodies – the Christian churches – whose tradition has been patriarchal and whose Scriptures have revealed a suspicion of women which has had profound effects upon women's lives for centuries. The story of Eve, as the architect of the Fall, the fact that very few women in the Old Testament are even named (though they lived in societies which took naming very seriously), the comments about women keeping 'silent in the churches' and being 'subordinate to their husbands' in the Epistles, were all used to justify a long history in which women were confined to the home, denied university education (or sometimes any educa- tion at all) and a chance to practise in any of the professions. Other texts were also used to justify the persecution of witches (almost, but not quite, exclusively women) in the early modern period and again later.

In the Church itself canards against women meant that women were largely excluded from attempts to include the laity in new forms of discussion in the late nineteenth and early twentieth century (obviously they were excluded from any participation at leadership level), that during the First World War they were explicitly forbidden to speak in churches except to other women and children, and as recently as the 1950s women neither preached nor read the lesson in church. Only in the later twentieth century would the Church seriously examine the possibility of women priests, a move that was strongly resisted.

Another problem highlighted by feminists is that God had always been seen and discussed in entirely male terms, although presumably femaleness emanates from God no less than maleness. (Some of the Fathers and Julian of Norwich did use female imagery for God, but over the centuries this usage gradually fell away.) Since maleness had this God-like connotation, men somehow derived kudos from this aura. 'If God is male' as Mary Daly succinctly put it, 'male is God.' 'God was Lord, King, Judge, Father: a greater patriarch than the patriarchs at the top of the human pyramid.'[47] Over against all this display of power, woman was 'the other'. Despite her relative powerlessness, she was frequently described as a threat, perhaps because her suppression produced guilt, as well as the fear of her revenge.

Another problem feminists highlighted was the maleness of Jesus. Could a woman be saved by a male saviour, some of them wondered. Those who did not find this a problem had to deal with the fact that one of the reasons those opposed to ordaining women as priests was that, since women were not physically male, and in this sense identical with Christ, they could not 'represent' Christ at the altar. Despite other sanctions used against them in the Church, it had not occurred to most women before this that they were in some sense 'second-class' Christians – they had imagined that baptism, the sacrament when they 'put on Christ', made them as capable of representing Christ as a man.

Feminists finally confronted the Church with these problems, as well as with problems about language – being endlessly addressed as 'brethren' and 'man', something which had been ignored as late as 1980 when the Alternative Service Book was published. The Liturgical Commission had a go at addressing objections to 'exclusive language' with a report *Making Women Visible* (1989), which was not without its comic aspects, with a cover printed in lipstick colours (now withdrawn in favour of a plain grey cover, I notice), and a sense of distaste for the whole difficult subject throughout. However, there was now public recognition that language that excluded women might be a problem.

Christian feminists objected to the emphasis on hierarchy in church thought (as it happened it was, of course, male hierarchy they were objecting to, but they were against hierarchy in principle), and in their own meetings and liturgies they attempted to replace it with something different – a sharing of power, a horizontal connectedness, which was often expressed by sitting in a circle. Different images for God were used by them – images of friendship, giving birth, motherhood, nurturing, which produced a very different feel from the images of God as rich aristocrat, judge, or king in the panoply of power. God was addressed as Mother, Sister, Friend, Creator, Jesus as Brother

These new insights came too late for many women in the Church and the churches. The derision, denial and refusal to 'see what all the fuss is about' that their attempts to open the subject for discussion induced, made the institution feel unappealing and unsympathetic. Many women simply opted out of the Church in the 1980s, describing themselves as 'post-Christian', or joining the Quakers or fringe groups right outside the Christian ethos – for example, Wicca, goddess worship and pagan circles. Some women theologians evolved elaborate theories why Christianity was finished. As yet the Church has shown no official interest in the mass defection of many feminists, nor made any attempt to refute their arguments, which are probably seen as not worth bothering with. It is noticeable how few professional theologians who are not women themselves do bother with them, just as few male church historians spend much time or trouble on women's historical experience in the Church.

There is a galling sense that women are not worth taking too seriously. Yet the effect on church numbers is not negligible, and the anger of many women deserves to be noticed and addressed. One cherished way of dealing with dissentient voices, of course, is simply to be deaf to them, to treat the speakers as non-existent.

Taking Leave of God and Finding Being

Another *persona non grata* for the Church is Don Cupitt, clergyman, famously Dean of Emmanuel College, Cambridge, and, since his retirement, a Life Fellow of Emmanuel. In 1987 he wrote a book *Taking Leave of God* which was the beginning of a long sequence of book about the 'non-realist God', the God who is structured from human imagination. In following on from a successful television series called *Sea of Faith* in the 1980s Cupitt helped to start a movement called The Sea of Faith, an organisation which holds conferences and publishes material discussing Cupitt's ideas and other ideas related to it. Quite a lot of clergy belong to it. One of them, Anthony Freeman, was sacked from his job in the Chichester diocese for refusing to defend traditional theology.

Since the mid-1980s Cupitt has produced a stream of slender books, sometimes more than one a year, in which he has talked about God, the churches, postmodernism, language, art and much else. He is quite simply the most interesting theologian around, not least because he tries to talk in everyday language and eschew the usual mandarin style which effectively excludes everyone not trained as a theologian. In spite of this he is not, in my view, particularly easy to read, but I value immensely his recognition that theology is of interest and importance outside its own little charmed circle. I am not saying that therefore I understand all that he says, only that I know he is trying to talk to me and others like me, not conducting a conversation from which I am carefully excluded. He is conducting a dialogue, not a monologue, with anyone interested enough to join in, and his side of the conversaion is conducted not only with great knowledge in all sorts of fields of study, but with the most extraordinary passion, the sort that ordinary believers in God rarely show nowadays. Cupitt's non-belief feels more religious than most people's belief.

Trick or Treat?

He is ready to use jokes, puns, even tricks, to make his readers think, in fact what has gradually emerged in his later writing is the image of 'the Trickster'. Many cultures, among them North American Indian, Inuit and Aboriginal Australian, regard the trickster as a sort of holy man. He is always going the opposite way from everyone else, not doing what is expected of him, making 'mistakes', having accidents, yet getting something fundamental right. By inverting the normal pattern of things, in particular the gravity and heavy solemnity of 'good people', he forces questions, doubts, crises, that might never occur to his community without his contribution.

Almost alone among contemporary theologians Cupitt admits to religious experience – quite a lot of it. In his most recent book (at the time of writing – another will undoubtedly have appeared before this is published), he describes, under the title of 'Bliss', a marvellous event which happened to him the previous year. He was sitting at his desk, writing a book, and looking out at Cambridge's Parker's Piece 'at moving clouds, kites, cars, groups of walkers and cyclists'.[48] Because of the writing he was doing he saw the scene as 'Being' coming into existence in the human context – 'the worlds of Being, of Meaning, and of human life'.

> These thoughts mounted. An all-round, unobstructed, clear understanding of things, which included me, seemed to dawn. There was an instant like the moment when a tightly-coiled spring begins to release its energy, and then a violent explosion of pure happiness which passed so rapidly that I became conscious of it and identified it only as something that was already fast receding and becoming forgotten. I found myself snatching at it as it slipped away, melting through my fingers.[49]

Such moments of ecstasy or *satori* are rare in most people's lives, if they have them at all. Cupitt has 'had such an experience, on average, every few years since early childhood'. One such incursion of 'the divine' came to him, in extreme pain, while watching sunlight through the window of a hospital ward.

What Cupitt does not do, as almost everyone else does, is to tie such experience immediately to 'God'. Since Cupitt does not believe in anyone as static as the old objective God, when he speaks of 'the divine' he forces us to stretch our minds to understand the incomprehensible (which is what primitive peoples value about the trickster), and we learn that he is speaking of something continually in flux, a flux of which we ourselves are a part. Like the feminists speaking of God in female terms (though they don't really believe he is a woman any more than he is a man), and thereby jolting Christian complacency, Cupitt speaks of 'the divine' in terms of flux, the flux of Being, and moves us on, like a needle in the groove of an old-fashioned record, to listen to a new bit of tune. It is exciting, but disturbing, and many Christians don't like it much.

What I notice is that a number of other theologians, George Pattison and 'radical orthodoxy' among them, seem to have been affected by Cupitt's work, if only, in some cases, because it makes them cross; they seem to be contradicting, or answering or working around his ideas. The trickster cannot be ignored. 'Radical orthodoxy' does not, for example, 'go with' the fragmentation of postmodernism with the ready cheerfulness that Cupitt does. (Like Ross Thompson's 'map folk' they are all for going back.) I have a feeling that Cupitt has annoyed them so much that it has sharpened up their ideas a good deal.

God in the Genes
A BBC television series on twins in July 1999 produced some interesting evidence from the huge research project on twins by Dr Bouchard of the University of Minnesota. In the 1950s and 1960s, as a result of bizarre social work policy, many pairs of orphaned twins were separated and adopted by different families without usually being told that they were twins. Appalling as this happening was in itself, it has made it possible to undertake a very unusual piece of research which has had considerable bearing on the nature/nurture debate. The twins, now grown up, had identical genes but had had different upbringings, often strikingly so in terms of class, wealth and education. In spite of separation, and different nurture, the life resemblances were shown to be extraordinary – not only of the children/adults having identical illnesses at the same time, but also of their marrying men or women with the same Christian names often at around the same stage in their lives, entering the same professions and sometimes the same companies, having the same number of children, etc. One of the most interesting findings was that both twins either were or were not religious, which Bouchard felt was a strong, if not conclusive, argument for the fact that 'being religious' has a genetic component.

If this is the case one must assume that in the 'ages of faith' when virtually everyone claimed Christian allegiance, some simply went along with it and picked up the universal jargon, rather as an unmusical child in a musical family could scarcely fail to learn the musical vocabulary even if untouched by music at a deeper level.

Yet it seems as if we now have the opposite situation – that of living in a society in which the practice of religion, at least (many people say they believe in God), seems to matter little, which poses problems for those who have a religious gene. It is as if a musical child is born into a family where the others are tone-deaf, and is left to pursue its bent blindly and in isolation until by luck it falls in with others who talk its language. (And the Church has fulfilled a function a bit like this for many people over the years.)

Despite the shortcomings of the Church, it is not easy to understand the way religion has almost dropped out of the common vocabulary in a generation or so. The psychologist R. D. Laing, who died in 1989, believed that we had given science too much power, and that its ideas had been used, in a sense, to curtail experience. What it robbed us of was the understanding of the world as 'magical'. 'Every child is aware of that until persuaded otherwise.'[50] He felt that this had reduced us to an 'aberrant civilization' which had lost the capacity for ecstasy. Like children in a too strict home we became fatally adjusted to 'the abdication of ecstasy, the betrayal of our true potentialities . . . many of us are only too successful in acquiring a false self to adapt to false realities'.[51] This abdication of ourselves was what we called 'normal'. Drugs, not religion, became the blind search of the young for what was missing from their lives – interestingly the most popular drug in use now among the young is called 'ecstasy'.

What is most frightening about this diagnosis, if it is true, is that it is very difficult for us to know what we have lost, or even that we have lost it at all. Yet many straws in the wind – our over-working and stress, our neglect of the natural environment, our perverted sexuality, the triviality of our art, the squalor of our cities, our ceaseless 'tourism' – suggest that a sense of life and the world around us as 'magical', or full of wonder, has been lost, though we continue to search with little hope. Laing says elsewhere that we are a generation that has 'repressed the transcendent'. Our world does not shine with the glory of the wider awareness. We have been robbed or have misguidedly tossed away 'the pearl of great price'.

I imagine that Laing, who was interested in Continental philosophy, may have been influenced by Heidegger. In a precis of Heidegger's *Being and Time* (1927) George Pattison quotes the philosopher. 'We, the children of the secular age, are, it seems, metaphysically dispossessed, immersed in the world of immediate, short-term and local undertakings and understandings, without any vision of the whole.'[52]

Heidegger went on to draw conclusions from this about whether a philosophical way forward from our deprived state might even be possible, damaged and 'inauthentic' as we are. Yet it does at least suggest the possibility that we could attempt to refind 'the magic', or if we cannot do that, at least to give it a place of primary importance, and try to learn from those – primitive peoples, children, some artists – for whom it is still the core of their lives. We could shape our lives – in terms of allowing ourselves space, silence, stability, the kinds of creativity that speak to our condition, and also in our refusal to overvalue money and busyness – in a way that might offer us a degree of restoration. Looking around me in religious circles – at retreats, pilgrimages, interest in the arts and in meditation – I sense that some such movement has been going on for some time.

24

Triumph and Disaster

Trying to take a long view of the Church I have been struck by the fact that, looking back, the outstanding achievements are almost invariably the fruit of imagination, courage and clear-headed intelligence, whereas the failures are about insensitivity, refusal to face conflict, fear of what religious extremists or the press will say, or sheer woolly-headedness and fudge.

In the first category comes the work of the Church Urban Fund. At the time of writing, ten years on from when the Fund was set up, the Fund recognises that one in four children in Britain grows up in abject poverty, that fifteen million people, more than a quarter of the population, are on means-tested benefits, and that during the last two decades the income of the poorest tenth of the population has fallen in real terms by 13 per cent. Working in Urban Priority Areas, the Fund sets out to help local people 'take charge of their own destiny', carefully using grants and supports to help the process along.

In the last year in the Diocese of London, for instance, awards amounting to £150,000 were made to thirty-one London community projects. Homework clubs for kids, and IT training for young adults, new community centres and kitchens which can be let out to support local ventures, paying Asian women the minimum wage to make clothes instead of sweatshop rates, special projects to bring 'disaffected children' back into the mainstream, total regeneration of some communities, with houses built or repaired, job training, crime reduction, raising educational attainment, and health and social facilities, are all part of this marvellous bit of Christian initiative. The Fund has helped nearly two thousand projects with grants, big and small, totalling £33 million, and continues to raise a million a year.

The overall direction of the Fund is regeneration, a bringing of hope to communities and individuals who had little to hope for previously.

On a smaller scale many parishes run projects – for the old, the young, the housebound, the homeless, the sick, refugees – which, while largely unsung, make a great deal of difference to people's happiness and wellbeing.

There is little doubt in the Christian mind that it is a duty to help those in need. The Church, whether in the parish, or the larger body of the Church Urban Fund, provides an excellent means of doing so, a channel, easy of access, through which people can make a difference and make an attempt to love their neighbour.

Christian Action

The forerunner of the Church Urban Fund, Christian Action, the very remarkable organisation for social action based on Christian principles, came into being in 1946. It was the brain child of Canon John Collins, who, as an RAF chaplain during the war, had realised how removed belief had tended to become from the realities of poverty and suffering. He and his wife Diana accommodated the new organisation in the basement of their house in Amen Court at St Paul's, though Collins designed it to be (and it remained) an ecumenical organisation. Christian Action's earliest achievements in the late 1940s concerned reconciliation with the erstwhile German enemy. Food parcels were sent to a starving Germany and elsewhere in Europe, German prisoners working in Britain were befriended, and their repatriation was encouraged, and cultural exchanges were arranged, such as bringing the Berlin Philharmonic Orchestra to Britain, and using the money raised at concerts for food and reconstruction in Europe.

Prophetically – long before such moves were popular – Christian Action ran a 'Don't Drink and Drive' campaign, and campaigned against advertising cigarettes. It was among the first in this country to speak out against apartheid in South Africa, and it joined the National Campaign for the Abolition of Capital Punishment in 1955. Over the years it worked at issues of world hunger, disarmament, race, East/West rapprochement. Two of its projects – the Homeless in Britain Campaign in the 1960s and the Newham Project, which came from an offshoot of Christian Action, Radical Alternatives to Prison, in the 1970s – were remarkably successful, the first setting up a number of housing associations and shelters, and the second showing itself successful in working with 112 ex-prisoners, very few of whom re-offended.

Trevor Beeson wrote of John Collins:

It seems obvious now that the churches and individual Christians

357

should be concerned about crime and punishment, the homeless, refugees, nuclear warfare and racism. But it seemed much less obvious in the 1950s. The premature death of William Temple in 1944 had removed the chief Christian social reformer of that time and in the aftermath of war the British churches were intent on reconstructing their own domestic life. Incredible though it now seems, the Church of England spent almost twenty years on the revision of its canon law. That this does seem incredible and that social action is on the agenda of all the churches, albeit in a much lower place than it ought to be, owes a very great deal to John Collins.[1]

From 1979 Eric James took up the baton of John Collins. A man from a working-class background as John was not, his emphases were different, and he had to work through the difficult political climate of the 1980s, and eighteen years of a right-wing government not sympathetic to social action.

Out of Eric's commitment came the Faith in the City Commission and Report, a cause to which he devoted himself tirelessly. Christian Action spent some £50,000 helping to get this initiative off the ground, partly by funding Eric to make it known. From 1979 Christian Action published a journal which drew attention to a huge range of social problems. Under Eric's leadership it also gave large sums of money to many organisations concerned with unemployment, race, education, sexual equality, poverty and housing.

A Mini-Success

It is much easier for organisations on the skirts of the Church to move lightly and easily in sensitive areas than it is for major changes to occur at the centre. Applause seems appropriate, therefore, for the Marriage document from the House of Bishops, just published at the time of writing in autumn 1999 (and preceding the Bishop of Winchester's report on the marriage of divorcees). It is not that the Marriage document is so startling in itself, though it was described by Bishop John Gladwin as 'the most important teaching document on marriage in this generation'.[2] But it braves the inevitable criticism aroused by a realistic recognition of second marriages, though it can be seen as reactive to the fact that second marriages among Christians are taking place whether the Church likes it or not.

It is puzzling that the document shows so little interest in the history and sociology of marriage. It is easy to dismiss its relative failure at present with remarks about 'a society with a false idea of freedom' which suffers from 'misleading fantasies about sex', as if this explains everything, but this ignores the sweeping social changes of the last generation or two. Surely an important comment that needs making is that marriages potentially last very much longer nowadays than they did in the past, when lives were shorter, and it was not uncommon for people to marry a second time because a partner had been lost in youth or early middle life. Both my paternal grandparents married for the second time for this reason, for example, my grandfather having lost his wife in childbirth and my grandmother having lost her husband in a cholera epidemic in India.

Another very important recognition about marriage is that it is the first time in history, in the last generation, that women who were unhappy in their marriages have had the financial means to get out of them. Before they were forced to remain and put up with whatever happened, including violence and cruelty.

In some circumstances a divorce can be positively a good and creative thing, sometimes for both partners, and sometimes for their children. It feels both morally and psychologically unreal to imply, as the Church constantly does, that for a marriage to continue is invariably a good thing. All of us have witnessed, and some have taken part in, mutually destructive marriages that were better ended. To end such a relationship can take courage and a sense of integrity – something the Church never seems able to allow.

It also will not do to suggest, as the document does, that relationships where one or both partners are unfit for marriage, physically or psychologically, applies to 'only a tiny fraction' of marriages. In a society where many marry very young and there is an unhelpful romantic haze around the drama of a wedding (watch any soap opera), all too many marry long before they are ready to take this most adult of responsibilities, and are simply unable to sustain what they have started. Since the Church is often implicated, it needs to be merciful to those who make this kind of mistake.

The Church adopts a gentler tone on marriage and divorce than it has done in the past, which is to be applauded, yet it still sounds, even in this latest document, as if it writes from above the battle – in what the New Zealand bishop Penny Jamieson deplores as the 'declamatory' style to which bishops are prone. It is miles away from life as lived on housing estates or even in most families. Yet by a cruel irony, in the same week as the document was reported, there was publicity for a bishop whose wife had left him to set up home with a priest in his former diocese. Bishops and clergy are no more immune from relationship disasters than are the rest of us. It would be salutary if the written style of church documents made this clear. The moral high ground is no place from which to hold forth.

The Disaster Department

It would be good if the Church was readier to disturb deeply held and damaging prejudices, which church people, who are often very conventional, find no easier to handle than anyone else. John Sentamu, a black bishop who was involved in the Stephen Lawrence enquiry, told the Synod, in July 1999, that it must take into its lifeblood the implications of the Lawrence report, in terms of its own attitudes to, and treatment of, different minority-ethnic groups in its body. Within the Church's own walls, he says, 'the expectation of the historic white, educated, élite, English norm is maintained, regardless of the make-up of a congregation'.[3] The bishop complained that the experience of different cultural and ethnic groups in the Church was one of not being drawn on in its education and teaching, in effect of being ignored except simply as pew-fodder.

This is a painful cry from the heart, a shaming and appropriate word to all of us who have not had the imagination, the daring, the originality, to stand where someone else stands, and see the world through their eyes. Timidity about going out to others and inviting their participation is inexcusable. But it is not only the black community who have this experience of exclusion, of course.

On not Celebrating Women

Many women too would say that the Church is run and ruled by the expectation of white English males, and is insensitive to the changed status and expectations of women, in a way that is now becoming increasingly rare in the world outside, at least in the corridors of power and business and other institutions, many of whom have made tremendous efforts to realise women's potential.

At the time of writing this chapter there has been a series of television programmes about St Paul's Cathedral at a peak viewing time on Sunday evenings on the BBC.[4] The first of these depicted the experiences of Lucy Winkett, on being appointed a minor Canon, the first woman priest in the Cathedral's history. The circumstances of her being invited to join 'the staff' of the Cathedral were puzzling, since it was clear in advance that one of the existing Canons was opposed to the idea, and a Minor Canon felt so bitterly about it that he soon left. Indeed the 'ethos' of the Cathedral seemed fairly hostile, and the most appalling scene in the film showed Lucy Winkett in tears when no one who had served mass for her had been prepared to receive communion from her. Could they really imagine that this is what Jesus would have recommended? Might it not have been better to swallow bread and wine incompletely consecrated (in their eyes), than to inflict such wanton and public hurt on another human being? Another shocking aspect of her appointment was that bread that she had consecrated could not be 'reserved' without some ludicrous and unkind chicanery to which they gave the preposterous term 'concomitance' – I think it meant someone else celebrating with her to make sure that her 'poisoned' bread and chalice might not infect any Christian who partook of it inadvertently.

What made it all particularly painful to watch was that she was clearly a fine priest who did her job superbly, though the principles would have been the same even if this had not been so. Dean John Moses defended the whole dreadful situation by saying that it showed the inclusiveness of the Church. He did not appear to notice that this was not at his expense but at Lucy Winkett's.

'It makes me ashamed to be a man,' said one person I talked to in the week following the showing of the programme. The Church pays a terrible price when such enormities are revealed to the public gaze – no amount of 'spin' can compensate for an organisation which is revealed as blatantly sexist, and which, far from expressing shame at this, finds in it grounds for self-congratulation.

Very little public support of women priests is spoken by church leaders, remarkable as their contribution has already been. I am told that in part of London's East End – Tower Hamlets, Islington and Hackney – the presence of women priests is thought, among other factors, to have helped bring about a 7 per cent increase in church attendance.

Difficult as the women's task has been in forging their way in a job where no women have been before them, and hampered as they are by a grossly discriminatory legislation, I find that I cannot remember a single word of recognition publicly paid to them by the bishops. One archbishop (John Habgood) on his retirement made no bones of the fact that he thought the Church should not have ordained women when it did (though he had supported the move). It is difficult to imagine such disloyalty to employed women occurring in any other business or public institution.

Women are often discriminated against in the Church, less perhaps from conscious prejudice than from a curiously old-fashioned view of women that takes no real account of how far and fast the world has changed. The first posters brought out by the Communications Department, meant to encourage men and women into the priest-hood, perfectly illustrated the problem, though amusingly. The woman was shown playing with a child, the man was at his desk doing something manly with a cheque book. It was laughable, and people did laugh. More seriously, the absence of all but token women from such Commissions as *Turnbull* and *Howe*, suggests an unawareness that women nowadays are excellently qualified in all sorts of new fields that would make them useful in working parties. The representation of women, who almost always outnumber men in the pews, would seem an important thing to achieve at the highest level. It is not a good idea for bishops and male clergy to assume that they are in a position to speak for women. On the whole, they are not, and in any case, women are perfectly capable of speaking for themselves.

The discrimination against women is, of course, noticed by the community as a whole. The political columnist Anthony Howard, writing in *The Times*, notes that Richard Chartres, the Bishop of London, strongly tipped as Carey's successor at Canterbury, is not prepared to ordain women as priests, though he is prepared to ordain deacons. To a world accustomed to a different attitude to women it all looks very odd. The Church, Howard notes, 'already has an Archbishop of York who has his own difficulties in acknowledging the validity of women's orders and if Chartres eventually gets to Canterbury that will make two *revanchistes* in the C of E's twin top places. Not quite what the two-thirds majority who in 1992 voted for the women's ordination measure can have had in mind.'[5]

Some dioceses, where the bishop is opposed to women priests, have an almost total absence of women as a result. Professor Walter James, who lives in the Chichester diocese, wrote a letter to *The Times* about what he called the 'gender cleansing' of that diocese, the creeping exclusion of women which he says is disappointing to those, like himself, who had looked forward to the ministry of women. One ordained woman told me of the depression that has set in since ordination. 'I wonder if it is worth the struggle.'

What is striking is how readily such discrimination is defended by senior churchmen. A priest who asked not to be identified, told me of a meeting he witnessed between the Archbishop of Canterbury and some sixth formers. The encounter moved slowly and awkwardly until the subject of women came up.

> Suddenly the whole thing took off and they were very clear that they wanted to know from him when there were going to be women bishops, when there was going to be a woman archbishop and would he resign in order to get a woman archbishop in! . . . One of the things he said back to them which I thought was a pretty poor show was 'Well, the Church is in a period where we have to settle down about this and women themselves are settling down.' Personally, I don't think women should be in a period of 'settling down' but of expanding, growing as priests.

The irony is that in the grassroots Church women priests are widely accepted and often hugely popular – they are one of the great success stories of the Church, and it is as if this is known everywhere except at the top. But, of course, to recognise this means that there is a necessity to make a decision on grounds of principle about whether to honour the decision General Synod took in November 1992. And to do this risks confrontation, and nothing at the moment scares the Church more. There is a kind of grudging attitude abroad – 'You women have got what you wanted, so now keep quiet'. It seems a pity.

Women, like John Sentamu's ethnic minorities, need to feel their gifts and qualities are fully valued and appreciated, and this can never happen while part of the Church, and some significant leaders, do not recognise their priesthood. The church leadership must make up its mind. Are women priests, or are they not? The parishes, I suggest, have, by and large, long ago decided the issue, and celebrate the creativity of women priests. When are the bishops going to join in?

Glad to be Gay?

When, for that matter, is the Church going to have the courage to celebrate the creativity of its homosexual members, who are more discriminated against than black people or women? For those gay people who wish to be ordained there is only one way to get through the initial interviews, and that is the humiliating one of keeping their sexuality concealed. 'Yes, well, I suppose I may get married one day.' It is painfully easy to remain in the closet ever afterwards, thinking that at some future date there will be an opportunity to come clean, only the day never comes. The Church, of course, encourages this silence. A description of a nervous breakdown, Jim Cotter's book *Brainsquall*, reveals what a terrible price gay clergy have been required to pay for such a double standard.

A gay priest friend of mine, in his fifties, with a fine history of work in the Church behind him, told me recently how helpful his diocesan and suffragan bishop have been. 'We've set up a group of gay clergy in this diocese, and they come and ask questions and really listen. And we've appreciated that enormously. The one thing they ask of us is that we won't go public about our homosexuality.' The irony of this statement is that this man lives openly with his man friend, who is accepted and much loved in the rather conservative working-class village that he serves. 'No one ever mentions homosexuality to me, except that someone sometimes says "It turns out my son is gay, and I wondered if you could advise me", or a young man who is worried about his sexuality comes to consult me.' Who has the problem here, the parish or the bishops?

Sometimes it seems as if the Church is almost the only body left which cannot deal with homosexuality. It is possible to get elected for Parliament as an openly gay man or woman, possible to be made a cabinet minister, possible for many eminent people to be quite straightforward about living with another man or woman, even possible, as I noticed recently, for *Good Housekeeping* to have a headline on its cover: 'Mum, I'm gay!' ('Not in the Church you're not, darling! Not if you know what's good for you!') Even the Ministry of Defence will soon be forced to employ known homosexuals because of European rulings.

Gayness arouses deep feelings among some Christians as the last Lambeth Conference revealed. Yet more and more in Britain it is being taken for granted; it is being understood not as something wicked or sinful or a sign of depravity but simply as how some people are, and there seems no good reason not to trust their account of the way love and sex seems to them, even if it is different from the way George Carey, or anyone else, happens to experience it. The evidence seems overwhelming that homosexual love can be rich, profound, consoling and creative, as heterosexual love can be. (And both can be degrading, selfish, a disgraceful exploitation of others.) Part of loving one's neighbour is allowing him or her to be different from oneself – if one cannot fully understand them, or imagine how their taste can be so different from one's own, at least one can try to give them the benefit of the doubt.

Change, of course, is inevitable. Just as the change of the status of women in society pushed the hand of the Church to ordain women; just as the change of the status of black people in Britain makes it imperative that they are seen as full members of the Church with their own distinctive contribution; just as the change in marital habits makes churches accepting of second marriages, so change in this field too is inevitable. Maybe not this year or next year, but before too long, the Church is going to have to get up its nerve (and it is not in a bold frame of mind) and accord homosexuals full status within the Church, because, like blacks or women, they are increasingly refusing the meek and silent status forced upon them. It is all very well for bishops to keep talking about 'listening' – but the only point of listening is to hear. The time is past for weasel words about 'compassion' – that is pure condescension – and the Church needs to remember, as Peter Tatchell unforgettably brought home to it, that those who live in glasshouses cannot afford to throw stones. Against personal truth neither Scripture nor tradition can ultimately prevail, but as we have seen so often in our history, from the burning of witches to the enslavement of black people, from the stoning of adulterers to the persecution of the Jews, both can be used to swell the sum of human unhappiness and despair. It is a very odd tribute to Jesus Christ, and it is unworthy of the Church of England and the many fine gay priests who have served it over the centuries.

Part Three

The Church As It May Be

It may be the will of God that our Church should have its heart broken. (Michael Ramsey, *The Christian Priest Today* (1972) p. 100)

When the Vandals are at the gates, there are three possible responses. One is simply to despair of the kingdom, of any ultimate meaning in the world or in human history; the second is to withdraw into a private, sacral sphere, a closed community, monastic or charismatic, abandoning the struggle for the secular state as irremediably corrupt; the third is to imitate Augustine himself, take a very sombre view but also a very long one, and retain in hope but without much evidence a Christian concern for the redeemability of the totality of things. (Adrian Hastings, *A History of English Christianity, 1920–1990* (SCM Press, 1991 edition), p. 660)

'I believe' said Alfred 'there are quiet victories and struggles, great sacrifices of self, and noble acts of heroism, in the world – even in many of its apparent lightnesses and contradictions – not the less difficult to achieve, because they have no earthly chronicle or audience – done every day in nooks and corners, and in little households, and in men's and women's hearts – any one of which might reconcile the sternest man to such a world, and fill him with belief and hope in it, though two fourths of its people were at war, and another fourth at law.' (Charles Dickens, *The Battle of Life*, *Christmas Books* (Oxford World Classics, 1988), p. 297)

'Jack has . . . what most people don't have – he has a developed heart. He doesn't need to watch it or take thought to educate it . . . [it] works like a kind of intelligence through all his actions.' (Rosamond Lehmann, *The Echoing Grove*, Collins, 1953)

25

The Educated Heart

Trying to write an account of the Church of England as it is now makes me sympathise with those artists (like Pieter Brueghel) who painted pictures full of people. Here in the foreground were two children playing with a whip and top and another being pulled along on a sled; there, through the window, were the town council chewing over a knotty problem; in the corner of the public square a man is sitting in the stocks; through yet another window we can see a couple *in flagrante delicto*; others are shopping, nursing babies, selling things, riding horses, cooking, skating, burying somebody, getting drunk. All human life is there, but which details are the most important, which activities matter most? Brueghel does not distinguish. He is not so much interested in the ladies and gentlemen as in the common people, and not all that much more interested in the Virgin and her baby than in the other doughy women with their doughy babies; neither she nor they have any particular beauty to recommend them. It is humanity itself that matters, fat, spotty, smelly, poor, crippled and old, and the Holy Family are as much a part of it as the rest of us, and share, as we all do, in the mystery of life, its ecstasy and suffering, its commonplace routines and its transcendent flights.

The Church of England is, mostly though not entirely, a more middle-class affair than Brueghel's Flemish towns, yet peopled with an extraordinary range of humanity, all of them plodding through the usual human chores, some of them performing acts of loving originality that have a transformative effect. The place to see the Church at its best is nearly always in the parishes, away from the religious-speak at the centre. Not that every church is a little powerhouse of loving energy. The admirable freedom which the Church has offered to clergy and people has meant that, at least up till now, there has necessarily been freedom not only for attractive liturgy and warm community but also for laziness, incompetence, bigotry or bloody-mindedness, if people were inclined that way. This is not a new phenomenon. Judith Maltby[1] describes post-Reformation churches where clergy and people were at daggers drawn – where, in the case of one vicar with Puritan sympathies, he refused to say the funeral service, but simply buried the corpse in silence – and another where the vicar would ring the church bell at a whim, and by the time the congregation arrived they would find he had intentionally galloped through the service so fast that it was practically over! As well as good clergy and good churches, and averagely lively ones, there have always been dead churches, and churches full of struggle and conflict. Sometimes this is the doing of the priest, sometimes one or two people in a congregation can stir up problems with an almost psychopathic manipulation; sometimes something beyond everybody's control happens, as when the movement of population gradually wipes out the life of a church. This is only to say the church communities have most of the qualities of all other communities – streets, neighbourhoods, offices, factories, institutions, families: they are vulnerable in all sorts of ways, they don't always get along together, and certain environments are more toxic or more beneficial than others, for reasons which we can speculate about, but never fully understand.

Perhaps in a new climate for the Church more plain speaking is necessary in parish communities. British reserve has to dissolve if the caring for one another is to be real. People need to know one another better, to the point where, as in families, they are not on their best behaviour all the time. This level of trust is costly to achieve, not least because it involves the recognition of anger, always difficult for Christians, but it is a way out of loneliness in a society where loneliness is endemic – the experience of knowing and being known. The most cheering bit of my research was in seeing how well churches achieved just that – people, black and white, men and women, old and young, working class and middle class, adults and children – simply enjoying being together. Not simply praying together, but doing other things together, and using this closeness as a base to help others – children, the homeless, refugees, the elderly. It was difficult to think of many other places in our fragmented society where that happens quite so effectively and not because it is someone's paid job to do it.

This kind of achievement was not limited to one kind of church or one kind of churchmanship – it was as impressive in a 'Catholic' parish in Hackney, as in a charismatic parish in south-east London or in a housing estate on the outskirts of Coventry. Numerically, there is no doubt that the charismatic and Evangelical churches are growing the fastest, not just because they offer certainty, though they do, but because they offer three things: instruction (to a generation which knows little about Christianity), a warm social environment (to many, particularly young adults, who are lonely), and religious experience (the Holy Spirit seems to come as part of the package).

I admire the charismatic and Evangelical success, and very much enjoyed being part of their services. I think, and hope, that they will go on from strength to strength.

But there are other streams that run through the Church of England, as the Archbishop himself pointed out, and they too need to find a new voice and new success. Religion is much more a matter of temperament than is often owned up to, which does not mean that while some are waving their arms, singing hymns written up on overhead projectors, and humming along to guitars, others need to sit in constipated isolation. It is possible to be vibrantly Catholic or vibrantly Liberal, to feel part of a community that is rich, satisfying, generous, and can make a difference to its members, if the right kind of effort has been made to make that community alive.

Wistfulness for God

There seems to be a wistfulness in the world outside the churches for a religion that feels do-able – there is certainly a belief in God. This is the churches' big opportunity to listen, to respond, to make the church a safe and rewarding place to visit and its community a satisfying place to be. Sometimes the power of history, and of the love the Church longs to stand for, works almost in spite of our individual failures. The journalist Celia Haddon in her book *If God Is My Father How Can He Love Me?* (Hodder and Stoughton, 1998)[2] describes in haunting detail her nervous breakdown in middle age, largely precipitated by a childhood made painful by a terrifying father, who had left her feeling permanently worthless.

> As an atheist I had usually visited churches when I was passing through towns or villages. Now, as I passed through London, I would drop into a church for perhaps two minutes. I did not pray. I did not dare to . . . I would merely sit there for a while. Sometimes I would cry. Then I started saying 'I am here, God.' Just those four words. It was the first prayer in my new life . . . The empty stillness of churches was calming and gave me some moments of peace of mind. As I began to feel better I worked out a morning prayer. It consisted of visualising myself back in my childhood home . . . only this time I was there as an adult and also as a child. I took the

child by the hand, and we walked together towards a great light which was God . . . The light shone on me. It was a loving, accepting light.[3]

Here is an example of someone who, without any human agency, felt able to use the Church for her own healing, a moving example of how being can help as well as doing.

There is an awful joke about a clergyman being summoned to visit a man who was desperately ill in hospital. When he got there he found him in an oxygen tent. Unable to speak to him, he sat beside him for a while feeling increasingly helpless. Finally he took out a piece of paper and pencil, wrote 'Can I help you?' on it, and pushed it into the oxygen tent. The patient scribbled violently on the paper, and then suddenly fell back and died. As the shocked and upset clergyman was going out through the hospital grounds he suddenly remembered the piece of paper in his hand and looked down and read it. It said 'You are standing on my breathing-tube.'

For 'clergyman' read the churches, or the Church, including, of course, the laity. Is the problem that, despite our loving intentions, we are ourselves standing on the breathing-tube that cuts people off from the Christian religion? If so, what is it that we have to do to reverse that horrifying possibility? The tendency is to rush into some kind of furious activity, which says more about our anxiety than a true assessment of the situation.

Perhaps the most important thing in the joke about the breathing-tube is the clergyman's sense of helplessness, and his inability to bear it. Suppose he had been able just to sit with his frustration, praying quietly for the man beside him, not feel that it was up to him to 'do' something? Many clergy know, with acute pain, a sense of helplessness. As long ago as 1966 when the Church had much more support than it enjoys now, I was asked to go and speak at a clergy conference in the Wakefield diocese. 'Be gentle,' the bishop said when he briefed me. 'A lot of the clergy are pretty depressed.'

They were depressed then, so far as I could make out, partly because they felt that other disciplines – social work, counselling – were taking over their territory. They were not 'experts', and increasingly they felt themselves part of a world where only experts were wanted. Since then, partly perhaps because some clergy themselves have explored the pastoral disciplines which abut on their own work, and discovered just how distinct a task the priestly one is, that particular fear seems to me to have abated somewhat. Yet clergy with small and often elderly congregations, and few resources to change that situation, still suffer a good deal from a sense of loss, as congregations diminish and become less able to do very much at all. And such clergy, like all Christians to a greater or lesser extent, can scarcely fail to be affected by the winds of secularism blowing around them.

Christian Jingoism

Yet official statements, with the best of intentions, have a way of being relentlessly gung-ho in a style one might describe as 'Christian jingoism'. The gap between the reality of actual clergy experience and rosy statements about ' a Church on the move' is too great. Many clergy struggle with small congregations, or, in the country, shuttle breathlessly between one church and another, or live and try to bring up children in dangerous city parishes, enduring vandalism to church and their own houses, and sometimes getting mugged themselves. This is the sharp end of the Church, but comfortable 'leafy' suburban parishes can be depressing in a different way, with people managing perfectly nicely thank you, too busy with the house, the car(s), the holidays, Sunday shopping, to bother with a religion that is about loving God and loving one's neighbour.

In the days when pennies were large and beautiful, children used to place a piece of tracing paper over the head of the monarch and scribble on the penny with a pencil. I remember the sense of wonder as the head gradually, magically, as it seemed at the age of about six, suddenly stood out amid the surrounding scribble. Writing this book there was an image which, somewhat to my surprise, began to stand out for me with ever greater clarity, and that was the image of the laity. In a Church whose roots are both feudal and strongly clerical, the laity have been an undervalued and under-used resource. They have been bred to passivity, expecting neither to become theologically aware, nor to be held financially responsible for their own parish churches. Only in the past generation in which lay education has improved unimaginably, in which theology is no longer the exclusive preserve of clergy, and in which certain groups have felt themselves unwanted by the Church, has this picture begun to change. But the financial difficulties in which the Church finds itself, for a number of reasons, have meant that the laity have quite suddenly found themselves not merely worrying about looking after the roof and the spire but contributing to clergy stipends and pensions. This may be the best thing that has ever happened to them because, for the first time in Church of England history, it forces a grown-up role upon the laity – it is like moving from living on pocket money to having a wage, and deciding how to spend it. And with this comes the possibility of laity 'owning' their Church and what goes on in it, not in order to boss their clergy and tell them what to do, but in order to for both to recognise each other as equal partners with their own views on God, liturgy and Christian fellowship. (And I don't just mean the churchwardens and the PCC. Whole congregations need to be fully roused to become adult, which, to the dread of clergy, means at least initially, to become critical, rather as adolescent children become critical as an essential part of their growing up.)

The great irony of the present situation is that this need for a highly active, aware and responsive laity comes at a time when the central structures of the Church are moving in the opposite direction, towards a controlling clerical oligarchy. I think if this strain in church thinking 'wins', as it were, then the Church is dead in the water. Only a vital laity prepared to 'own' every detail of church life – which means to understand it, think about it, practise it, be critical about it – can save the situation. This is not because there is anything fundamentally wrong with the clergy (well, not with most of them), but because the world picks up the condescension built into the old system (and rediscovered in the new) and will have none of it. The choice now, I believe, is between a 'people's church' or, in time, no church at all.

A Church in Denial?

Not to admit how painful all this is and to insist that everything is going swimmingly is to deny the truth that many are experiencing. The Church has suffered a steep decline since the beginning of the twentieth century, as well as an immense loss of status and influence. There is no need to dwell on pessimism, gloom and doom, but rather to let ourselves know what we are actually feeling, acknowledge the bewilderment of loss, face it, live through it, as those who suffer from bereavement have to do. Loss needs to be accepted not once but repeatedly if it is to be fully integrated and, eventually, used creatively to revision a new life. Pushing it out of sight or refusing to look at it or talk about it, means that it remains unhealed and will return later in the form of depression or physical symptoms.

The Roman Catholic writer Gerald Arbuckle thinks it is vital for the churches to undertake this acceptance, though he acknowledges the temptation of denial. He describes the experience of a consultant brought in two decades after Vatican II to help religious congregations and dioceses look at the rapid way their resources and prospects had dwindled.

Very often, participants denied in a variety of ways disturbing truths about themselves in the surveys' findings. Generally, denial would show itself first by a personal attack, for example: 'Who do *you* think you are? Stop wasting our time. There is nothing wrong with [us], until some fool like you comes round and tells us otherwise!' . . . Another comments: 'How could you write such harsh things about [us]? Your criticism shows that you lack charity and compassion!'[4]

When this did not deflect the consultant they attacked his professional competence, or said that they noted what he said in his report but had decided that 'the time was not right' to act on its conclusions. Or they adopted what he called 'the bottom drawer method': 'We are most grateful for your fine report, and we expect to act on it in due course.' They had no intention of acting on it. There was 'spiritual escapism'. 'God is never tied down by the findings of surveys!'[5]

Another way of dealing with loss that Arbuckle describes is what he called 'the grand gesture'. He describes a religious community which decided that the way out of decline was to do 'something spectacular'.

> They opened a new school [and another important 'faith initiative'] and explained to the province that 'all must have faith'. . . For a while the province felt good about the new initiatives, because, said the congregational leader, 'they show we are alive and well'. However, morale collapsed again later, but the team still felt all would be well if they could find yet another grand gesture to undertake. They were wrong.[6]

The Church of England has been tempted in recent years by grand gestures which, together with the upbeat 'positive thinking', are meant to solve everything. Now the major restructuring is more or less complete, the Church is now 'swept and garnished' as it says in the Gospels, but what will fill the emptiness?

My belief is that the answer must come from a very much deeper level than this, a much more accurate and caring response to people's real needs. Arbuckle sees the beginning of such a process as a 'sitting with' the shock and pain of loss as much as is humanly possible (nobody can do it continually), a willing entering of the chaos that comes when what you already know no longer seems to work for you, and a new way forward has to be discovered, something that many individuals discover for themselves after crises in their lives – illness, divorce, bereavement, loss of job, or breakdown. It is a 'natural' resurrection constantly evident in the world around us.

The Breaking Heart

Michael Ramsay said many years ago that the Church of England might need to have its heart broken, and perhaps that is precisely the process that is going on, if it would only consent to notice. Arbuckle would add that those most needed at the moment are the 'loyal dissenters' – those who are not happy with the current Church but feel on their pulses that there is another way forward.

The Question of Guilt

One of the problems with denial is that it makes it impossible to tackle the problem of guilt. If the churches are half empty, then it must be our fault, runs the painful subtext behind many Christian statements. Guilt, no less than depression, needs to be taken out and looked at. Is it the fault of the churches? The answer, confusingly, is both yes and no. There are things the churches should have done in the past and should be doing now that could, and can, make a difference to their decline, but it is too late to worry about the errors of the past (though not too late to learn from them). And in any case all the Church can do is offer its treasures to others. The others have the right to refuse.

The S Curve

But suppose some of the problem is simply inevitable, whatever we Christians had done or not done? The business guru Charles Handy charts the way businesses rise and fall in what he calls 'the S or Sigmoid Curve'.[7] The fate of institutions, in his view, is inevitable. 'We wax, and then we wane.' Businesses, if they succeed at all, start hesitantly and falteringly – the first dip of the S – then go down a bit, and then they rise in a promising curve. At that stage everyone is happy, everyone feels it is all going swimmingly. It is then, says Handy, at the point of maximum success, that plans should start to be laid for the business to develop along quite different lines in the future. Because what is quite certain is that after the curve there will be a dramatic fall in its prospects. If the managing director is clever enough to know this he will start work on it while his enterprise is at the top, because this is the easiest moment to take this action. Most managing directors, most businesses, don't do anything of the kind, because at this point all the messages are so promising, so that the business goes over the top and down into decline, until it reaches a point where it is very much more difficult for it to start the painful journey upwards again. This is hard, but Handy says that 'all that we know of change, be it personal change or change in organisations, tells us that the real energy for change only comes when you are looking disaster in the face'.[8]

He goes on to say that this law of change is true for institutions as well as businesses, and even applies it to marriage. He describes how there came a time in his own marriage when he and his wife, who had been deeply 'in love', realised that they had to renegotiate their relationship, painful as this was, and let certain things go, in order to glide onwards into another upward curve (which they did).

Going back to institutions he describes how they can go on to a second upward curve.

> The second curve, be it a new product, a new way of operating, a new strategy or a new culture, is going to be noticeably different from the old. It has to be. The people also have to be different. Those who lead the second curve are not going to be the people who led the first curve ... they will find it temperamentally difficult to abandon their first curve ... even if they recognise that a new curve is needed. For a time, therefore, new ideas and new people have to coexist with the old until the second curve is established and the first begins to wane.[9]

As I read Handy I observed that the great Marks and Spencer, which always seemed impregnable, was getting rid of executives, laying off staff and changing its buying policies, as its shares dropped in value to half what they had once been. No institution is safe from this kind of reverse. It is not easy to know where to place an institution like the Church of England on Handy's S curve – it has been going for so long and I am not sure what sort of time spans Handy is talking in – but if the Edwardian period is taken as the first big curve in the twentieth century, and the 1950s as the second, it would look as if a new direction was needed in the 1960s and 1970s. There *were* some new directions in that period, most importantly perhaps the placing of the parish eucharist at the centre of Sunday worship, but the changes were not profound enough to stop the Church sweeping over into severe decline, with all the painful nostalgic longing for what Arbuckle calls 'restorationism', the attempted return to the old status quo. There have been other lively moments, most notably *Faith in the City* and the remarkable success of the Church Urban Fund, which showed the Church was ready to put money where its mouth was and set an impressive social example. There was Runcie's Falklands sermon which, in the aftermath of war, said clearly and unequivocally that our enemies were as dear to God as we were. There was the ordination of women, but the fatal loss of nerve in the year after the favourable vote, which issued in the Act of Synod, largely deprived the Church of the goodwill it accrued by being seen to do something new, generous and, in the context, daring. Placating its traditionalists mattered more than reaching out towards a changed society, and this kind of failure costs it more dearly than it knows.

The act of creation is to do something that is new, not for the sake of new, but new because new-minted out of changed collective Christian understanding, which may be, and often is, spurred on by developments in secular society. Once the need for this newness becomes plain it must be carried through with determination and courage, and without having second thoughts and looking over one's shoulder. But before such understandings become plain to us, there is a lot of sitting around with the chaos and uncertainty and listening to the 'loyal dissenters', or perhaps being such dissenters ourselves.

At the moment 'loyal dissent' can only point at possibilities. The whole 'Establishment' issue is one of these. Establishment is a lying mirror for the Church, one which, because it not only places it at the heart of the nation but also proclaims that it is 'there for everyone' is narcissistically satisfying to a profoundly insecure institution. It may be that it still feels 'becoming' for Governments to have the Church around – though for how long? – but the idea, or the ideal, grows further and further from the facts. Another way to put it might be that the Church of England is there for people to stay away from. The grain of goodness in all this is the sense of love for those outside the institution and the wish to serve them, but this would not suddenly cease with disestablishment – at least it did not do so in Wales or Ireland. The most damaging aspect of all about Establishment is the sense of the Church of England as 'one up' on the other churches, something they feel and mind. If the organisation of the Church is, however remotely, intended to reveal its beliefs, then a re-Establishment seems called for in which the other mainstream churches enjoy parity with the Church of England. It would be impressive if this could be offered voluntarily – most Church reforms occur only when a minority somehow shames people into it.

What is necessary now is for the three main streams of Christianity in this country – the Roman Catholic, Anglican and Free Church – to be seen to be united at a deeper level than they are at present. Real affection and respect is now evident at so many levels – the Queen presenting the Order of Merit to Cardinal Hume shortly before his death, the attendance of Archbishop Carey at the Cardinal's funeral, the resuming of talk between Methodists and Anglicans. There must be ways, without entering interminable debates about doctrine and orders, which would bring us still closer.

'Loyal dissent' also suggests that, partly for historical reasons harking back to a time, not so many years ago, when the clergy were often the only university-educated people in their churches, the gifts of the laity have been neglected in our churches. This is not only a pity in itself, but it has affected the sense of 'ownership' that might have been fostered. The local church often seemed to belong to the clergy, and this fostered a kind of parent-and-child relationship which tended to make churchgoers either dutiful or defiant, usually a bit of both. Partly because of the shortage of clergy, partly because evangelical churches have a stronger sense of the vocation of the laity, real inroads are being made into this attitude, and the fact that the laity are going to be asked to play a bigger financial role in the future can only increase their sense of their own value.

Daring to be a Daniel
I have often been shocked by clergy who felt unable to stick up for one principle or another – even in the days when they were almost universally protected by the freehold – because it might affect their job prospects. In this they were 'mirroring' the Church which often shrinks from doing what it knows it should because it dreads public scorn, as well as internal dissension. Ground between the millstones of being accused, usually by Tories, of abandoning its traditional moral territory, on the one hand, and of those within the Church threatening either to desert to Rome (over the ordination of women), or refusing to pay their quota (over issues of homosexuality in the case of Reform parishes), it vacillates, goes forward, backslides, plays safe, and makes itself morally contemptible, as it defends itself by claiming that it is holding dissentient voices within it when it is simply frightened to make up its mind. Expediency, too often, is all. By not making up its mind, it does not exist in a moral vacuum – it sins against vulnerable people whom it should be defending and supporting. There is only one way through this sort of impasse (and it is almost embarrassing to say something so straightforwardly old-fashioned), which is to decide what is right and stick to the decision, no matter how many brickbats get thrown by the *Daily Telegraph* and the *Daily Mail*, or how many threaten to refuse to pay their quota or defect to Rome. There is only one effective way to deal with blackmailers.

Nonsense about not ordaining homosexual priests, when for centuries homosexual priests have worked magnificently for the Church, nonsense about women being priests, but then again not being priests, according to the eye of the beholder, do incalculable damage to the Church's witness in a society that has radically changed its mind about women, and is bravely learning to face an irrational dread of homosexuality. If only the Church could lead the battle

379

against prejudice for once instead of always struggling along in the rear, and finding moral reasons for doing so. As one of the clergy earlier in this book remarks, 'Outsiders watch the Church, waiting to see whether it has changed.' The perception that the Church, for all its claims of love, reveals prejudice against vulnerable groups – women, gays, blacks – in its actions if not its public words, quickly unravels the most elaborate confections of spin. Joe and Jane Public are not fools.

Part of the Church's problem is its unthinking 'maleness'. (It is not that I think women are superior to men, but that their life experience has been, and is, a very different one, and it is one which is vital to the Church, as a number of excellent women priests have already demonstrated.)

One of the things that often seems lacking in the Church is what Rosamond Lehmann calls 'the educated heart', the emotional sensitivity that responds delicately and gracefully to others because it has a developed imagination, and knows how to stand in their shoes. It is this quality, I suspect, which many people found irresistibly attractive in Jesus Christ. Imagination is perhaps the quality most strikingly lacking in public statements about sexuality. Can the bishops imagine what it is like to be a woman, a homosexual man, a homosexual priest, a person who has made a bad choice in marriage, a divorced person? Either they cannot imagine it, or they know it all too well and find it too threatening to deal with.

Cutting a Figure
Style seems another issue, since outward show tells a story that those with eyes to see cannot ignore. The Prime Minister of Britain, who heads a government which rules more than fifty million people, lives in a relatively modest residence at 10 Downing Street; the Archbishop, with a charge of a million or so, inhabits the seedy splendour of Lambeth Palace. Might not a more modest residence set off a modern archbishop better? Again does he need a substantial separate staff? Might it not be better (and even *Turnbull* seems a little wistful over this) to unify the Church in a way that had Lambeth staff working in Church House along with the Church House staff and the Church Commissioners? A separatist Lambeth gives the wrong message.

If it is going to be separate, however, then should not Lambeth be more of a meeting place not just for the great and the good, but for as many church people as is practically possible? At present most churchgoers have more chance of going to a Buckingham Palace garden party than going to Lambeth, yet Lambeth costs the Church money, and churchgoers are being asked to fund their Church. On a slightly different level, the Queen long ago pioneered lunch parties of people whom she might not choose to spend the weekend with, or hope to find alongside her at Ascot, but whom she recognised to be people who mattered in society as a whole because they shaped it and gave it its flavour – clergy, academics, scientists, doctors, lawyers, writers, actors, artists, musicians. It would be encouraging to think that archbishops, thirsting for knowledge of contemporary Britain, spread their nets this wide in a world not necessarily Christian, but part of modern Britain. If they do so, they have kept uncharacteristically quiet about it.

The whole question of lifestyle and more particularly of houses – for bishops, deans, cathedral canons – seems to need at least thinking through. Of course, they need houses suitable for working and entertaining in, but the size and splendour of some of them seems to have little to do with the twentieth century. *Turnbull* talks of a 'slimmed-down' Church, but it is important that all the belt-tightening, sacrificial giving, and heart-searching is not confined to parish clergy and laity.

In this interim 'waiting' period how should we Anglican Christians think of ourselves? I find myself repeating the words of the architect of the church resurrected after the fire. 'I saw myself designing for you "a clearing in the forest".' The Church itself, damaged by a number of things, some of which are its own fault, some of which are not, is perhaps a clearing in the forest. It exists in a society cluttered with consumerism, with a multiplicity of possibilities, driven by a hunger which seems to want to devour the world itself. In the clearing there is nothing, merely a space in which first of all to find oneself, to locate one's hunger, and to live in the perspective of God. That perspective, and the story of Jesus, living and dying and living again, are all that the Church has to offer, and nothing could be more appropriate to society's need.

In the 'new style' of Church that we are going to need, I hope we are going to be much more like the way George Pattison describes the 'new style' theologian, not the one who knows it all, and is waiting for you to keep quiet to come up with the answer, but the 'fellow worker' and puzzler, who is capable of some 'negative capability' (being able to admit that one does not know without getting too worried about it), and does not necessarily think that truth can always be supported by argument. Or that one needs to win every argument.

It is natural to worry about total rejection and the collapse of the Church in any form in which we now understand it. I don't actually think that will happen. Fashions change, and the fashion for rejecting the Church now may, almost certainly will, turn into finding it attractive and desirable, and we shall sweep into another one of Handy's curves. Better than that, because fashion is a fickle nonsense, however deeply rooted in the the human unconscious, there are already numerous signs of local churches radically revisioning themselves, asking what they are there for, trying painfully hard to talk honestly to one another, shedding all kinds of liturgical and ecclesiastical nonsense in the struggle for clarity. Slimmed to a core of those who, whatever the world thinks of them, find something vital in Christian faith, there is now an almost total absence of those who go to church because convention demands it. Those who remain are not content with easy answers of what the faith *is*, or how it is to be lived out.

The Church would look more attractive if it was not continually yearning, like a neglected lover, over those who stay away. It could try celebrating the clientele it has got. I was interested in some remarks by the new Controller of Radio 3, Roger Wright. 'I'd like us to have more listeners – and I do care about what they say – but it may be that two and a half million is all we are going to get. And I refuse to believe that that is a small number. Surely the main thing is that we do what we do really well?'

I'd love to see the Church of England talking in that vein: 'We'd love to have more members, and we do listen to criticism, but maybe for now we must accept that we'll never have more than a million. That is a lot of people. Let us try to make sure that that million have the best quality of Christian life we can manage – good teaching, marvellous liturgy, sermons, good community life, a capacity for having fun together, and for helping those who need it.' In other words, a general lightening up.

Yet the old texts of 'heroic leadership' are still very seductive and it will need a lot of loyal dissent to subvert them. Questioning of beliefs, living with doubts and uncertainties, 'negative capability', must be built in to a modern Christianity, if only so that we do not make idols of a fixed and final idea, and lose sight of a God who is neither fixed nor final.

'"What a pity' remarks Hugh Dickinson, the former Dean of Salisbury 'that Jesus did not live in the age of the bicycle. "On this bicycle I will found my Church" would have a less static feel to it than "On this rock . . ."'[10] For those who must have rocks this will be an unnerving idea, but perhaps we are placed as no earlier Christian generation has been to know that the only stability for the rock is for it to flow.

Stevie Smith, not a churchgoer as far as I know, though fascinated by the Christian religion, saw the life and death of Jesus not as a programme for rules and doctrines, especially the kind that exclude people, but as a song that we are invited to listen to, and perhaps to join in.

> Those who truly hear the voice, the words, the happy song,
> Never shall need working laws to keep from doing wrong.
>
> Deaf men will pretend sometimes they hear the song, the words,
> And make excuse to sin extremely; this will be absurd.
>
> Heed it not. Whatever foolish men may do the song is cried
> For those who hear, and the sweet singer does not care that he
>   was crucified.
>
> For he does not wish that men should love him more than
>   anything
> Because he died; he only wishes they would hear him sing.[11]

Notes

Introduction

1 Gerald A. Arbuckle, *Refounding the Church: Dissent for Leadership* (Geoffrey Chapman, 1993), p. 1.

Part One: The Church as It Was

Chapter 1: *'An Old World of Devotion'*

1 Judith Maltby, ' "Circular as Our Way Is" – Recent Revisions of the English Reformation and some Ecumenical Reflections'. Paper read at the Oxford Society for Historical Theology, 29 February 1996.
2 John Guy, 'The Tudor Age: 1485–1603' in *The Oxford Illustrated History of Britain*, ed. Kenneth O. Morgan (Oxford University Press, 1984), p. 237.
3 Diarmaid MacCulloch, *Thomas Cranmer: A Life* (Yale University Press, 1996), p. 3.
4 Eamon Duffy, T*he Stripping of the Altars: Traditional Religion in England 1400–1580* (Yale University Press, 1992), p. 11.
5 Richard Marius, *Thomas More* (J. M. Dent & Sons, 1984), pp. 89–90.
6 Marius, *Thomas More*, p. 518.
7 MacCulloch, *Cranmer*, p. 89.

Chapter 2: *Anglicana Ecclesia*

1 Diarmaid MacCulloch, *Thomas Cranmer: A Life* (Yale University Press, 1996), p. 121.
2 MacCulloch, *Cranmer*, p. 159.

3 J. R. H. Moorman, *A History of the Church in England* (A. & C. Black, 1954), p. 175.
4 John Guy, 'The Tudor Age' in *The Oxford Illustrated History of Britain*, ed. Kenneth O. Morgan (Oxford University Press, 1984), p. 238.
5 MacCulloch, *Cranmer*, p. 275.
6 David L. Edwards, *A Concise History of English Christianity* (HarperCollins, 1998), p. 52.
7 Leslie Paul, *A Church by Daylight: A Reappraisement of the Church of England and its Future* (Geoffrey Chapman, 1973), p. 18.
8 Geoffrey Elton, *Reform and Reformation: England 1509–1558* (Cambridge, MA, 1977), p. 301.
9 There are various versions. One is *The Letters and Papers of Henry VIII*, Vol. 20 (HMSO, 1907), ii, 1031, p. 513.

Chapter 3: *The Evangelical Hour*

1 Eamon Duffy, *The Stripping of the Altars: Traditional Religion in England 1400–1580* (Yale University Press, 1992), p. 451.
2 Duffy, *Stripping of the Altars*, p. 453.
3 Duffy, *Stripping of the Altars*, p. 454.
4 Diarmaid MacCulloch, *Thomas Cranmer: A Life* (Yale University Press, 1996), p. 381.
5 MacCulloch, *Cranmer*, p. 417.
6 Judith Maltby, *Prayer Book and People in Elizabethan and Early Stuart England* (Cambridge University Press, 1998), p. 3.
7 Maltby, *Prayer Book and People*, p. 41.
8 Duffy, *Stripping of the Altars*, p. 473.
9 Duffy, *Stripping of the Altars*, p. 474f.
10 Duffy, *Stripping of the Altars*, p. 475.
11 MacCulloch, *Cranmer*, p. 613f.
12 Duffy, *Stripping of the Altars*, p. 473.
13 MacCulloch, *Cranmer*, p. 511.
14 Ibid.
15 Maltby, *Prayer Book and People*, p. 2.
16 Maltby, *Prayer Book and People*, p. 4.
17 Maltby, *Prayer Book and People*, p. 13f.
18 Maltby, *Prayer Book and People*, p. 24, quoting from correspondence between Judith Maltby and the historian Ian Green.

Chapter 4: *The Fall of Cranmer – Queen Mary*

1 Eamon Duffy, *The Stripping of the Altars: Traditional Religion in England 1400–1580* (Yale University Press, 1992), p. 530.
2 Duffy, *Stripping of the Altars*, p. 532.
3 Duffy, *Stripping of the Altars*, p. 536.
4 Diarmaid MacCulloch, *Thomas Cranmer: A Life* (Yale University Press, 1996), p. 582.
5 MacCulloch, *Cranmer*, p. 591.
6 MacCulloch, *Cranmer*, p. 606.
7 Leslie Paul, *A Church by Daylight: An Appraisement of the Church of England and Its Future* (Geoffrey Chapman, 1973), p. 22.

Chapter 5: *The Elizabethan Settlement: The Golden Mediocrity*

1 The Act of Supremacy (1559), quoted by Leslie Paul in *A Church by Daylight: A Reappraisement of the Church of England and Its Future* (Geoffrey Chapman, 1973), p. 23.
2 David Edwards, *A Concise History of English Christianity* (HarperCollins, 1998), p. 64.
3 Eamon Duffy, *The Stripping of the Altars: Traditional Religion in England 1400–1580* (Yale University Press, 1992), p. 586.
4 Duffy, *Stripping of the Altars*, p. 588.
5 Owen Chadwick, *The Reformation*, Pelican History of the Church, Vol. 3 (Penguin Books, 1964), p. 369.
6 John Morrill, 'The Stuarts' in *The Oxford Illustrated History of Britain*, ed. Kenneth O. Morgan (Oxford University Press, 1984), p. 343.
7 Paul, *Church by Daylight*, p. 25.
8 Edwards, *Concise History*, p. 68.
9 Morrill, 'The Stuarts', p. 343.
10 Paul, *Church by Daylight*, p. 27.
11 Paul, *Church by Daylight*, p. 29.
12 Edwards, *Concise History*, p. 78.
13 Edwards, *Concise History*, p. 80.

Chapter 6: *A Different Debate*

1 W. M. Jacob, *Lay People and Religion in the Early Eighteenth Century* (Cambridge University Press, 1995), p. 1.
2 Jacob, *Lay People*, p. 1.
3 Peter Laslett, *The World We have Lost* (1965), quoted by Jacob, Lay People, p. 4.

4 Jacob, *Lay People*, p. 4.
5 Ibid.
6 Jacob, *Lay People*, p. 17.
7 Jonathan Swift, 'Voyage to the Houyhnhnms', *Gulliver's Travels* (1726), fourth part, quoted in Leslie Paul, *A Church by Daylight* (Geoffrey Chapman, 1973), p. 40.
8 David Hume, *Treatise of Human Nature* Bk I, Pt III, Sec. VIII.
9 James Woodforde, *The Diary of a Country Parson* (Oxford University Press, abridged edn 1978).
10 Richard Sharp, 'New Perspectives on the High Church Tradition: Historical Background 1730–1780' in *Tradition Renewed*, ed. Geoffrey Rowell (Darton, Longman & Todd, 1986), p. 14.
11 Sharp, 'New Perspectives', p. 4.
12 Peter Nockles, 'The Oxford Movement: Historical Background 1780–1833' in *Tradition Renewed*, p. 24.
13 Sharp, 'New Perspectives', p. 9.
14 Paul, *Church by Daylight*, pp. 45–7.
15 Gordon S. Wakefield, 'A Mystical Substitute for the Glorious Gospel? A Methodist Critique of Tractarianism' in *Tradition Renewed*, p. 187.
16 Paul, *Church by Daylight*, p. 50.
17 J. F. C. *Harrison, Early Victorian Britain, 1832–51* (Fontana, HarperCollins, 1988), p. 128.
18 Harrison, *Early Victorian Britain*, p. 128.
19 Ibid.
20 Harrison, *Early Victorian Britain*, p. 129.
21 Paul, *Church by Daylight*, p. 52.
22 Harrison, *Early Victorian Britain*, p. 131.
23 Paul, *Church by Daylight*, p. 56.
24 A. P. Stanley, *The Life of Thomas Arnold* (1904), p. 178.

Chapter 7: *'The Stammering Lips of Ambiguous Formularies'*

1 S. L. Ollard, *A Short History of the Oxford Movement* ([1915] A. R. Mowbray, 1983), p. 24.
2 Owen Chadwick, *The Victorian Church* (A. & C. Black, 1966), Part I, p. 169.
3 Chadwick, *Victorian Church*, Part I, pp. 169–170.
4 Richard Hurrell Froude, *Remains* (1838–9), quoted in Ollard, *Oxford Movement*, p. 54.
5 Richard Church, *Letters, Occasional Papers* ii, 386, quoted in Ollard, *Oxford Movement*, p. 83.

6 Chadwick, *Victorian Church*, p. 495.
7 Owen Chadwick, *The Mind of the Oxford Movement* (A. & C. Black, 1960), p. 55.
8 Ibid.
9 Chadwick, *Victorian Church*, p. 499.
10 Chadwick, *Victorian Church*, p. 501.
11 Ollard, *Oxford Movement*, p. 99.
12 W. S. F. Pickering, 'Anglo-Catholicism: Some Sociological Observations' in *Tradition Renewed: The Oxford Movement Conference Papers*, ed. Geoffrey Rowell (Darton, Longman & Todd, 1986), p. 156.
13 Pickering, 'Anglo-Catholicism', p. 154.
14 John Hick (ed.), *The Myth of God Incarnate* (SCM Press, 1977), p. ix.

Chapter 8: *New Definitions and Structures*

1 *Census of Religious Worship, England and Wales: Report and Tables* (London, 1853).
2 J. F. C. Harrison, *Early Victorian Britain 1832–51* (Fontana, HarperCollins, 1988).
3 Harrison, *Early Victorian Britain*, p. 124.
4 José Harris, 'Private Lives, Public Spirit: Britain 1870–1914', *The Penguin Social History of Britain* (Penguin Books, 1994), p. 151.
5 Ibid.
6 Harris, *Social History*, p. 154.
7 Ibid.
8 Harrison, *Early Victorian Britain*, p. 126.
9 Edward Norman, 'Stewart Headlam and the Christian Socialists' in *Victorian Values: Personalities and Perspectives in Nineteenth Century Society*, ed. Gordon Marsden (Longman, 1990), p. 200.
10 Brian Heeney, *The Women's Movement in the Church of England 1850–1930* (Clarendon Press, 1988), p. 95.
11 Ibid.
12 Heeney, *Women's Movement*, p. 96.
13 Heeney, *Women's Movement*, p. 97.
14 Heeney, *Women's Movement*, p. 98.
15 Heeney, *Women's Movement*, p. 7.
16 Ibid.
17 Heeney, *Women's Movement*, p. 16.
18 Heeney, *Women's Movement*, p. 27.

19 Sheila Fletcher, *Maude Royden: A Life* (Blackwell, 1989), p. 177.
20 Harris, *Social History*, p. 165.
21 Ibid.

Chapter 9: *The Twentieth Century*

1 Adrian Hastings, *A History of English Christianity 1920–90*, 3rd edn (SCM Press, 1991), p. 45.
2 Hastings, *English Christianity*, p. 47.
3 Ibid.
4 Leslie Paul, *A Church by Daylight: A Reappraisement of the Church of England and Its Future* (Geoffrey Chapman, 1973), p. 97.
5 Paul, *Church by Daylight*, p. 98.
6 W. R. Matthews, *Memories and Meanings* (Hodder & Stoughton, 1969), p. 144.
7 Paul, *Church by Daylight*, p. 99.
8 W. S. F. Pickering, 'Anglo-Catholicism: Some Sociological Observations' in *Tradition Renewed: The Oxford Conference Papers*, ed. Geoffrey Rowell (Darton, Longman & Todd, 1986), p. 165.
9 Pickering, 'Anglo-Catholicism', p. 171.
10 Ibid.
11 Ibid.
12 A. M. Allchin, 'The Understanding of Unity in Tractarian Theology and Spirituality' in *Tradition Renewed*, ed. Rowell, p. 228.
13 Oliver Barclay, *Evangelicalism in Britain 1935–1995: A Personal Sketch* (InterVarsity Press, 1997), p. 25.
14 Barclay, *Evangelicalism*, p. 26.
15 Hastings, *English Christianity*, p. 255f.

Chapter 10: *Postwar Christianity*

1 Adrian Hastings, *A History of English Christianity 1920–1990* (SCM Press, 1991), p. 510.
2 Ibid.
3 Hastings, *English Christianity*, p. 523.
4 Hastings, *English Christianity*, p. 531.
5 Interview with Canon Eric James, 28 February 1997.
6 Alec Vidler (ed.), *Soundings: Essays concerning Christian Understanding* (Cambridge University Press, 1962).
7 John A. T. Robinson, *Honest to God* (SCM Press, 1963).

8 William James, *Varieties of Religious Experience* (New York: Longmans, Green & Co., 1902; Penguin Classics, 1985).

9 Aldous Huxley, *The Doors of Perception* (New York: Harper & Row, 1954).

10 Huxley, *Doors of Perception*, p. 12.

11 R. D. Laing, interview with the author, 1966.

12 Betty Friedan, *The Feminine Mystique* (1963; Penguin Books, 1965).

13 Germaine Greer, *The Female Eunuch* (Macgibbon & Kee, 1970; Flamingo, 1973).

14 Interview with the Reverend Sir Derek Pattinson, 5 March 1997.

15 John Hick (ed.), *The Myth of God Incarnate* (SCM Press, 1977), p. x.

16 Hastings, *English Christianity*, p. 548.

Chapter 11: *The End of the Century*

1 Interview with the Reverend Sir Derek Pattinson, 5 March 1997.

2 Ibid.

3 Ibid.

4 Humphrey Carpenter, *Robert Runcie: The Reluctant Archbishop* (Hodder & Stoughton, 1996).

5 Carpenter, *Reluctant Archbishop*, p. 256f.

6 *Faith in the City: The Report of the Archbishop of Canterbury's Commission on Urban Priority Areas* (Church House Publishing, 1985).

7 Adrian Hastings, *Robert Runcie* (Mowbray, 1991).

8 *Faith in the City*.

9 William Oddie, *The Crockford's File: Gareth Bennett and the Death of the Anglican Mind* (Hamish Hamilton, 1989).

10 Interview with the Reverend Sir Derek Pattinson, 5 March 1997.

11 *The Cutting Edge of Mission: Mid Point Review of the Decade of Evangelism* (Anglican Communion Publications, 1996).

12 Judith Maltby, quoting Donald Anderson of the Anglican Communion Office, in *Prayer Book and People in Elizabethan and Early Stuart England* (Cambridge University Press, 1998), p. 237.

13 *Cutting Edge*, p. 104.

14 *Cutting Edge*, p. 105.

15 *Cutting Edge*, p. 10.

16 *Issues in Human Sexuality: A Statement by the House of Bishops* (Church House Publishing, 1991).
17 Reform is an extreme Anglican group which was originally concerned with opposing women's ordination, but later moved on to oppose any move by the Church to recognise homosexual relations as acceptable.
18 *A Pastoral Statement to Lesbian and Gay Anglicans from Some Member Bishops of the Lambeth Conference* (5 August 1998).
19 *Issues in Human Sexuality.*
20 *Pastoral Statement.*

Part Two: The Church as It Is

Chapter 12: *The Lambeth Walk*

1 *Working as One Body: The Report of the Archbishops' Commission on the Organisation of the Church of England*, the Turnbull Report (Church House Publishing, 1995), p. 79 (7.9).
2 Humphrey Carpenter, *Robert Runcie: The Reluctant Archbishop* (Hodder & Stoughton, 1996), p. 204.
3 Ibid.
4 Carpenter, *Reluctant Archbishop*, p. 205.
5 Dominic Milroy OSB, *The Tablet*, 26 June 1999.
6 Madeleine Bunting, *The Guardian*, 9 May 1998.
7 Ibid.
8 Ibid.
9 Ibid.
10 Ibid.
11 Interview with His Grace the Archbishop of Canterbury, 15 April 1999.

Chapter 13: *Ruritania Revisited*

1 Terry Lovell, *Number One Millbank: The Financial Downfall of the Church of England* (HarperCollins, 1997), p. 159.
2 Lovell, *Number One Millbank*, p. 6.
3 Lovell, *Number One Millbank*, p. 126.
4 Lovell, *Number One Millbank*, p. 29.
5 Lovell, *Number One Millbank*, p. 3.
6 Keith Bladon, 'The Gracious Gift: Church of England Finances and Resources' in *A Church for the 21st Century*, ed. Robert Hannaford (Gracewing, 1998), p. 46.
7 Bladon, 'Gracious Gift', p. 50.

8 *Working as One Body: The Report of the Archbishops' Commission on the Organisation of the Church of England*, the Turnbull Report (Church House Publishing, 1995).

Chapter 14: *All Change – the Clean Sweep*

1 *Synodical Government in the Church of England: A Review*, the Bridge Report (Church House Publishing, 1997), Section 2: 'Theological Principles and Historical Development'.
2 *Working as One Body: The Report of the Archbishops' Commission on the Organisation of the Church of England*, the Turnbull Report (Church House Publishing, 1995).
3 Interview with Bishop Michael Turnbull, 30 January 1997.
4 Madeleine Bunting, *The Guardian*, 9 May 1998.
5 *Working as One Body*, p. 119.
6 Interview with member of Church House staff, 18 June 1999.
7 Ibid.
8 *Working as One Body*, p. 37.
9 Wesley Carr, 'The Church of England in the Next Millennium' in *A Church for the 21st Century: The Church of England Today and Tomorrow: An Agenda for the Future*, ed. Robert Hannaford (Gracewing, 1998), p. 31.
10 *Working as One Body*, p. 45.
11 *Working as One Body*, p. 35.
12 Ibid.
13 Robin Gill, *Vision of Growth* (SPCK, 1994), p. 85.
14 *Working as One Body*, p. 35.
15 Report by House of Bishops, June 1998.
16 Ibid.
17 Ibid.
18 *Church Times*, 12 February 1999.
19 *Church Times*, 19 February 1999.
20 Thomas Merton, 'Bureaucrats and Diggers' in *Collected Poems* (Sheldon Press, 1978), p. 694.
21 First Report of the Archbishops' Council, June 1999.
22 Leader, *Church Times*, 18 June 1999.
23 *Church Times* letter column, 25 June 1999.
24 Staff Survey by Surveys and Audits Consultants of the Industrial Society, June 1998.
25 Ibid.
26 Ibid.
27 Ibid.
28 Ibid.

29 Ibid.
30 Ibid.
31 Ibid.
32 Ibid.
33 Ibid.
34 Ibid.
35 Ibid.
36 Ibid.
37 Ibid.
38 Ibid.
39 Church House staff interviewed by author, 27 January 1999.
40 Ibid.
41 Ibid.
42 'Fr Jones' interviewed 27 January 1999.
43 Ibid.
44 Ibid.
45 Ibid.
46 Philip Mawer, Secretary-General of General Synod, interviewed 21 June 1999.

Chapter 15: *Statistics, Spin and Management*

1 General Synod Board of Education, *Youth a Part: Young People and the Church* (National Society and Church House Publishing, 1996).
2 Betty Saunders, *O Blest Communion! The Home Life of the Church of England* (Darton, Longman & Todd, 1996).
3 Clifford Longley in *Church Times*, 16 January 1999.
4 William Beaver in *Church Times*, 23 January 1999.
5 Clifford Longley in *Church Times*, 30 January 1999.
6 William Beaver in *Church Times*, 6 February 1999.
7 Peter Brierley (ed.), *Religious Trends* (Christian Research, 1998-9).
8 *The Church of England Today: A Summary of Current Statistics* (Church House Publishing, 1999).
9 Ibid.
10 Ibid.
11 Interview with Philip Mawer, 21 June 1999.
12 See note 7 above.
13 Interview with Peter Brierley, 12 February 1998.
14 Brierley, *Religious Trends*.
15 Interview with Peter Brierley.
16 T. S. Eliot, *Choruses from 'The Rock'*, I, lines 27–30, 35; II, lines

44–5, 47, *Collected Poems 1909–1962* (Faber & Faber, 1963).
17 'And the Church Saw that Business Was Good', *The Guardian*, 18 October 1997.

Chapter 16: *Bright the Vision: Ways of Thinking about the Church*

1 Robin Gill, *A Vision for Growth* (SPCK, 1993), p. 12.
2 Robert Hannaford (ed.), *A Church for the 21st Century: The Church of England Today and Tomorrow: An Agenda for the Future* (Gracewing, 1998).
3 Lynne Leeder, 'New Wine in Old Skins: An Examination of the Legal Position' in Hannaford, *A Church for the 21st Century*.
4 Robin Gill, *The Myth of the Empty Church* (SPCK, 1993), p. 9 (précis).
5 Gill, *Vision for Growth*, p. 20.
6 Gill, *Vision for Growth*, p. 21.
7 Gill, *Vision for Growth*, p. 105.
8 Gill, *Vision for Growth*, p. 56.
9 Gill, *Vision for Growth*, p. 65.
10 Ibid.
11 Gill, *Vision for Growth*, p. 73.
12 Ibid.
13 Gill, *Vision for Growth*, p. 86.
14 Gill, *Vision for Growth*, p. 85.
15 Gill, *Vision for Growth*, p. 77.
16 Gill, *Vision for Growth*, p. 116.
17 Wesley Carr, 'Is There a Future for the Church of England?' in Wesley Carr and others, *Say One for Me: The Church of England in the Next Decade* (SPCK, 1992), p. 7.
18 Ibid.
19 Carr, 'Is There a Future', p. 10.
20 Carr, 'Is There a Future', p. 12.
21 Carr, 'Is There a Future', p. 16.
22 Bernice Martin, 'Church and Culture' in Carr and others, *Say One for Me*, p. 103.
23 Ibid.
24 Martin, 'Church and Culture', p. 104.
25 Gerald A. Arbuckle, *Refounding the Church: Dissent for Leadership* (Geoffrey Chapman, 1993).
26 Interview with Canon Vincent Strudwick, 11 August 1999.

Chapter 17: 'Stablish'd It Fast by a Changeless Decree'

1 Adrian Hastings, *A History of English Christianity 1920–1990* (SCM Press, 1991), p. 49.
2 Ibid.
3 Hastings, *English Christianity*, p. 52.
4 Colin Buchanan, *Cut the Connection: Disestablishment and the Church of England* (Darton, Longman & Todd, 1994).
5 *The Tablet*, 19 June 1999.
6 Buchanan, *Cut the Connection*, p. 8.
7 John Moses, *A Broad and Living Way: Church and State: A Continuing Establishment* (The Canterbury Press, Norwich, 1995).
8 Moses, *Broad and Living Way*, p. 9.
9 *Senior Church Appointments: A Review of the Methods of Appointment of Area and Suffragan Bishops, Deans, Provosts, Archdeacons and Residentiary Canons* (Church House Publishing, 1992), Memorandum of Dissent by Mr Frank Field MP, p. 116, para. 4.
10 Peter Brierley (ed.), *Religious Trends* (Christian Research, 1998–9).
11 Field, Memorandum of Dissent.
12 Leader, *The Tablet*, 31 January 1998.

Chapter 18: *In the Purple*

1 Inaugural homily of Cardinal Basil Hume in Westminster Cathedral, 25 March 1976.
2 *Working as One Body: The Report of the Archbishops' Commission on the Organisation of the Church of England, the Turnbull Report* (Church House Publishing, 1995), p. 75.
3 Ibid.
4 'The Ordination or Consecration of a Bishop', *The Alternative Service Book 1980*.
5 Peter Selby, *Grace and Mortgage: The Language of Faith and the Debt of the World* (Darton, Longman & Todd, 1997).
6 Colin Buchanan, *Cut the Connection: Disestablishment and the Church of England* (Darton, Longman & Todd, 1994).
7 Interview with Canon June Osborne, 16 May 1997.
8 *Church Times*, 23 July 1999.
9 Peter Selby, *BeLonging: Challenge to a Tribal Church* (SPCK, 1991).
10 Selby, *BeLonging*, p. 60.

11 Ibid.
12 Selby, *BeLonging*, p. 61.
13 Ibid.
14 *Senior Church Appointments: A Review of the Methods of Apppointment of Area and Suffragan Bishops, Deans, Provosts, Archdeacons and Residentiary Canons* (Church House Publishing, 1992), Memorandum of Dissent by Mr Frank Field MP.
15 Lesley Bentley, 'At the Grassroots: The Act in the Parishes' in *Act of Synod – Act of Folly*, ed. Monica Furlong (SCM Press, 1998).
16 Bentley, 'At the Grass roots', p. 113f.
17 *The Times*, 4 March 1999.
18 Lynne Leeder, 'New Wine in Old Skins: An Examination of the Legal Position' in *A Church for the 21st Century: The Church of England Today and Tomorrow: An Agenda for the Future*, ed. Robert Hannaford (Gracewing, 1998), p. 111, note 110.
19 Paul Welsby, *How the Church of England Works* (CIO Publishing, 1985).
20 *Synodical Government in the Church of England: A Review*, the *Bridge Report* (Church House Publishing, 1997).

Chapter 19: *The Poor Parson*

1 Interview with Canon Vincent Strudwick, 11 August 1999.
2 Revd Simon Tebbutt, letter to the *Church Times*, 10 September 1999.
3 Hugh Wilcox, 'Review of the Year 1998: A Personal View', Preface to *The Church of England Year Book 1999* (Church House Publishing, 1999).
4 Revd Maurice Stanton-Saringer, letter to the *Church Times*, 5 February 1999.
5 Report in the *Church Times* (6 August 1999), about clergy joining the clergy section of the MSF Trade Union.
6 Ibid.
7 Report in the Church Times (3 September 1999) of *Explaining and Forecasting Job Satisfaction* (University of Bath, 1999).

Chapter 21: *Cathedrals – Popular Icons*

1 *Heritage and Renewal: The Report of the Archbishops' Commission on Cathedrals*, the Howe Report (Church House Publishing, 1994).
2 *Heritage and Renewal*, p. 3.

3 Interview with Canon June Osborne, 16 May 1997.
4 Ibid.
5 Ibid.
6 Ibid.
7 Interview with the Very Revd Trevor Beeson, 3 February 1997.
8 *Heritage and Renewal*, p. ix.
9 Interview with Trevor Beeson.
10 Ibid.
11 Interview with the Very Revd Hugh Dickinson, 24 April 1997.

Chapter 22: *Forms of Divine Worship*

1 Gordon P. Jeanes, 'Liturgy and Worship' in *A Church for the 21st Century: The Church of England Today and Tomorrow: An Agenda for the Future* (Gracewing, 1998), p. 243.
2 David Stancliffe, 'Performance and Presence: The Quest for Reality in Liturgical Worship' in *New Soundings*, ed. Stephen Platten, Graham James and Andrew Chandler (Darton, Longman & Todd, 1997), p. 37.
3 Martin Reardon, *Christian Initiation: A Policy for the Church of England* (Church House Publishing, 1991).
4 Stancliffe, 'Performance and Presence', p. 42.

Chapter 23: *Belief: the Longest Journey*

1 Ross Thompson, *Is There an Anglican Way? Scripture, Church and Reason: New Approaches to an Old Triad* (Darton, Longman & Todd, 1997).
2 Thompson, *Anglican Way*, pp. 1f.
3 Thompson, *Anglican Way*, pp. 2f.
4 Thompson, *Anglican Way*, p. 4.
5 Ibid.
6 Thompson, *Anglican Way*, p. 4.
7 Interview with Dr Rachel Waterhouse, 21 June 1997.
8 Ibid.
9 Ibid.
10 Ibid.
11 Ibid.
12 Interview with Canon June Osborne, 16 May 1997.
13 Ibid.
14 Michael Saward, 'At Root It's a Matter of Theology' in Graham Cray and others, *The Post-Evangelical Debate* (Triangle, 1997).
15 Saward, 'A Matter of Theology', p. 79f.

16 Jonathan Margolis, 'Party for Jesus', article in *The Guardian*, 22 September 1999.

17 Ibid.

18 Ibid.

19 Dave Tomlinson, *The Post-Evangelical* (Triangle, 1995), p. 61f.

20 Betty Saunders, *O Blest Communion! The Home Life of the Church of England* (Darton, Longman & Todd, 1996), p. 86f.

21 Ibid.

22 Ibid.

23 Ibid.

24 Ibid.

25 W. R. Matthews, *Memories and Meanings* (Hodder & Stoughton, 1969), p. 149.

26 Ibid.

27 John Saxbee, *Liberal Evangelism: A Flexible Response to the Decade* (SPCK, 1994), p. 3.

28 Martyn Percy, 'The New Liberalism' in *Faith for the Third Millennium*, ed. Jonathan Clatworthy (Modern Churchpeople's Union, 1998), p. 12.

29 Percy, 'New Liberalism', p. 12.

30 Percy, 'New Liberalism', p. 14.

31 Ibid.

32 Interview with the Revd Richard Truss, 12 July 1998.

33 Ibid.

34 Ibid.

35 *Called to New Living: The World of Lay Discipleship, Report prepared by Working Group of the Board of Education* (Church House Publishing, 1999).

36 Ibid.

37 Ibid.

38 George Pattison, *The End of Theology – and the Task of Thinking about God* (SCM Press, 1998), p. xi.

39 Pattison, *End of Theology*, p. 6.

40 Pattison, *End of Theology*, p. 18.

41 Pattison, *End of Theology*, p. 31.

42 Pattison, *End of Theology*, p. 32.

43 Ibid.

44 Pattison, *End of Theology*, p. 75.

45 John Milbank, Catherine Pickstock and Graham Ward (eds), *Radical Orthodoxy* (Routledge, 1999), 'Introduction': 'Suspending the Material: The Turn of Radical Orthodoxy'.

46 Ibid.

47 Daphne Hampson, *After Christianity* (SCM Press, 1996), p. 5.

48 Don Cupitt, *The Revelation of Being* (SCM Press, 1998), p. 8.
49 Ibid.
50 R. D. Laing, quoted by John Clay in *R. D. Laing: A Divided Self* (Hodder & Stoughton, 1996), p. 216.
51 R. D. Laing, quoted by Clay, *Divided Self*, p. 118.
52 Heidegger, quoted by Pattison, *End of Theology*, pp. 25–9.

Chapter 24: *Triumph and Disaster*

1 Trevor Beeson, 'Profiles of Two Directors' in *Christian Action 1946–1996* (Christian Action, 1999).
2 Report in *Church Times*, 24 September 1999.
3 Bishop John Sentamu, quoted in *Church Times*, 16 July 1999.
4 *St Paul's: Behind the Scenes of One of Britain's most Famous Landmarks*, shown on BBC1, 27 June 1999.
5 Anthony Howard, *The Times*, 27 July 1999.

Part Three: The Church as It May Be

Chapter 25: *The Educated Heart*

1 Judith Maltby, *Prayer Book and People in Elizabethan and Early Stuart England* (Cambridge University Press, 1998).
2 Celia Haddon, *If God Is My Father How Can He Love Me?* (Hodder & Stoughton, 1998).
3 Haddon, *If God Is My Father*, p. 184.
4 Gerald A. Arbuckle, *Refounding the Church: Dissent for Leadership* (Geoffrey Chapman, 1993), p. 188.
5 Ibid.
6 Arbuckle, *Refounding the Church*, p. 189.
7 Charles Handy, *The Empty Raincoat: Making Sense of the Future* (Hutchinson, 1994; Arrow Books, 1995), pp. 49ff.
8 Handy, *The Empty Raincoat*, p. 51.
9 Handy, *The Empty Raincoat*, p. 52.
10 Interview with the Very Revd Hugh Dickinson, 24 April 1997.
11 Stevie Smith, 'The Airy Christ', *Penguin Modern Poets* 8 (1966), p. 108.

Bibliography

Church of England Publications

Apostolicity and Succession. House of Bishops Occasional Paper. Church House Publishing, 1994.

Called to New Living: The World of Lay Discipleship. Church House Publishing, 1999.

Church Representation Rules. Church House Publishing, 1999.

Church Statistics. Central Board of Finance of the Church of England, 1996.

Faith in the City: The Report of the Archbishop of Canterbury's Commission on Urban Priority Areas. Church House Publishing, 1985.

Heritage and Renewal: The Report of the Archbishops' Commission on Cathedrals. The Howe Report. Church House Publishing, 1994.

Issues in Human Sexuality: A Statement by the House of Bishops. Church House Publishing, 1991.

Synodical Government in the Church of England: A Review. The Bridge Report. Church House Publishing, 1997.

The Christian Year: Calendar, Lectionary and Collects. Church House Publishing, 1997.

The Church of England A-Z: A Glossary of Terms. Church House Publishing, 1994.

The Cutting Edge of Mission: Mid Point Review of the Decade of Evangelism. Anglican Communion Publications, 1996.

Working as One Body: Report of the Archbishops' Commission on the Organisation of the Church of England. The Turnbull Report. Church House Publishing, 1995.

Youth a Part: Young People and the Church. Report from the General Synod Board of Education. National Society and Church House Publishing, 1996.

Other Sources

A Pastoral Statement to Lesbian and Gay Anglicans from Some Member Bishops of the Lambeth Conference. 5 August 1998.

Arbuckle, Gerald, *Refounding the Church: Dissent for Leadership.* Geoffrey Chapman, 1993.

Baptism, Eucharist and Ministry 1982–1990: Report on the Processes and Responses. WCC Publications, Geneva, 1992.

Barclay, Oliver, *Evangelicalism in Britain: A Personal Sketch 1935–1995.* InterVarsity Press, 1997.

Beeson, Trevor, *A Dean's Diary: Winchester 1987–1996.* SCM Press, 1997.

Beeson, Trevor, *Window on Westminster: A Canon's Diary 1976–1987.* SCM Press, 1998.

Beeson, Trevor, *Christian Action 1946–1996.* Christian Action, 1999.

Brierley, Peter, *Religious Trends.* Christian Research, 1998–9.

Buchanan, Colin, *Cut the Connection: Diestablishment and the Church of England.* Darton, Longman & Todd, 1994.

Carpenter, Humphrey, *Robert Runcie: The Reluctant Archbishop.* Hodder & Stoughton, 1996.

Catherwood, Fred, *At the Cutting Edge: A Lifetime of Politics, Industry and Faith.* Hodder & Stoughton, 1996.

Carr, Wesley and others, *Say One for Me: The Church of England in the Next Decade.* SPCK, 1992.

Chadwick, Owen, *The Mind of the Oxford Movement.* A. & C. Black, 1960.

Chadwick, Owen, *The Reformation.* Pelican History of the Church, Penguin Books, 1964.

Chadwick, Owen, *The Victorian Church.* A. & C. Black, 1966.

Clatworthy, Jonathan (ed.), *The New Liberalism: Faith for the Third Millennium.* MCU, 1998.

Clay, John, *R. D. Laing: A Divided Self.* Hodder & Stoughton, 1996.

Collinson, Patrick, *The Elizabethan Puritan Movement.* Clarendon Press, 1990.

Cray, Graham and others, *The Post-Evangelical Debate.* Triangle, 1997.

Cupitt, Don, *After God: The Future of Religion.* Weidenfeld & Nicolson, 1997.

Cupitt, Don, *The Religion of Being.* SCM Press, 1998.

Cupitt, Don, *The Revelation of Being.* SCM Press, 1998.

De-la-Noy, Michael, *The Church of England: A Portrait.* Simon & Schuster, 1993.

Duffy, Eamon, *The Stripping of the Altars: Traditional Religion in England 1400–1580.* Yale University Press, 1992.

Edwards, David, *Religion and Change*. Hodder & Stoughton, 1969.

Edwards, David, *A Concise History of English Christianity*. Fount, 1998.

Eliot, T. S., *Collected Poems 1909–1962*. Faber & Faber, 1963.

Elton, Geoffrey, *Reform and Reformation: England 1509–1558*. Cambridge, MA, 1977.

Ferris, Paul, *The Church of England*. Gollancz, 1962.

Fletcher, Sheila, *Maude Royden: A Life*. Blackwell, 1989.

Fowler, James W. and others, *Stages of Faith and Religious Development: Implications for Church, Education and Society*. SCM Press, 1992.

Friedan, Betty, *The Feminine Mystique*. New York, 1963; Penguin Books, 1965.

Furlong, Monica (ed.), *Act of Synod – Act of Folly?* SCM Press, 1998.

Gill, Robin, *The Myth of the Empty Church*. SPCK, 1993.

Gill, Robin, *Vision of Growth*. SPCK, 1994.

Gill, Sean, *Women and the Church of England: From the Eighteenth Century to the Present*. SPCK, 1994.

Green, Maxine and Chandu Christian, *Accompanying: Young People on Their Spiritual Quest*. The National Society and Church House Publishing, 1998.

Greer, Germaine, *The Female Eunuch*. MacGibbon & Kee, 1970.

Habgood, John, *Church and Nation in a Secular Age*. Darton, Longman & Todd, 1983.

Haddon, Celia, *If God Is My Father, How Can He Love Me?* Hodder & Stoughton, 1998.

Hampson, Daphne, *After Christianity*. SCM Press, 1996.

Hampson, Daphne (ed.), *Swallowing a Fishbone? Feminist Theologians Debate Christianity*. SPCK, 1996.

Handy, Charles, *The Empty Raincoat: Making Sense of the Future*. Hutchinson, 1994.

Handy, Charles, *The Hungry Spirit: Beyond Capitalism: A Quest for Purpose in the Modern World*. Hutchinson, 1997.

Hannaford, Robert (ed.), *A Church for the 21st Century: The Church of England Today and Tomorrow: An Agenda for the Future*. Gracewing, 1998.

Hardy, D. W. and P. H. Sedgwick (eds), *The Weight of Glory: The future of Liberal Theology*. T. & T. Clark, 1991.

Harris, José, *Private Lives, Public Spirit: Britain 1870–1914*. Oxford University Press, 1993. (Penguin Books, 1994).

Harrison, J. F. C., *Early Victorian Britain, 1832–51*. Fontana, 1988.

Harvey, Anthony, *Theology in the City*. SPCK, 1989.

Hastings, Adrian, *A History of English Christianity 1920–1990*. SCM

Press, 1991. (Earlier editions William Collins & Sons, 1986 and 1987.)

Hastings, Adrian, *Robert Runcie*. Mowbray, 1991.

Hebblethwaite, Brian, *The Ocean of Truth*. Cambridge University Press, 1988.

Heeney, Brian, *The Women's Movement in the Church of England 1850–1930*. Clarendon Press, 1988.

Hick, John (ed.), *The Myth of God Incarnate*. SCM Press, 1977.

Hinton, Michael, *The Anglican Parochial Clergy: A Celebration*. SCM Press, 1994.

Huxley, Aldous, *The Doors of Perception*. New York, Harper & Row, 1954.

Jacob, W. M., *Lay People and Religion in the Early Eighteenth Century*. Cambridge University Press, 1996.

James, William, *Varieties of Religious Experience*. 1902; Penguin Classics, 1985.

Livingstone, E. A. (ed.), *The Concise Oxford Dictionary of the Christian Church*. Oxford University Press, 1977, 1980.

Lovell, Terry, *Number One Millbank: The Financial Downfall of the Church of England*. HarperCollins, 1997.

MacCulloch, Diarmaid, *Thomas Cranmer: A Life*. Yale University Press, 1996.

Maltby, Judith, *Prayer Book and People in Elizabethan and Early Stuart England*. Cambridge University Press, 1998.

Marius, Richard, *Thomas More*. J. M. Dent & Sons, 1984.

Marsden, Gordon (ed.), *Victorian Values: Personalities and Perspectives in Nineteenth Century Society*. Longman, 1998.

Maxtone-Graham, Ysenda, *The Church Hesitant*. Hodder & Stoughton, 1993.

Milbank, John, Catherine Pickstock, Graham Ward and others, *Radical Orthodoxy*. Routledge, 1999.

Moorman, J. R. H., *A History of the Church in England*. A. & C. Black, 1954.

Morgan, Kenneth O. (ed.), *The Oxford Illustrated History of Britain*. Oxford University Press, 1984.

Moses, John, *A Broad and Living Way: Church and State: A Continuing Establishment*. The Canterbury Press, Norwich, 1995.

Neuberger, Julia, *On Being Jewish*. Heinemann, 1995.

Oddie, William, *The Crockford's File: Gareth Bennett and the Death of the Anglican Mind*. Hamish Hamilton, 1989.

Ollard, S. L., *A Short History of the Oxford Movement*. 1915; Oxford Movement Centenary Edition, 1932; Faith Press, 1963; Mowbray, 1983.

Bibliography

Pattison, George, *The End of Theology – and the Task of Thinking about God*. SCM Press, 1998.
Paul, Leslie, *A Church by Daylight: A Reappraisement of the Church of England and Its Future*. Geoffrey Chapman, 1973.
Platten, Stephen, Graham James and Andrew Chandler (eds), *New Soundings: Essays on Developing Tradition*. Darton, Longman & Todd, 1997.
Reardon, Martin, *Christian Initiation: A Policy for the Church of England*. Church House Publishing, 1991.
Robinson, John A. T., *Honest to God*. SCM Press, 1963.
Rowell, Geoffrey (ed.), *Tradition Renewed: The Oxford Movement Conference Papers*. Darton, Longman & Todd, 1986.
St Hilda Community, *Women Included: A Book of Services and Prayers*. SPCK, 1991.
Saunders, Betty, *O Blest Communion! The Home Life of the Church of England*. Darton, Longman & Todd, 1996.
Saxbee, John, *Liberal Evangelism: A Flexible Response to the Decade*. SPCK, 1994.
Selby, Peter, *BeLonging: Challenge to a Tribal Church*. SPCK, 1991.
Selby, Peter, *Grace and Mortgage: The Language of Faith and the Debt of the World*. Darton, Longman & Todd, 1997.
Stibbe, Mark, *O Brave New Church*. Darton, Longman & Todd, 1995.
Sykes, Stephen, *Unashamed Anglicanism*. Darton, Longman & Todd, 1995.
Thompson, Ross, *Is There an Anglican Way? Scripture, Church and Reason: New Approaches to an Old Triad*. Darton, Longman & Todd, 1997.
Tomlinson, Dave, *The Post-Evangelical*. Triangle, 1995.
Wakeman, Hilary (ed.), *Women Priests: The First Years*. Darton, Longman & Todd, 1996.
Walsh, John and Stephen Taylor (eds), *The Church of England c.1689–c.1833: From Toleration to Tractarianism*. Cambridge University Press, 1993.
Webster, Alison, *Found Wanting: Women, Christianity and Sexuality*. Cassell, 1995.
Webster, Margaret, *A New Strength, A New Song*. Mowbray, 1994.
Wesley, John, *The Journal of John Wesley*, ed. Elisabeth Jay. Oxford University Press, 1987.
Woodforde, James, *The Diary of a Country Parson*. Oxford University Press, abridged edition, 1978.

Index

413

Index

St Stephen's House theological
    college, Oxford 265-6
Stacey, Nick 115
staff, of Church House 178-9, 182,
    185, 186, 189-90, 193-5, 199-
    201, 206-7, 380
staff, of Lambeth Palace 151-2, 193,
    199-200, 380
stage and Church, link between 262
Stages of Faith and Development (James
    W. Fowler, 1992) 324
Stancliffe, David 316, 318, 323
Standing Committee 163, 180, 183,
    186, 202, 207
Stanton, Arthur Henry 82
Stanton-Saringer, Maurice 268
statistics, Church 212-14 *see also*
    Church attendance
Stibbe, Mark 229
stipends 107, 268, 270
Stockwood, Mervyn 114-15
Stokesley, John 29
Stott, John 159
Stripping of the Altars, The (Eamon
    Duffy, 1992) 17-19, 262
Strudwick, Vincent 230-33, 264-5
Stuart era 58-9
Studdert Kennedy, G.A. ('Woodbine
    Willie') 97
students: rise of Evangelical
    Christianity amongst 335-6;
    Student Christian Federation 157;
Student Christian Movement 103
'submission of the clergy' (1532) 28
subsidiarity 184, 198, 220-21
suffragan bishop 246
Sunday Schools 83, 88, 278
Swift, Jonathan 64-5
Sykes, Stephen 249
Synod: debates about ordination of
    women 134-7, 253; impact of
    Archbishops' Council on 162-3,
    164, 196-7, 201-3; impact of
    Turnbull Report on 176-81,
    185-6; relationship to House of
    Bishops 204-5; synodical
    government 122-4, 227-8, 237,
    329

Tablet, the 211, 239
'taint', doctrine of 136, 257
Tait, Archbishop 81
Taking Leave of God (Don Cupitt,
    1987) 351

Tanner, Mary 138
Tatchell, Peter 142, 364
Taylor, Jeremy 159
temperance movement 73, 92
Temple, Archbishop William 104-5,
    109, 159, 235, 236, 248
'Ten Articles', the 30-31
Test Act, the (1673) 60
Tetley, Joy 259
Thatcher, Margaret 129, 153, 255
theological colleges 153, 154, 160,
    264, 265-6, 278, 300
theology, limitations of 345-8
Thirty-Nine Articles, the (1571)
    56-7, 89, 100
Thompson, Ross 325, 329, 331, 332,
    338, 353
tied accommodation, clergy 268-9
Tillich, Paul 118
Tomlinson, Dave 304, 336
tongues, gift of 298, 334
Tory party, relationship to C of E
    67, 87, 129, 130-31
Toronto Blessing 272
tourism, impact on and importance
    to cathedrals 309-10
Tractarianism *see* Oxford Movement
Tracts for the Times 76, 77, 78-9
trade union membership, clergy 270
tradition: growing emphasis on in
    Elizabethan Church 55-6; place
    of 326, 327; relationship to
    innovation in worship 315-16
traditions, holding together 159,
    160, 161, 316, 327-46
training of clergy 264-5, 266-70; *see*
    also theological colleges
transcendent, rediscovery of 354-5
trans-sexuality, Church's hostility to
    263
transubstantiation 33, 38, 50, 57, 60,
    81
trialogue of the deaf 326-7
Trinity College, Bristol 153, 154,
    160, 300
Truss, Richard 339-40
Tudor, Mary 22, 41, 45, 46
Turnbull Report (*Working as One
    Body*, 1995) impact of 2, 149, 150,
    158, 163, 174-5, 179-209, 220;
    neglect of Establishment issue
    238; token women's
    representation on Commission
    361-2; recommendations on role
    of bishops 246-7

417